P9-CSU-738

How to Be
a Perfect Stranger
————5th Edition————

NOV   2011

Books in the
"Perfect Stranger" Series

How to Be a Perfect Stranger, 5th Edition:
The Essential Religious Etiquette Handbook

The Perfect Stranger's Guide to Funerals and Grieving Practices:
A Guide to Etiquette in Other People's Religious Ceremonies

The Perfect Stranger's Guide to Wedding Ceremonies:
A Guide to Etiquette in Other People's Religious Ceremonies

NOV 2011

How to Be
a Perfect Stranger

—————— 5th Edition ——————

The Essential Religious
Etiquette Handbook

Edited by Stuart M. Matlins
& Arthur J. Magida

Walking Together, Finding the Way ®
SKYLIGHT PATHS ®
PUBLISHING
Woodstock, Vermont

How to Be a Perfect Stranger, 5th Edition:
The Essential Religious Etiquette Handbook

2011 Fifth Edition, Quality Paperback, First Printing
©2011 and 2006 by SkyLight Paths Publishing

All rights reserved. No part of this book may be reproduced or transmitted in any form or by any means, electronic or mechanical, including photocopying, recording, or by any information storage and retrieval system, without permission in writing from the publisher.

For information regarding permission to reprint material from this book, please mail or fax your request in writing to SkyLight Paths Publishing, Permissions Department, at the address / fax number listed below, or e-mail your request to permissions@skylightpaths.com.

Library of Congress Cataloging-in-Publication Data

How to be a perfect stranger : the essential religious etiquette handbook / edited by Stuart M. Matlins & Arthur J. Magida.—5th ed.
  p. cm.
 ISBN 978-1-59473-294-2 (quality pbk.)
 1. Religious etiquette. 2. Church etiquette. I. Matlins, Stuart M. II. Magida, Arthur J.
 BJ2010.H68 2010
 203'.8—dc22

                                                                          2010031668

10   9   8   7   6   5   4   3   2   1

SkyLight Paths Publishing is creating a place where people of different spiritual traditions come together for challenge and inspiration, a place where we can help each other understand the mystery that lies at the heart of our existence.

SkyLight Paths sees both believers and seekers as a community that increasingly transcends traditional boundaries of religion and denomination—people wanting to learn from each other, *walking together, finding the way.*

Manufactured in the United States of America

SkyLight Paths, "Walking Together, Finding the Way," and colophon are trademarks of LongHill Partners, Inc., registered in the U.S. Patent and Trademark Office.

Walking Together, Finding the Way®
Published by SkyLight Paths Publishing
A Division of LongHill Partners, Inc.
Sunset Farm Offices, Rte. 4, P.O. Box 237
Woodstock, VT 05091
Tel: (802) 457-4000   Fax: (802) 457-4004
www.skylightpaths.com

Contents

Foreword

The religious landscape of North America has been in flux to one degree or another since the arrival of the first Europeans to these shores. Despite this, the cultural consciousness of North American people was largely Protestant Christian until fairly recently. However, from about the middle of the 20th century, the *rate* of change and diversification of religious affiliation within the United States and Canada has increased appreciably. Today, any residual sense of North America as a religious monolith has been dispelled even in small towns and throughout the countryside.

In the United States, for example, about 92 percent of our citizens profess a belief in God, and the nation continues to reflect one of the highest rates of religious affiliation among industrialized countries. The confluence of recent immigration patterns and a growing awareness among North Americans of world religions has helped produce in our country today a more open and vital attitude toward all faiths.

In an earlier era, those who practiced a faith other than the Protestant or Roman Catholic traditions of Christianity often did so in relative obscurity. Today, the vigorous religious rites and customs of a host of faiths take place in full public view. This reality, which is the manifestation of the venerable North American right to free exercise of religions, is a national treasure of great worth.

The great North American experiment in a pluralistic republic democracy is well served by the growing religious pluralism and the diversity of our people. It is freshly infused in each generation as new people bring their religious and cultural legacy to the workplace, the public square and their newly founded houses of worship, reinvigorating our land and our sense of the holy.

How to Be a Perfect Stranger provides all North Americans with an inviting point of entry into the world of religious pluralism. As we become more comfortable with the ways in which others pray, marry, bury and celebrate, we can move more effectively toward a sense of our single yet diverse peoplehood. Although we are diverse racially, religiously and culturally, we are united by principles and ideals that celebrate our very differences.

How to Be a Perfect Stranger equips each of us to enter into the religious realm of our neighbors. By providing us with practical information concerning what to bring, where to sit or stand, when to participate and when to refrain from participating, this volume serves as a great encouragement for all of us to know the faith traditions of each other, and to help erode the walls of ignorance that too often separate or confuse us. By bringing us out of our respective religious communities, each of which has a tendency to be more insular than we might like, *How to Be a Perfect Stranger* can help us appreciate and know the vast variety of our religious voices. Together, these voices create an extraordinary choir of ritual and celebration, piety and devotion, faith and resilience that is truly part of the bedrock of our nation.

Schools, businesses, public libraries and libraries in churches, synagogues and mosques will want to have a copy of *How to Be a Perfect Stranger* on hand, a volume that can reap big dividends during celebrations of our quintessential North American right of religious liberties.

Rev. Dr. Joan Brown Campbell

Preface

The truism that 11:00 on Sunday morning is the most segregated hour in North American life does not refer to race only. For most people, religious practice is an exercise in the familiar. Those of us who participate in congregational worship and observance—and many do in Canada and the United States, the most religiously observant nations in the industrialized West—do so with people who live like us, look like us and pretty much think and believe like us. So while white Americans and black Americans, for example, do not, as a rule, worship together in large numbers, neither do evangelical and liberal Lutherans, Satmar and Lubavitcher Hasidim, Sunni and Shiite Muslims. Let alone Jews and Presbyterians, or Greek Orthodox and Quakers, or Methodists and Buddhists.

The vitality experienced in these communities is usually enjoyed in isolation: Faith communities in North America often don't have much to do with each other. Many North Americans live in geographic, cultural, economic and social isolation from one another and are ill-prepared to speak honestly across racial, religious and cultural lines. To them, others' ways are strange ways.

Yet, a sense of estrangement is not necessarily a stranger to religious tradition. For example, the earliest writings at the core of the Abrahamic religions—Islam, Christianity and Judaism—use the experience of otherness and isolation from other religious traditions as a pretext to reflect on being strangers in strange lands. Little wonder, then, that many religions exalt the stranger and offer numerous spiritual injunctions about the obligations of hospitality, the right of protection and the general caution, expressed in one form or another, to take care with strangers "lest," as the Christian saint Paul wrote in his Letter to the Hebrews (13:2), "we entertain angels unawares."

If the ancient wisdom suggests caution, contemporary circumstances suggest urgency. Indeed, the publication of *How to Be a Perfect Stranger* comes at a time when the airwaves and radio talk shows are dominated by those who would use religious faith as a cover for intolerance, who exploit eternal truths for short-term political gain and who cynically use the spark of faith to ignite culture wars and divide North America into bickering camps.

Having seen how religion can be abused, it is up to us, as citizens, to step out of our isolated communities and into dialogue with those different from ourselves if we are ever to reach the common ground that defines us as citizens, parents, neighbors and human beings. For shared values can get us past the superficial barriers of language and skin color to catch a glimpse, however fleeting, of the spirit that exists in equal measure in all people. Only around those shared values can we hope to find solutions to many of the problems vexing society as a whole.

For understanding to increase, our differences need not disappear. But they must be understood before we come to know that the values we share are far greater in number and importance than any real or perceived differences. Without that understanding, perception threatens to become reality. Unless we find new ways to talk to each other, we'll be left talking about each other. And we know where that can lead us.

It's time we stopped ignoring the racial, ethnic, cultural and religious fault lines that divide us and our experiences and start finding the way forward for all communities. *How to Be a Perfect Stranger* makes that task seem much more doable and much less daunting. Here, presented in clear, direct prose, is the kind of social, cultural and logistical nuts and bolts you would expect to find in traveler's guides if congregations were your ports of call instead of, say, the island nations of the South Pacific.

How to Be a Perfect Stranger is a conscientious labor in the service of intergroup understanding. It expresses as few sermons could fundamental convictions about the value of all creation. It especially conveys truths about those who worship via differing paths than our own. It is a living demonstration of the truth and power of its own central conviction that religious belief can be particular without being intolerant, that it can be fervently held without being divisive, that it can ennoble life with a concern for the common interests of a society reflective of many different traditions.

The editors and researchers of this book have done their work. Now it is time for people of goodwill to do theirs. *How to Be a Perfect Stranger* shows us the way. For that, we are in its debt.

Sanford Cloud, Jr.

Former President and CEO,
The National Conference for
Community and Justice

Acknowledgments

A book such as this is the product of many contributions by many people. It could be no other way given the broad tapestry of religions in North America. This essential handbook on religious etiquette is based on the two award-winning volumes of *How to Be a Perfect Stranger: A Guide to Etiquette in Other People's Religious Ceremonies*.

Instrumental in the evolution of *How to Be a Perfect Stranger* were Richard A. Siegel and William Shanken, who developed the original concept and helped get the first volume into gear. Stuart M. Matlins, publisher of SkyLight Paths, developed the methodology for obtaining the information, and with Arthur J. Magida oversaw the research and writing and provided the impetus for the project. Sandra Korinchak, editor, shepherded the project from start to finish with the help of Jennifer Goneau, editorial assistant. Research assistant Susan Parks helped ensure that certain denominations responded promptly to our requests. And Jordan D. Wood generously assumed an initiative that delighted us all. Michael Schwartzentruber, series editor of Northstone Publishing, helped in compiling the Canadian data.

The Native American/First Nations information was provided by Dan Wildcat, a member of the Wyuchi Tribe of Oklahoma and a sociology professor at the Haskell Indian Nations University in Lawrence, Kansas.

All other chapters were based on information obtained from an extensive questionnaire filled out by clergy and other religious experts coast-to-coast. Without the help of the following, this book would never have become a reality:

Dr. Satyendra Banerjee, priest and Past President,
Bengali Cultural Society of British Columbia

Rabbi Gary M. Bretton-Granatoor, Director of Interreligious Affairs,
Union of American Hebrew Congregations (Reform), New York, New York

Ellen K. Campbell, Executive Director,
Canadian Unitarian Council, Toronto, Ontario

Marj Carpenter, former Mission Interpreter,
Presbyterian Church (USA), Louisville, Kentucky

Glenn Cooper, former Director of Communications,
The Presbyterian Church in Canada, Pictou, Nova Scotia

Archpriest George Corey, Vicar,
Antiochian Orthodox Archdiocese, New York, New York

Scott Dickson, Public Affairs (Canada), Jehovah's Witnesses,
Watch Tower Bible and Tract Society of Canada

Alf Dumont (member, First Nations),
St. John's United Church, Alliston, Ontario

Rabbi Moshe Edelman, Director of Programs and Leadership Development,
United Synagogue of Conservative Judaism, New York, New York

Eugene J. Fisher, Associate Director of the Secretariat for Ecumenical
and Interreligious Affairs of the National Conference of Catholic Bishops,
Washington, D.C.

Ted George, Librarian, Greek Orthodox Cathedral of the Annunciation,
Baltimore, Maryland

Rev. Lance Gifford, Rector, St. John's Episcopal Church,
Baltimore, Maryland

James S. Golding, Editor, *The [Greek] Orthodox Observer,*
New York, New York

Steven D. Goodman, Professor of Indian and Tibetan Buddhism,
Institute of Buddhist Studies, Berkeley, California

Father Gregory Havrilak, Director of Communications,
Orthodox Church in North America, New York, New York

Hoyt Hickman, now retired from the General Board of Discipleship,
United Methodist Church, Nashville, Tennessee

Hans Holznagel, Public Relations Manager,
United Church of Christ, Cleveland, Ohio

Ibrahim Hooper, Council on American-Islamic Relations, Washington, D.C.

Bede Hubbard, Assistant General Secretary,
Canadian Conference of Catholic Bishops, Ottawa, Ontario

John Hurley, Archivist and Public Relations Officer,
Unitarian Universalist Association of Congregations, Boston, Massachusetts

Ralph Janes, Communications Director,
Seventh-day Adventist Church in Canada

Hari Dharam Kaur Khalsa, The Mukhia Sardarni Sahiba,
Sikh Dharma of New Mexico, Española, New Mexico

Rev. Dr. Ralph Lebold, Past President, Conrad Grebel College,
University of Waterloo, Waterloo, Ontario

Don LeFevre, Manager of Public Affairs Department,
The Church of Jesus Christ of Latter-day Saints, Salt Lake City, Utah

Barbara Liotscos, Consultant for Ministry and Worship,
The Anglican Church of Canada, Toronto, Ontario

Stan Litke, Executive Director,
Christian Church (Disciples of Christ) in Canada, Calgary, Alberta

Rev. David Mahsman, Director of News and Information,
The Lutheran Church–Missouri Synod, St. Louis, Missouri

Mike McDonald, Pulpit Minister, The Church of Christ, Monahans, Texas

The Very Reverend Protopresbyter Frank P. Miloro,
The American Carpatho-Russian Orthodox Greek Catholic
Diocese of the U.S.A., Johnstown, Pennsylvania

Ronald R. Minor, General Secretary,
The Pentecostal Church of God, Joplin, Missouri

Dana Mullen, Clerk–Representative Meeting,
Canadian Yearly Meeting, Ottawa, Ontario

Dr. Paul Nelson, Director for Worship,
Evangelical Lutheran Church in America, Chicago, Illinois

Father Louis Noplos, Assistant Pastor,
Greek Orthodox Cathedral of the Annunciation, Baltimore, Maryland

Rev. Dr. David Ocea, The Romanian Orthodox
Episcopate of North America, Grass Lake, Minnesota

Sara Palmer, Program Secretary, The Wider Quaker Fellowship,
Philadelphia, Pennsylvania

Mark Parent, Ph.D., Pereaux United Baptist Church, Pereaux, Nova Scotia

Richard Payne, Dean, Institute of Buddhist Studies,
Berkeley, California

Wardell Payne, Research Consultant on African American
Religions, Washington, D.C.

Laurie Peach, Staff Writer,
The First Church of Christ, Scientist, Boston, Massachusetts

Pal S. Purewal, former President, Sikh Society of Alberta, Edmonton, Alberta

Rev. Frank Reid, Senior Pastor,
Bethel African Methodist Episcopal Church, Baltimore, Maryland

Dr. George W. Reid, Director of the Biblical Research Institute,
Seventh-day Adventists, Silver Spring, Maryland

Raymond Richardson, Writing Department,
Jehovah's Witnesses, Brooklyn, New York

Rev. John Roberts, Pastor,
Woodbrook Baptist Church, Baltimore, Maryland

Michael R. Rothaar, Acting Director for Worship,
Evangelical Lutheran Church in America, Chicago, Illinois

John Schlenck, Librarian and Music Director,
Vedanta Society of New York, New York

Bhante Seelawimala, Professor of Theravada Buddhism,
Institute of Buddhist Studies, Berkeley, California

Bruce Smith, Public Affairs,
The Church of Jesus Christ of Latter-day Saints, North York, Ontario

Rabbi David Sulomm Stein, Beit Tikvah Congregation
(Reconstructionist), Baltimore, Maryland

Dr. Suwanda Sugunasiri, President, Buddhist Council of Canada;
Teaching Staff and Research Associate in Buddhist Studies,
Trinity College, University of Toronto

Trish Swanson, Former Director, Office of Public Information, Bahá'ís of the
United States, New York, New York

James Taylor, United Church of Canada,
co-founder Wood Lake Books Inc., Okanagan Centre, British Columbia

Imam Michael Abdur Rashid Taylor,
Islamic Chaplaincy Services Canada, Bancroft, Ontario

Dr. David A. Teutsch, President,
Reconstructionist Rabbinical College, Wyncote, Pennsylvania

Juleen Turnage, Secretary of Public Relations,
Assemblies of God, Springfield, Missouri

Jerry Van Marter, Mission Interpreter and International News,
Presbyterian Church (USA), Louisville, Kentucky

Rev. Kenn Ward, editor of *Canada Lutheran*, Winnipeg, Manitoba

Deborah Weiner, Director, Public Relations,
Unitarian Universalist Association of Congregations, Boston, Massachusetts

Rabbi Tzvi Hersh Weinreb, Shomrei Emunah Congregation
(Orthodox), Baltimore, Maryland

M. Victor Westberg, Manager, Committees on Publications,
The First Church of Christ, Scientist, Boston, Massachusetts

Clifford L. Willis, Director of News and Information,
The Christian Church (Disciples of Christ), Indianapolis, Indiana

Pamela Zivari, Director, Office of Public Information,
Bahá'ís of the United States, New York, New York

Introduction

When the first volume of *How to Be a Perfect Stranger* received the Benjamin Franklin Award for the "Best Reference Book of the Year," we were pleased and proud. From our research, we had known that many people were looking forward to this practical, helpful book. What we did not expect was that so many people would tell us in letters and in person that they not only referred to this intriguing volume, they were reading it from cover to cover—and they wanted, and needed, more. Therefore, we compiled the second volume of *How to Be a Perfect Stranger*. People were hungry for information about their neighbors' faiths, and needed it at a most practical level.

We had always planned to keep the *Perfect Stranger* volumes up-to-date with current statistics, dates and other information; however, we decided that the material might be even more useful to people if it were combined into a single essential handbook. Besides redesigning the text, we came up with a few more helpful resources to add to the third edition, including a checklist that people could photocopy and complete before venturing out to a new experience at a religious ceremony outside their own faith, and a special feature designed as a handy reference for clergy and others who regularly interact with religious leaders outside their own faith: "Summary of Proper Forms for Addressing Leaders of Various Faiths" (see pages 401–402). In addition to the many updates to the fourth edition—including statistics, holiday dates and supplements to the glossary—we added a helpful new section on popular religious symbols. This section provides a clear, thorough explanation of their meanings, allowing for an even deeper understanding of the many religious traditions. In the fifth edition, we added more resources to encourage understanding of the many different religious traditions in our communities.

The denominations in *How to Be a Perfect Stranger*, 5th Edition, range from the largest in North America, with membership, in many cases, running into the millions, to denominations with fewer members, but most still over 50,000—and those that are less frequently encountered, such as Native American religions and the Baháʼí and Sikh faiths.

As you will see, the chapter on Native faiths differs in presentation and content from the other chapters. Because there is not a single Native American/First Nations faith, we found the standard question-and-answer format used in these chapters inadequate to properly explain the practices and spirituality of indigenous North American peoples. At the same time, their faith differs so basically from those religions in the Judeo-Christian and Islamic traditions or from Hinduism or Buddhism that adhering to the standard format would have been more a disservice than a virtue. For example, ceremonies and their content vary greatly among tribal groups, and even native religions' basic concept of a Creator bears little relation to concepts of a Creator in most Western and Asian religions.

The enthusiastic reception from readers and reviewers to the first two volumes of *How to Be a Perfect Stranger* suggests that, while each denomination in North America worships in its own unique and idiosyncratic way, we fervently want to know what is going on in the churches and mosques and synagogues and meeting halls that sustain our spiritual life. But perhaps even more fervent is the urge to be personally comfortable and inwardly and outwardly respectful of other beliefs and traditions, customs and rituals when dealing with a faith not our own. While we may not subscribe to another's religious beliefs, we just as surely wish to understand the basis of that faith and the purposes and manner of its rituals and ceremonies.

This impulse is certainly rooted in the fact that we North Americans live in a remarkably fluid society. There is movement between class and race; between the many cultures that form the patchwork known as "American culture"; and between religions, that most personal—and often most deeply embedded—of the institutions that shape us, inform us, inspirit us, enlighten us.

As North Americans, we often celebrate the diverse ways we worship God. This pluralism and cross-fertilization, we say, is part of what makes North America special, and it often occurs at the most personal of levels. It is not uncommon, for instance, to be invited to a wedding, a funeral or a religious celebration in the home of a relative or friend of a different faith from one's own. Such exposure to the religious ways of others can give us a deep appreciation for the extraordinary diversity of faith and the variety of ways it surfaces.

Also, as the insightful Catholic writer Father Andrew M. Greeley has observed, religion is "a collection of ...'pictures'" that we use to give order and meaning to our lives and everything around them. Viewing others' "religious 'pictures'" and noting the contrast between what we see and what we've experienced in our own religious traditions can also deepen and solidify our own faith by making us consider how our tradition speaks to us, comforts us and challenges us.

Yet, we may be uncomfortable or uncertain when we meet "the other" on his or her own turf: What does one do? Or wear? Or say? What should one avoid doing, wearing, saying? What will happen during the ceremony? How long will it last? What does each ritual mean? What are the basic beliefs of this particular religion?

Will there be a reception? Will there be food? Will there be grace before we eat? Are gifts expected? When can I leave?

These are just some of the practical questions that arise because of the fundamental foreignness of the experience. *How to Be a Perfect Stranger* addresses these concerns in a straightforward and nonjudgmental manner. Its goal is to make a well-meaning guest feel comfortable, participate to the fullest extent feasible and avoid violating anyone's religious principles. It is not intended to be a comprehensive primer on theology. It's a guidebook to a land where we may be strangers, but where, on the whole, those on whose celebratory turf we will soon be treading want us to be as comfortable, relaxed and unperturbed as possible.

After all, as the philosopher George Santayana said, "Religion in its humility restores man to his only dignity, the courage to live by grace." And there is nothing more mutually grace-full than to welcome "the stranger"—and for "the stranger" to do his or her homework before entering an unfamiliar house of worship or religious ceremony.

We've all been strangers at one time or another or in one place or another. If this book helps turn the "strange" into the less "exotic" and into the less confusing (but not into the ordinary), then it will have satisfied its goal of minimizing our anxiety and our confusion when face-to-face with another faith—while, at the same time, deepening our appreciation and our understanding of that faith. While we pray and worship in thousands of churches, synagogues, mosques, temples and meeting halls around the country, these denominational fences are not insurmountable. Indeed, these fences come complete with gates. It is often up to us to find the key to those gates. We hope that this book helps in the search for that key.

A few notes on the way in which *How to Be a Perfect Stranger* was compiled and structured:

Each chapter is devoted to a particular religion or denomination; each is organized around that religion's life cycle events, religious calendar and home celebrations.

Basic research was conducted through an extensive questionnaire that was completed in almost all cases by the national office of each religion and denomination. For those denominations whose national office did not respond to the questionnaire, we obtained responses from clergy of that particular faith. To minimize error in nuance, drafts of each chapter were forwarded for comments to those who had filled out the questionnaire.

How to Be a Perfect Stranger is not intended as a substitute for the social common sense that should prevail at social or religious events. For example, if a chapter advises readers that "casual dress" is acceptable at a religious service, this is not to suggest that it is appropriate to show up in Bermuda shorts. Or if a certain denomination allows visitors to use a flash or a video camera, the equipment should not be used in such a way that it disrupts the religious ceremony or disturbs worshipers or other visitors.

The guidelines in this book are just that. They should not be mistaken for firm and unbendable rules. Religious customs, traditions and rituals are strongly influenced by where people live and the part of the world from which their ancestors originated. As a result, there may be a variety of practices within a single denomination. This book is a general guide to religious practice, and it's important to remember that particulars may sometimes vary broadly within individual denominations.

Terms within each chapter are those used by that religion. For example, the terms "New Testament" and "Old Testament" appear in almost every chapter about various Christian denominations. Some Jewish people may find this disconcerting, since they recognize only one testament. The purpose is not to offend, but to portray these religions as they portray themselves. The goal of this book, one must remember, is to enable us to be "a perfect stranger." And "perfection" might well begin with recognizing that when we join others in celebrating events in their religion's vernacular, we are obliged, as guests, to know the customs, rituals and language of the event.

For future editions of *How to Be a Perfect Stranger,* we encourage readers to write to us and suggest ways in which this book could be made more useful to them and to others. Are there additional subjects that future editions should cover? Have important subtleties been missed? We see this book—and the evolution of our unique North American society— as an ongoing work-in-progress, and we welcome your comments. Please write to:

Editors, *How to Be a Perfect Stranger*
SkyLight Paths Publishing
Sunset Farm Offices, Rte. 4
P.O. Box 237
Woodstock, Vermont 05091
www.skylightpaths.com

The "Everything You Need to Know Before You Go" Checklist

The Essentials

Review the appropriate chapter(s) to answer at least these basic questions:

How should I be dressed?

What will happen during the service?

What will happen after the service?

Should I bring a gift?

Will I be expected to participate in any way?

This material is from *How to Be a Perfect Stranger*, 5th Edition, by Stuart M. Matlins and Arthur J. Magida, published by SkyLight Paths Publishing, P.O. Box 237, Woodstock, VT 05091. (802) 457-4000; www.skylightpaths.com. The Publisher grants permission to you to copy this handout. All rights to other parts of this book are still covered by copyright and are reserved to the Publisher. Any other copying or usage requires written permission.

African American Methodist Churches

(known as the African Methodist Episcopal Church; the African Methodist Episcopal Zion Church; the Christian Methodist Episcopal Church; the Union American Methodist Episcopal Church, Inc.; and the African Union First Colored Methodist Protestant Church)

1 • HISTORY AND BELIEFS

The African American Methodist churches began in the late 18th century and throughout the 19th century as a reaction to racial discrimination. The broader Methodist Church had originated in the early 18th century in England under the preaching of John Wesley, an Anglican priest who was a prodigious evangelical preacher, writer and organizer. While a student at Oxford University, he and his brother had led the Holy Club of devout students, whom scoffers called the "Methodists."

Wesley's teachings affirmed the freedom of human will as promoted by grace. He saw each person's depth of sin matched by the height of sanctification to which the Holy Spirit, the empowering spirit of God, can lead persons of faith.

Although Wesley remained an Anglican and disavowed attempts to form a new church, Methodism eventually became another church body. During a conference in Balti-more, Maryland, in 1784, the Methodist Church was founded as an ecclesiastical organization and the first Methodist bishop in the United States was elected.

Blacks had originally been attracted to the Methodist Church because its original evangelism made no distinctions between the races and John Wesley, the founder of Methodism, had strongly denounced slavery and the African slave trade on the grounds that they were contrary to the will of God. Initially, many Methodists—clergy and laity—opposed slavery, called upon church members to desist from trafficking in slaves, and urged them to free any slaves they did own. But as Methodists became more numerous in the South, the Church gradually muted its opposition to slavery.

In 1787, black members of Philadelphia's St. George's Methodist Episcopal Church withdrew from the church after experiencing discrimination, and the African Methodist Episcopal Church was officially established as a denomination on April 16, 1816.

1

The African Methodist Episcopal Zion Church was founded in 1796 after blacks were denied the sacraments and full participation in the John Street Methodist Church in New York City, located in a state with the largest slave population outside of the South.

And the Christian Methodist Episcopal Church was founded in 1870, four years after African-American members of the Methodist Episcopal Church, South (M.E.C.S.) petitioned the Church to be allowed to create a separate church that would be governed by the M.E.C.S. In 1870, the General Conference of the M.E.C.S. voted to let black members be constituted as an independent church, not as a subordinate body. This reflected the post–Civil War period's imperatives calling for independence for African Americans and the reconstruction of American society.

Two smaller African American Methodist churches are the Union American Methodist Episcopal Church, Inc., with 15,000 members in 55 congregations, and the African Union First Colored Methodist Protestant Church, with 5,000 members in 33 congregations. Both of these were founded in 1865.

Local African American Methodist churches are called "charges." Their ministers are appointed by the bishop at an annual conference, and each church elects its own administrative board, which initiates planning and sets local goals and policies.

U.S. churches:
African Methodist Episcopal: 4,174
African Methodist Episcopal Zion:
    3,393
African Union First Colored
    Methodist Protestant Church: 33
Christian Methodist Episcopal Church:
    3,300
Union American Methodist Episcopal
    Church, Inc.: 55

U.S. membership:
African Methodist Episcopal:
    2.5 million
African Methodist Episcopal Zion:
    1.4 million
African Union First Colored Methodist
    Protestant Church: 5,000
Christian Methodist Episcopal Church:
    850,000
Union American Methodist Episcopal
    Church, Inc.: 15,000
    (data from the 1995 Directory of African
    American Religious Bodies *and the* 2010
    Yearbook of American and Canadian
    Churches*)*

For more information, contact:
African Methodist Episcopal Church
3801 Market Street, Suite 300
Philadelphia, PA 19104
(215) 662-0506
www.ame-church.com

African Methodist Episcopal
    Zion Church
Department of Records and Research
3225 West Sugar Creek Road
Charlotte, NC 28269
(704) 599-4630
www.amez.org

African Union Methodist
    Protestant Church
602 Spruce Street
Wilmington, DE 19801
(302) 994-3410

Christian Methodist Episcopal Church
4466 Elvis Presley Boulevard
Memphis, TN 38116
(901) 345-0580
www.c-m-e.org

2. THE BASIC SERVICE

To the African American Methodist denominations, worship is a congregation's encounter and communion with God and with one another in God's name. It includes praise and prayer, Scripture readings, a sermon and sometimes Holy Communion.

Most African American Methodist services last about one hour.

APPROPRIATE ATTIRE

Men: A jacket and tie. No head covering is required.

Women: A dress. The arms do not necessarily have to be covered nor do hems have to be below the knees. Open-toed shoes and modest jewelry are permissible. No head covering is required.

There are no rules regarding colors of clothing.

THE SANCTUARY

What are the major sections of the church?
The platform or chancel: A raised section at the front of the church. This is where the leaders and the choir function.
The nave: Where congregants sit on pews.

THE SERVICE

When should guests arrive and where should they sit? Arrive at the time for which the service has been called. An usher will indicate where to sit. There are usually no restrictions on where to sit.

If arriving late, are there times when a guest should *not* enter the service? Yes. Ushers will seat you when appropriate.

Are there times when a guest should *not* leave the service? No.

Who are the major officiants, leaders or participants and what do they do?
The pastor, who presides, preaches and celebrates communion.
The associate pastor or the assisting layperson, who aids the senior pastor in leading the service.
The choir or soloists, who sing hymns and psalms.

What are the major ritual objects of the service?
Bread, which is eaten during Holy Communion and which signifies the body of Jesus Christ.
Grape juice, which the pastor presents to congregants to drink during Holy Communion and signifies the blood of Jesus Christ.

What books are used? Books vary from congregation to congregation within each of the African American Methodist denominations, but the Bibles usually used are the King James Version, the New Revised Standard or the New International Version. Also, most African Methodist Episcopal churches use *The AMEC Hymnal* (Nashville, Tenn.: The African Methodist Episcopal Church, 1984); African Methodist Episcopal Zion churches use *The Songs of Zion* (Nashville, Tenn.: Abingdon Press, 1999); and Christian Methodist Episcopal churches use *The Hymnal of the Christian Methodist Episcopal Church* (Memphis, Tenn.: The CME Publishing House, 2000).

To indicate the order of the service: A program will be provided and periodic announcements will be made by the pastor or another leader.

GUEST BEHAVIOR DURING THE SERVICE

Will a guest who is not a member of an African American Methodist denomination be expected to do anything other than sit? Standing and kneeling with the congregation and reading prayers aloud and singing with congregants are all optional. Guests are welcome to participate if this does not compromise their personal beliefs. If guests do not wish to kneel or stand, they may remain seated at these times.

Are there any parts of the service in which a guest who is not a member of an African American Methodist denomination should *not* participate? Yes. Methodists invite all to receive Holy Communion, but guests should be aware that partaking of Communion is regarded as an act of identification with Christianity. Feel free to remain seated as others go forward for Communion. Likewise, if Communion bread and cups are passed among the pews, feel free to pass them along without partaking.

If not disruptive to the service, is it okay to:
Take pictures? Possibly. Ask an usher.
Use a video camera? Possibly. Ask an usher.
Use a flash? Possibly. Ask an usher.
Use a tape recorder? Possibly. Ask an usher.
(Note: Many African American Methodist churches have audio-visual ministries that enable congregants and guests to purchase copies of services at a modest cost. Information on obtaining these audio or video tapes is available from the offices of local churches.)

Will contributions to the church be collected at the service? Yes. The offering plate will be passed through the congregation during the service. This usually occurs immediately before or after the sermon.

How much is it customary to contribute? The customary offering is about $10.

AFTER THE SERVICE

Is there usually a reception after the service? Possibly. If so, it will be held in the church's reception area. It usually lasts less than 30 minutes, and pastry, coffee and tea are ordinarily served.

Also, many congregations operate a kitchen after services, where low-cost meals can be purchased. These will be served in the church's dining area.

A brief prayer or blessing may be recited during the service or just before the meal in the church dining area.

Is there a traditional form of address for clergy who may be at the reception? "Reverend" or "Pastor."

Is it okay to leave early? Yes.

GENERAL GUIDELINES AND ADVICE

The chief potential for mistake occurs during Holy Communion. Feel free not to partake if you cannot in good conscience do so. Christian guests should be aware that the African American Methodist denominations never refuse Communion to anyone.

The cups at Holy Communion

always contain grape juice, not wine. Children, as well as adults, are welcome to partake.

SPECIAL VOCABULARY

None provided.

DOGMA AND IDEOLOGY

African American Methodists believe:

The doctrine of the Trinity: God is the Father, the Son (embodied by Jesus Christ), and the Holy Spirit (the empowering spirit of God).

The natural sinfulness of humanity.

Humanity's fall from grace and the need for individual repentance.

Freedom of will.

In practice, Methodists are highly diverse in their beliefs and tend to emphasize right living more than orthodoxy of belief.

A basic book to which a guest can refer to learn more about the African American Methodist tradition: *Directory of African American Religious Bodies: A Compendium* by the Howard University School of Divinity, edited by Wardell J. Payne (Washington, D.C.: Howard University Press, 1995).

3. HOLY DAYS AND FESTIVALS

Advent. Begins four weeks before Christmas. The purpose is to prepare for Christmas and to focus on Christ. There is no traditional greeting for Advent.

Christmas. Occurs on the evening of December 24 and the day of December 25. Marks the birth and the incarnation of God as a man. The traditional greeting is "Merry Christmas."

Lent. Begins on Ash Wednesday, which occurs six weeks before Easter. The purpose is to prepare for Easter. Between Lent and Easter, fasting and abstention from entertainment are encouraged, as is increased giving to the poor. Often, there are midweek worship services. There are no traditional greetings for this holiday.

Easter. Always falls on the Sunday after the first full moon that occurs on or after the spring equinox of March 21. Celebrates the Resurrection of Jesus Christ. The traditional greeting to Methodists is "Happy Easter."

Pentecost Sunday. The seventh Sunday after Easter. Celebrates the coming of the Holy Spirit, which is the empowering spirit of God in human life. This is often considered the birth of the Christian church. There are no traditional greetings for this holiday.

4. LIFE CYCLE EVENTS

Birth Ceremony

Baptism initiates an infant into Christianity. It is administered once to each person, usually during infancy. The pastor sprinkles or pours water on the person's head or immerses the person in water. This signifies the washing away of sins. God is invoked to strengthen this new Christian, and the congregation, as well as the parents and godparents, pledge to nurture him or her in the Christian faith and life.

Baptism is part of the larger weekly congregational Sunday morning service, which usually lasts about an hour.

BEFORE THE CEREMONY

Are guests usually invited by a formal invitation? Yes.

If not stated explicitly, should one assume that children are invited? Yes.

If one can't attend, what should one do? Either of these is appropriate: Send flowers or a gift, or telephone the parents with your congratulations and your regrets that you can't attend.

APPROPRIATE ATTIRE

Men: A jacket and tie. No head covering is required.

Women: A dress. The arms do not necessarily have to be covered nor do hems have to be below the knees. Open-toed shoes and modest jewelry are permissible. No head covering is required.

There are no rules regarding colors of clothing.

GIFTS

Is a gift customarily expected? No, but it is appropriate. Gifts such as U.S. savings bonds or baby clothes or toys are commonly given.

Should gifts be brought to the ceremony? Usually gifts can be brought to the reception.

THE CEREMONY

Where will the ceremony take place? In the parents' church.

When should guests arrive and where should they sit? Arrive at the time for which the service has been called. Ushers will indicate where to sit. There are usually no restrictions on where to sit.

If arriving late, are there times when a guest should *not* enter the ceremony? Yes. Ushers will seat you when appropriate.

Are there times when a guest should *not* leave the ceremony? No.

Who are the major officiants, leaders or participants at the ceremony and what do they do?
The pastor, who will baptize the child.
The child and his or her parents.

What books are used? Books vary from congregation to congregation within each of the African American Methodist denominations, but the Bibles usually used are the King James Version, the New Revised Standard or the New International Version. Also, most African Methodist Episcopal churches use *The AMEC Hymnal* (Nashville, Tenn.: The African Methodist Episcopal Church, 1984); African Methodist Episcopal Zion churches use *The Songs of Zion* (Nashville, Tenn.: Abingdon Press, 1999); and Christian Methodist Episcopal churches use *The Hymnal of the Christian Methodist Episcopal Church* (Memphis, Tenn.: The CME Publishing House, 2000).

To indicate the order of the ceremony: A program will be provided and periodic announcements will be made by the pastor or his or her assistant.

Will a guest who is not a member of an African American Methodist denomination be expected to do anything other than sit? Standing and kneeling with the congregation and reading prayers aloud and singing with congregants are all optional. Guests are welcome to participate if this does not compromise their personal beliefs. If guests do not wish to kneel or stand, they may remain seated at these times.

Are there any parts of the ceremony in which a guest who is not a member of an African American Methodist denomination should *not* participate? Yes. Methodists invite all to receive Holy Communion, but guests should be aware that partaking of Communion is regarded as an act of identification with Christianity. Feel free to remain seated as others go forward for Communion. Likewise, if Communion bread and cups are passed among the pews, feel free to pass them along without partaking. Christian guests should be aware that the Methodist church never refuses Communion to anyone. The cups at Holy Communion always contain grape juice, not wine. Children, as well as adults, are welcome to partake.

If not disruptive to the ceremony, is it okay to:
Take pictures? Possibly. Ask ushers.
Use a flash? Possibly. Ask ushers.
Use a video camera? Possibly. Ask ushers.
Use a tape recorder? Possibly. Ask ushers.
(Note: Many African American Methodist churches have audio-visual ministries that enable congregants and guests to purchase copies of services at a modest cost. Information on obtaining these audio or video tapes is available from the offices of local churches.)

Will contributions to the church be collected at the ceremony? Yes. The offering plate will be passed through the congregation during the service. This usually occurs immediately before or after the sermon.

How much is it customary to contribute? The customary offering is about $10.

AFTER THE CEREMONY

Is there usually a reception after the ceremony? Possibly. If so, it will be held in the church's reception area. It usually lasts less than 30 minutes, and pastry, coffee and tea are ordinarily served.

Also, many congregations operate a kitchen after services, where low-cost meals can be purchased. These will be served in the church's dining area.

Would it be considered impolite to neither eat nor drink? No.

Is there a grace or benediction before eating or drinking? A brief prayer or blessing may be recited during the service or just before the reception or the meal.

Is there a grace or benediction after eating or drinking? No.

Is there a traditional greeting for the family? No. Just offer your congratulations.

Is there a traditional form of address for clergy who may be at the reception? "Reverend" or "Pastor."

Is it okay to leave early? Yes.

Initiation Ceremony

Confirmation is conferred to an early adolescent. It is a Methodist's first profession of faith. The candidates affirm for themselves the Christian faith and church into which they were baptized (usually as infants).

Teens participate in the ceremony with members of their confirmation class. The 15-minute ceremony is part of a larger Sunday morning service, which lasts about an hour.

BEFORE THE CEREMONY

Are guests usually invited by a formal invitation? No.

If not stated explicitly, should one assume that children are invited? Yes.

If one can't attend, what should one do? Either of these is appropriate: Send flowers or a gift, or telephone the parents with your congratulations and your regrets that you can't attend.

APPROPRIATE ATTIRE

Men: A jacket and tie. No head covering is required.

Women: A dress. The arms do not necessarily have to be covered nor do hems have to be below the knees. Open-toed shoes and modest jewelry are permissible. No head covering is required.

There are no rules regarding colors of clothing.

GIFTS

Is a gift customarily expected? No.

THE CEREMONY

Where will the ceremony take place? Usually at the front of the main sanctuary of the church.

When should guests arrive and where should they sit? Arrive at the time for which the service has been called. An usher will indicate where to sit. There are usually no restrictions on where to sit.

If arriving late, are there times when a guest should *not* enter the ceremony? Yes. Ushers will seat you when appropriate.

Are there times when a guest should *not* leave the ceremony? No.

Who are the major officiants, leaders or participants at the ceremony and what do they do?
The pastor, who confirms the teen(s).
The teen(s) being confirmed.

What books are used? Books vary from congregation to congregation within each of the African American Methodist denominations, but the Bibles usually used are the King James Version, the New Revised Standard or the New International Version. Also, most African Methodist Episcopal churches use *The AMEC Hymnal* (Nashville, Tenn.: The African Methodist Episcopal Church, 1984); African Methodist Episcopal Zion churches use *The Songs of Zion* (Nashville, Tenn.: Abingdon Press, 1999); and Christian Methodist Episcopal churches use *The Hymnal of the Christian Methodist Episcopal Church* (Memphis, Tenn.: The CME Publishing House, 2000).

To indicate the order of the ceremony: A program will be provided, and periodic announcements will be made by the pastor or his assistant.

Will a guest who is not a member of an African American Methodist denomination be expected to do anything other than sit? Standing and kneeling with the congregation and reading prayers aloud and singing with congregants are all optional. Guests are welcome to participate if this does not compromise their personal beliefs. If guests do not wish to kneel or stand, they may remain seated at these times.

Are there any parts of the ceremony in which a guest who is not a member of an African American Methodist denomination should *not* participate? Yes. Methodists invite all to receive Holy Communion, but guests should be aware that partaking of Communion is regarded as an act of identification with Christianity. Feel free to remain seated as others go forward for Communion. Likewise, if Communion bread and cups are passed among the pews, feel free to pass them along without partaking. Christian guests should be aware that the Methodist Church never refuses Communion to anyone. The cups at Holy Communion always contain grape juice, not wine. Children, as well as adults, are welcome to partake.

If not disruptive to the ceremony, is it okay to:
Take pictures? Possibly. Ask ushers.
Use a flash? Possibly. Ask ushers.
Use a video camera? Possibly. Ask ushers.
Use a tape recorder? Possibly. Ask ushers.
(Note: Many African American Methodist churches have audio-visual ministries that enable congregants and guests to purchase copies of services at a modest cost. Information on obtaining these audio or video tapes is available from the office of a local church.)

Will contributions to the church be collected at the ceremony? Yes. The offering plate will be passed through the congregation during the service. This usually occurs immediately before or after the sermon.

How much is it customary to contribute? The customary offering is about $10.

AFTER THE CEREMONY

Is there usually a reception after the ceremony? Possibly. If so, it will be held in the church's reception area. It usually lasts less than 30 minutes, and pastry, coffee and tea are ordinarily served.

Also, many congregations operate a kitchen after services, where low-cost meals can be purchased. These will be served in the church's dining area.

Would it be considered impolite to neither eat nor drink? No.

Is there a grace or benediction before eating or drinking? A brief prayer or blessing may be recited during the service or just before the reception or the meal.

Is there a grace or benediction after eating or drinking? No.

Is there a traditional greeting for the family? No. Just offer your congratulations.

Is there a traditional form of address for clergy who may be at the reception? "Reverend" or "Pastor."

Is it okay to leave early? Yes.

Marriage Ceremony

Marriage is the uniting of a man and a woman in a union that is intended—and pledged—to be lifelong. The marriage ceremony is a service in itself. It may last between 15 and 30 minutes.

BEFORE THE CEREMONY

Are guests usually invited by a formal invitation? Yes.

If not stated explicitly, should one assume that children are invited? No.

If one can't attend, what should one do? RSVP with your regrets and send a gift.

APPROPRIATE ATTIRE

Men: A jacket and tie. No head covering is required.

Women: A dress. The arms do not necessarily have to be covered nor do hems have to be below the knees. Open-toed shoes and modest jewelry are permissible. No head covering is required.

There are no rules regarding colors of clothing.

GIFTS

Is a gift customarily expected? Yes. Such gifts as small appliances, sheets, towels or other household gifts are appropriate.

Should gifts be brought to the ceremony? No, send them to the home of the newlyweds.

THE CEREMONY

Where will the ceremony take place? Usually in the main sanctuary of a church.

When should guests arrive and where should they sit? Arrive early. Depending on the setting, ushers may show guests where to sit.

If arriving late, are there times when a guest should *not* enter the ceremony? Ushers will usually assist latecomers.

Are there times when a guest should *not* leave the ceremony? No.

Who are the major officiants, leaders or participants at the ceremony and what do they do?
The pastor, who officiates.
The bride and groom and their wedding party.

What books are used? Books vary from congregation to congregation within each of the African American Methodist denominations, but the Bibles usually used are the King James Version, the New Revised Standard or the New International Version. Also, most African Methodist Episcopal churches use *The AMEC Hymnal* (Nashville, Tenn.: The African Methodist Episcopal Church, 1984); African Methodist Episcopal Zion churches use *The Songs of Zion* (Nashville, Tenn.: Abingdon Press, 1999); and Christian Methodist Episcopal churches use *The Hymnal of the Christian Methodist Episcopal Church* (Memphis, Tenn.: The CME Publishing House, 2000).

To indicate the order of the ceremony: A program will be provided.

Will a guest who is not a member of an African American Methodist denomination be expected to do anything other than sit? Standing and kneeling with the congregation and reading prayers aloud and singing with congregants are all optional. Guests are welcome to participate if this does not compromise their personal beliefs. If guests do not wish to kneel or stand, they may remain seated at these times.

Are there any parts of the ceremony in which a guest who is not a member of an African American Methodist denomination should *not* participate? Yes. Holy Communion may be offered at the service. Methodists invite all to receive Holy Communion, but guests should be aware that partaking of Communion is regarded as an act of identification with Christianity. Feel free to remain seated as others go forward for Communion. Likewise, if Communion bread and cups are passed among the pews, feel free to pass them along without partaking.

If not disruptive to the ceremony, is it okay to:
Take pictures? Possibly. Ask ushers.
Use a flash? Possibly. Ask ushers.
Use a video camera? Possibly. Ask ushers.
Use a tape recorder? Possibly. Ask ushers.

Will contributions to the church be collected at the ceremony? No.

AFTER THE CEREMONY

Is there usually a reception after the ceremony? There is often a reception that may last one to two hours. It may be at a home, a catering facility or in the same building as the ceremony. Ordinarily, food and beverages are served and there is dancing and music. Alcoholic beverages may be served.

Would it be considered impolite to neither eat nor drink? No.

Is there a grace or benediction before eating or drinking? No.

Is there a grace or benediction after eating or drinking? No.

Is there a traditional greeting for the family? No. Just offer your congratulations.

Is there a traditional form of address for clergy who may be at the reception? "Reverend" or "Pastor."

Is it okay to leave early? Yes, but usually only after toasts have been made and the wedding cake has been served.

Funerals and Mourning

African American Methodist denominations affirm that life is eternal and that, in faith, one can look forward to life with God after death.

African American Methodists have diverse beliefs about afterlife and are generally content to look forward to it as a glorious mystery. Funerals have as their purposes: (1) expressing grief and comforting one another in our bereavement, (2) celebrating the life of the deceased, and (3) affirming faith in life with God after death. Which of these is most emphasized at the funeral depends on the circumstances of the death and the extent of the faith of the deceased.

BEFORE THE CEREMONY

How soon after the death does the funeral usually take place? Usually within two to three days.

What should one who is not a member of an African American Methodist denomination do upon hearing of the death of a member of

that faith? Telephone or visit the bereaved.

APPROPRIATE ATTIRE

Men: A jacket and tie. No head covering is required.

Women: A dress. Open-toed shoes and modest jewelry are permissible. No head covering is required.

There are no rules regarding colors of clothing, but somber, dark colors are recommended for men and women.

GIFTS

Is it appropriate to send flowers or make a contribution? Yes. Send flowers to the home of the bereaved. Contributions are also optional. The recommended charity may be mentioned in the deceased's obituary.

Is it appropriate to send food? Yes. Send it to the home of the bereaved.

THE CEREMONY

Where will the ceremony take place? At a church or funeral home.

When should guests arrive and where should they sit? Arrive early. Ushers will advise them where to sit.

If arriving late, are there times when a guest should *not* enter the ceremony? No.

Will the bereaved family be present at the church or funeral home before the ceremony? Possibly.

Is there a traditional greeting for the family? Simply express your condolences.

Will there be an open casket? Usually.

Is a guest expected to view the body? This is entirely optional.

What is appropriate behavior upon viewing the body? Silent prayer.

Who are the major officiants at the ceremony and what do they do? *The pastor,* who officiates.

To indicate the order of the ceremony: A program will be provided.

Will a guest who is not a member of an African American Methodist denomination be expected to do anything other than sit? No.

Are there any parts of the ceremony in which a guest who is not a member of an African American Methodist denomination should *not* participate? No.

If not disruptive to the ceremony, is it okay to:
Take pictures? No.
Use a flash? No.
Use a video camera? No.
Use a tape recorder? No.

Will contributions to the church be collected at the ceremony? No.

THE INTERMENT

Should guests attend the interment? Yes.

Whom should one ask for directions? The funeral director.

What happens at the graveside? Prayers are recited by the pastor and the body is committed to the ground. If there has been a cremation, which is done privately before the service, the ashes are either buried or put in a vault.

Do guests who are not members of an African American Methodist denomination participate at the graveside ceremony? No. They are simply present.

COMFORTING THE BEREAVED

Is it appropriate to visit the home of the bereaved after the funeral? Yes, at any mutually convenient time. How long one stays depends on your closeness to the bereaved. Typically, one stays about 30 to 45 minutes.

Will there be a religious service at the home of the bereaved? No.

Will food be served? No.

How soon after the funeral will a mourner usually return to a normal work schedule? This is entirely at the discretion of the bereaved.

How soon after the funeral will a mourner usually return to a normal social schedule? This is entirely at the discretion of the bereaved.

Are there mourning customs to which a friend who is not a member of an African American Methodist denomination should be sensitive? No.

Are there rituals for observing the anniversary of the death? There may be a service commemorating the deceased.

5 · HOME CELEBRATIONS

Not applicable to African American Methodist denominations.

2

Assemblies of God

1. HISTORY AND BELIEFS

In 1914, when the Assemblies of God was formed, America had, for several years, been in the midst of a major revival movement. Many involved spontaneously spoke "in tongues" (or in a language unknown to those speaking it) and claims were made of divine healing that saved lives. Since many of these experiences were associated with the coming of the Holy Spirit (the empowering quality of God) on the Day of Pentecost, participants in the revival were called Pentecostals.

After mainline churches divorced themselves from the revival phenomenon, about 300 Pentecostal leaders met in Hot Springs, Arkansas. After three days of prayer, they decided to organize themselves not as a new denomination, but as a loose-knit fellowship called the General Council of the Assemblies of God. Two years later, the council realized the need to establish standards of doctrinal truths.

In part, this Statement of Fundamental Truths asserts that the Bible is divinely inspired and is infallible; the one true God created earth and heaven, redeems humanity from its sins and consists of the Father, the Son (Jesus Christ) and the Holy Spirit; Jesus has always existed and is without beginning or end; humanity was created good and upright, but, by falling into sin, incurred physical and spiritual death; humanity's only hope for salvation from sin and spiritual death is through Christ.

The Assemblies of God is one of the more quickly growing churches in the United States: Since 1960, membership has grown from around 500,000 to nearly 3 million. The Church is especially keen on using conversion to swell its ranks. In recent years, the largest number of conversions has been in the Church's southwest region (California, Nevada, Arizona and Colorado). Many of these new members are Spanish-speaking.

U.S. churches: 12,377
U.S. membership: 2.9 million
(data from the 2010 Yearbook of American and Canadian Churches)

For more information, contact:

The Assemblies of God
1445 North Boonville Avenue
Springfield, MO 65802
(417) 862-2781
www.ag.org

Not present in Canada

2 · THE BASIC SERVICE

The Sunday morning service usually begins with singing, Scripture reading or prayer. This is usually followed with hymns, prayer and worship to God, a sermon by the pastor and individuals making either a public commitment to Christ as their Savior or publicly praying for needs and concerns in their lives.

At some point during the service, there will be special prayers for the needs of congregants. Also, the sick may be anointed with oil and prayed for.

Churches observe Communion once a month. During this ritual, bread signifying the body of Christ and juice symbolizing his blood are distributed among congregants.

The Assemblies of God encourages various styles of worship: Some congregants may pray silently, some audibly, some may weep openly. Common to most Assemblies of God services is the clapping and raising of hands. This is used as a form of adoration to God. Raised hands during prayer are another expression common to the Church and are an outward sign of surrender to God's will.

The service may last about 30 to 60 minutes.

APPROPRIATE ATTIRE

Men: A jacket and tie or more casual attire. No head covering is required.

Women: A dress or a skirt and blouse. Clothing need not cover the arms and hems need not reach below the knees (although miniskirts, shorts and halters are frowned upon). Open-toed shoes and modest jewelry are permissible. No head covering is required.

There are no rules regarding colors of clothing.

THE SANCTUARY

What are the major sections of the church?

The foyer or lobby: Where guests and congregants are greeted upon arrival.

The main floor: Where congregants sit.

The platform: Where leaders of the service gather.

The pulpit: Where the service leaders lead prayer or read Scriptures and preach.

THE SERVICE

When should guests arrive and where should they sit? Arrive shortly before the time for which the service has been called. Ushers usually seat guests.

If arriving late, are there times when a guest should *not* enter the service? Do not enter during prayers.

Are there times when a guest should *not* leave the service? No.

Who are the major officiants, leaders or participants and what do they do?

The pastor, who leads prayer and delivers a sermon.

The minister of music, who directs the choir and leads the congregation's musical worship.

What are the major ritual objects of the service? There are none. Also, most Assemblies of God churches have little, if any, adornment and usually lack statues and stained glass windows. The cross is the most commonly displayed symbol.

What books are used? Several translations of the Old and New Testaments are used throughout the Church. Most commonly used is the New International Version of the King James translation of the Bible, which is released by several publishers. The hymnals used also vary from congregation to congregation, although the Church publishes its own hymnal, *Sing His Praise* (Springfield, Mo.: Gospel Publishing House, 1991), as well as two earlier hymnals still in use, *Hymns of Glorious Praise* and *Melodies of Praise*, all available from www.gospelpublishing.com.

To indicate the order of the service: A program will be distributed and periodic announcements will be made.

GUEST BEHAVIOR DURING THE SERVICE

Will a guest who is not a member of the Assemblies of God be expected to do anything other than sit? No. It is entirely optional for guests of other faiths to stand, kneel and sing with congregants and read prayers aloud with them.

Are there any parts of the service in which a guest who is not a member of the Assemblies of God should *not* participate? No.

If not disruptive to the service, is it okay to:
Take pictures? Possibly.

Use a flash? Possibly.
Use a video camera? Possibly.
Use a tape recorder? Possibly.
(Note: Policies regarding still and video cameras and tape recorders vary with each church. Check with the local pastor before using such equipment during a service.)

Will contributions to the church be collected at the service? Yes.

How much is it customary to contribute? If one chooses to give, a contribution between $1 and $10 is appropriate.

AFTER THE SERVICE

Is there usually a reception after the service? No.

Is there a traditional form of address for clergy whom a guest may meet? Either "Pastor" or "Reverend."

GENERAL GUIDELINES AND ADVICE

None provided.

SPECIAL VOCABULARY

Key words or phrases that it might be helpful for a visitor to know:
Ordinance: The Church's term for water baptism and Communion because they were practices ordained or established by Jesus. Many other churches call these practices "sacraments," a term the Assemblies of God rejects, it states, because "'sacraments' carries for many people the idea that a spiritual work takes place in a person when the sacrament is received or experienced."

DOGMA AND IDEOLOGY

Members of the Assemblies of God believe:

Each person may commune directly with God.

God exists in the Father, the Son (Jesus Christ) and the Holy Spirit (the empowering quality of God).

As a result of Adam's fall in the Garden of Eden, all people are born in a sinful condition. Children are covered by grace until they reach an age of accountability, but everyone else needs redemption that is provided only through the life, death and Resurrection of Jesus. Only by receiving Jesus' forgiveness and accepting him as Lord can people be forgiven of their sins.

Divine healing for the sick is provided in Christ's death.

Baptism endows upon believers:
1. The power to witness and serve others.
2. A dedication to the work of God.
3. A more intense love for Christ.
4. Certain spiritual gifts.

When the Holy Spirit initially fills a believer, that person will speak in an unknown tongue.

Some pamphlets to which a guest can refer to learn more about the Assemblies of God: *Assemblies of God: Our Church & Fellowship* and *Assemblies of God: Our 16 Doctrines*. Both are available from the Gospel Publishing House, (800) 641-4310.

3. HOLY DAYS AND FESTIVALS

Christmas. Always falls on December 25.

Celebrates the birth of Christ. The traditional greeting is "Merry Christmas."

Good Friday. Three days before Easter. Commemorates the crucifixion, death and burial of Jesus.

Easter. Always falls on the Sunday after the first full moon that occurs on or after the spring equinox of March 21. Commemorates the death and Resurrection of Jesus. The traditional greeting is "Happy Easter."

Pentecost. Occurs 50 days after Easter because this is when the Holy Ghost (the spirit of Jesus) descended on his apostles. Celebrates the power of the Holy Spirit and its manifestation in the early Christian church. There is no traditional greeting for this holiday.

4. LIFE CYCLE EVENTS

Birth Ceremony

This ceremony, which is called a Dedication, is based on the biblical account of Jesus calling young children to him and blessing them. The Church does not believe that the Dedication constitutes salvation, but rather that it lets the child's parents publicly commit themselves to their intentions to raise the child in the teachings of Jesus.

During the Dedication, which is for infants or young children, the pastor asks the parents to pledge to live in such a way that, at an early age, their child will be a Christian. They respond with, "We do." Some pastors also charge the congregation to help the parents by role-modeling Christian living for the child.

The Dedication, which is the same for males and females, usually lasts about three to five minutes. It is part of a larger service (usually a Sunday morning worship service) that lasts from 30 to 60 minutes.

BEFORE THE CEREMONY

Are guests usually invited by a formal invitation? No. They are usually invited informally and orally by the parents of the newborn.

If not stated explicitly, should one assume that children are invited? Yes.

If one can't attend, what should one do? RSVP orally with regrets.

APPROPRIATE ATTIRE

Men: A jacket and tie or more casual attire. No head covering is required.

Women: A dress or a skirt and blouse. Clothing need not cover the arms and hems need not reach below the knees (although miniskirts, shorts and halters are frowned upon). Open-toed shoes and modest jewelry are permissible. No head covering is required.

There are no rules regarding colors of clothing.

GIFTS

Is a gift customarily expected? No.

THE CEREMONY

Where will the ceremony take place? In the main sanctuary of the church.

When should guests arrive and where should they sit? Arrive shortly before the time for which the service has been called. Ushers will usually seat guests.

If arriving late, are there times when a guest should *not* enter the ceremony? Do not enter during prayers.

Are there times when a guest should *not* leave the ceremony? No.

Who are the major officiants, leaders or participants at the ceremony and what do they do?

The pastor, who leads the prayer of dedication and makes comments about the infant.

What books are used? None, although the Old and New Testaments are used during the service that includes the Dedication. Most commonly used is the New International Version of the King James translation of the Bible, which is released by several publishers. The hymnals used also vary from congregation to congregation, although the Church publishes its own hymnal, *Sing His Praise* (Springfield, Mo.: Gospel Publishing House, 1991), as well as two earlier hymnals still in use, *Hymns of Glorious Praise* and *Melodies of Praise.*

To indicate the order of the ceremony: A program will be distributed.

Will a guest who is not a member of the Assemblies of God be expected to do anything other than sit? No.

Are there any parts of the ceremony in which a guest who is not a member of the Assemblies of God should *not* participate? No.

If not disruptive to the ceremony, is it okay to:
Take pictures? Possibly.
Use a flash? Possibly.
Use a video camera? Possibly.
Use a tape recorder? Possibly.
(Note: Policies regarding still and video cameras and tape recorders vary with each church. Check with the local pastor before using such equipment during a service.)

Will contributions to the church be collected at the ceremony? Contributions will be collected as part of the larger service of which the Dedication is just one component.

How much is it customary to contribute? If one chooses to give, a contribution between $1 and $10 is appropriate.

AFTER THE CEREMONY

Is there usually a reception after the ceremony? No.

Is there a traditional greeting for the family? Just offer your congratulations.

Is there a traditional form of address for clergy whom a guest may meet? Either "Pastor" or "Reverend."

Initiation Ceremony

This ceremony, which is the same for males and females, is called a baptism. During it, children who have reached the "age of accountability," which is usually considered to be eight to 10 years of age (although children as young as five or six have been baptized), are fully immersed in the baptismal waters.

Baptism is necessary because all people are born in a sinful condition and it fills one with the purging, cleansing and zeal of the Holy Spirit, the empowering quality of God. Baptism is a public testimony of the death of the individual's sinful nature and of one's new birth in the spirit of Jesus. It endows believers with the power to witness and serve others, a dedication to the work of God, a more intense love for Jesus, and certain spiritual gifts. Baptism, which is performed once for any individual, can occur at any time during one's life.

The baptismal service is usually part of a regular Sunday morning or evening church service. The baptism itself may last about 15 to 30 minutes, depending on the number of persons being baptized.

BEFORE THE CEREMONY

Are guests usually invited by a formal invitation? They are usually invited informally and orally by the parents of the child.

If not stated explicitly, should one assume that children are invited? Yes.

If one can't attend, what should one do? RSVP orally with regrets.

APPROPRIATE ATTIRE

Men: A jacket and tie or more casual attire. No head covering is required.

Women: A dress or a skirt and blouse. Clothing need not cover the arms and hems need not reach below the knees (although mini-skirts, shorts and halters are frowned upon). Open-toed shoes and modest jewelry are permissible. No head covering is required.

There are no rules regarding colors of clothing.

GIFTS

Is a gift customarily expected? No.

Should gifts be brought to the ceremony? See above.

THE CEREMONY

Where will the ceremony take place? In the main sanctuary of the church.

When should guests arrive and where should they sit? Arrive shortly before the time for which the service has been called. Ushers will usually seat guests.

If arriving late, are there times when a guest should *not* enter the ceremony? Do not enter during prayers.

Are there times when a guest should *not* leave the ceremony? No.

Who are the major officiants, leaders or participants at the ceremony and what do they do?
The pastor, who performs the baptism.

What books are used? None, although a Bible and hymnal are used during the service that includes the baptism. Several translations of the Old and New Testaments are used throughout the Church. Most commonly used is the New International Version of the King James translation of the Bible, which is released by several publishers. The hymnals used vary from congregation to congregation, although the Church publishes its own hymnal, *Sing His Praise* (Springfield, Mo.: Gospel Publishing House, 1991), as well as two earlier hymnals still in use, *Hymns of Glorious Praise* and *Melodies of Praise*.

To indicate the order of the ceremony: A program will be distributed.

Will a guest who is not a member of the Assemblies of God be expected to do anything other than sit? No.

Are there any parts of the ceremony in which a guest who is not a member of the Assemblies of God should *not* participate? No.

If not disruptive to the ceremony, is it okay to:
Take pictures? Possibly.
Use a flash? Possibly.
Use a video camera? Possibly.
Use a tape recorder? Possibly.
(Note: Policies regarding still and video cameras and tape recorders vary with each church. Check with the local pastor before using such equipment during a service.)

Will contributions to the church be collected at the ceremony? Contributions will be collected as part of the larger service of which the baptism is just one component.

How much is it customary to contribute? If one chooses to give, a contribution between $1 and $10 is appropriate.

AFTER THE CEREMONY

Is there usually a reception after the ceremony? No.

Is there a traditional greeting for the family? Just offer your congratulations.

Is there a traditional form of address for clergy whom a guest may meet? Either "Pastor" or "Reverend."

Marriage Ceremony

The Assemblies of God teaches that the family was the first institution ordained by God in the Garden of Eden. The basis for a family is marriage between two consenting adults. Marriage, which is not to be entered into lightly, is said to be "until death do us part."

The marriage ceremony is a ceremony in itself and may last 30 to 60 minutes.

BEFORE THE CEREMONY

Are guests usually invited by a formal invitation? Yes.

If not stated explicitly, should one assume that children are invited? No.

If one can't attend, what should one do? RSVP by card or letter with regrets.

APPROPRIATE ATTIRE

Men: A jacket and tie. No head covering is required.

Women: A dress. Clothing need not cover the arms and hems need not reach below the knees. Open-toed shoes and modest jewelry are permissible. No head covering is required.

There are no rules regarding colors of clothing.

GIFTS

Is a gift customarily expected? Yes. Cash or bonds or small household items are most frequently given.

Should gifts be brought to the ceremony? Yes.

THE CEREMONY

Where will the ceremony take place? In the main sanctuary of the church.

When should guests arrive and where should they sit? Arrive shortly before the time for which the ceremony has been called. Ushers will usually advise guests about where to sit.

If arriving late, are there times when a guest should *not* enter the ceremony? Do not enter during the processional or recessional of the wedding party.

Are there times when a guest should *not* leave the ceremony? No.

Who are the major officiants, leaders or participants at the ceremony and what do they do?
The pastor, who officiates.

What books are used? Ordinarily, the pastor uses various wedding ceremonies chosen by the bride and groom. These include references to and passages from the Scriptures.

To indicate the order of the ceremony: A program will be distributed.

Will a guest who is not a member of the Assemblies of God be expected to do anything other than sit? Guests of other faiths are expected to stand when other guests rise during the ceremony. It is optional for them to kneel and to sing with the congregants and to join them in reading prayers aloud.

Are there any parts of the ceremony in which a guest who is not a member of the Assemblies of God should *not* participate? No.

If not disruptive to the ceremony, is it okay to:
Take pictures? Possibly.
Use a flash? Possibly.
Use a video camera? Possibly.
Use a tape recorder? Possibly.
(Note: Policies regarding still and video cameras and tape recorders vary with each church. Check with the local pastor before using such equipment during a service.)

Will contributions to the church be collected at the ceremony? No.

AFTER THE CEREMONY

Is there usually a reception after the ceremony? Yes. It may be in the same building where the wedding ceremony was held or in a catering hall. Receptions vary from full-course meals to a stand-up reception at which cake, mints, nuts and punch are served. There will be no alcoholic beverages. The reception may last 30 to 60 minutes.

Would it be considered impolite to neither eat nor drink? No.

Is there a grace or benediction before eating or drinking? No.

Is there a grace or benediction after eating or drinking? No.

Is there a traditional greeting for the family? Just offer your congratulations.

Is there a traditional form of address for clergy who may be at the reception? Either "Pastor" or "Reverend."

Is it okay to leave early? Yes, unless it is a formal meal.

Funerals and Mourning

Members of the Assemblies of God believe that all Christians who have died will one day rise from their graves and meet the Lord in the air. Meanwhile, Christians who are still alive will be raptured (or caught up with those who have risen from their graves) and will also be with the Lord. All who have thus joined with God will live forever.

An Assemblies of God funeral usually begins with singing, Scripture reading or prayer. This is followed with hymns, prayer and worship to God, and a sermon by the pastor.

A ceremony in itself, the funeral service lasts about 30 to 60 minutes.

BEFORE THE CEREMONY

How soon after the death does the funeral usually take place? Usually, within two to three days; sometimes, within one week.

What should someone who is not a member of the Assemblies of God do upon hearing of the death of a member of that faith? Telephone or visit the bereaved to offer condolences and sympathies and offer to assist in any way possible.

APPROPRIATE ATTIRE

Men: A jacket and tie. No head covering is required.

Women: A dress or a skirt and blouse. Clothing need not cover the arms and hems need not reach below the knees. Open-toed shoes and modest jewelry are permissible. No head covering is required.

Dark, somber colors for clothing are advised.

GIFTS

Is it appropriate to send flowers or make a contribution? Flowers may be sent to the funeral home or church where the funeral service is held. Con-tributions may be sent to the home of the bereaved after the funeral.

Is it appropriate to send food? Yes.

THE CEREMONY

Where will the ceremony take place? Either in a church or in a funeral home.

When should guests arrive and where should they sit? Arrive at the time for which the service has been scheduled. Ushers usually advise guests where to sit.

If arriving late, are there times when a guest should *not* enter the ceremony? No.

Will the bereaved family be present at the church or funeral home before the ceremony? Not usually.

Is there a traditional greeting for the family? Just offer your condolences.

Will there be an open casket? Usually.

Is a guest expected to view the body? This is optional.

What is appropriate behavior upon viewing the body? Walk past the casket, then take a seat in the church sanctuary or the room in the funeral parlor where the service will be held.

Who are the major officiants at the ceremony and what do they do?
The pastor, who delivers a brief sermon and tribute to the deceased.
Musicians, who sing one or two songs.

What books are used? The Old and

New Testaments. Most commonly used is the New International Version of the King James translation of the Bible, which is released by several publishers.

To indicate the order of the ceremony: A program will be distributed.

Will a guest who is not a member of the Assemblies of God be expected to do anything other than sit? Guests of other faiths are expected to stand when other guests rise during the service. It is optional for them to kneel and to sing with the congregants and to join them in reading prayers aloud.

Are there any parts of the ceremony in which a guest who is not a member of the Assemblies of God should *not* participate? No.

If not disruptive to the ceremony, is it okay to:
Take pictures? Possibly.
Use a flash? Possibly.
Use a video camera? Possibly.
Use a tape recorder? Possibly.
    (Note: Policies regarding still and video cameras and tape recorders vary with each church. Check with the local pastor before using such equipment during a service.)

Will contributions to the church be collected at the ceremony? No.

THE INTERMENT

Should guests attend the interment? Attendance is optional.

Whom should one ask for directions? An usher or the funeral director.

What happens at the graveside?

There are prayers, songs and Scripture readings.

Do guests who are not members of the Assemblies of God participate at the graveside ceremony? No, they are simply present.

COMFORTING THE BEREAVED

Is it appropriate to visit the home of the bereaved after the funeral? Yes, if one knows the family well.

Will there be a religious service at the home of the bereaved? No.

Will food be served? Possibly.

How soon after the funeral will a mourner usually return to a normal work schedule? A week or two, depending upon individual preference. The Church has no set tradition.

How soon after the funeral will a mourner usually return to a normal social schedule? This is entirely the choice of the bereaved, since the Church has no set tradition. It may be one or two weeks, or more, and is often primarily determined by local cultural traditions.

Are there mourning customs to which a friend who is not a member of the Assemblies of God should be sensitive? No.

Are there rituals for observing the anniversary of the death? No.

5 · HOME CELEBRATIONS

Not applicable to the Assemblies of God.

3
Bahá'í Faith

1. HISTORY AND BELIEFS

The Bahá'í Faith is an independent world religion. It sprang out of an Islamic movement known as the Bábí faith, which was founded in the mid-19th century in Persia (now southern Iran) by Mírzá 'Alí- Muhammad, a direct descendant of the Prophet Muhammad. By proclaiming himself to be The Báb, which literally means "gate" or "door," 'Alí-Muhammad announced that he was the forerunner of the Universal Messenger of God, who would usher in an era of justice and peace.

In 1850, The Báb was killed by a firing squad in Tabriz, Persia, upon the order of the grand vizier of the new Shah of Iran. The grand vizier was acting on behalf of traditional Islamic clergy in his country, who were alarmed at what they perceived to be the heretical doctrine being taught by The Báb and also by the fact that he was gaining followers.

In 1863, one of The Báb's 18 original closest disciples, Bahá'u'lláh, made his public declaration, while he was in exile in Iraq, that he was

"He Whom God Shall Manifest," the messianic figure whom The Báb had predicted. He was soon banished by the Iraqi government to Istanbul and then to Adrianapole, where he stayed for five years.

Agitation from opponents caused the Turkish government to send the exiles to Acre, Palestine, where Bahá'u'lláh spent his last years. Upon his death, his eldest son, 'Abdu'l-Bahá, "The Servant of Baha," led the faith, as had been determined in his father's will. With his death in 1921, leadership fell, as stipulated in 'Abdu'l-Bahá's will, to his eldest grandson, Shoghi Effendi, "The Guardian of the Cause of God," who devoted himself to expanding the worldwide Bahá'í community, establishing its central administrative offices in Haifa, and translating the writings of his great-grandfather, Bahá'u'lláh.

Central to Bahá'í beliefs is the unity of all religions and of all humanity. God, Bahá'ís teach, may be unknowable, but the divine presence manifests itself in various ways. Among these are the creation of the world and the prophets, beginning with Adam, and continuing through the Jewish prophets, Buddha, Krishna, Zoroaster, Jesus and Muhammad, who was succeeded by Bahá'u'lláh. Each prophet represents a divine message that was appropriate for the era in which he appeared. Bahá'ís believe that other prophets may come in the future, and that there is no last revelation or final prophet.

Bahá'ís live in some 100,000 localities around the globe and thousands of these localities elect a local spiritual assembly each year. In the United States there are about 1,100 local assemblies and 248 in Canada. These culminate in a Universal House of Justice, which has administrative, judicial and legislative functions and the authority to frame new rules for situations not provided for in the writings of Bahá'u'lláh.

The Bahá'í Faith has more than 5 million members and is established in virtually every country and in many dependent territories and overseas departments of countries. Most nations and a few territories have a National Spiritual assembly elected by the Bahá'ís of that jurisdiction. Throughout the world, the Bahá'í Faith has only seven houses of worship, one on each continent. The house of worship in North America is in Wilmette, Illinois. Locally, Bahá'ís may meet for worship or for communal activities in homes or Bahá'í centers. The minimum number of Bahá'ís that can compose a local community is two, but nine are required for a local spiritual assembly.

U.S. communities: 9,455
U.S. membership: More than 168,000
(2010 data from the Office of Communications, Bahá'í National Center)

For more information, contact:
Office of Communications
Bahá'í National Center
1233 Central Street
Evanston, IL 60201
(847) 733-3559
www.bahai.us

Canadian communities: 1,759
Canadian membership: 37,597
(2010 data from the Department of External Affairs, Bahá'í National Centre)

For more information, contact:
Department of External Affairs
Bahá'í National Centre
7200 Leslie Street
Thornhill, ON L3T 6L8
(905) 889-8168
www.ca.bahai.org

2 · THE BASIC SERVICE

The centerpiece of the Bahá'í community is the Nineteen Day Feast, which is held every 19 days and is the local community's regular worship gathering—and more. The feast day is held on the first day of each of the 19 months in the Bahá'í calendar.

The Nineteen Day Feast functions both as a worship service and a business meeting for the local Bahá'í community. For this reason, Feasts are generally restricted to members of the Bahá'í Faith. In addition to Feast, however, most Bahá'í communities also hold regular prayer gatherings in their homes or community centers, as well as adult study circles and classes for children and teens, which are open to anyone.

The Nineteen Day Feast helps sustain the unity of the local Bahá'í community. While Bahá'í feasts around the world adapt to local cultural and social needs, they always contain spiritual devotions, administrative consultation and fellowship.

The word *feast* is used to imply not that a large meal will be served, but that a "spiritual feast"—worship, companionship and unity—will be available.

During devotions, selections from the writings of the Bahá'í Faith and, often, other faiths, will be read aloud. This is followed by a general discussion, which allows every member of the community to have a voice in community affairs.

Devotions plus the discussion that follows usually lasts about 90 minutes.

APPROPRIATE ATTIRE

Men: Personal preference for attire, plus one's own sense of reverence, are the only criteria. This may range from jacket and tie to slacks or jeans. No head covering is required.

Women: Personal preference for attire, plus one's own sense of reverence, are the only criteria. This may range from a dress or skirt to slacks or jeans. Clothing need not cover the arms or reach below the knees. No head covering is required. Women may wear open-toed shoes and/or modest jewelry.

There are no rules regarding colors of clothing.

THE SANCTUARY

What are the major sections of the house of worship? The only Bahá'í house of worship in North America is in Wilmette, Illinois, and has no "sanctuary." Instead, it has an entirely open, domed interior with a podium at the front. Elsewhere, Bahá'ís may meet in homes or in Bahá'í community centers.

THE SERVICE

When should guests arrive and where should they sit? Arrive at the time for which the service has been called. Guests may sit wherever they wish. There are no ushers to guide them to their seats.

If arriving late, are there times when a guest should *not* enter the service? Yes. Do not enter during prayers.

Are there times when a guest should *not* leave the service? No.

Who are the major officiants, leaders or participants and what do they do?

The chairperson or host, who will conduct the flow of activities during the service. There are no clergy in the Bahá'í Faith. The method of selecting the host varies among local Bahá'í communities. They usually either are elected or simply volunteer for the position. Often, the person in whose home a Nineteen Day Feast is held is the host for that occasion.

What are the major ritual objects of the service? There are no ritual objects in the Bahá'í Faith.

What books are used? A prayer book, which is usually *Bahá'í Prayers* (Wilmette,

Ill.: National Spiritual Assembly of the Bahá'ís of the United States, 2002; reprinted 2007). This is a selection of writings by Bahá'u'lláh, 'Abdu'l-Bahá, and Shoghi Effendi. Also, readings from sacred Bahá'í writings are often taken from *Gleanings from the Writings of Bahá'u'lláh* by Bahá'u'lláh (Wilmette, Ill.: Bahá'í Publishing, 2005) and other sacred texts. Selected writings of the Bahá'í Faith can be found at www.reference.bahai.org.

To indicate the order of the service: Periodic announcements will be made by the chairperson or host.

GUEST BEHAVIOR DURING THE SERVICE

Will a guest who is not a Bahá'í be expected to do anything other than sit? No, although it is optional for guests to sing with the congregation.

Are there any parts of the service in which a guest who is not a Bahá'í should *not* participate? Yes. Guests should not participate in the business portion. Often, this will be suspended if guests are present out of consideration for them. The business portion consists of reports from the secretary and the treasurer, after which those present can make recommendations to the local spiritual assembly or the national spiritual assembly. Such recommendations may address any aspect of the Bahá'í Faith, from the secular to the religious. Members may, for example, express a desire to have more music during a worship service or to schedule a fund-raiser for the local religious school.

If not disruptive to the service, is it okay to:
Take pictures? Yes.
Use a flash? Yes.

Use a video camera? Yes.
Use a tape recorder? Yes.

Will contributions to the church be collected at the service? No. But even if there were collections, only Bahá'ís may contribute to the Bahá'í Faith. The primary reason for this is to make Bahá'ís solely responsible for their faith. Also, contributing to the faith is considered a sacred privilege that rests on recognizing Bahá'u'lláh as the Manifestation for this day.

AFTER THE SERVICE

Is there usually a reception after the service? There may be a reception, depending on the customs of the individual community, each of which sets its own policy. If there is a reception, which is called the "social portion," it may last about 30 minutes to several hours. Food will definitely be served at a reception, but not alcoholic beverages, since alcohol is forbidden to Bahá'ís.

Is there a traditional form of address for clergy who may be at the reception? No, since there are no clergy in the Bahá'í Faith.

Is it okay to leave early? Yes.

GENERAL GUIDELINES AND ADVICE

None provided.

SPECIAL VOCABULARY

Key words or phrases that it might be helpful for a visitor to know:

Bahá'u'lláh ("Bah-HAH-oo-LAH"): Prophet. The founder of the Bahá'í Faith, whose name means "Glory of God."

'Abdu'l-Bahá ("Ab-DOOL-bah-HAH"): Son of Bahá'u'lláh, whose name means "Servant of Baha."

Shoghi Effendi ("SHOW-gey Eh-FEN-dee"): Grandson of 'Abdu'l-Bahá, also called "the Guardian."

Allah'u'Abhá ("Ah-lah-oo-ab-HAH"): "God is most glorious."

Bahá'í ("Ba-HIGH"): A follower of Bahá'u'lláh.

DOGMA AND IDEOLOGY

Bahá'ís believe:

Humanity is one.

Men and women are equal.

Any apparent inequality between the capacities of men and women is due solely to the lack of educational opportunities currently available to women.

Prejudice, religious intolerance and the extremes between wealth and poverty must be eliminated.

In addition to the Ten Commandments, behavior should be guided by avoiding such activities as gambling, drinking alcohol, drug abuse, gossip and backbiting.

Ethical work is a form of worship.

In establishing a world federation and a world language.

In universal education for all.

That science and religion are in fundamental agreement about the cosmos, since God would not have given humanity two systems that attempt to explain existence that are in conflict.

Some basic books to which a guest can refer to learn more about the Bahá'í Faith:

Bahá'u'lláh and the New Era: An Introduction to the Bahá'í Faith by J. E. Esslemont (Wilmette, Ill.: Bahá'í Publishing, 2006).

God Speaks Again: An Introduction to the Bahá'í Faith by Kenneth E. Bowers (Wilmette, Ill.: Bahá'í Publishing, 2004).

The Story of Bahá'u'lláh Promised One of All Religions by Druzelle Cederquist (Wilmette, Ill.: Bahá'í Publishing, 2005).

The above books may be obtained from:

Bahá'í Distribution Service
415 Linden Avenue
Wilmette, IL 60091
(800) 999-9019
(847) 425-7950
Fax: (847) 425-7951
bds@usbnc.org
www.bahaibookstore.com

3 · HOLY DAYS AND FESTIVALS

World Religion Day. Occurs on the third Sunday in January. The purpose is to proclaim the oneness of religion and the belief that world religion will unify the peoples of the earth. There is no traditional greeting for this holiday.

Ayyám-i-Há ("Ah-yah-mee-HAH") or "Days of Ha." Celebrated from February 26 through March 1. The holiday is devoted to hospitality, charity and gift-giving and to spiritually preparing one's self for the annual fast for the entire length of the last month in the Bahá'í calendar. The fast continues from sunrise to sundown for 19 days. Ayyám-i-Há is celebrated during the four days (five in a leap year) before the last month of the Bahá'í year. There is no traditional greeting for this holiday.

Naw-Rúz ("Naw-ROOZ"). The Bahá'í New Year's Day, which occurs on March 21. The day is astronomically fixed to commence the year on the first day of spring. Bahá'ís attend neither work nor school on this day. While there are no set rituals for observing the holiday, it is often marked by prayers, feasts and possible festive communal field trips. There is no traditional greeting for this holiday.

Festival of Ridván ("RIZ-von"). Celebrated from April 21 through May 2. This 12-day holiday commemorates the 12 days from April 21 through May 2, 1863, when Bahá'u'lláh, the prophet-founder of the Bahá'í Faith, publicly proclaimed in a garden in Baghdad his mission as God's messenger for this age. The garden was called "Ridván." Three days during the Festival of Ridván are holy days during which work and school are suspended: The first day (April 21), the ninth day (April 29) and the twelfth day (May 2). There is no traditional greeting for this holiday.

The Declaration of The Báb. Occurs on May 23. Commemorates the date in 1844 when The Báb, the prophet-herald of the Bahá'í Faith, announced in Shiraz, Persia, that he was the new herald of a new messenger of God. Work and school are suspended on this day, for which there is no traditional greeting.

Race Unity Day. Occurs on the second Sunday in June. A Bahá'í-sponsored observance intended to promote racial harmony and understanding and the essential unity of humanity. Established in 1957 by the Bahá'ís of the United States. There is no traditional greeting for this holiday.

The Martyrdom of The Báb. Occurs on July 9, and commemorates the anniversary of the execution by a firing squad in Tabriz, Persia, of Mírzá 'Alí-Muhammad, The Báb, the prophet-herald of the Bahá'í Faith. The martyrdom is marked with prayers at noon, which is when The Báb was executed. There is no traditional greeting for this holiday.

The Birth of The Báb. Celebrated on October 20. Commemorates the anniversary of the birth of The Báb, which means "the Gate," and who was the prophet-herald of the Bahá'í Faith. The Báb was born with the name Siyyid 'Alí-Muhammad in 1819. Work and school are suspended on this holiday. While there are no set rituals for observing the holiday, it is often marked by prayers, feasts and possibly festive communal field trips. There is no traditional greeting for this holiday.

The Birth of Bahá'u'lláh ("Bah-HAH-oo-LAH"). Celebrated on November 12. Commemorates the birth of Bahá'u'lláh, who was born Mírzá Husayn Ali in 1817 in Nur, Persia. Bahá'u'lláh, which means "Glory of God," was the prophet-founder of the Bahá'í Faith. Work and school are suspended on this holiday. While there are no set rituals for observing the holiday, it is often marked by prayers, feasts and possibly festive communal field trips. There is no traditional greeting for this holiday.

The Day of the Covenant. Occurs on November 26. Commemorates Bahá'u'lláh's appointing his son, 'Abdu'l-Bahá, as the Center of his Covenant. While there are no set rituals for observing the holiday, it is often marked by prayers, feasts and possibly festive communal field trips. There is no traditional greeting for this holiday.

4 · LIFE CYCLE EVENTS

Birth Ceremony

Not applicable to the Bahá'í Faith.

Initiation Ceremony

Not applicable to the Bahá'í Faith.

Marriage Ceremony

The Bahá'í Faith teaches that the family is the basic unit of society and that monogamous marriage is the foundation of family life. Also, preparation for marriage is essential for ensuring a happy marriage. Preparation includes parental approval for the choice of a spouse. This does not mean that Bahá'í marriages are arranged, since Bahá'ís marry the person of their choice. But once the choice is made, parents have the right and the obligation to weigh carefully whether to give their consent and, thus, to guide their offspring in one of life's most important decisions.

Bahá'ís encourage interracial marriages, since these stress humanity's essential oneness. The faith also does not discourage interfaith marriages.

The Bahá'í Faith allows divorce, although it strongly discourages it. If a Bahá'í couple decides to seek a divorce, they must live apart from each other for at least one year—the "year of patience"—while they attempt to reconcile. If they still desire a divorce after those 12 months, it is granted.

The Bahá'í Faith does not have a standard wedding service. Its only stipulation for a wedding is that the bride and groom must exchange vows in front of two witnesses designated by the local Bahá'í spiritual assembly. The vow repeated by the bride and groom is, "We will all verily abide by the Will of God." For a Bahá'í, that Will implies all of the commitments associated with marriage, including to love, honor and cherish; to care for each other, regardless of health or wealth; and to share with and serve each other.

Other than meeting the criteria regarding witnesses and the bride and groom reciting the vows, a Bahá'í wedding may be as simple or elaborate as a couple wishes.

The length of the wedding varies, depending on its content.

BEFORE THE CEREMONY

Are guests usually invited by a formal invitation? Either by a written invitation or by a telephone call.

If not stated explicitly, should one assume that children are invited? Yes.

If one can't attend, what should one do? Depending on your personal preference, you may send flowers or a gift to the couple along with writing or telephoning your regrets that you cannot attend.

APPROPRIATE ATTIRE

Men: A jacket and tie. No head covering is required.

Women: Personal preference for attire, and one's own sense of reverence, are the only criteria. This may range from a dress or skirt to slacks or jeans. Clothing need not cover the arms or reach below the knees. No head covering is required. Women may wear open-toed shoes and/or modest jewelry.

There are no rules regarding colors of clothing.

GIFTS

Is a gift customarily expected? Yes. Appropriate gifts are whatever is the norm in one's culture.

Should gifts be brought to the ceremony? They may be brought to the ceremony or the reception or sent to the home of the newlyweds.

THE CEREMONY

Where will the ceremony take place? Bahá'í weddings may be held wherever the bride and groom desire.

When should guests arrive and where should they sit? Arrive at the time for which the service has been called. At some weddings, there may be ushers to advise guests on where to sit.

If arriving late, are there times when a guest should *not* enter the ceremony? No.

Are there times when a guest should *not* leave the ceremony? No.

Who are the major officiants, leaders or participants at the ceremony and what do they do?

The bride, the groom and two witnesses approved by the local spiritual assembly and who need not be Bahá'ís.

What books are used? There are no standard readings at Bahá'í weddings. Whatever is read is chosen by the bride and groom and usually includes writings from Bahá'í and other faiths, and other poetry and prose.

To indicate the order of the ceremony: There may be a program or periodic announcements.

Will a guest who is not a Bahá'í be expected to do anything other than sit? No.

Are there any parts of the ceremony in which a guest who is not a Bahá'í should *not* participate? No.

If not disruptive to the ceremony, is it okay to:
Take pictures? Yes.
Use a flash? Yes.
Use a video camera? Yes.
Use a tape recorder? Yes.

Will contributions to the house of worship be collected at the ceremony? No.

AFTER THE CEREMONY

Is there usually a reception after the ceremony? Possibly, depending on personal preference. If there is a reception, there will probably be food, but no alcoholic beverages, since members of the Bahá'í Faith do not drink alcohol. There may also be music and dancing at the reception.

Would it be considered impolite to neither eat nor drink? No.

Is there a grace or benediction before eating or drinking? No.

Is there a grace or benediction after eating or drinking? No.

Is there a traditional greeting for the family? No.

Is there a traditional form of address for clergy who may be at the reception? No, since there are no clergy in the Bahá'í Faith.

Is it okay to leave early? Yes.

Funerals and Mourning

The Bahá'í Faith teaches that there is a separate, rational soul for every human. It provides the underlying animation for the body and is our real self. Upon the death of the body, the soul is freed from its ties with the physical body and the surrounding physical world, and begins its journey through the spiritual world. Bahá'ís understand the spiritual world to be a timeless, placeless extension of our own universe, and not a physically remote or removed place.

Heaven is envisioned partly as a state of nearness to God; hell is a state of remoteness from God. Each state is a natural consequence of the efforts of an individual—or the lack of them—to develop spiritually. The key to spiritual progress is to follow the path outlined by the various prophets of God, who include Adam, Moses, Buddha, Krishna, Zoroaster, Jesus and Muhammad, and Bahá'u'lláh.

Beyond this, the exact nature of afterlife remains a mystery.

While the Bahá'í Faith is relatively free of teachings regarding the actual rituals of funerals, it does advise that the deceased should not be embalmed, unless it is required by state law. Also the deceased should be buried within one hour's travel time from the place of death, since the Bahá'í Faith teaches that we are all world citizens and should not be attached to any particular geographic site.

BEFORE THE CEREMONY

How soon after the death does the funeral usually take place? Usually within two or three days.

What should a non-Bahá'í do upon hearing of the death of a member of that faith? Convey your condolences to the bereaved either by telephone or by a visit to their home.

APPROPRIATE ATTIRE

Men: Personal preference for attire, and one's own sense of reverence, are the only criteria. This may range from jacket and tie to slacks or jeans. No head covering is required.

Women: Personal preference for attire, and one's own sense of reverence, are the only criteria. This may range from a dress or skirt to slacks or jeans. Clothing need not cover the arms or reach below the knees. No head covering is required.

Women may wear open-toed shoes and/or modest jewelry.

There are no rules regarding colors of clothing, but these should conform to social and cultural custom.

GIFTS

Is it appropriate to send flowers or make a contribution? Yes. Flowers may be sent either to the home of the bereaved before or after the funeral or to the funeral itself. Contributions may be made to a fund or charity designated by the bereaved or before death by the deceased, but non-Bahá'ís cannot contribute to a Bahá'í fund.

Is it appropriate to send food? Food may be sent to the home of the bereaved before or after the funeral. No specific types of food are best to send or are prohibited.

THE CEREMONY

Where will the ceremony take place? At the local house of worship or at a funeral home.

When should guests arrive and where should they sit? Arrive early or at the time for which the service has been called. Ushers may be available to advise guests on where to sit.

If arriving late, are there times when a guest should *not* enter the ceremony? Yes. Do not enter during prayers.

Will the bereaved family be present before the ceremony? Possibly.

Is there a traditional greeting for the family? No. Simply express your condolences.

Will there be an open casket? Rarely, since the Bahá'í Faith does not allow embalming.

Is a guest expected to view the body? This is entirely optional.

What is appropriate behavior upon viewing the body? The Bahá'í Faith does not ordain certain behavior at such moments, since open caskets are so rare.

Who are the major officiants at the ceremony and what do they do? Whoever the family asks to officiate. They will see that the service is carried out according to the family's wishes.

What books are used? A prayer book, which is usually *Bahá'í Prayers* (Wilmette, Ill.: National Spiritual Assembly of the Bahá'ís of the United States, 2002; reprinted 2007). This is a selection of writings by Bahá'u'lláh, 'Abdu'l-Bahá, and Shoghi Effendi. Readings from sacred Bahá'í writings are often taken from *Gleanings from the Writings of Bahá'u'lláh* by Bahá'u'lláh (Wilmette, Ill.: Bahá'í Publishing, 2005). Other religious writings, prose or poetry may be also be read.

To indicate the order of the ceremony: There may be periodic announcements or a program may be distributed.

Will a guest who is not a Bahá'í be expected to do anything other than sit? No.

Are there any parts of the ceremony in which a guest who is not a Bahá'í should *not* participate? No.

If not disruptive to the ceremony, is it okay to:

Take pictures? Possibly, depending on the preference of the family members.

Use a flash? Possibly, depending on the preference of the family members.

Use a video camera? Possibly, depending on the preference of the family members.

Use a tape recorder? Possibly, depending on the preference of the family members.

Will contributions to the Bahá'í Faith's fund be collected at the ceremony? No.

THE INTERMENT

Should guests attend the interment? Yes.

Whom should one ask for directions? Family members or the funeral director.

What happens at the graveside? A particular Bahá'í prayer for the deceased may be recited at the graveside.

Do guests who are not Bahá'ís participate at the graveside ceremony? Depending on a guest's relationship with the deceased, the bereaved family may possibly ask a guest to read aloud some prayers to those gathered at the funeral.

COMFORTING THE BEREAVED

Is it appropriate to visit the home of the bereaved after the funeral? Yes. The timing of the visit entirely depends on the personal preference of the visitor and the bereaved.

Will there be a religious service at the home of the bereaved? No.

Will food be served? Probably.

How soon after the funeral will a mourner usually return to a normal work schedule? The Bahá'í Faith ordains no particular mourning period. The length of a mourner's absence from work depends entirely on the individual mourner.

How soon after the funeral will a mourner usually return to a normal social schedule? The Bahá'í Faith ordains no particular mourning period. The length of a mourner's absence from social events depends entirely on the individual mourner.

Are there mourning customs to which a friend who is not a Bahá'í should be sensitive? No, since the Bahá'í Faith ordains no particular mourning customs.

Are there rituals for observing the anniversary of the death? No.

5 · HOME CELEBRATIONS

Not applicable to the Bahá'í Faith.

4

Baptist

1. HISTORY AND BELIEFS

The Baptist churches descend from the spiritual ferment generated by 17th-century English Puritanism. Essentially, Baptists believe in the authority of the Bible, the right to privately interpret it, baptizing only those old enough to profess belief for themselves, and strict separation of church and state.

Although there are about two dozen different branches and divisions of Baptist churches in the United States, there are essentially two separate schools of the faith: The General and the Particular. General Baptists believe in a universal atonement in which Christ died for all; Particular Baptists believe in the limited or "particular" death of Christ for believers only.

The movement began in England in the early 17th century. Its founder, John Smyth, moved to Holland in 1607 seeking religious liberty. Some early founders of Massachusetts, including the first president of Harvard, held Baptist beliefs. Although the first Baptist church in the colonies was founded in Providence, Rhode Island, in 1639, Philadelphia became the center of Baptist life during the colonial era.

In 1845, the white Baptist churches had separated into a northern and a southern group, with the northern division opposed to the extension of slavery. After the Civil War, the number of black churches increased swiftly, mostly because Baptist principles appealed to blacks and also because the autonomy allowed in individual churches meant that black Baptist churches could operate without interference from white society. Canadian Baptists did not suffer from racial disunity but from theological disunity arising out of the Fundamentalist-Modernist controversy of the 1920s.

Today, the two largest Baptist denominations are the Southern Baptist Convention and the National Baptist Convention, U.S.A., Inc. The former has more than 16 million members and its founding in 1845 centered around a missionary impulse. The latter, with about five million members, is the largest African-American religious association in the United States.

In Canada, three Baptist groups are significant: the Federation Baptists, divided into four conventions; the Fellowship Baptists; and the North American Baptists (German descent).

U.S. churches: 88,403
U.S. membership: 34.1 million
(*data from the* 2010 Yearbook of American and Canadian Churches)

For more information, contact:

The Southern Baptist Convention
901 Commerce Street
Nashville, TN 37203
(615) 244-2355
www.sbc.net

The National Baptist Convention,
U.S.A., Inc.
1700 Baptist World Center Drive
Nashville, TN 37207
(615) 228-6292

Canadian churches: 3,201
Canadian membership: 383,116
(*data from the* 2010 Yearbook of American and Canadian Churches)

For more information, contact:

Canadian Baptist Ministries
7185 Millcreek Drive
Mississauga, ON L5N 5R4
(905) 821-3533
www.cbmin.org

North American Baptist Conference
1 S. 210 Summit Avenue
Oakbrook Terrace, IL 60181
(630) 495-2000
www.nabconference.org

2. THE BASIC SERVICE

The sermon is at the heart of the Baptist service. The sermon usually flows from that day's Scripture lesson, as do the hymns chosen for that service. The sermon is followed by "the invitation," which asks those present either to become members of the church or to rededicate themselves to Christ. One or more hymns are sung as congregants or guests come forward to accept "the invitation." The service lasts about one hour.

APPROPRIATE ATTIRE

Men: A suit or sport jacket and tie or more casual attire, depending on the specific church. No head covering is required.

Women: A dress or a skirt and blouse. Clothing should cover the arms, and hems should reach below the knees. Open-toed shoes and modest jewelry allowed. No head covering is required.

There are no rules regarding colors of clothing.

THE SANCTUARY

What are the major sections of the church?

The sanctuary: The part of the church where the altar is located and where ministers lead congregants in prayer. It is usually elevated above the floor level and is invariably at the front of the church.

The pulpit or lectern: The stand at which scriptural lessons and psalm respon-ses are read and the word of God is preached.

Seating for congregants: Seats and sometimes kneeling benches, usually in front and/or to the side of the altar or Communion table.

Communion table: The place from which the Lord's Supper is served.

Baptistery: The place for administering baptism.

THE SERVICE

When should guests arrive and where should they sit? Arrive at the time for which the service has been called. Ushers will advise guests and congregants where to sit.

If arriving late, are there times when a guest should *not* enter the service? Do not enter while prayers are being recited or while announcements are being made.

Are there times when a guest should *not* leave the service? Do not leave during the sermon or during the benediction.

Who are the major officiants, leaders or participants and what do they do?

The pastor, who presides during the service and preaches.

The associate pastor, who helps the pastor when needed with the service.

The minister of music, who leads congregational singing and directs the choir.

The choir, which provides music.

The hostess or usher, who welcomes visitors and who sometimes makes announcements about church activities.

What are the major ritual objects of the service?

Bread and grape juice (rarely is wine served), which compose the Communion (or the Lord's Supper) and are considered a memorial to the body and blood of Jesus Christ, as well as a reminder of his Second Coming.

The Communion table, from which the bread and grape juice are offered to congregants. On it may be a crucifix, candles or flowers.

What books are used? Several translations of the Bible may be used, especially the King James Version, the New International Version and the New Revised Standard Version. All are distributed by several publishers. Most Southern Baptist churches use *The Baptist Hymnal* (Nashville, Tenn.: Convention Press, 2008). Many Canadian Baptist churches use *The Hymnal* (Brantford, Ont.: Baptist Federation of Canada, 1973; or other editions).

To indicate the order of the service: A program or bulletin will be distributed.

GUEST BEHAVIOR DURING THE SERVICE

Will a guest who is not a Baptist be expected to do anything other than sit? Guests of other faiths are expected to stand, kneel, read prayers aloud and sing with those present, unless this violates their religious beliefs. If one chooses to neither kneel nor stand, remain seated.

Are there any parts of the service in which a guest who is not a Baptist should *not* participate? In some churches, Communion (or the Lord's Supper) is offered only to members of that congregation.

If not disruptive to the service, is it okay to:

Take pictures? Yes, but only with prior permission of the pastor.

Use a flash? Yes, but only with prior permission of the pastor.

Use a video camera? Yes, but only with prior permission of the pastor.
Use a tape recorder? Yes, but only with prior permission of the pastor.

Will contributions to the church be collected at the service? Yes.

How much is it customary to contribute? It is not expected that guests will contribute. If they choose to do so, between $1 and $10 is appropriate.

AFTER THE SERVICE

Is there usually a reception after the service? No.

Is there a traditional form of address for clergy whom a guest may meet? "Pastor" or "Reverend."

Is it okay to leave early? Yes.

GENERAL GUIDELINES AND ADVICE

None provided.

SPECIAL VOCABULARY

None provided.

DOGMA AND IDEOLOGY

Baptists believe:
Jesus Christ is Lord.
The sacred Scriptures are the sole norm for faith and practice.
The New Testament church is composed of baptized believers.
Local congregations are autonomous.
Religious liberty is guaranteed only by strictly separating church and state.

A basic book to which a guest can refer to learn more about the Baptist faith:
The Baptist Heritage, by N. Leon McBeth (Nashville, Tenn.: Broadman Press, 1987).

3 · HOLY DAYS AND FESTIVALS

Christmas. Always falls on December 25. Celebrates the birth of Christ. The traditional greeting is "Merry Christmas."

Easter. Always falls on the Sunday after the first full moon that occurs on or after the spring equinox of March 21. Commemorates the death and Resurrection of Jesus. The traditional greeting is "Happy Easter."

Pentecost. Occurs 50 days after Easter because this is when the Holy Ghost (the spirit of Jesus) descended on his apostles. Celebrates the power of the Holy Spirit and its manifestation in the early Christian church. There is no traditional greeting for this holiday.

Ash Wednesday. Occurs 40 days before Easter. Commemorates the beginning of Lent, which is a season for preparation and penitence before Easter itself. There is no traditional greeting for this holiday.

Maundy Thursday. Falls four days before Easter. Commemorates the institution of the Lord's Supper (also known as Communion) and Jesus' subsequent arrest and trial. There is no traditional greeting.

Good Friday. Three days before Easter. Commemorates the crucifixion, death and burial of Jesus.

Christmas, Easter and Pentecost are joyful celebrations. Ash Wednesday, Maundy Thursday and Good Friday are somber, penitential commemorations. During the services for these latter three holidays, decorum and discretion are of great importance.

4 · LIFE CYCLE EVENTS

Birth Ceremony

Baptists practice a child dedication service in which parents present their child and themselves to God in dedication. The congregation is also asked at this time to help the parents nurture their child in the Christian faith. This service usually takes place within the child's first year of life.

Initiation Ceremony

During this ceremony, which is called a baptism, an individual is completely immersed into the baptismal waters. The ceremony represents an active, volitional, public declaration of one's commitment to the Church. One's downward movement into the baptismal waters symbolizes the death of Jesus; the upward movement symbolizes his Resurrection.

Baptism occurs at the "age of accountability," which the Church has not defined, but which is assumed to usually occur between the ages of nine and 12 years old. The actual baptism takes about five to ten minutes, although the larger basic service of which it is a part lasts about one hour.

BEFORE THE CEREMONY

Are guests usually invited by a formal invitation? Guests are usually invited orally, either by telephone or in person.

If not stated explicitly, should one assume that children are invited? Yes.

If one can't attend, what should one do? RSVP with regrets. Gifts are not expected.

APPROPRIATE ATTIRE

Men: A suit or a sport jacket and tie. No head covering is required.

Women: A dress or skirt. Clothing should cover the arms, and hems should reach below the knees. Open-toed shoes and modest jewelry allowed. No head covering is required.

There are no rules regarding colors of clothing.

GIFTS

Is a gift customarily expected? No.

Should gifts be brought to the ceremony? See above.

THE CEREMONY

Where will the ceremony take place? In the main sanctuary.

When should guests arrive and where should they sit? Arrive at the time for which the service has been called. Ushers will advise guests and congregants where to sit.

If arriving late, are there times

when a guest should *not* enter the ceremony? Do not enter while prayers are being recited or while announcements are being made.

Are there times when a guest should *not* leave the ceremony? Do not leave during the sermon or during the benediction.

Who are the major officiants, leaders or participants at the ceremony and what do they do?

The pastor, who presides during the service and preaches.

The associate pastor, who helps the pastor when needed with the service.

The minister of music, who leads congregational singing and directs the choir.

The choir, which provides music.

The hostess or usher, who welcomes visitors and who sometimes makes announcements about church activities.

What books are used? Several translations of the Bible may be used, especially the King James Version, the New International Version, and the New Revised Standard Version. All are released by several publishers. Most Southern Baptist churches use *The Baptist Hymnal* (Nashville, Tenn.: Convention Press, 2008). Many Canadian Baptist churches use *The Hymnal* (Brantford, Ont.: Baptist Federation of Canada, 1973; or other editions).

To indicate the order of the ceremony: A program or bulletin may be distributed.

Will a guest who is not a Baptist be expected to do anything other than sit? Guests of other faiths are expected to stand, kneel, read prayers aloud and sing with those present, unless this violates their religious beliefs. If one chooses to neither kneel nor stand, remain seated.

Are there any parts of the ceremony in which a guest who is not a Baptist should *not* participate? In some churches, Communion (or the Lord's Supper) is offered only to members of that congregation.

If not disruptive to the ceremony, is it okay to:

Take pictures? Yes, but only with prior permission of the pastor.

Use a flash? Yes, but only with prior permission of the pastor.

Use a video camera? Yes, but only with prior permission of the pastor.

Use a tape recorder? Yes, but only with prior permission of the pastor.

Will contributions to the church be collected at the ceremony? Yes.

How much is it customary to contribute? It is not expected that guests will contribute. If they choose to do so, between $1 and $10 is appropriate.

AFTER THE CEREMONY

Is there usually a reception after the ceremony? There may possibly be a reception. If so, it is usually held in the fellowship hall of the church or at the home of the individual who has been baptized. Light food, such as punch, cookies or cake, may be served. The reception may last up to two hours.

Would it be considered impolite to neither eat nor drink? No.

Is there a grace or benediction before eating or drinking? Yes.

Is there a grace or benediction after eating or drinking? No.

Is there a traditional greeting for the family? Just offer your congratulations.

Is there a traditional form of address for clergy who may be at the reception? "Pastor" or "Reverend."

Is it okay to leave early? Yes.

Marriage Ceremony

Marriage is considered to be a three-way covenant between a woman, a man and God, who is represented at the marriage ceremony by the pastor, the congregation and the Holy Spirit (the empowering spirit of God). The ceremony takes about 30 to 60 minutes and is a ceremony in itself.

BEFORE THE CEREMONY

Are guests usually invited by a formal invitation? Yes.

If not stated explicitly, should one assume that children are invited? No.

If one can't attend, what should one do? RSVP with regrets and send a gift.

APPROPRIATE ATTIRE

Men: A suit or a jacket and tie. No head covering is required.

Women: A dress or skirt. Clothing should cover the arms, and hems should reach below the knees. Open-toed shoes and modest jewelry allowed. No head covering is required.

There are no rules regarding colors of clothing.

GIFTS

Is a gift customarily expected? Yes. Often appropriate are such household items as sheets, kitchenware or small household appliances.

Should gifts be brought to the ceremony? Send gifts to the home of the newlyweds.

THE CEREMONY

Where will the ceremony take place? In either a church or a home.

When should guests arrive and where should they sit? Arrive about 10 minutes before the time for which the ceremony has been called. Ushers will advise guests where to sit.

If arriving late, are there times when a guest should *not* enter the ceremony? Do not enter during the procession or recession of the wedding party.

Are there times when a guest should *not* leave the ceremony? Do not leave before the ceremony has ended.

Who are the major officiants, leaders or participants at the ceremony and what do they do?
The pastor, who performs the ceremony.
The bride and groom.
Musicians, who provide music before, during and after the ceremony.

What books are used? Only the pastor uses a text, which is invariably the Bible. Several translations of the Bible may be used, especially the King James Version, the New International Version and the New Revised Standard Version. All are released by several publishers. Many Canadian Baptist churches use *The Hymnal* (Brantford, Ont.: Baptist Federation of Canada, 1973).

To indicate the order of the ceremony: No such guidance is needed for those present, since the ceremony is relatively brief and there is no participation by guests.

Will a guest who is not a Baptist be expected to do anything other than sit? No.

Are there any parts of the ceremony in which a guest who is not a Baptist should *not* participate? No.

If not disruptive to the ceremony, is it okay to:
Take pictures? Yes, but only with prior permission of the pastor.
Use a flash? Yes, but only with prior permission of the pastor.
Use a video camera? Yes, but only with prior permission of the pastor.
Use a tape recorder? Yes, but only with prior permission of the pastor.

Will contributions to the church be collected at the ceremony? No.

AFTER THE CEREMONY

Is there usually a reception after the ceremony? Yes. It may be held at the church where the ceremony is conducted or in a home or a catering hall. Depending on the choice of the couple and of the bride's family, a full-course meal may be served. Alcoholic beverages are rarely served. There may be music and dancing. The reception may last more than two hours.

Would it be considered impolite to neither eat nor drink? Yes.

Is there a grace or benediction before eating or drinking? Possibly.

Is there a grace or benediction after eating or drinking? Possibly. If guests arrive and start eating at different times, grace may be said after the meal.

Is there a traditional greeting for the family? Offer your congratulations when you meet the family in the reception line after the service.

Is there a traditional form of address for clergy who may be at the reception? "Pastor" or "Reverend."

Is it okay to leave early? Yes.

Funerals and Mourning

There are two schools of belief in the Baptist faith about afterlife. One maintains that one enters Paradise immediately after death. This is based on Jesus' words on the cross to the penitent thief, "This day thou shalt be with Me in Paradise" (Luke 23:43). The other school maintains that upon Jesus' Second Coming, a trumpet will sound and the dead will be raised to Paradise. This is based on Paul's writings in First Corinthians (15:32). The funeral service, which is a ceremony in itself, lasts about 30 to 60 minutes.

BEFORE THE CEREMONY

How soon after the death does the funeral usually take place? Within one week.

What should a non-Baptist do upon hearing of the death of a member of that faith? Telephone or visit the bereaved to offer condolences and sympathies.

APPROPRIATE ATTIRE

Men: A suit or a sport jacket and tie. No head covering is required.

Women: A dress or skirt. Clothing should cover the arms, and hems should reach below the knees. Open-toed shoes and modest jewelry allowed. No head covering is required.

Dark, somber colors are advised.

GIFTS

Is it appropriate to send flowers or make a contribution? Flowers may be sent to the home of the bereaved before the funeral or to the church or funeral home where the funeral will take place. Contributions to a particular charity may be sent to the home of the bereaved before or after the funeral. The amount of the contribution is at the discretion of the donor. Such gifts should be presented to the spouse or adult children of the deceased.

Is it appropriate to send food? Food may be sent to the home of the bereaved after the funeral.

THE CEREMONY

Where will the ceremony take place? In either a church or a funeral home.

When should guests arrive and where should they sit? Arrive about 10 minutes before the time for which the ceremony has been called. Ushers will advise guests where to sit.

If arriving late, are there times when a guest should *not* enter the ceremony? Do not enter when the bereaved family is entering or during prayers.

Will the bereaved family be present at the church or funeral home before the ceremony? No.

Is there a traditional greeting for the family? No. Just offer your condolences.

Will there be an open casket? Usually.

Is a guest expected to view the body? This is optional.

What is appropriate behavior upon viewing the body? Join the line of viewers and view the body silently and somberly.

Who are the major officiants at the ceremony and what do they do? *The pastor*, who performs the service. *Musicians*, who provide music before, during and after the service.

What books are used? Several translations of the Bible may be used, especially the King James Version, the New International Version, and the New Revised Standard Version. All are released by several publishers.

To indicate the order of the ceremony: A program or bulletin will be distributed.

Will a guest who is not a Baptist be expected to do anything other

than sit? Guests of other faiths are expected to stand, kneel, read prayers aloud and sing with those present, unless this violates their religious beliefs. If one chooses not to kneel or stand, remain seated.

Are there any parts of the ceremony in which a guest who is not a Baptist should *not* participate? No, although, very rarely, Communion (or the Lord's Supper) is offered at funeral ceremonies. In some churches, Communion is offered only to members of that congregation. In such cases, follow the cues of those present, ask a fellow guest for guidance or ask a pastor for advice before the service begins.

If not disruptive to the ceremony, is it okay to:
Take pictures? No.
Use a flash? No.
Use a video camera? No.
Use a tape recorder? No.

Will contributions to the church be collected at the ceremony? No.

THE INTERMENT

Should guests attend the interment? Yes.

Whom should one ask for directions? Either ask the funeral director or follow the funeral procession to the cemetery.

What happens at the graveside? During a brief service, Scriptures are read, prayers are recited and the casket is committed to the ground.

Do guests who are not Baptists participate at the graveside ceremony? No. They are simply present.

COMFORTING THE BEREAVED

Is it appropriate to visit the home of the bereaved after the funeral? Yes. It is appropriate to do so after the burial. During such visits, happy times during the life of the deceased are recalled and spoken about. A visit of no more than 30 minutes is fitting.

Will there be a religious service at the home of the bereaved? No.

Will food be served? Yes, but no alcoholic beverages. It would be considered impolite for a visitor not to eat. No grace or benediction will be recited before or after eating or drinking.

How soon after the funeral will a mourner usually return to a normal work schedule? Possibly in one week, although there are no doctrinal prescriptions.

How soon after the funeral will a mourner usually return to a normal social schedule? Possibly two months, although there are no doctrinal prescriptions.

Are there mourning customs to which a friend who is not a Baptist should be sensitive? No.

Are there rituals for observing the anniversary of the death? There is usually no formal remembrance in a church, but there are often quiet commemorations of the death within the family of the deceased.

5 · HOME CELEBRATIONS

Not applicable to Baptists.

5

Buddhist

1 · HISTORY AND BELIEFS

Buddhism was founded in the sixth century B.C.E. in northern India by Siddhartha Gautama, who was born as the son to a king in what is now southern Nepal. Warned by a sage that his son would become either an ascetic or a universal monarch, the king confined his son to home. A few years after marrying and having a child of his own, Siddhartha escaped from his father's palace around the age of 29. Since he had been sheltered for his entire life from the pains of life, he was shocked when he beheld three men. The first was old and weak; the second was ill and diseased; the last was dead. Each represented different aspects of the impermanence inherent in all forms of earthly existence. He also saw a religious ascetic, who represented the possibility of a solution to these frailties.

Wandering in search of peace, Siddhartha tried many disciplines, including severe asceticism, until he came to the Bodhi Tree (the Tree of Enlightenment). He sat there in meditation until, at the age of 35,

he became a Buddha, or one who is enlightened.

In his first sermon after achieving enlightenment, the Buddha spoke of the Four Noble Truths and the Noble Eightfold Path. These succinctly comprise the Buddha's insights into the essential ways of life and how to achieve spiritual liberation. The Buddha died at the age of 80. His last words were for his disciples to depend not on him, but on the *dharma*, or Buddhist teachings.

In subsequent centuries, Buddhism flowered in Asia. Asian immigrants to the United States from the early third of the 19th century to the present have brought Buddhism to America. The first significant influence of Buddhist values and ideas on American intellectuals seems to have occurred in the 1830s in the writings of the New England transcendentalists. More recently, Buddhism has appealed to members of the Beat culture of the 1950s, the counterculture of the 1960s and the subsequent New Age movement, as well as today's spiritual seekers.

In Canada, Buddhism may have arrived as early as the middle of the 19th century when the Chinese arrived, first from California and then from Hong Kong. World Buddhism (i.e., the many cultural Buddhisms from all over the world) began to impact Canada only after the Canadian multiculturalism policy of the late 1960s. The three major Buddhist centers are Toronto, Vancouver and Montreal.

U.S. temples: Not available.
U.S. membership: 2.2 million
(data from The CIA World Factbook*)*

For more information, contact:

Buddhist Churches of America
1710 Octavia Street
San Francisco, CA 94109
(415) 776-5600
www.buddhistchurchesofamerica.org

Canadian temples: Not available.
Canadian membership: 300,345
(data from the 2001 Census*)*

2 · THE BASIC SERVICE

There are many varieties of Buddhist congregational gatherings. Some are almost entirely devoted to silent meditation; others include talks and teachings by a priest, monk or nun, and announcements by the president or lay leader of the Buddhist temple. Elements most common to Buddhist congregational gatherings are chanting, an incense offering, silent meditation and a sermon or talk by a priest or monk.

The gathering may last one to two hours.

APPROPRIATE ATTIRE

Men: Standards for attire vary widely. A minority of temples expect men to wear a jacket and tie; the vast majority allow much more casual dress. Loose, comfortable, casual clothing is especially recommended for those temples in which members and guests sit on meditation cushions on the floor. (Guests are advised to call the temple prior to the service for details on seating.) No head covering is required in any Buddhist temple.

Women: A minority of temples expect women to wear a dress or a skirt and blouse. The vast majority allow more casual attire. Loose, comfortable, casual clothing is especially recommended for those temples in which members and guests sit on meditation cushions on the floor. (Guests are advised to call the temple prior to the service for details on seating.) Open-toed shoes and modest jewelry are permissible. No head covering is required in any Buddhist temple.

There are no rules regarding colors of clothing.

THE SANCTUARY

What are the major sections of the temple? The architecture of Buddhist temples varies widely. These elements will be found in many, but not all, temples:
The altar: Contains a statue of the main Buddha for that particular temple.

This is at the front of the sanctuary. (Each temple is devoted to one of the hundreds of buddhas in Buddhism.)

Side altars: Contain statues or pictures of the founder of the particular lineage adhered to by a temple. A lineage is a line of teachers and their students who, in turn, also become teachers.

Pews or meditation cushions: Where congregants sit. Some temples have pews; others have pillows on the floor.

THE SERVICE

When should guests arrive and where should they sit? It is customary to arrive early. Where one sits depends on the particular tradition of that temple. If there is a seated meditation, a visitor will probably be directed to a meditation cushion.

If arriving late, are there times when a guest should *not* enter the service? Do not enter during meditation.

Are there times when a guest should *not* leave the service? Do not leave during meditation.

Who are the major officiants, leaders or participants and what do they do?

A minister or priest, monk or nun, who leads the service, including chanting.

The temple president, a layperson who may lead the service in some temples in lieu of a monk or priest.

What are the major ritual objects of the service?

An incense burner, which is usually at the front of the altar and contains an offering of incense. The incense is offered to Buddha and is lit by a priest or monk.

An ouzo ("oo-ZOH") *or a mala* ("MAH-lah"), a string of beads that is used to count recitations of a mantra, a verbal expression to keep the Buddha in one's mind or to sharpen concentration. The prayer beads are used by priests and/or monks and by congregants.

A bell, used by priests or monks to announce the beginning or end of meditation.

What books are used? All Buddhist traditions and sects quote from the sutras, which are the collected sayings of the Buddha.

To indicate the order of the service: Periodic announcements may be made by the temple president or instructions may be given by the priest or monk.

GUEST BEHAVIOR DURING THE SERVICE

Will a guest who is not a Buddhist be expected to do anything other than sit? It is entirely optional for a guest from another faith to chant with the congregation or stand when congregants do so.

Are there any parts of the service in which a guest who is not a Buddhist should *not* participate? No.

If not disruptive to the service, is it okay to:

Take pictures? Only with prior approval of a priest or monk.

Use a flash? Only with prior approval of a priest or monk.

Use a video camera? Only with prior approval of a priest or monk.

Use a tape recorder? Only with prior approval of a priest or monk.

Will contributions to the temple be collected at the service? Possibly. In some temples, there may be an offertory box near the front door of the temple.

How much is it customary to contribute? From $1 to $10.

AFTER THE SERVICE

Is there usually a reception after the service? There may be a reception in the temple's reception area at which light food may be served. There is usually no alcohol. The reception may last 60 minutes. It is not considered impolite to neither eat nor drink. Some temples have a form of grace before or after eating or drinking.

Is there a traditional form of address for clergy who may be at the reception? Depending on the particular Buddhist denomination, the form of address may be "Reverend," "Lama" ("LAH-mah") or "Roshi" ("ROH-shee").

Is it okay to leave early? Yes.

GENERAL GUIDELINES AND ADVICE

It is fine not to participate in rituals or meditations if one is uncomfortable about them. Guests who do not participate should sit quietly and still.

A typical mistake that guests should avoid is talking during the service.

SPECIAL VOCABULARY

Key words or phrases that it might be helpful for a visitor to know:

Gassho ("GASH-oh"): To place one's hands together in reverence.

Osenko ("oh-SEN-koh"): To burn incense in offering to Buddha.

DOGMA AND IDEOLOGY

Buddhists believe:

The Four Noble Truths, originally enunciated by the Buddha, comprise the essence of Buddhist teaching and practice:

1. All life (birth, aging, death) is suffering.
2. Suffering is caused by craving or desire.
3. Cessation of suffering is possible.
4. The Noble Eightfold Path can lead to the extinction of suffering.

The Noble Eightfold Path consists of:

1. Right understanding of the nature of reality.
2. Right thought, which is free from sensuous desire, ill will and cruelty.
3. Right speech, which should be absent of falsehoods, harsh words and useless chatter.
4. Right action, which includes refraining from killing, stealing and wrong conduct in matters of bodily pleasure, intoxicants and gambling.
5. Right livelihood, which forbids any conduct contrary to right speech and right action and any trickery or fraud in the service of commerce or one's trade.

6. Right effort, which seeks to avoid generating new, unwholesome actions and encourages purifying the mind (by avoiding and overcoming unwholesome states of mind, while developing and maintaining wholesome states).
7. Right mindfulness, or meditative practices that encourage greater alertness and awareness of one's self.
8. Right concentration, or striving for mental "one-pointedness." Right effort and right mindfulness together develop right concentration—and vice versa.

A basic book to which a guest can refer to learn more about Buddhism: *How the Swans Came to the Lake*, by Rick Fields (Boston: Shambhala Books, 1992).

3 · HOLY DAYS AND FESTIVALS

The three events listed below are celebrated by all Buddhist traditions, but not on the same dates. The examples given below represent the Japanese tradition.

Nirvana Day, or *Nehan E* in Japanese. Observed on February 15, which commemorates the death of the Buddha. The Sanskrit word *nirvana* ("neer-VAH-nah") means "a blowing out as of a flame," or the extinction of worldly illusions and passions. The doctrine of nirvana is closely associated with the condition of *samsara* ("SAHM-sahr-ah"), or recurrent birth-and-death, from

which one is finally liberated. Nirvana and samsara are the themes of the service for Nirvana Day. There is no traditional greeting for this holiday, but guests should be aware that, instead of shaking hands, traditional Buddhists place their palms together in front of their chest and bow slightly when greeting each other.

Hanamatsuri Day, or Buddha Day. Observed on April 8 to celebrate the birth of the Buddha. There is no traditional greeting for this holiday, but guests should be aware that, instead of shaking hands, traditional Buddhists place their palms together in front of their chest and bow slightly when greeting each other.

Bodhi Day. Observed on December 8 as the day on which Siddhartha Gautama vowed to meditate under the Bodhi Tree until attaining enlightenment. There is no traditional greeting for this holiday, but guests should be aware that, instead of shaking hands, tradi-tional Buddhists place their palms together in front of their chest and bow slightly when greeting each other.

4 · LIFE CYCLE EVENTS

Birth Ceremony

Not applicable to Buddhism.

Initiation Ceremony

In certain Japanese Buddhist sects, there is a lay initiation into the faith known as *Jukai*. It is also a name-giving ceremony. It can occur at any age and is the same for males and females. This is a fairly brief ceremony and is usually part of a larger congregational gathering.

BEFORE THE CEREMONY

Are guests usually invited by a formal invitation? Yes.

If not stated explicitly, should one assume that children are invited? No.

If one can't attend, what should one do? RSVP with regrets and send flowers.

APPROPRIATE ATTIRE

Men: Standards for attire vary widely. A minority of temples expect men to wear a jacket and tie; the vast majority allow much more casual dress. Loose, comfortable, casual clothing is especially recommended for those temples in which members and guests sit on meditation cushions on the floor. (Guests are advised to call the temple prior to the service for details on seating.) No head covering is required in any Buddhist temple.

Women: A minority of temples expect women to wear a dress or a skirt and blouse. The vast majority allow more casual attire. Loose, comfortable, casual clothing is especially recommended for those temples in which members and guests sit on meditation cushions on the floor. (Guests are advised to call

the temple prior to the service for details on seating.) Open-toed shoes and modest jewelry are permissible. No head covering is required in any Buddhist temple.

There are no rules regarding colors of clothing.

GIFTS

Is a gift customarily expected? No.

Should gifts be brought to the ceremony? See above.

THE CEREMONY

Where will the ceremony take place? Either in the main sanctuary of the temple or in a special area elsewhere in the temple.

When should guests arrive and where should they sit? It is customary to arrive early. Where one sits depends on the particular tradition of that temple. If there is a seated meditation, a visitor will probably be directed to a meditation cushion.

If arriving late, are there times when a guest should *not* enter the ceremony? Do not enter during meditation.

Are there times when a guest should *not* leave the ceremony? Do not leave during meditation.

Who are the major officiants, leaders or participants at the ceremony and what do they do?
The minister or priest, who leads the service, including chanting.
The temple president, a layperson who may lead the service in lieu of the

minister or priest in some temples.

What books are used? All Buddhist traditions and sects quote from the sutras, which are the collected sayings of the Buddha.

To indicate the order of the ceremony: Periodic announcements are usually made by the temple president or instructions may be given by a priest or monk.

Will a guest who is not a Buddhist be expected to do anything other than sit? No. It is entirely optional for a guest from another faith to chant with the congregation or stand when congregants do so.

Are there any parts of the ceremony in which a guest who is not a Buddhist should *not* participate? No.

If not disruptive to the ceremony, is it okay to:

Take pictures? Only with prior approval of the priest or monk.

Use a flash? Only with prior approval of the priest or monk.

Use a video camera? Only with prior approval of the priest or monk.

Use a tape recorder? Only with prior approval of the priest or monk.

Will contributions to the temple be collected at the ceremony? Yes. There is usually an offertory box near the front door of the temple.

How much is it customary to contribute? From $1 to $10.

AFTER THE CEREMONY

Is there usually a reception after the ceremony? There may be a reception in the temple's reception area at which light food may be served. There is usually no alcohol. The reception may last 60 to 90 minutes.

Would it be considered impolite to neither eat nor drink? No.

Is there a grace or benediction before eating or drinking? Some temples have a form of grace before eating or drinking.

Is there a grace or benediction after eating or drinking? Some temples have a form of grace after eating or drinking.

Is there a traditional greeting for the family? Just offer your congratulations.

Is there a traditional form of address for clergy who may be at the reception? Depending on the particular Buddhist denomination, the form of address may be "Reverend," "Lama" or "Roshi."

Is it okay to leave early? Yes.

Marriage Ceremony

There is no standard Buddhist marriage ceremony in the United States or Canada. In some cases, the ceremony may be modeled after a standard Protestant wedding service. Regardless of the structure of the ceremony, the overall purpose is to remind those present of the essential Buddhist principle of non-harmfulness to all sentient beings.

The ceremony may last from 15 to 30 minutes.

BEFORE THE CEREMONY

Are guests usually invited by a formal invitation? Guests will be invited orally, either in person or on the telephone, or through a written invitation.

If not stated explicitly, should one assume that children are invited? The broad variables of Buddhist practice make this impossible to answer. Ask the couple or family members.

If one can't attend, what should one do? RSVP with regrets. Ordinarily, no present is expected.

APPROPRIATE ATTIRE

Men: Standards for attire vary widely. A minority of temples expect men to wear a jacket and tie; the vast majority allow much more casual dress. Loose, comfortable, casual clothing is especially recommended for those temples in which members and guests sit on meditation cushions on the floor. (Guests are advised to call the temple prior to the service for details on seating.) No head covering is required in any Buddhist temple.

Women: A minority of temples expect women to wear a dress or a skirt and blouse. The vast majority allow more casual attire. Loose, comfortable, casual clothing is especially recommended for those temples in which members and guests sit on meditation cushions on the floor. (Guests are advised to call the temple prior to the service for details on seating.) Open-toed shoes and modest jewelry are permissible. No head covering is required in any Buddhist temple.

There are no rules regarding colors of clothing.

GIFTS

Is a gift customarily expected? No.

Should gifts be brought to the ceremony? See above.

THE CEREMONY

Where will the ceremony take place? Either in a temple or outdoors.

When should guests arrive and where should they sit? It is customary to arrive early. Where one sits depends on the particular tradition of that temple. Guests should be aware that a temple may have meditation cushions on the floor and not pews in which to sit.

If arriving late, are there times when a guest should *not* enter the ceremony? Do not enter during meditation.

Are there times when a guest should *not* leave the ceremony? No.

Who are the major officiants, leaders or participants at the ceremony and what do they do?
A minister or priest, who officiates.
The bride and groom.

What books are used? There are no standard texts for Buddhist wedding ceremonies, although any readings will usually refer to kindness and compassion.

To indicate the order of the ceremony: Since the ceremony is fairly brief and only the priest or monk does any recitations, there is little need to indicate the order of the event.

Will a guest who is not a Buddhist be expected to do anything other than sit? Perhaps only to stand when others do.

Are there any parts of the ceremony in which a guest who is not a Buddhist should *not* participate? No.

If not disruptive to the ceremony, is it okay to:
Take pictures? Only with prior approval of a priest or monk.
Use a flash? Only with prior approval of a priest or monk.
Use a video camera? Only with prior approval of a priest or monk.
Use a tape recorder? Only with prior approval of a priest or monk.

Will contributions to the temple be collected at the ceremony? No.

AFTER THE CEREMONY

Is there usually a reception after the ceremony? There may be a reception in the temple's reception area or at another site chosen by the newlyweds. Light food may be served, but not meat. There is usually no alcohol. The reception may last 60 minutes.

Would it be considered impolite to neither eat nor drink? No.

Is there a grace or benediction before eating or drinking? Possibly, depending on the particular Buddhist denomination and sect.

Is there a grace or benediction after eating or drinking? Possibly, depending on the particular Buddhist denomination and sect.

Is there a traditional greeting for the family? Just offer your congratulations.

Is there a traditional form of address for clergy who may be at the reception? Depending on the particular Buddhist denomination, the form of address may be "Reverend," "Lama" or "Roshi."

Is it okay to leave early? Yes.

Funerals and Mourning

According to Buddhist belief, each individual passes through many reincarnations until he or she is liberated from worldly illusions and passions. They have then entered nirvana, Sanskrit for "a blowing out as of a flame." One enters a new incarnation immediately after death. Although the resulting being is not fully realized for nine months, a new incarnation can be interpreted as entering the womb of a woman.

Three components of any Buddhist funeral ceremony are sharing; the practice of good conduct; and developing a calm mind, or meditation.

A funeral ceremony in several Japanese Buddhist traditions resembles a Christian ceremony in the West, with a eulogy and prayers at a funeral home. It may last one hour and 15 minutes. Cambodian, Thai and Ceylonese traditions may have up to three ceremonies, each lasting about 45 minutes. (See below for details on these ceremonies.)

BEFORE THE CEREMONY

How soon after the death does the funeral usually take place? This varies, depending on the specific Buddhist tradition of the bereaved. In certain Japanese traditions, the funeral is usually within one week. In the Buddhist traditions of Cambodia, Ceylon and Thailand, there are three ceremonies. In the first, which is held within two days after death, monks hold a ceremony at the home of the bereaved. In the second, which is held within two to five days after death, monks conduct a service at a funeral home. In the third, which is held seven days after the burial or cremation, monks lead a ceremony either at the home of the bereaved or at a temple. This last ceremony, called a "merit transference," seeks to generate good energy for the deceased in his or her new incarnation.

What should a non-Buddhist do upon hearing of the death of a member of that faith? It is usually not considered appropriate to communicate with the bereaved before the funeral.

APPROPRIATE ATTIRE

Men: Standards for attire vary widely. A minority of temples expect men to wear a jacket and tie; the vast majority allow more casual dress. Loose, comfortable, casual clothing is especially recommended for those temples in which members and guests sit on meditation cushions on the floor. (Guests are advised to call the temple prior to the service for details on seating.) No head covering is required in any Buddhist temple.

Women: A minority of temples expect women to wear a dress or a skirt and blouse. The vast majority allow more casual attire. Loose, comfortable, casual clothing is especially recommended for those temples in which members and guests sit on meditation cushions on the floor. (Guests are advised to call the temple prior to the service for details on seating.) Open-toed shoes and modest jewelry are permissible. No head covering is required in any Buddhist temple.

In Japanese Buddhist traditions, dark, somber colors for clothing are advised. In Cambodian, Thai or Ceylonese traditions, white colors are advised.

GIFTS

Is it appropriate to send flowers or make a contribution? It is appropriate to send flowers to the funeral or to make a donation of $5 to $100, depending on one's relation to the deceased. Typically, the bereaved family recommends a specific charity or cause as the recipient of donations.

Is it appropriate to send food? No.

THE CEREMONY

Where will the ceremony take place? In certain Japanese traditions, the ceremony is usually held at a funeral home. In Cambodian, Thai and Ceylonese traditions, the first ceremony is at the home of the bereaved, the second is at a funeral home and the third is either at the home of the bereaved or at a temple.

When should guests arrive and where should they sit? Arrive at the time for which the service has been called. Sit wherever you wish. If the ceremony is in a funeral home, there will be pews for sitting. If held at the home or the temple of an adherent of the Cambodian, Thai or Ceylonese traditions, sitting will probably be on the floor on meditation cushions.

If arriving late, are there times when a guest should *not* enter the ceremony? No.

Will the bereaved family be present at the temple or funeral home before the ceremony? Yes.

Is there a traditional greeting for the family? Just offer your condolences.

Will there be an open casket? Always.

Is a guest expected to view the body? Yes, because Buddhism deems viewing the body to be a valuable reminder of the impermanence of life.

What is appropriate behavior upon viewing the body? Bow slightly toward the body as a sign of appreciation of its lesson regarding impermanence.

Who are the major officiants at the ceremony and what do they do?
A *minister or priest*, who officiates in the Japanese tradition.
A *monk*, who officiates in the Cambodian, Thai and Ceylonese traditions.

What books are used? All Buddhist traditions and sects quote from the sutras, which are the collected sayings of the Buddha.

To indicate the order of the ceremony: Announcements may be made by the priest or monk.

Will a guest who is not a Buddhist be expected to do anything other than sit? Stand when others do so.

Are there any parts of the ceremony in which a guest who is not a Buddhist should *not* participate? No.

If not disruptive to the ceremony, is it okay to:
Take pictures? No.
Use a flash? No.
Use a video camera? No.
Use a tape recorder? No.

Will contributions to the temple be collected at the ceremony? No.

THE INTERMENT

Should guests attend the interment or cremation? If so desired.

Whom should one ask for directions? The funeral director or a monk or priest.

What happens at the graveside? Prayers are recited and the body is committed to the ground.

Do guests who are not Buddhists participate at the graveside ceremony? No.

COMFORTING THE BEREAVED

Is it appropriate to visit the home of the bereaved after the funeral? Yes.

Will there be a religious service at the home of the bereaved? In Cambodian, Thai and Ceylonese traditions, monks lead a "merit transference" ceremony seven days after the burial or cremation. The purpose is to generate good energy for the deceased in his or her new incarnation.

Will food be served? Yes.

How soon after the funeral will a mourner usually return to a normal work schedule? This totally depends on the individual mourner. There are no religious prescriptions regarding refraining from work.

How soon after the funeral will a mourner usually return to a normal social schedule? Usually not until three months after the death.

Are there mourning customs to which a friend who is not a Buddhist should be sensitive? No.

Are there rituals for observing the anniversary of the death? Japanese, Cambodian, Thai and Ceylonese traditions have a memorial service 90 days after the death. A year after the death, all four traditions have "merit transference" ceremonies, whose purpose is to generate good energy for the deceased in his or her new incarnation. These may be held either at the home of the bereaved or at a temple. Food will be served, since sharing is an integral part of all Buddhist ceremonies.

5 · HOME CELEBRATIONS

Not applicable to Buddhism.

6

Christian Church (Disciples of Christ)

1. HISTORY AND BELIEFS

Reacting against the sectarianism common among religions on the American frontier of the early 1800s, the founders of the Christian Church urged a union of all Christians. Two independently developing groups, the "Disciples" and the "Christians," formally united in 1832.

They advocated adult baptism by immersion, weekly observance of the Lord's Supper (more commonly known as Communion) and autonomy of local congregations.

The Canadian church traces its heritage to this new American group and to a similar movement within the Scotch Baptist movement in Britain.

One joins the Church after simply declaring his or her faith in Jesus and being baptized by immersion. The highly ecumenical Christian Church was among the founders of the National Council of Churches and the World Council of Churches. Its secular-oriented programs focus on such issues as helping the mentally challenged, aiding war victims, bolstering farms and improving cities and education.

The Church is highly democratic. Local congregations own their own property and control their budgets and programs. Each congregation votes in the General Assembly that meets every two years.

U.S. churches: 3,714
U.S. membership: 679,563
   (data from the 2010 Yearbook of American and Canadian Churches*)*

For more information, contact:
The Christian Church (Disciples of Christ)
Disciples Center
130 East Washington St.
P.O. Box 1986
Indianapolis, IN 46206-1986
(317) 635-3100
www.disciples.org

Canadian churches: 25
Canadian membership: 2,631
   (data from the 2010 Yearbook of American and Canadian Churches*)*

For more information, contact:
The Christian Church (Disciples of Christ) in Canada
P.O. Box 23030
417 Wellington Street
St. Thomas, ON N5R 6A3
(519) 633-9083

2 · THE BASIC SERVICE

The basic worship service is a relatively simple formal liturgy that emphasizes the preaching of God's word and celebration of the Lord's Supper. (The ritual commemorating the Lord's Supper is known as Holy Communion.) The service includes hymns, psalms, responsive readings, Bible readings, a sermon and, always, the Communion liturgy.

Disciples of Christ believe that the Lord's Supper is a celebration and a thanksgiving to God and an affirmation of Christ's spiritual presence.

The service usually lasts less than one hour.

APPROPRIATE ATTIRE

Men: Jacket and tie or slacks and a sport shirt. Attire varies from congregation to congregation. No head covering is required.

Women: A dress, skirt and blouse or pants suit is acceptable. Open-toed shoes and modest jewelry are fine. Neither a head covering nor hems below the knees are required.

There are no rules regarding colors of clothing.

THE SANCTUARY

What are the major sections of the church?

The nave: Where congregants sit.
The choir loft: Where the choir sits.
The chancel: Includes the altar and pulpit and seating for clergy. The pastor conducts the worship from this area.

THE SERVICE

When should guests arrive and where should they sit?
It is generally appropriate to arrive a few minutes early to be seated, since services typically begin at the hour called. Usually, ushers will help you find a seat.

If arriving late, are there times when a guest should *not* enter the service?
Do not enter during spoken or silent prayers. Entry during songs is advised.

Are there times when a guest should *not* leave the service?
Do not leave during the message (or sermon), the Scripture reading, prayer or Communion.

Who are the major officiants, leaders or participants and what do they do?
The pastor, who preaches, oversees others who participate in the service and administers the sacraments.
Elders, who in some congregations will preside at the table. Their role varies from simply giving a prayer or meditation to the actual administering of the sacraments.
Liturgists or readers, and assisting ministers, who assist with prayers and read the scripture lessons.
An acolyte, who lights candles, assists with Communion and other tasks. This is usually a youth of elementary school age.
The choir, which leads the singing.
Ushers and greeters, who welcome and seat guests and distribute books.
The music leader, who plays the organ, directs the choir and leads singing.

What are the major ritual objects of the service?

The altar, which symbolizes the presence of God.

The pulpit, behind which the pastor stands while preaching.

The lectern, where scripture is read.

The baptismal font, which is used for baptizing. This is usually near the front of the church.

A crucifix, a cross with a representation of the body of Jesus Christ on it. This may be on the altar or incorporated in a church's interior design.

A Communion table, the site from which the Lord's Supper (Communion) is served.

What books are used? The New Revised Standard Version of the Bible (New York: National Council of Churches' Division of Christian Education, 1989) and *The Chalice Hymnal* (St. Louis, Mo.: Chalice Press, 1995).

To indicate the order of the service: Ushers will distribute a program.

GUEST BEHAVIOR DURING THE SERVICE

Will a guest who is not a Disciple of Christ be expected to do anything other than sit? The level of participation depends on whether or not the guest is Christian. Christians will generally be expected to stand and sing with congregants and read prayers aloud. Non-Christians are expected to stand with congregants and are invited to sing and pray with them.

Are there any parts of the service in which a guest who is not a Disciple of Christ should *not* participate? No, unless these parts violate or compromise their own religious beliefs. In most, although not all, congregations, it is permissible for visitors to take Communion. However, in a minority of congregations this would not be allowed. If possible, check the local practice beforehand.

If not disruptive to the service, is it okay to:
Take pictures? Yes.
Use a flash? Yes.
Use a video camera? Yes.
Use a tape recorder? Yes.

Will contributions to the church be collected at the service? Generally, ushers pass an offering plate or basket among the seated congregants. It is the guest's choice whether or not to contribute.

How much is it customary to contribute? A donation (by cash or check) of $1 to $10 is appropriate.

AFTER THE SERVICE

Is there usually a reception after the service? Usually, there is a 30- to 60-minute reception in the church's reception area. Light food will be served, but not alcoholic beverages. It is not considered impolite to neither eat nor drink. There is no grace or benediction before or after eating or drinking.

Is there a traditional form of address for clergy who may be at the reception? "Pastor" or "Reverend."

Is it okay to leave early? Yes.

GENERAL GUIDELINES AND ADVICE

Generally, model your behavior and your movements on those of the other worshipers and follow the instructions of the leaders of the service.

SPECIAL VOCABULARY

Key words or phrases that it might be helpful for a visitor to know:

Holy Communion: A rite through which Disciples believe they receive Christ's body and blood as assurance that God has forgiven their sins.

Lessons: Readings from the Bible (or "Scripture"), including the Old Testament (the Hebrew Scriptures, written before the birth of Jesus), the Epistle (generally from one of the letters of St. Paul or another New Testament writer) and the Gospel (a reading from Matthew, Mark, Luke or John, the "biographers" of Jesus).

DOGMA AND IDEOLOGY

Disciples of Christ believe:

Communion is shared weekly and all Christians are welcome to participate in its offering. Disciples believe that Christ is the Host of the table and invite all Christians, regardless of their denomination, to take part. Communion unites Disciples with other Christians.

Worship is led by lay leaders in conjunction with ordained clergy. Unlike certain other Christian denominations, no confession, or statement that Jesus is the Christ, is required for membership.

The Law of God, as found, for example, in the Ten Commandments, tells what God expects of us and how we are to live. The Law also shows us that we fall short of God's expectations and that we are dis-obedient to God.

The Gospel is the good news of how God remains faithful to his justice, love and mercy, and does not want to see any of us punished or separated from him because of our sin. The good news (which is what *Gospel* means) is that the eternal Son of God, who is himself fully God, became a man in the person of Jesus of Nazareth, lived a life of perfect obedience that we cannot live, and suffered God's own punishment for our sins so we don't have to. Instead, we are freely forgiven through Jesus Christ and given eternal life with God as a free gift.

Individuals are encouraged to interpret Scripture in light of science, reason, faith and tradition.

A basic book to which a guest can refer to learn more about the Disciples of Christ:

A Handbook for Today's Disciples in the Christian Church (Disciples of Christ) by D. Duane Cummins (St. Louis, Mo.: Chalice Press, 2010).

3 · HOLY DAYS AND FESTIVALS

Advent. Begins four weeks before Christmas. The purpose is to prepare for Christmas and to focus on Christ. There is no traditional greeting among church members for Advent.

Christmas. Occurs on the evening of December 24 and the day of December 25. Marks the birth and the incarnation of God as a man. The traditional greeting is "Merry Christmas."

Lent. Begins on Ash Wednesday, which

occurs six weeks before Easter. The purpose is to prepare for Easter. There is no traditional greeting among church members for this holiday.

Between Lent and Easter, abstention from entertainment and increased giving to the poor are encouraged. Often, there are midweek worship services. Some church members fast, although it is not mandated by the Church. Those who fast may choose to abstain from certain foods or from certain meals.

Easter. Always falls on the Sunday after the first full moon that occurs on or after March 21. Celebrates the Resurrection of Jesus Christ. The traditional greeting to Disciples of Christ is "Happy Easter."

Pentecost Sunday. The seventh Sunday after Easter. Celebrates the coming of the Holy Spirit, which is the empowering spirit of God in human life. This is often considered the birth of the Christian church. There is no traditional greeting among church members for this holiday.

4 · LIFE CYCLE EVENTS

Birth Ceremony

The "blessing and dedication service" acknowledges an infant's presence in the Christian community, and seals a covenant between its parents, sponsors and congregation to guide the child.

The service is part of a larger morning worship service. The entire service usually lasts about one hour.

BEFORE THE CEREMONY

Are guests usually invited by a formal invitation? They are usually invited by a note or phone call.

If not stated explicitly, should one assume that children are invited? Yes.

If one can't attend, what should one do? RSVP with regrets, either by phone or by sending a note to the parents.

APPROPRIATE ATTIRE

Men: Jacket and tie. No head covering is required.

Women: A dress, skirt and blouse, or pants suit is acceptable. Open-toed shoes and modest jewelry are fine. Neither a head covering nor hems below the knees are required.

There are no rules regarding colors of clothing.

GIFTS

Is a gift customarily expected? While this is entirely optional, such gifts as cash or bonds or baby toys or clothing are certainly appreciated.

Should gifts be brought to the ceremony? No. Bring them to the reception afterward.

THE CEREMONY

Where will the ceremony take place? Just below the chancel area in the main sanctuary of the parents' church. The chancel includes the altar and pulpit and seating for clergy.

When should guests arrive and where should they sit? It is generally appropriate to arrive a few minutes early to be seated, since services typically begin at the hour called. Usually, ushers will be available to assist you in finding a seat.

If arriving late, are there times when a guest should *not* enter the ceremony? Do not enter during prayers.

Are there times when a guest should *not* leave the ceremony? Do not leave during the message (or sermon), the Scripture reading, prayer or Communion.

Who are the major officiants, leaders or participants at the ceremony and what do they do?
The pastor, who presides.
The child's parents.
The child's godparents.

What books are used? The New Revised Standard Version of the Bible (New York: National Council of Churches' Division of Christian Education, 1989) and *The Chalice Hymnal* (St. Louis, Mo.: Chalice Press, 1995).

To indicate the order of the ceremony: Ushers will distribute a program.

Will a guest who is not a Disciple of Christ be expected to do anything other than sit? The level of participation depends on whether or not the guest is Christian. Christians will generally be expected to stand and sing with congregants and read prayers aloud. Non-Christians are expected to stand with congregants and are invited to sing and pray with them.

Are there any parts of the ceremony in which a guest who is not a Disciple of Christ should *not* participate? No, unless they violate or compromise their own religious beliefs.

If not disruptive to the ceremony, is it okay to:
Take pictures? Yes.
Use a flash? Yes.
Use a video camera? Yes.
Use a tape recorder? Yes.

Will contributions to the church be collected at the ceremony? Generally, ushers pass an offering plate or basket among the seated congregants. It is the guest's choice whether or not to contribute.

How much is it customary to contribute? A donation (by cash or check) of $1 to $10 is appropriate.

AFTER THE CEREMONY

Is there usually a reception after the ceremony? Yes, usually in the church's reception area. This may last about 30 to 60 minutes. Light food is ordinarily served, but not alcoholic beverages.

Would it be considered impolite to neither eat nor drink? No.

Is there a grace or benediction before eating or drinking? No.

Is there a grace or benediction after eating or drinking? No.

Is there a traditional greeting for the family? No. Just offer your congratulations.

Is there a traditional form of address for clergy who may be at the reception? "Pastor" or "Reverend."

Is it okay to leave early? Yes.

Initiation Ceremony

Baptism by immersion is done for pre- or early adolescents, for adults or for children with parental consent. The sacrament is a symbolic participation in Christ's death, burial and Resurrection and also a purifying remission of sin. It is largely based upon Jesus' saying in the Gospel of John (3:5) that one can enter the Kingdom of God only if he is "born of water and the Spirit."

For Disciples of Christ, baptism may be done either individually or with one's Sunday school classmates.

BEFORE THE CEREMONY

Are guests usually invited by a formal invitation? Guests are usually invited by a note or phone call.

If not stated explicitly, should one assume that children are invited? Yes.

If one can't attend, what should one do? Telephone the parents and the adolescent. Offer your congratulations.

APPROPRIATE ATTIRE

Men: Jacket and tie. No head covering is required.

Women: A dress, skirt and blouse, or pants suit is acceptable. Open-toed shoes and modest jewelry are fine. Neither a head covering nor hems below the knees are required.

There are no rules regarding color of clothing.

GIFTS

Is a gift customarily expected? This is entirely optional. Usual gifts are a Bible, a bookmark or something equally modest and fitting to the occasion.

Should gifts be brought to the ceremony? They are usually brought to the reception afterward.

THE CEREMONY

Where will the ceremony take place? At the baptismal font near the chancel in the main sanctuary of the church. The chancel includes the altar and pulpit and seating for clergy.

When should guests arrive and where should they sit? It is generally appropriate to arrive a few minutes early to be seated since services typically begin at the hour called. Usually, ushers will be available to assist you in finding a seat.

If arriving late, are there times when a guest should *not* enter the ceremony? Do not enter during spoken or silent prayers. Entry during songs is advised.

Are there times when a guest should *not* leave the ceremony? Do not leave during the message (or sermon), the Scripture reading, prayer or Communion.

Who are the major officiants,

leaders or participants at the ceremony and what do they do? *The pastor and/or the elder,* who presides. *The candidate for baptism.*

What books are used? The New Revised Standard Version of the Bible (New York: National Council of Churches' Division of Christian Education, 1989) and *The Chalice Hymnal* (St. Louis, Mo.: Chalice Press, 1995).

To indicate the order of the ceremony: Ushers will distribute a program.

Will a guest who is not a Disciple of Christ be expected to do anything other than sit? The level of participation depends on whether or not the guest is Christian. Christians will generally be expected to stand and sing with congregants and read prayers aloud. Non-Christians are expected to stand with congregants and are invited to sing and pray with them.

Are there any parts of the ceremony in which a guest who is not a Disciple of Christ should *not* participate? No, unless they violate or compromise their own religious beliefs.

If not disruptive to the ceremony, is it okay to:
Take pictures? Yes.
Use a flash? Yes.
Use a video camera? Yes.
Use a tape recorder? Yes.

Will contributions to the church be collected at the ceremony? Generally, ushers pass an offering plate or basket among the seated congregants. It is the guest's choice whether or not to contribute.

How much is it customary to contribute? A donation (by cash or check) of $1 to $10 is appropriate.

AFTER THE CEREMONY

Is there usually a reception after the ceremony? Usually, a 30- to 60-minute reception is held in the church's reception area. Light food is served, but not alcoholic beverages.

Would it be considered impolite to neither eat or drink? No.

Is there a grace or benediction before eating or drinking? No.

Is there a grace or benediction after eating or drinking? No.

Is there a traditional greeting for the family? No. Just offer your congratulations.

Is there a traditional form of address for clergy who may be at the reception? "Pastor" or "Reverend."

Is it okay to leave early? Yes.

Marriage Ceremony

A church wedding is an act of worship in which the couple profess their love for and their commitment to each other before God and ask his blessing on their marriage. The same decorum exercised in any worship service should be exercised in the wedding service.

The wedding is a ceremony in itself. In it, the wedding party progresses in, then the pastor reads appropriate lessons from the Bible and asks the bride and groom about their commitment to one another. The pastor delivers a brief homily, wedding vows and rings are exchanged and the couple are pronounced husband and wife.

The ceremony lasts between 15 and 30 minutes.

BEFORE THE CEREMONY

Are guests usually invited by a formal invitation? Yes.

If not stated explicitly, should one assume that children are invited? Yes.

If one can't attend, what should one do? RSVP and send a gift.

APPROPRIATE ATTIRE

Men: Jacket and tie. No head covering is required.

Women: A dress, skirt and blouse, or pants suit is acceptable. Open-toed shoes and modest jewelry are fine. Neither a head covering nor hems below the knees are required.

There are no rules regarding colors of clothing.

GIFTS

Is a gift customarily expected? Yes, ordinarily cash or items for the household such as small appliances, dishes, towels or blankets.

Should gifts be brought to the ceremony? Either bring a gift to the ceremony and place it on the gift table or send it to the home of the newlyweds.

THE CEREMONY

Where will the ceremony take place? In the main sanctuary of the House of Worship. The wedding party will stand near the altar in the chancel, the area in front of the sanctuary that includes the altar and pulpit and seating for clergy.

When should guests arrive and where should they sit? It is appropriate to arrive before the time called for the ceremony. An usher will advise you where to sit.

If arriving late, are there times when a guest should *not* enter the ceremony? Do not enter during the processional or recessional or during prayer.

Are there times when a guest should *not* leave the ceremony? Do not leave during the processional or recessional or during prayer.

Who are the major officiants, leaders or participants at the ceremony and what do they do?
The pastor, who presides.

What books are used? The New Revised Standard Version of the Bible (New York: National Council of Churches' Division of Christian Education, 1989) and the worship book with the wedding liturgy.

To indicate the order of the ceremony: Ushers will distribute a program.

Will a guest who is not a Disciple of Christ be expected to do anything other than sit? The level of participation depends on whether or not the guest is Christian. Christians will generally be expected to stand and sing with congregants and read prayers aloud. Non-Christians are expected to stand with congregants and are invited to sing and pray with them.

Are there any parts of the ceremony in which a guest who is not a Disciple of Christ should *not* participate? No, unless they violate or compromise their own religious beliefs.

If not disruptive to the ceremony, is it okay to:
Take pictures? Yes.
Use a flash? Yes.
Use a video camera? Yes.
Use a tape recorder? Yes.

Will contributions to the church be collected at the ceremony? No.

AFTER THE CEREMONY

Is there usually a reception after the ceremony? Yes. It may be at the church, at home or in a catering hall. It may last between one to two hours. Food will be served. Alcoholic beverages may be served if the reception is not held at the church. There will probably be music and dancing.

Would it be considered impolite to neither eat nor drink? No. If you have dietary restrictions, inform your host or hostess in advance.

Is there a grace or benediction before eating or drinking? Guests should wait for the saying of grace before eating.

Is there a grace or benediction after eating or drinking? No.

Is there a traditional greeting for the family? Congratulate the new couple and their parents.

Is there a traditional form of address for clergy who may be at the reception? "Pastor" or "Reverend."

Is it okay to leave early? Yes.

Funerals and Mourning

For Disciples of Christ, death is not the end of life, but the beginning of new life. While Disciples will grieve, they do not mourn as do those who have no hope of ever seeing the deceased again or who are without the sure hope that those who die in faith in Jesus Christ are assured eternal life with God.

The funeral is a service in itself. A pastor presides. Pallbearers carry or push the casket on rollers into the funeral home or church sanctuary.

The service will last between 15 and 30 minutes. All attending are expected to remain to the end.

BEFORE THE CEREMONY

How soon after the death does the funeral usually take place? Within one week.

What should someone who is not a Disciple of Christ do upon hearing of the death of a member of that faith? Call the bereaved or visit or send a note to express your sympathy at their loss. Express your concern for them.

APPROPRIATE ATTIRE

Men: Jacket and tie. No head covering is required.

Women: A dress or skirt and blouse is acceptable. Open-toed shoes and modest jewelry are fine. No head covering is required.

Dark, somber colors are recommended.

GIFTS

Is it appropriate to send flowers or make a contribution? It is appropriate to send flowers unless the family expresses otherwise. Send them to the deceased's home or to the funeral home where the funeral will be held.

It is also appropriate to make a donation in memory of the deceased. The family will often announce, through either the funeral home or a classified ad in a local newspaper, the preferred cause or charity for memorial contributions.

There is no standard amount to be donated.

Is it appropriate to send food? You may want to send food to the home of the bereaved for the family and their guests.

THE CEREMONY

Where will the ceremony take place? Either in the church of the deceased or in a funeral home.

When should guests arrive and where should they sit? It is customary to arrive early enough to be seated when the service begins. Someone will tell you where and when to sit.

If arriving late, are there times when a guest should *not* enter the ceremony? Do not enter during the procession or during prayer.

Will the bereaved family be present at the church or funeral home before the ceremony? There is often a visitation at the funeral home the night before the service.

Is there a traditional greeting for the family? Express your sorrow and regrets.

Will there be an open casket? Usually.

Is a guest expected to view the body? This is entirely optional.

What is appropriate behavior upon viewing the body? Stand quietly near the casket, view the body and extend your condolences to the family.

Who are the major officiants at the ceremony and what do they do? *The pastor*, who presides.

What books are used? The New Revised Standard Version of the Bible (New York: National Council of Churches' Division of Christian Education, 1989).

To indicate the order of the ceremony: A program will be distributed.

Will a guest who is not a Disciple of Christ be expected to do anything other than sit? The level of participation depends on whether or not the guest is Christian. Christians will generally be expected to stand and sing with congregants and read prayers aloud. Non-Christians are expected to stand with congregants and are invited to sing and pray with them.

Are there are any parts of the service in which a guest who is not a Disciple of Christ should *not* participate? No, unless these parts violate or compromise their own religious beliefs.

If not disruptive to the ceremony, it is okay to:
Take pictures? No.
Use a flash? No.
Use a video camera? No.
Use a tape recorder? No.

Will contributions to the church be collected at the ceremony? No.

THE INTERMENT

Should guests attend the interment? This is optional. If one decides to do so, join the funeral procession.

Whom should one ask for directions? The funeral director.

What happens at the graveside? The casket is carried to the grave. Prayers and readings are offered. The pastor blesses the earth placed on the casket.

Do guests who are not Disciples of Christ participate at the graveside service? No, they are simply present.

COMFORTING THE BEREAVED

Is it appropriate to visit the home of the bereaved after the funeral? Yes. More than once is appropriate. The length of the visit depends on one's judgment and sensitivities.

Will there be a religious service at the home of the bereaved? No.

Will food be served? Yes. Wait for grace to be said before eating. It would not be considered impolite not to eat.

How soon after the funeral will a mourner usually return to a normal work schedule? Within three days to a week.

How soon after the funeral will a mourner usually return to a normal social schedule? Within three days to a week.

Are there mourning customs to which a friend who is not a Disciple of Christ should be sensitive? No.

Are there rituals for observing the anniversary of the death? No.

5 · HOME CELEBRATIONS

Not applicable to Disciples of Christ.

Christian Science
(Church of Christ, Scientist)

1. HISTORY AND BELIEFS

Christian Science was founded in 1879 by Mary Baker Eddy, who was healed of a serious injury in 1866 while reading an account in the New Testament of Jesus' healings. Thirteen years later, she established the Church of Christ, Scientist, in Boston. Mrs. Eddy died in 1910.

The Church consists of the Mother Church—the First Church of Christ, Scientist—in Boston and over 2,000 branch churches in about 75 countries around the world.

Christian Science theology holds that God created man in his image and likeness. Christian Scientists also believe that God is good and that his creation is all that is real and eternal. This belief is based on the first chapter of Genesis, which states: "So God created man in His own image, in the image of God created He him; male and female created He them.... And God saw everything that He had made, and, behold, it was good."

Therefore, Christian Scientists believe that sin, disease and death do not originate in God. Rather, they are considered to be distortions of the human mind.

The Church is grounded in the teachings of the King James Bible and relies on spiritual means for healing. According to the Church, its spiritual healing "is not popular faith healing or human mind cure. It is not self-hypnosis, mere positive thinking, autosuggestion, or spontaneous remission. Nor is it to be confused with Scientology or New Age thinking....

"Christian Scientists find the Christian healing they experience is the reinstatement of the healing method practiced by Jesus 2,000 years ago. It is based on understanding the laws of God revealed in the Bible, and conforming to them. These laws are available for all mankind to practice and thereby obtain full salvation from sickness as well as sin.

"Christian Science healing involves more than healing sick bodies. It heals broken hearts and minds as well as broken homes, and is directly applicable to all of society's ills."

U.S. churches: 1,200
U.S. membership: Not available
(data from denomination headquarters)

For more information, contact:

The First Church of Christ, Scientist
210 Massachusetts Avenue
Boston, MA 02115
(617) 450-2000
www.christianscience.com and
    www.spirituality.com

Canadian churches: More than 35
Canadian membership: Not
    available
No Canadian contact address
available.

(data from denomination headquarters)

2 . THE BASIC SERVICE

Christian Science's basic religious service is held on Sunday morning in a Christian Science church. The 60-minute service includes congregational singing, silent and audible prayer, and reading a Lesson-Sermon consisting of passages from the King James Version of the Bible and *Science and Health with Key to the Scriptures,* written by the founder of Christian Science, Mary Baker Eddy.

Communion is held twice a year: on the second Sunday in January and the second Sunday in July, when the congregation kneels for a moment of silent prayer followed by the audible repetition of the Lord's Prayer. No bread or wine is given.

Each church holds a Wednesday evening testimony meeting, in which the First Reader chooses a subject, prepares readings from the King James Bible and Mary Baker Eddy's *Science and Health,* and selects the hymns. The meeting also includes spontaneous sharing of testimonies of healing and remarks on Christian Science by individuals in the congregation.

The public is welcome to Sunday and Wednesday services.

APPROPRIATE ATTIRE

Men: Jacket and tie are not expected. Casual attire is acceptable. No head covering is required.

Women: A dress, a skirt and blouse, a pants suit or slightly more casual attire is recommended. Arms do not have to be covered by clothing nor do hems need to reach below the knees. Modest jewelry and open-toed shoes are permissible. No head covering is required.

There are no rules regarding colors of clothing.

THE SANCTUARY

What are the major sections of the church? A Christian Science church has no altar. The service is conducted from a platform that has no ritual significance.

THE SERVICE

When should guests arrive and where should they sit? People are welcome whenever they arrive. Usually, an usher will greet latecomers at the door and seat them. If not, guests should sit wherever they wish.

If arriving late, are there times when a guest should *not* enter the service? No, but usually ushers will help you determine when to enter.

Are there times when a guest should *not* leave the service? No.

Who are the major officiants, leaders or participants and what do they do?
The "pastor" in a Christian Science church is the King James Version of the Bible and *Science and Health with Key to the Scriptures* by Mary Baker Eddy. Other than that, there are two primary participants in the service:
The First Reader, elected for a term of one to three years by congregants. He or she conducts the service. Reads mainly from *Science and Health* on Sunday and equally from the King James Bible and *Science and Health* on Wednesday.
The Second Reader, elected by members to read from the Bible at the Sunday service. He or she shares the platform with the First Reader and presides over the service in the absence of the First Reader.

What are the major ritual objects of the service? Simplicity is the mark of a Christian Science service. There are no ritual objects—and few rituals.

What books are used? The King James Version of the Bible, *Science and Health with Key to the Scriptures,* the *Christian Science Quarterly* and the *Christian Science Hymnal.*

To indicate the order of service: Refer to the second page of the *Christian Science Quarterly,* which is provided by ushers. The First Reader may give cues to the service by saying "Let us sing" or "Let us pray."

GUEST BEHAVIOR DURING THE SERVICE

Will a guest who is not a Christian Scientist be expected to do anything other than sit? No. The following behavior is optional: Standing, kneeling or singing with the congregation; saying or repeating the Lord's Prayer, which is the only prayer said orally; contributing to collections; and giving testimony at Wednesday services.

Are there any parts of the service in which a guest who is not a Christian Scientist should *not* participate? No.

If not disruptive to the service, is it okay to:
Take pictures? Only with permission of an usher.
Use a flash? Only with permission of an usher.
Use a video camera? Only with permission of an usher.
Use a tape recorder? Only with permission of an usher.

Will contributions to the church be collected at the service? Only on Sundays. Collection is taken by ushers after the Lesson-Sermon is read. No one is required to contribute.

How much is it customary to contribute? Whatever congregants and guests wish to give. Usually $1 to $10.

AFTER THE SERVICE

Is there usually a reception after the service? No.

Is there a traditional form of address for clergy whom a guest might meet? No. Christian Science has no clergy.

GENERAL GUIDELINES AND ADVICE

The congregation stands only while singing hymns. At the end of the third hymn, congregants remain standing while the First Reader reads the "Scientific Statement of Being," passages from 1 John, and the benediction. After the "Amen," worshipers may leave.

After the second hymn at the Wednesday testimony meeting, worshipers are invited to give testimonies of healing, or just expressions of gratitude to God and Christian Science. Guests are not expected to do this, but may if they wish.

SPECIAL VOCABULARY

Key words or phrases that it might be helpful for a visitor to know:

Mind, Spirit, Soul, Principle, Life, Truth, Love: When capitalized, these are interchangeable names for God.

Prayer: Desire for good; a total turning to and trusting in God; searching to understand the relationship between humans and God.

Healing: A realization of God's goodness and the perfection of humanity; regeneration of thought reflected on the body.

Error: Mary Baker Eddy's word for "evil"; the opposite of God and good; defined in *Science and Health* as something that "seemeth to be and is not."

Mortal Mind: Another name for error or evil; the belief in a mind or life separate from God.

Matter: That which appears "real" to the five senses.

Mortal: A concept of each person as born and dying. The opposite of the "real" person.

DOGMA AND IDEOLOGY

This summary of Christian Science's religious tenets appears in *Science and Health:*

1. As adherents of Truth, we take the inspired Word of the Bible as our sufficient guide to eternal truth.

2. We acknowledge and adore one supreme and infinite God. We acknowledge his Son, one Christ; the Holy Ghost or divine Comforter; and man in God's image and likeness.

3. We acknowledge God's forgiveness of sin in the destruction of sin and the spiritual understanding that casts out evil as unreal. But the belief in sin is punished so long as the belief lasts.

4. We acknowledge Jesus' atonement as the evidence of divine, efficacious Love, unfolding man's unity with God through Christ Jesus the Way-shower; and we acknowledge that man is saved through Christ, through Truth, Life and Love as demonstrated by the Galilean Prophet in healing the sick and overcoming sin and death.

5. We acknowledge that the crucifixion of Jesus and his Resurrection served to uplift faith to understand eternal life, even the allness of Soul, Spirit and the nothingness of matter.

6. And we solemnly promise to watch, and pray for that Mind to be in us which was also in Christ

Jesus; to do unto others as we would have them do unto us; and to be merciful, just and pure.

Some basic books or resources to which a guest can refer to learn more about Christian Science:

Science and Health with Key to the Scriptures, by Mary Baker Eddy (Boston: Christian Science Publishing Society).

Two magazines, the weekly *Christian Science Sentinel* and the monthly *Christian Science Journal.* These may be obtained in any Christian Science Reading Room or ordered from www.spirituality.com, the website for the Christian Science Publishing Society.

A website where people may visit for background or to write and ask for more information. The address is www.christianscience.com.

Ask a librarian in a Christian Science Reading Room to help you find appropriate materials. The locations of these reading rooms can be found on www.christianscience.com or listed on the back of the *Christian Science Journal.*

3 · HOLY DAYS AND FESTIVALS

Christian Science has no special holidays or festivals.

With the religion's emphasis on the metaphysical, it does not hold a special Christmas service, since that would honor the physical nature of Jesus.

A special Thanksgiving service is held on the morning of that holiday. This reflects Mary Baker Eddy's emphasis on gratitude. Similar to a Wednesday testimony meeting, it includes a Lesson-Sermon, silent and audible prayer, and a period for expressions of gratitude. No collection is taken at this service.

4 · LIFE CYCLE EVENTS

Birth Ceremony

There is no special ceremony for the birth or naming of a child.

Initiation Ceremony

There is no initiation ceremony. A participant may join the Mother Church and his or her local church as early as the age of 12. But one is not required to do so and may join whenever one feels it is appropriate. On the day one joins the local church, he or she is welcomed by the entire congregation and invited to sign the membership book.

At the age of 20, students graduate from Sunday school and may be informally presented with a copy of *The Mother Church Manual.* Again, there is no formal ceremony.

Marriage Ceremony

There is no set marriage ceremony. Since Christian Science has no ordained clergy, it has no one who can legally perform a marriage. In accord with the laws where they reside, Christian Scientists may be married by the clergy of another faith.

Funerals and Mourning

The church does not designate special arrangements or rituals for funerals or mourning. A funeral service is optional.

BEFORE THE CEREMONY

How soon after the death does the funeral usually take place? About two to four days.

What should someone who is not a Christian Scientist do upon hearing of the death of a member of that faith? Telephone or visit the bereaved or send a condolence card or personal letter.

APPROPRIATE ATTIRE

Men: A jacket and tie. No head covering is required.

Women: A dress, a skirt and blouse or a pants suit. Arms do not have to be covered by clothing nor do hems need to reach below the knees. Modest jewelry and open-toed shoes are permissible. No head covering is required.

There are no rules regarding colors of clothing, but slightly subdued colors are preferable.

GIFTS

Is it appropriate to send flowers or make a contribution? Both flowers to the bereaved family and contributions in the name of the deceased are appropriate. Flowers may be sent to the homes of the bereaved. Contributions are often made to the church of the deceased.

Is it appropriate to send food? Yes, any kind.

THE CEREMONY

Where will the ceremony take place? Christian Science churches are used only for public worship services. Private funeral or memorial services are arranged by the families concerned and are usually held in their own homes or in funeral homes.

When should guests arrive and where should they sit? Arrive early. Sit wherever you wish.

If arriving late, are there times when a guest should *not* enter the ceremony? No.

Will the bereaved family be present at the church or funeral home before the ceremony? This depends on the family's wishes.

Is there a traditional greeting for the family? No.

Will there be an open casket? Rarely. While most Christian Scientists do not have open viewing at the memorial service, this is done at the discretion of the individual.

Who are the major officiants at the ceremony and what do they do? Since the Christian Science Church has no clergy, the service is conducted by a Christian Scientist who might be a Reader or a Christian Science practitioner or teacher, or a friend of the deceased.

(A "practitioner" is an experienced

Christian Scientist who, on a professional basis, devotes full time to the healing ministry. Individuals enter the public practice of Christian Science as a life work only after demonstrating a consistent ability to heal others through Christian Scientific prayer.)

What books are used? The format and content of a Christian Science funeral service are determined by the family or whoever conducts the service. However, the service typically consists of readings from the King James Bible and from *Science and Health with Key to the Scriptures* or some other writing by Mrs. Eddy. Silent prayer, followed by those attending repeating the Lord's Prayer, may also be included. If music is desired, the *Christian Science Hymnal* contains hymns suitable for funerals.

The service usually includes no personal remarks or eulogy, but the family's wishes are taken into account. If they request, a poem or hymn that is not in the *Christian Science Hymnal* may be read or sung.

Will a guest who is not a Christian Scientist be expected to do anything other than sit? No.

Are there any parts of the ceremony in which a guest who is not a Christian Scientist should *not* participate? No.

If not disruptive to the ceremony, is it okay to:
Take pictures? No.
Use a flash? No.
Use a video camera? No.
Use a tape recorder? No.

Will contributions to the church be collected at the ceremony? No.

THE INTERMENT

Cremation or burial is solely the bereaved family's decision.

COMFORTING THE BEREAVED

Is it appropriate to visit the home of the bereaved after the funeral? Yes.

Will there be a religious service at the home of the bereaved? No.

Will food be served? Sometimes, but not alcoholic beverages.

How soon after the funeral will a mourner usually return to a normal work schedule? This is solely an individual decision. Christian Scientists do not have a prescribed period of mourning or specific customs of mourning.

Are there rituals for observing the anniversary of the death? No.

5 · HOME CELEBRATIONS

Not applicable to Christian Science.

8

Churches of Christ

1. HISTORY AND BELIEFS

Churches of Christ are autonomous congregations; there are no central governing offices or officers, and Church publications and institutions are either under local congregational control or independent of any one congregation. Members of the Churches of Christ appeal to the Bible alone to determine matters involving their faith and practice.

In the 19th century, Churches of Christ shared a common fellowship with the Christian Churches/Churches of Christ and with the Christian Church (Disciples of Christ). This relationship became strained after the Civil War because of emerging theories of interpreting the Bible and the centralizing of church-wide activities through a missionary society.

The Church teaches that Jesus Christ was divine, that the remission of sins can be achieved only by immersing oneself into Christ, and that the Scriptures were divinely inspired.

U.S. churches: 13,000
U.S. membership: 1.6 million
(data from the 2010 Yearbook of American and Canadian Churches)

For more information, contact:
Gospel Advocate
1006 Elm Hill Pike
Nashville, TN 37202
(800) 251-8446

Canadian churches: 149
Canadian membership: 6,857
(data from the 2010 Yearbook of American and Canadian Churches)

For more information, contact:
Gospel Herald
4904 King Street
Beamsville, ON L0R 1B6
(905) 563-7503
www.gospelherald.org

2. THE BASIC SERVICE

In most churches, there are a worship service and Bible classes on Sunday morning and another worship service Sunday evening. Both services last about an hour.

On Wednesday evenings, there is a Bible class, which is followed, in some churches, by a brief devotional service.

APPROPRIATE ATTIRE

Men: Jacket and tie are the norm for the Sunday morning service, but are not required. More casual attire, such as slacks or nice jeans and a sport shirt, are appropriate for the Wednesday evening service. No head covering is required.

Women: A casual dress is recommended. It is not necessary to cover the arms. Open-toed shoes and modest jewelry permissible. No head covering is required.

There are no rules regarding colors of clothing.

THE SANCTUARY

What are the major sections of the church?

The pews. Where members sit for worship.

The podium/pulpit area. Where song and prayer leaders and the preacher sit and from where the service is led.

THE SERVICE

When should guests arrive and where should they sit? Arrive early or at the time called. You may sit in any seat. No usher will seat you.

If arriving late, are there times when a guest should *not* enter the service? It's preferable to enter between songs rather than during them.

Are there times when a guest should *not* leave the service? It's preferable to leave between songs rather than during them.

Who are the major officiants, leaders or participants and what do they do?

The announcement maker, who greets congregants and makes announcements during the service.

The song leader, who leads singing.

The prayer leader, who leads prayers.

The preacher, who preaches the sermon.

What are the major ritual objects of the service?

Grape juice and unleavened bread, such as thin crackers, are used during Communion to symbolize the body and blood of Jesus Christ.

What books are used? A hymnal and a Bible (which includes the Old and New Testaments). Among the more commonly used hymnals are *Songs of Faith and Praise* (West Monroe, La.: Alton Howard Publishers, 1993) and *Praise for the Lord* (Nashville, Tenn.: Praise Press, 1997). The church does not endorse a particular translation of the Bible.

Often, several different translations of the Bible are used by congregants at the same service. It is suggested that guests bring their own Bible.

To indicate the order of the service: Sometimes a program is distributed. At other times, prayers and songs are announced by the song leader.

GUEST BEHAVIOR DURING THE SERVICE

Will a guest who is not a member of the Churches of Christ be expected to do anything other than sit? Guests are expected to sing with congregants during the service, unless the songs being sung are contrary to their religious beliefs. It is optional for them to stand when the congregation rises.

Are there are any parts of the service in which a guest who is not a member of the Churches of Christ should *not* participate? Only members of the Churches of Christ or other Christians take Communion. If a visitor is not a Christian or is uncomfortable in partaking of Communion, he or she should just pass the Communion plate to the next person.

If not disruptive to the service, is it okay to:
Take pictures? Yes.
Use a flash? Yes, but use sparingly.
Use a video camera? Yes.
Use a tape recorder? Yes.

Will contributions to the church be collected at the service? Usually, there is a collection immediately after Communion. It is entirely optional for guests to contribute.

How much is it customary to contribute? About $1 to $10.

AFTER THE SERVICE

Is there usually a reception after the service? No, but there often is a fellowship luncheon immediately after the service. It may last about one hour. Guests are always welcome and are not expected to bring any food.

Often, a church will have a potluck luncheon one Sunday a month. Everyone is invited. Members bring a variety of foods. No alcoholic beverages are served. A prayer is usually said before eating. There is no concluding ritual after eating.

Is there a traditional form of address for clergy whom a guest may meet? Churches of Christ do not have titles for clergy. Ministers or preachers are addressed no differently than are lay members. All church members are considered to be living lives of integrity and each should be trying to live a life as holy as the minister's.

Is it okay to leave early? Yes.

GENERAL GUIDELINES AND ADVICE

None provided.

SPECIAL VOCABULARY

None provided.

DOGMA AND IDEOLOGY

Members of the Churches of Christ believe:

Going back to the Bible does not mean establishing another denomination, but rather returning to the original church. Members call themselves "a people of restoration spirit," meaning they want to restore in our time the original New Testament church. They do not consider themselves belonging to a separate denomination, but as members of the church that Jesus established and for which he died.

Each congregation is independent of every other congregation. The only tie binding the many congregations is a common allegiance to Christ and the Bible.

3 · HOLY DAYS AND FESTIVALS

Churches of Christ celebrate the death and Resurrection of Jesus every week by partaking of Communion.

Thus, every Sunday is seen as a "holy day."

Both *Easter* (which is always the Sunday following the first full moon on or after March 21 and which celebrates the Resurrection of Jesus Christ) and *Christmas* (which occurs on December 25 and marks the birth and the incarnation of God as Jesus) may be celebrated in churches with a special service or with a special sermon. This reflects the autonomous nature of the Churches of Christ. The traditional greeting for Easter is "Happy Easter" and for Christmas "Merry Christmas."

Good Friday (the Friday before Easter, which commemorates the day on which Jesus was crucified) is not observed because the Crucifixion is observed every Sunday in the Churches of Christ.

4 · LIFE CYCLE EVENTS

Birth Ceremony

Churches of Christ have no birth ceremony.

Initiation Ceremony

The Churches of Christ teach that children are innocent of sin until they reach an age when they can truly understand right from wrong and make a conscious decision about it. This age is usually considered to be around 13, although it may be as young as 11 or 12.

Baptism is an expression of one's faith in God and in Christ. At this time, a person repents of the sin in his or her life, renounces sinful ways of living and confesses that Jesus is the Son of God. He or she is immersed during baptism as a sign of participating in the death, burial and Resurrection of Jesus.

The participant is usually baptized individually, although the ceremony may be done with someone else.

BEFORE THE CEREMONY

Are guests usually invited by a formal invitation? Sometimes.

If not stated explicitly, should one assume that children are invited? Yes.

If one can't attend, what should one do? RSVP with regrets, possibly by telephone, and congratulate the person being baptized.

APPROPRIATE ATTIRE

Men: Jacket and tie, if the baptism occurs during worship service. If the baptism is a separate service, dress more casually, for example, in slacks or nice jeans and a sport shirt. No head covering is required.

Women: A casual dress if baptism occurs during worship service or if it is a separate service. Open-toed shoes and modest jewelry permissible. No head covering is required.

There are no rules regarding colors of clothing.

GIFTS

Is a gift customarily expected? No.

Should gifts be brought to the ceremony? See above.

THE CEREMONY

Where will the ceremony take place? In the church's baptistery. This is usually located behind the pulpit.

When should guests arrive and where should they sit? Arrive early or at the time called. You may sit in any seat. No usher will seat you.

If arriving late, are there times when a guest should *not* enter the ceremony? It's preferable to enter between songs rather than during them.

Are there times when a guest should *not* leave the ceremony? It's preferable to leave between songs rather than during them.

Who are the major officiants, leaders or participants in the ceremony and what do they do?
The person being baptized.
The person doing the baptizing.
Often there is *a song leader* who leads the congregation in singing as preparations for the baptism are being made.

What books are used? A hymnal and a Bible (which includes the Old and New Testaments). Among the more commonly used hymnals are *Songs of Faith and Praise* (West Monroe, La.: Alton Howard Publishers, 1993) and *Praise for the Lord* (Nashville, Tenn.: Praise Press, 1997). The church does not endorse a particular version of the Bible.

Often, several different translations of the Bible are used by congregants at the same service. It is suggested that guests bring their own Bible.

To indicate the order of the ceremony: Usually the minister or song leader will give directions.

Will a guest who is not a member of the Churches of Christ be expected to do anything other than sit? You are only expected to sit. It is optional for a guest to sing with the congregation while the participant is changing clothes before and after the baptism.

Are there are any parts of the ceremony in which a guest who is not a member of the Churches of Christ should *not* participate? Only members of the Churches of Christ or other Christians take Communion. If a visitor is not a Christian or is uncomfortable in partaking of Communion, he or should just pass the Communion plate to the next person.

If not disruptive to the ceremony, is it okay to:
Take pictures? Yes.
Use a flash? Yes.
Use a video camera? Yes.
Use a tape recorder? Yes.

Will contributions to the church be collected at the ceremony? Only if the baptism takes place at the Sunday morning worship. In that case, the collection is part of the worship and not part of the baptism. Collections immediately follow the Communion (the passing of the bread and fruit of the vine). Whether guests contribute to this is completely optional.

How much is it customary to contribute? About $1 to $10.

AFTER THE CEREMONY

Is there usually a reception after the ceremony? There is no formal reception after the ceremony.

Is there a traditional greeting for the family? No, simply offer your best wishes.

Is there a traditional form of address for clergy whom a guest may meet? Churches of Christ do not have titles for clergy. Ministers or preachers are addressed no differently than are lay members. All church members are considered to be living lives of integrity and each should be trying to live a life as holy as the minister's.

Marriage Ceremony

The Churches of Christ teach that marriage "originated in the mind of God," who "created woman especially to be a companion for the man.... There can be no doubt that God intended for man and woman to marry," since God said, "For this cause shall a man leave his father and mother, and shall cleave unto his wife."

God "officiated" at the marriage between Adam and Eve, and "continues to officiate at all scriptural marriages today."

This is why the church states that marriage is "divine" and that "those who marry not only have obliga-

tions to each other, but they also have obligations to God."

Usually, Churches of Christ marriage ceremonies last about 30 minutes.

BEFORE THE CEREMONY

Are guests usually invited by a formal invitation? Yes. Often, general invitations are published in the church bulletin.

If not stated explicitly, should one assume that children are invited? Yes.

If one can't attend, what should one do? RSVP by phone or card, along with your congratulations. Most friends will send a gift either to a wedding shower or to the couple.

APPROPRIATE ATTIRE

Men: Jacket and tie, although occasionally less formal clothes may be suitable. No head covering is required.

Women: Dress modestly. Hems slightly above the knees are fine. Open-toed shoes and modest jewelry permissible. No head covering is required, but hats or scarfs may be worn.

There are no rules regarding colors of clothing.

GIFTS

Is a gift customarily expected? Yes, either for the bridal shower or for the wedding itself. Such gifts as small household appliances, sheets or towels or other household goods are appropriate.

Should gifts be brought to the ceremony? If you bring a gift to the wedding, place it on the table in the reception area for that purpose. Gifts can also be sent to the home of the newlyweds.

THE CEREMONY

Where will the ceremony take place? In the main sanctuary of the church.

When should guests arrive and where should they sit? Arrive early. Sit wherever you wish.

If arriving late, are there times when a guest should *not* enter the ceremony? Do not enter the service during the processional.

Are there times when a guest should *not* leave the ceremony? Do not leave during the processional.

Who are the major officiants, leaders or participants at the ceremony and what do they do?
The minister, who performs the ceremony.
Singers.

What books are used? Usually, the minister has a Bible, from which he reads. Other books are usually not used.

To indicate the order of the ceremony: A program will be provided.

Will a guest who is not a member of the Churches of Christ be expected to do anything other than sit? Guests are only expected to enjoy the celebration.

Are there any parts of the ceremony in which a guest who is not a member of the Churches of Christ should *not* participate? No.

If not disruptive to the ceremony, is it okay to:
Take pictures? Yes.
Use a flash? Yes.
Use a video camera? Yes.
Use a tape recorder? Yes.

Will contributions to the church be collected at the ceremony? No.

AFTER THE CEREMONY

Is there usually a reception after the ceremony? There is often a reception in the same building as the ceremony. It lasts about one hour. There may be finger foods, fruit, vegetables and dip. Alcohol in any form is discouraged, as is smoking inside the building.

Would it be considered impolite to neither eat nor drink? No.

Is there a grace or benediction before eating or drinking? Sometimes a prayer is said before eating.

Is there a grace or benediction after eating or drinking? No. But usually after the reception, rice or bird seed is thrown at the newlyweds when they leave. (Bird seed has generally replaced rice because of ecological concerns.)

Is there a traditional greeting for the family? No, just offer your congratulations.

Is there a traditional form of address for clergy who may be at the reception? Churches of Christ do not have titles for clergy. Ministers or preachers are addressed no differently than are lay members. All church members are considered to be living lives of integrity and each should be trying to live a life as holy as the minister's.

Funerals and Mourning

Members of the Churches of Christ believe that, upon death, the souls of those who are faithful Christians are taken to a place called Paradise to await the Final Judgment. The souls of those who are unfaithful or are not Christians are taken to a place called Tartarus to await judgment. On Judgment Day (which is the second coming of Jesus), the faithful will be taken to heaven and the unfaithful to hell.

The funeral service usually lasts about 30 minutes.

BEFORE THE CEREMONY

How soon after the death does the funeral usually take place? Usually within two to three days. If family members cannot arrive for the funeral immediately, it may be delayed for four or five days. But this is rare.

What should someone who is not a member of the Churches of Christ do upon hearing of the death of a member of that faith? Visit or telephone the bereaved before the funeral.

APPROPRIATE ATTIRE

Men: Jacket and tie. No head covering is required.

Women: A dress or skirt and blouse. Hems slightly above the knees are fine. Open-toed shoes and modest jewelry are permissible. No head covering is required.

There are no rules regarding colors of clothing, but black or other somber colors or patterns are recommended.

GIFTS

Is it appropriate to send flowers or make a contribution? Flowers, plants and cards are appropriate. They may be sent upon hearing the news of the death or shortly thereafter. They may be sent to the home of the deceased before or after the funeral, or to the funeral home before the funeral.

Contributions are not customary unless the family indicates they are appropriate.

Is it appropriate to send food? Yes, to the home of the bereaved before or after the funeral.

THE CEREMONY

Where will the ceremony take place? At a church or a funeral home.

When should guests arrive and where should they sit? Arrive early. Register upon entry. No one will tell guests where to sit. Sit wherever there is an available seat.

If arriving late, are there times when a guest should *not* enter the ceremony? Do not enter when the family is entering.

Will the bereaved family be present at the church or funeral home before the ceremony? Yes, but there is no formal receiving line before the service.

Is there a traditional greeting for the family? Express your condolences.

Will there be an open casket? Usually.

Is a guest expected to view the body? This is optional.

What is appropriate behavior upon viewing the body? Most will pause briefly to look one last time at their friend or loved one. Occasionally, someone may pat the hand of the deceased or place a flower in the casket.

Who are the major officiants at the ceremony and what do they do?
One or more ministers will deliver eulogies.
Singers will lead songs.

What books are used? A hymnal and a Bible (which includes the Old and New Testaments). Among the more commonly used hymnals are *Songs of Faith and Praise* (West Monroe, La.: Alton Howard Publishers, 1993) and *Praise for the Lord* (Nashville, Tenn.: Praise Press, 1997). The church does not endorse a particular version of the Bible.

Often, several different translations of the Bible are used by congregants at the same service. It is suggested that guests bring their own Bible.

To indicate the order of the ceremony: The minister or funeral director will explain any involvement by those present and cue them should they be asked to do anything, such as view the body.

Will a guest who is not a member of the Churches of Christ be expected to do anything other than sit? Guests can sing with the congregation, if the words are not contrary to their religious beliefs. Otherwise, nothing is expected of them.

Are there any parts of the ceremony in which a guest who is not a member of the Churches of Christ should *not* participate? No.

If not disruptive to the ceremony, is it okay to:
Take pictures? No.
Use a flash? No.
Use a video camera? No.
Use a tape recorder? Yes.

Will contributions to the church be collected at the ceremony? No.

THE INTERMENT

Should guests attend the interment? Their attendance is optional.

Whom should one ask for directions? The funeral director.

What happens at the graveside? There is prayer, readings from the Scriptures, and the minister gives comments about the deceased.

Do guests who are not members of the Churches of Christ participate at the graveside ceremony? No. They are simply present.

COMFORTING THE BEREAVED

Is it appropriate to visit the home of the bereaved after the funeral? Yes, either after the service at the cemetery or later.

Will there be a religious service at the home of the bereaved? No.

Will food be served? Possibly, but no alcoholic beverages.

How soon after the funeral will a mourner usually return to a normal work schedule? Usually, the bereaved can be expected to return to work after one week of mourning.

How soon after the funeral will a mourner usually return to a normal social schedule? Social occasions are usually avoided for about one month after the death, but this depends on the individual mourner.

Are there rituals for observing the anniversary of the death? There is no formal ritual, although occasionally friends or relatives may call or visit each other on the anniversary of the death.

5 · HOME CELEBRATIONS

Not applicable to the Churches of Christ.

Episcopalian and Anglican

1 · HISTORY AND BELIEFS

The Episcopal/Anglican Church is derived from the Church of England and shares with it traditions of faith as set forth in its *Book of Common Prayer.*

The English who settled in Jamestown, Virginia, in 1607 brought the seeds of the Episcopal Church to America. After the American Revolution, the Church became independent from the Anglican Church and adopted the name Protestant Episcopal Church in the United States of America. This was shortened in 1967 when the Episcopal Church became the Church's official alternate name.

To many Americans after the Revolution, the Church was suspect because it had been closely linked with the British Crown and because many of its leaders and members had sided with England during the war. But extensive missionary efforts in the fledgling nation's new territories (as well as in Africa, Latin America and the Far East) and an eventual network of dioceses from the Atlantic to the Pacific helped it to finally establish its own identity.

In Canada, the first known service was performed by a chaplain in Sir Martin Frobisher's expedition in Frobisher Bay on September 2, 1578. In subsequent years, Anglicanism spread as a result of emigration from the British Isles and the coming of Loyalists, many of whom were Anglicans, after the American Revolution.

The Church is a fairly nondoctrinaire institution. It teaches that the Holy Scriptures were written by people, and inspired by the Holy Spirit (the empowering spirit of God), and that reason helps members penetrate to the full depths of God's truths. It does not control interpretation and practice, and urges members to make responsible moral decisions under the guidance of scripture, tradition and ordained ministry and in response to sincere prayer.

The Episcopal/Anglican Church is democratically structured. Each diocese, which consists of a group of parishes (or churches), is presided over by a bishop, who is democratically elected by a diocesan synod.

According to the *Book of Common Prayer,* "the duty of all Christians is to follow Christ, to come together week by week for corporate worship; and to work, pray and give for the spread of the Kingdom of God."

U.S. churches: 6,964
U.S. membership: 2.1 million
(*data from the* 2010 Yearbook of American and Canadian Churches)

For more information, contact:
The Episcopal Church Center
815 Second Avenue
New York, NY 10017
(800) 334-7626
(212) 716-6240
www.ecusa.anglican.org
www.episcopalchurch.org

Canadian churches: 2,884
Canadian membership: 681,845
(*data from the* 2010 Yearbook of American and Canadian Churches)

For more information, contact:
Church House
80 Hayden Street
Toronto, ON M4Y 3G2
(416) 924-9192
www.anglican.ca

2 · THE BASIC SERVICE

To Episcopalians/Anglicans, worship is a joyous response to God's love, an expression of hope for salvation, a chance to praise God and receive strength and forgiveness, and a way to share faith with other believers.

Ordinarily, the Sunday morning Episcopal/Anglican service lasts between 30 and 60 minutes.

APPROPRIATE ATTIRE

Men: Jacket and tie or more casual clothing. No head covering required.

Women: Dress or a skirt and blouse or a pants suit. Open-toed shoes and jewelry are permissible. No head covering required.

There are no rules regarding colors of clothing.

THE SANCTUARY

What are the major sections of the church?

The sanctuary: The part of the church where the altar is located and where ministers lead congregants in prayer. It is set off from the body of the church by a distinctive structural feature, such as an elevation above the floor level or by ornamentation. It is usually at the front of the church, but may be centrally located.

The pulpit or lectern: The stand at which scriptural lessons and psalm responses are read and the word of God is preached.

Seating for congregants: Seats and kneeling benches, usually in front and/or to the side of the altar.

Baptistery or font: The place for administering baptism. Some churches have baptisteries adjoining or near their entrance. This position indicates that through baptism, one is initiated, or "enters," the church.

Aumbry light: A lamp that burns continuously in a small box or niche in which the Communion sacrament that has not been totally consumed during services is kept. This Communion bread and wine may be brought, for instance, by the priest to a congregant who has been hospitalized. The light symbolizes the presence of Christ. The aumbry box is usually either along the wall near the altar or on a table at the rear of the altar.

THE SERVICE

When should guests arrive and where should they sit? It is customary to arrive early. An usher will indicate where to sit. There are usually no restrictions on where to sit.

If arriving late, are there times when a guest should *not* enter the service? Check with the ushers.

Are there times when a guest should *not* leave the service? No, but guests should plan to remain for the entire service.

Who are the major officiants, leaders or participants and what do they do?

A priest, who presides, preaches and celebrates Communion.

A lector, who reads from the Old Testament and/or the Epistles or apostolic letters, which are a part of the New Testament.

A deacon, who reads from the Gospels, which record the life and ministry of Jesus.

A lay minister, or chalicist, who assists with the distribution of Communion.

An intercessor, who reads the "prayers of the people," which are petitions, intercessions and thanksgivings by the congregation.

What are the major ritual objects of the service?

Bread and wine, which are consecrated into the body and blood of Jesus Christ.

The chalice and paten, which hold, respectively, the consecrated wine and bread.

The altar, or table where the bread and wine are consecrated.

The Gospel book or Bible, which may be processed into the midst of the congregation before the Gospel is read.

What books are used? A hymnal and *The Book of Common Prayer* (New York: Church Publishing, 1979). In Canada, *The Book of Alternative Services* (Toronto: The Anglican Book Center, 1985) may also be used. Occasionally, the Bible lessons are included in the program.

To indicate the order of the service: A program will be provided.

GUEST BEHAVIOR DURING THE SERVICE

Will a guest who is not Episcopalian/Anglican be expected to do anything other than sit? They are expected to stand and kneel with the congregation, read prayers aloud and sing with congregants, if this does not compromise their personal beliefs. If one does not wish to kneel, sit when congregants do so. The only behavior that would be considered "offensive" would be not to stand for the reading of the Gospel.

Are there any parts of the service in which a guest who is not Episcopalian/Anglican should *not* participate? Yes. Do not receive Communion or say any prayers contradictory to the beliefs of your own faith. Only baptized Christians may receive Communion.

If not disruptive to the service, is it okay to:
Take pictures? No.

Use a flash? No.
Use a video camera? No.
Use a tape recorder? No.

Will contributions to the church be collected at the service? Yes. The offertory takes place about midway through the service. Ushers usually pass the plate for offerings.

How much is it customary to contribute? The customary offering is from $1 to $10.

AFTER THE SERVICE

Is there usually a reception after the service? Yes, in the church's reception area. It may last less than 30 minutes. Usually food and light beverages are served. It is not impolite to refrain from eating. Usually there is no blessing before or after eating or drinking.

Is there a traditional form of address for clergy who may be at the reception? "Mr.," "Ms." or "Mrs." is usually sufficient. "Reverend" for more formal situations.

Is it okay to leave early? Yes.

GENERAL GUIDELINES AND ADVICE

Episcopalians/Anglicans are quite diverse—socially, racially and ethnically. Generally, they rejoice in this diversity and celebrate it. Most consider their church an extension of their family life. What represents "good manners" at home would be considered "good manners" in church. Politeness is the key.

Appearing overly reserved or noncommunicative—which can imply disapproval—is a typical mistake that guests can avoid. Conviviality implies acceptance and approval.

SPECIAL VOCABULARY

Key words or phrases that it might be helpful for a visitor to know:

Gospel: As used during worship, this means a reading from one of the accounts of the life of Jesus as written in the New Testament by four of his apostles.

Sermon: An explication of the Gospel text that is read during the service.

Communion or Eucharist: The common meal instituted by Jesus Christ at the Last Supper.

Morning (or Evening) Prayer: A worship service that includes prayer and possibly a sermon, but not Communion.

DOGMA AND IDEOLOGY

Episcopalians/Anglicans believe:

While interpretation of Church teachings may vary from parish to parish, an essential Episcopalian/Anglican belief is that God has three prime qualities as reflected in the Holy Trinity: the Father (who is infinite, good and omnipotent), the Son (Jesus Christ, whose life, death and Resurrection liberated humanity from sin and death), and the Holy Spirit (God's power of love appearing within men and women in mysterious and unexpected ways).

The Episcopal/Anglican Church recognizes our sinfulness and God's love for his creation as demonstrated by Jesus, whose life and death affirms our salvation and is celebrated with praise and thanksgiving.

The Book of Common Prayer states that private worship alone is inadequate and that religion is a fellowship. Episcopalians/Anglicans must relate to the entire Church through their respective parish and local church community.

Some basic books to which a guest can refer to learn more about the Episcopal/Anglican faith:

This Anglican Church of Ours by Patricia Bays (Winfield, B.C.: Wood Lake Books, 1995).

Welcome to the Book of Common Prayer by Vicki K. Black (New York: Morehouse, 2005).

Welcome to the Episcopal Church: An Introduction to Its History, Faith, and Worship by Christopher L. Webber (New York: Morehouse, 2002).

3 · HOLY DAYS AND FESTIVALS

Christmas. Always falls on December 25. Celebrates the birth of Christ. The traditional greeting is "Merry Christmas."

Easter. Always falls on the Sunday after the first full moon that occurs on or after the spring equinox of March 21. Commemorates the death and Resurrection of Jesus. The traditional greeting is "Happy Easter."

Pentecost. Occurs 50 days after Easter because this is when the Holy Ghost (the spirit of Jesus) descended on his apostles. Celebrates the power of the Holy Spirit and its manifestation in the early Christian church. There is no traditional greeting for this holiday.

Ash Wednesday. Occurs 40 days before Easter. Commemorates the beginning of Lent, which is a season for preparation and penitence before Easter itself. There is no traditional greeting for this holiday.

Maundy Thursday. Falls four days before Easter. Commemorates the institution of the Eucharist (also known as Communion) and Jesus' subsequent arrest and trial. There is no traditional greeting.

Good Friday. Three days before Easter. Commemorates the crucifixion, death and burial of Jesus.

Christmas, Easter and Pentecost are joyful celebrations. Ash Wednesday, Maundy Thursday and Good Friday are somber, penitential commemorations. During the services for these latter three holidays, decorum and discretion are of great importance.

4 · LIFE CYCLE EVENTS

Birth Ceremony

Baptism is administered once to each person, usually as an infant. During the 30- to 60-minute ceremony, which is part of a larger Sunday morning service, a priest pours water on the head of the child or immerses the child in water. This symbolizes the washing away of sins. The Holy Trinity is also called upon to strengthen the new church member.

Baptism is a pledge of repentance and obedience to divine will. It also initiates the individual into the Christian community and in the larger family of the children of a loving God.

BEFORE THE CEREMONY

Are guests usually invited by a formal invitation? Yes.

If not stated explicitly, should one assume that children are invited? Yes.

If one can't attend, what should one do? RSVP with regrets and send a gift.

APPROPRIATE ATTIRE

Men: Jacket and tie or more casual clothing. No head covering required.

Women: Dress or a skirt and blouse or a pants suit. Open-toed shoes and jewelry are permissible. No head covering required.

There are no rules regarding colors of clothing.

GIFTS

Is a gift customarily expected? No. If you attend, your presence is the gift. If you cannot attend, sending a gift would be appropriate.

Should gifts be brought to the ceremony? See above.

THE CEREMONY

Where will the ceremony take place? Some churches have a special baptistery, which is usually near or adjoins the church entrance. In more modest churches, the font (which holds the water for baptism) is near the church entrance.

When should guests arrive and where should they sit? Arrive early. Ushers will indicate where to sit.

If arriving late, are there times when a guest should *not* enter the ceremony? Check with the ushers.

Are there times when a guest should *not* leave the ceremony? Guests should plan to stay for the entire service.

Who are the major officiants, leaders or participants in the ceremony and what do they do?
A priest, who will baptize the child.
The child's parents.
Sponsors, who will speak for the child and agree to aid in the child's upbringing.

What books are used? A hymnal and *The Book of Common Prayer* (New York: Church Publishing, 1979). In Canada, *The Book of Alternative Services* (Toronto: The Anglican Book Center, 1985) may be used. Occasionally, the Bible lessons are included in the program.

To indicate the order of the ceremony: A program will be distributed by ushers.

Will a guest who is not Episcopalian/Anglican be expected to do anything other than sit? They are expected to stand and kneel with the congregation, read prayers aloud and sing with congregants, if this does not compromise their personal beliefs. If one does not wish to kneel, sit when congregants do so. The only behavior that would be considered "offensive" would be not to stand for the reading of the Gospel.

Are there any parts of the ceremony in which a guest who is not Episcopalian/Anglican should *not* participate? Do not receive Communion or say any prayers contradictory to the beliefs of your own faith. Only baptized Christians may receive Communion.

If not disruptive to the ceremony, is it okay to:
Take pictures? No.
Use a flash? No.
Use a video camera? No.
Use a tape recorder? No.

Will contributions to the church be collected at the ceremony? Yes. The offertory takes place about midway through the service. Ushers usually pass the plate for offerings.

How much is it customary to contribute? The customary offering is from $1 to $10.

AFTER THE CEREMONY

Is there usually a reception after the ceremony? Possibly. It is solely at the discretion of the parents. If so, it will probably last less than 30 minutes. Food and light beverages will be served.

Would it be considered impolite to neither eat nor drink? No.

Is there a grace or benediction before eating or drinking? Usually there is no blessing prior to eating.

Is there a grace or benediction after eating or drinking? No.

Is there a traditional greeting for the family? No, simply offer your best wishes.

Is there a traditional form of address for clergy who may be at the reception? "Mr.," "Ms." or "Mrs." is usually sufficient. "Reverend" is used for more formal occasions.

Is it okay to leave early? Yes.

Initiation Ceremony

Confirmation is conferred, by a bishop, on an early adolescent (or occasionally on an adult who seeks church membership). It strengthens the commitment made by Christians at baptism, which occurs shortly after birth, and initiates one into the adult life of the church.

Episcopalians/Anglicans also believe that confirmation gives them courage to witness Christ in the world and to selflessly serve each other.

Teens participate in the ceremony with members of their confirmation class. The ceremony, which lasts between 30 and 60 minutes, is part of a larger Sunday morning service.

BEFORE THE CEREMONY

Are guests usually invited by a formal invitation? No.

If not stated explicitly, should one assume that children are invited? Yes.

If one can't attend, what should one do? RSVP with regrets and send a gift.

APPROPRIATE ATTIRE

Men: Jacket and tie or more casual clothing. No head covering required.

Women: Dress or a skirt and blouse or a pants suit. Open-toed shoes and jewelry are permissible. No head covering required.

There are no rules regarding colors of clothing.

GIFTS

Is a gift customarily expected? Yes. This is usually a modest present, more of a token of affection.

Should gifts be brought to the ceremony? Usually they are brought to the reception afterward.

THE CEREMONY

Where will the ceremony take place? In the main sanctuary of the confirmand's church.

When should guests arrive and where should they sit? Arrive early. Ushers will help you with seating.

If arriving late, are there times when a guest should *not* enter the ceremony? Check with the ushers.

Are there times when a guest should *not* leave the ceremony? Guests should plan to remain for the entire service.

Who are the major officiants, leaders or participants in the ceremony and what do they do?
The bishop, who alone has the authority to confirm.

What books are used? A hymnal and *The Book of Common Prayer* (New York: Church Publishing, 1979). In Canada, *The Book of Alternative Services* (Toronto: The Anglican Book Center, 1985) may

be used. Occasionally, the Bible lessons are included in the program.

To indicate the order of the ceremony: A program will be distributed by ushers.

Will a guest who is not Episcopalian/Anglican be expected to do anything other than sit? They are expected to stand and kneel with the congregation, read prayers aloud and sing with congregants, if this does not compromise their personal beliefs. If one does not wish to kneel, sit when congregants do so. The only behavior that would be considered "offensive" would be not to stand for the reading of the Gospel.

Are there any parts of the ceremony in which a guest who is not Episcopalian/Anglican should *not* participate? Do not receive Communion or say any prayers contradictory to the beliefs of your own faith. Only baptized Christians may receive Communion.

If not disruptive to the ceremony, is it okay to:
Take pictures? No.
Use a flash? No.
Use a video camera? No.
Use a tape recorder? No.

Will contributions to the church be collected at the ceremony? Yes. The offertory takes place about midway through the service. Ushers usually pass the plate for offerings.

How much is it customary to contribute? The customary offering is from $1 to $10.

AFTER THE CEREMONY

Is there usually a reception after the ceremony? Yes, in the church's reception area. It ordinarily lasts less than 30 minutes. Usually light food and beverages are served.

Would it be considered impolite to neither eat nor drink? No.

Is there a grace or benediction before eating or drinking? Usually there is no blessing prior to eating.

Is there a grace or benediction after eating or drinking? No.

Is there a traditional greeting for the family? No, simply offer your best wishes.

Is there a traditional form of address for clergy who may be at the reception? "Mr.," "Ms." or "Mrs." is usually sufficient.

Is it okay to leave early? Yes.

Marriage Ceremony

The Episcopal/Anglican Church believes that, through the sacrament of marriage, God joins together man and woman in physical and spiritual union.

The marriage ceremony may either be a ceremony in itself or part of a Holy Communion service. It may last between 30 and 60 minutes.

BEFORE THE CEREMONY

Are guests usually invited by a formal invitation? Yes.

If not stated explicitly, should one assume that children are invited? No.

If one can't attend, what should one do? RSVP with your regrets and send a gift.

APPROPRIATE ATTIRE

Men: Jacket and tie or more casual clothing (depending on the style of the wedding. This may be indicated in the invitation.) No head covering required.

Women: Dress or a skirt and blouse or a pants suit. Open-toed shoes and jewelry are permissible. No head covering required.

There are no rules regarding colors of clothing.

GIFTS

Is a gift customarily expected? Yes, costing between $20 and $40.

Should gifts be brought to the ceremony? Yes, or they can be sent to the home.

THE CEREMONY

Where will the ceremony take place? Depending on the wishes of the couple being married, it may be in the main sanctuary of a church, in another part of the church, in a home or banquet hall, or in another setting of their choice.

When should guests arrive and where should they sit? Arrive early.

Depending on the setting, ushers may show guests where to sit.

If arriving late, are there times when a guest should *not* enter the ceremony? Check with the ushers.

Are there times when a guest should *not* leave the ceremony? Guests should plan to remain for the entire service.

Who are the major officiants, leaders or participants at the ceremony and what do they do? Depending on the setting and the wishes of the couple, there may be:

A priest, who presides, preaches and celebrates Communion.

A lector, who reads from the Old Testament and/or the Epistles or apostolic letters, which are a part of the New Testament.

A deacon, who reads the Gospel, which records the life and ministry of Jesus.

A lay minister, or chalicist, who assists with the distribution of Communion.

An intercessor, who reads the "prayers of the people," which are petitions, intercessions and thanksgivings by the congregation.

What books are used? *The Book of Common Prayer* (New York: Church Publishing, 1979) and a hymnal. In Canada, *The Book of Alternative Services* (Toronto: The Anglican Book Center, 1985) may be used. Occasionally, the Bible lessons are included in the program.

To indicate the order of the ceremony: A program will be provided.

Will a guest who is not Episcopalian/Anglican be expected to do anything other than sit? They are expected to stand and kneel with the congregation, read prayers aloud and sing with congregants, if this does not compromise their personal beliefs. If one does not wish to kneel, sit when congregants do so. The only behavior that would be considered "offensive" would be not to stand for the reading of the Gospel.

Are there any parts of the ceremony in which a guest who is not Episcopalian/Anglican should *not* participate? Do not receive Communion or say any prayers contradictory to the beliefs of your own faith. Only baptized Christians may receive Communion.

If not disruptive to the ceremony, is it okay to:
Take pictures? No.
Use a flash? No.
Use a video camera? No.
Use a tape recorder? No.
(Photos and videos are usually taken after the ceremony.)

Will contributions to the church be collected at the ceremony? No.

AFTER THE CEREMONY

Is there usually a reception after the ceremony? There is usually a reception that may last one to two hours. It may be at a home or at a catering facility. Food and beverages may be served and there may be dancing and music.

Would it be considered impolite to neither eat nor drink? No.

Is there a grace or benediction before eating or drinking? Not normally, but there may be a blessing if the reception is a "sit-down" affair.

Is there a grace or benediction after eating or drinking? No.

Is there a traditional greeting for the family? Extend your congratulations and best wishes.

Is there a traditional form of address for clergy who may be at the reception? "Mr.," "Ms." or "Mrs." is usually sufficient.

Is it okay to leave early? Yes, but usually only after toasts have been made and the wedding cake is cut and served.

Funerals and Mourning

In the Episcopal/Anglican Church, a funeral service can be either part of a larger service or a ceremony in itself. If it is part of a larger service, that service is called a "requiem," which includes a Holy Communion service.

Episcopalians/Anglicans believe that Christ will come and judge all, the living and dead. Some will be consigned to heaven, where they will spend eternal life in the enjoyment of God. Others will be consigned to hell, where they will spend eternal death in the rejection of God.

BEFORE THE CEREMONY

How soon after the death does the funeral usually take place? Usually within two to three days.

What should a non-Episcopalian/Anglican do upon hearing of the death of a member of that faith? Telephone or visit the bereaved. There is no specific "ritual" for calling or expressing sympathy to someone who is mourning.

APPROPRIATE ATTIRE

Men: Jacket and tie. No head covering is required.

Women: A dress. Clothing should be modest, with arms covered and hems below the knee. Open-toed shoes and modest jewelry are permissible. No head covering is required.

Somber colors are recommended for clothing.

GIFTS

Is it appropriate to send flowers or make a contribution? Frequently, obituary notices will indicate if flowers are appropriate and may list specific charities for which contributions can be made in memory of the deceased.

Is it appropriate to send food? Ask the bereaved.

THE CEREMONY

Where will the ceremony take place? At a church or a funeral home.

When should guests arrive and where should they sit? Arrive early. Sit wherever you choose.

If arriving late, are there times when a guest should *not* enter the ceremony? No.

Will the bereaved family be present at the church or funeral home before the service? Yes.

Is there a traditional greeting for the family? No.

Will there be an open casket? Rarely.

Is a guest expected to view the body? This is entirely optional.

What is appropriate behavior upon viewing the body? A moment of silent prayer.

Who are the major officiants at the ceremony and what do they do? *A priest*, who leads the service.

What books are used? *The Book of Common Prayer* (New York: Church Publishing, 1979) and a hymnal. In Canada, *The Book of Alternative Services* (Toronto: The Anglican Book Center, 1985) may be used. Occasionally, the Bible lessons are included in the program.

To indicate the order of the ceremony: A program will be provided.

Will a guest who is not Episcopalian/Anglican be expected to do anything other than sit? They are expected to stand and kneel with the congregation, read prayers aloud and sing with congregants, if this does not compromise their personal beliefs. If one does not wish to kneel, sit when congregants do so.

Are there any parts of the ceremony in which a guest who is not Episcopalian/Anglican should *not* participate? Do not receive Communion or say any prayers contradictory to the beliefs of your own faith. Only baptized Christians may receive Communion.

If not disruptive to the ceremony, is it okay to:
Take pictures? No.
Use a flash? No.
Use a video camera? No.
Use a tape recorder? No.

Will contributions to the church be collected at the ceremony? No.

THE INTERMENT

Should guests attend the interment? Yes, especially if the deceased was a close friend.

Whom should one ask for directions? The funeral director or another guest.

What happens at the graveside? The body is committed to the ground. If there has been a cremation, the ashes are either buried or put in a vault.

Do guests who are not Episcopalian/Anglicans participate at the graveside ceremony? No. They are simply present.

COMFORTING THE BEREAVED

Is it appropriate to visit the home of the bereaved after the funeral? Yes, although there is no specific "ritual" for calling or expressing sympathy to someone who is mourning. Nor is there a "ritual" that guides the behavior of the mourners.

Will there be a religious service at the home of the bereaved? No.

Will food be served? This is at the discretion of the bereaved.

How soon after the funeral will a mourner usually return to a normal work schedule? One week.

How soon after the funeral will a mourner usually return to a normal social schedule? This is entirely at the discretion of the bereaved.

5 . HOME CELEBRATIONS

Not applicable to Episcopalians/ Anglicans.

10

Hindu

1. HISTORY AND BELIEFS

There are extraordinary differences between Hindu culture and beliefs and the prevailing Judeo-Christian religions and cultures in North America. Yet, from the transcendentalists in New England in the early 19th century through the beatniks of the 1950s and the spiritual seekers of today, Hinduism has held a fascination for many thousands of North Americans. Most of these were either influenced tangentially by Hinduism or became actual practitioners of certain aspects of it for a while. But today, the vast majority of Hindus in the United States and Canada are immigrants from Asia, especially from India.

Unlike other religions, Hinduism has no founder and no common creed or doctrine. Generally, it teaches that God is within being and object in the universe and transcends every being and object, that the essence of each soul is divine, and that the purpose of life is to become aware of that divine essence. The many forms of worship ritual and meditation in Hinduism are intended to lead the soul toward direct experience of God or Self.

In general, the different gods and goddesses in Hinduism are different ways of conceiving and approaching the one God beyond name and form. Different forms of worship through images, symbols and rituals are helpful to different kinds of persons. Some do not need external worship. The goal is to transcend these forms and the world as it is ordinarily perceived and to realize the divine presence everywhere.

U.S. temples: 160
U.S. membership: 1.5 million
(2005 data from the Secretariat of the Council of Hindu Temples of North America)

For more information, contact:
Hindu American Foundation
(301) 770-7835
www.hafsite.org

Canadian temples: 60+
Canadian membership: 100,000+
(data from the Canadian Council of Hindus)

For more information, contact:
Vedanta Society of Toronto
120 Emmett Avenue
Toronto, ON M6M 2E6
(416) 240-7262
www.vedantatoronto.ca

2 · THE BASIC SERVICE

Hindu temples are understood to be the residence of a particular god or goddess, or many gods and goddesses. At their center is a small room where a main image of that deity is kept.

Hindu services differ from typical congregational services in North America. Usually, Hindus recite prayer or are engaged in rituals at their own pace. In North America, however, some Hindu groups have attempted to modify Hindu customs so they conform more closely to North American practices, such as meeting at certain times on Sundays.

During the typical *puja*, or ritual worship that is held before a specific deity, the god is treated as a "guest" and the devotee is its "host." Prayers are directed to it, flowers are draped around or near it and incense is lit near it. It may even be bathed in special oils. The intention is to offer the best things to the "guest."

During the service, sacramental food called *prasad* may be served to those present. Guests who wish to abstain may do so without offending congregants. During the ritual called *bhog*, which is performed prior to eating, the food is blessed. No alcoholic beverages or nonvegetarian dishes are served as part of *prasad*.

APPROPRIATE ATTIRE

Men: Dress casually. No head covering is required.

Women: Dress casually. Not required are a head covering, clothing that covers the arms or hems that reach below the knees. Open-toed shoes and modest jewelry are permissible.

There are no rules regarding colors of clothing.

THE SANCTUARY

What are the major sections of the temple? There are many variables in Hindu temple architecture, especially in North America. But generally, both here and in India, there is a large room called a *natmandir*, where worshipers sit or stand. This faces a smaller section where the deity of the temple resides and where rituals honoring it are performed.

THE SERVICE

When should guests arrive and where should they sit? Arrive at the time for which the service is called. Sit wherever you wish on the floor, as do the congregants.

If arriving late, are there times when a guest should *not* enter the service? No.

Are there times when a guest should *not* leave the service? No.

Who are the major officiants, leaders or participants and what do they do?
Priests, who conduct the service.

What are the major ritual objects of the service?
Statues or pictures that represent any of the thousands of Hindu deities.
Narayana shalagram, a black round stone that symbolizes totality.

Flowers, which may be placed in front of a picture or statue of the temple's deity.

Incense, which is usually burned near the deity to perfume the air.

Water from the Ganges River, the river in India that is holy to Hindus. Often brought to the United States and Canada by traveling Hindus.

Lamps with five wicks dipped in clarified butter, and rotated near the deity by the worshipers.

What books are used? The Bhagavad Gita, the epic Sanskrit poem that relates the dialogue between the human Arjuna and the god, Lord Krishna. It consists of 700 two-line stanzas in 18 chapters in which Krishna expounds on the nature of reality. Also used are various scriptures favored by each Hindu sect. Readings from the Vedas and Upanishads and commentaries on the scriptures are regularly performed instead of sermons.

To indicate the order of the service: Periodic announcements will be made by a copriest.

GUEST BEHAVIOR DURING THE SERVICE

Will a guest who is not a Hindu be expected to do anything other than sit? No.

Are there any parts of the service in which a guest who is not a Hindu should *not* participate? Guests of other faiths are welcome to participate in any aspects of the service if these do not compromise or violate their own religious beliefs.

If not disruptive to the service, is it okay to:

Take pictures? Yes, with permission of the priest.

Use a flash? Yes, with permission of the priest.

Use a video camera? Yes, with permission of the priest.

Use a tape recorder? Yes, with permission of the priest.

Will contributions to the temple be collected at the service? Yes.

How much is it customary to contribute? There is no usual amount, although $1 to $10 would be appropriate.

AFTER THE SERVICE

Is there usually a reception after the service? No.

Is there a traditional form of address for clergy whom a guest may meet? "Swamiji" ("SWAH-mee-jee") if a monk, "Panditji"("PUN-deet-jee") if a priest.

GENERAL GUIDELINES AND ADVICE

Remove your shoes before entering the main sanctuary.

Silence is expected from all present during the ceremony, except during chanting.

SPECIAL VOCABULARY

Key words or phrases that it might be helpful for a visitor to know:

Prasad ("PRAH-sahd"): Sacramental food.

Mantras ("MAHN-tras"): Repeated prayers.

Murti ("MOOR-ty"): A statue or picture representing a deity.

Thakur ("TAH-koor"): Lord or God.

DOGMA AND IDEOLOGY

Hindus believe:

Humans are cast in a recurring cycle of birth and rebirth called *samsara*. *Karma*, the consequences of one's actions, determines one's lot in a future reincarnation from one lifetime to another.

The Path of Desire, or the attractions of worldly success, is ephemeral and seductive.

The Path of Renunciation, which comes after one realizes the shortcomings of the Path of Desire, can lead to exhilaration and confidence in life's higher calling. The path includes discipline (of every form) and preferring difficult, time-consuming accomplishments to those that are easy and quick.

Four *yogas*, or disciplines, comprise four paths to enlightenment, or discerning the true nature of reality:

Jnana yoga, marshaling the powers of the intellect to cut through the veils of illusion. Includes meditative practices.

Bhakti yoga, directing one's love toward God.

Karma yoga, selfless service toward others.

Raja yoga, which incorporates the above yogas into a unified discipline that addresses the body, mind and emotions. Included in *raja yoga* is hatha yoga, which disciplines and subdues the body.

Some basic books to which a guest can refer to learn more about Hinduism:

Bhagavad Gita: Annotated & Explained annotated by Kendra Crossen Burroughs; translated by Shri Purohit Swami (Woodstock, Vt.: SkyLight Paths Publishing, 2001).

The Essentials of Hinduism by Swami Bhaskarananda (Seattle, Wash.: Viveka Press, 2002).

The Upanishads and the Bhagavad Gita, both of which are available in numerous translations from several publishers.

What You Will See Inside a Hindu Temple by Dr. Mahendra Jani and Dr. Vandana Jani with photographs by Neirah Bhargava and Vijay Dave (Woodstock, Vt.: SkyLight Paths Publishing, 2005).

3 · HOLY DAYS AND FESTIVALS

The specific dates of Hindu holidays vary from year to year in relation to the Western secular calendar because the Hindu calendar is lunar-based.

Shiva Ratri. An all-night worship of God as the god Shiva. Shiva's primary qualities are creation and destruction, and compassion and renunciation. This holiday usually occurs in late winter. There is no traditional greeting for this holiday.

Duhsehra/Durga Puja. Celebrates the triumph of good over evil. Usually occurs in early autumn. There is no traditional greeting for this holiday.

Rama Navami. Worship of Rama, who (along with the god Krishna) is regarded as God incarnate. This usually occurs in the spring. There is no traditional greeting for this holiday.

Krishna Janmashtami. The birthday celebration of Krishna, who (along with Rama) is regarded as God incarnate. Krishna is perhaps the most widely worshiped Hindu deity. This holiday occurs in the late summer. There is no traditional greeting for this holiday.

4 · LIFE CYCLE EVENTS

Birth Ceremony

The naming ceremony occurs when a newborn is six to eight months old. It is called the "rice eating ceremony" because it marks the first time the child has eaten solid food. Held at the child's home, it is a ceremony in itself.

BEFORE THE CEREMONY

Are guests usually invited by a formal invitation? Yes.

If not stated explicitly, should one assume that children are invited? Yes.

If one can't attend, what should one do? RSVP with regrets and send a gift.

APPROPRIATE ATTIRE

Men: Dress casually. No head covering required.

Women: Dress casually. Not required are a head covering, clothing that covers the arms or hems that reach below the knees. Open-toed shoes and modest jewelry are permissible.

There are no rules regarding colors of clothing.

GIFTS

Is a gift customarily expected? Yes. Such gift items as clothes or toys are usual. Less common are cash or bonds.

Should gifts be brought to the ceremony? Bring gifts to the ceremony itself and place them in the hands of the parents.

THE CEREMONY

Where will the ceremony take place? Usually in a home. Less frequently in a temple.

When should guests arrive and where should they sit? Arrive at the time called for the ceremony to begin. Sit wherever you wish.

If arriving late, are there times when a guest should *not* enter the ceremony? No.

Are there times when a guest should *not* leave the ceremony? No.

Who are the major officiants, leaders or participants at the ceremony and what do they do? If the ceremony is held at home, a priest may perform the ritual, but in some cases senior members of the family officiate. If held at a Hindu temple, a priest officiates.

What books are used? No standard books are used for the ceremony.

To indicate the order of the ceremony: The service is so brief that few, if any, directions are needed for those present.

Will a guest who is not a Hindu be expected to do anything other than sit? No.

Are there any parts of the ceremony in which a guest who is not a Hindu should *not* participate? Guests of other faiths are welcome to participate in any aspects of the service if these do not compromise or violate their own religious beliefs.

If not disruptive to the ceremony, is it okay to:

Take pictures? Yes, with permission of the priest.

Use a flash? Yes, with permission of the priest.

Use a video camera? Yes, with permission of the priest.

Use a tape recorder? Yes, with permission of the priest.

Will contributions to the temple be collected at the ceremony? No.

AFTER THE CEREMONY

Is there usually a reception after the ceremony? A reception is usually held both before and after the ceremony, often in the same place as the ceremony itself. Traditional Indian food will be served. No alcoholic beverages will be served. There will be singing and, possibly, music.

Prasad, or food offered to a deity, is given to the child before others are fed.

Would it be considered impolite to neither eat nor drink? No.

Is there a grace or benediction before eating or drinking? No.

Is there a grace or benediction after eating or drinking? No.

Is there a traditional greeting for the family? No. Just offer your congratulations.

Is there a traditional form of address for clergy who may be at the reception? "Swamiji" ("SWAH-mee-jee") if a monk, "Panditji" ("PUN-deet-jee") if a priest.

Is it okay to leave early? No.

Initiation Ceremony

There is an initiation ceremony only for males of the priest class. This is called the "sacred thread ceremony" and occurs between the ages of eight and 12. It is strictly private and is a ceremony in itself.

In this ritual, the boy is initiated into the priesthood. Thereafter, he is regarded as having had his second, or spiritual, birth.

Marriage Ceremony

Hindu marriages are generally arranged by the parents or guardians of the bride and groom. In those rare cases where males and females choose their own partners, permission must be obtained from both sets of parents. No premarital dating or free mixing is allowed between males and females of marriageable age.

A Hindu marriage has seven major ceremonies:

Vagdana, the verbal contract about the marriage between the fathers or guardians of the bride and groom.

Kanya Sampradana, the giving away of the daughter to the groom by her father or guardian.

Varana, welcoming the bride and groom.

Panigrahana, ritualistic holding of each

other's hands by the bride and groom.

Saptapadi, a seven-step walking ritual by the bride and groom.

Laj homa, creation of the holy fire that symbolizes the formless divinity. The bride and groom circle it four times and offer parched paddy rice as oblation.

Sindur dam, the groom puts red vermilion on the forehead and the furrow of the parted hair of the bride.

Marriage ceremonies are usually held after sunset and before sunrise.

BEFORE THE CEREMONY

Are guests usually invited by a formal invitation? Yes.

If not stated explicitly, should one assume that children are invited? Yes.

If one can't attend, what should one do? RSVP with regrets and send a gift.

APPROPRIATE ATTIRE

Men: Dress casually. No head covering is required.

Women: Dress casually. Not required are a head covering, clothing that covers the arms or hems that reach below the knees. Open-toed shoes and modest jewelry are permissible.

There are no rules regarding colors of clothing.

GIFTS

Is a gift customarily expected? Yes, usually household items.

Should gifts be brought to the ceremony? Yes.

THE CEREMONY

Where will the ceremony take place? In any area that is covered. This could be a temple, a home, a catering hall or outside under a canopy.

When should guests arrive and where should they sit? Arrive at the time specified for the ceremony to begin. Sit wherever you wish.

If arriving late, are there times when a guest should *not* enter the ceremony? No.

Are there times when a guest should *not* leave the ceremony? No.

Who are the major officiants, leaders or participants at the ceremony and what do they do?

Priests, who officiate.

Parents and/or guardians, who exchange verbal contracts about the marriage. Also, the bride's father gives her to the groom.

Bride and groom.

What books are used? Only the priests use books.

To indicate the order of the ceremony: Ordinarily, neither is a program distributed nor periodic announcements made by the officiating priests. The ceremony just proceeds, although in the United States and Canada, the priest may occasionally explain the ceremony to guests who are not Hindus.

Will a guest who is not a Hindu be expected to do anything other than sit? No.

Are there any parts of the ceremony in which a guest who is not a Hindu should *not* participate? No.

If not disruptive to the ceremony, is it okay to:
Take pictures? Yes.
Use a flash? Yes.
Use a video camera? Yes.
Use a tape recorder? Yes.

Will contributions to the temple be collected at the ceremony? No.

AFTER THE CEREMONY

Is there usually a reception after the ceremony? There is a reception before and after the ceremony. Traditional Indian foods are served. It may last for many hours.

Would it be considered impolite to neither eat nor drink? Yes.

Is there a grace or benediction before eating or drinking? No.

Is there a grace or benediction after eating or drinking? No.

Is there a traditional greeting for the family? No. Just offer your congratulations.

Is there a traditional form of address for clergy who may be at the reception? "Swamiji" ("SWAH-mee-jee") if a monk, "Panditji" ("PUN-deet-jee") if a priest.

Is it okay to leave early? Yes.

Funerals and Mourning

Although the physical body dies, *atman* ("AHT-mahn"), or the individual soul, has no beginning and no end. It may, upon death, pass into another reincarnation, the condition of which depends on the *karma*, or consequences of one's actions, reaped during the life that just ended, as well as during previous lifetimes.

But if, over many lifetimes, the deceased has realized the true nature of reality, the individuality of the soul will be lost upon death and it will become one with Brahman, the One, All-Encompassing soul.

BEFORE THE CEREMONY

How soon after the death does the funeral usually take place? Usually within 24 hours.

What should a non-Hindu do upon hearing of the death of a member of that faith? Telephone or visit the bereaved and offer your condolences.

APPROPRIATE ATTIRE

Men: Dress casually. No head covering is required.

Women: Dress casually. Not required are a head covering, clothing that covers the arms or hems that reach below the knees. Open-toed shoes and modest jewelry are permissible.

Wear white clothing. Black is not appropriate.

GIFTS

Is it appropriate to send flowers or make a contribution? It is appropriate to personally bring flowers to the home of the deceased upon hearing of the death. In Hinduism, there is no concept of a "funeral home," so the body remains at the home until taken to the place of cremation, which is usually 24 hours after death. Flowers are placed at the feet of the deceased.

Donations are not customary.

Is it appropriate to send food? No.

THE CEREMONY

Where will the ceremony take place? At the place of cremation.

When should guests arrive and where should they sit? Arrive at the time for which the ceremony has been called. Sit wherever you wish.

If arriving late, are there times when a guest should *not* enter the ceremony? No.

Will the bereaved family be present at the place of cremation before the ceremony? Yes.

Is there a traditional greeting for the family? No. Just offer your condolences.

Will there be an open casket? Always.

Is a guest expected to view the body? Yes.

What is appropriate behavior upon viewing the body? Look reverently upon the body and do not touch it.

Who are the major officiants at the ceremony and what do they do? *Priests* or senior members of the family.

What books are used? Special books containing mantras for funeral services. Only the priests use these.

To indicate the order of the ceremony: Ordinarily, neither is a program distributed nor are periodic announcements made by the officiating priests. The ceremony just proceeds, although in the United States and Canada, the priest may occasionally explain the ceremony to guests who are not Hindus.

Will a guest who is not a Hindu be expected to do anything other than sit? No.

Are there any parts of the ceremony in which a guest who is not a Hindu should *not* participate? Guests of other faiths are welcome to participate in any aspects of the service if these do not compromise or violate their own religious beliefs.

If not disruptive to the ceremony, is it okay to:
Take pictures? No.
Use a flash? No.
Use a video camera? No.
Use a tape recorder? No.

Will contributions to the temple be collected at the ceremony? No.

THE CREMATION

Should guests attend the crema-

tion? If they wish to.

Whom should one ask for directions? Ask family members.

What happens at the cremation? The last food offering is symbolically made to the deceased and then the body is cremated. The cremation ceremony is called *mukhagni* ("moo-KAHG-nee").

Do guests who are not Hindus participate at the cremation ceremony? No. They are simply present.

COMFORTING THE
BEREAVED

Is it appropriate to visit the home of the bereaved after the funeral? Yes. Visit the bereaved before the *shraddha* ("SHRAHD-hah") ceremony, which occurs 10 days after the death for members of the Brahman caste and 30 days after the death for members of other castes. The ceremony is intended to liberate the soul of the deceased for its ascent to heaven. Visitors are expected to bring fruit to the home of the bereaved.

Will there be a religious service at the home of the bereaved? The *shraddha* ceremony is performed at home. Guests are usually invited to it by phone.

Will food be served? Varies according to tradition.

How soon after the funeral will a mourner usually return to a normal work schedule? In 10 to 30 days, depending on when the *shraddha* ceremony is performed.

How soon after the funeral will a mourner usually return to a normal social schedule? After the *shraddha* ceremony, which occurs 10 to 30 days after the death.

Are there mourning customs to which a friend who is not a Hindu should be sensitive? For 10 to 30 days after the death, depending on when the *shraddha* ceremony is performed, mourners dress, eat and behave austerely.

Are there rituals for observing the anniversary of the death? Yes. These are performed by a priest in a temple. There is no name for these rituals.

5 · HOME CELEBRATIONS

Worship in the home is a paramount aspect of Hindu ritual. This is a private ceremony that centers around the small shrine for a god and goddess found in most Hindu homes.

Islam

1 · HISTORY AND BELIEFS

The Arabic word *islam* means "submission," and Islam is the religion of submission to the will of God ("Allah" in Arabic).

Muhammad, who is regarded as the last and final prophet of Allah, was born in Mecca (in present-day Saudi Arabia) in approximately 570 C.E. As a young man, he sought solitude in a cave on the outskirts of Mecca, where, according to Muslim belief, he received revelation from God. The basic creed that Muhammad taught is that the one God in heaven demands morality and monotheistic devotion from those he has created.

Initially, Muhammad's message was widely rejected, especially by Mecca's elite, who felt threatened by its egalitarian teachings. But by the time he died in 632 C.E., most of Arabia had embraced Islam.

Muslims revere the Qur'an, their holy book, as the earthly cornerstone of their faith.

Islam teaches that the Hebrew Bible and the New Testament were also authentic revelations from God and recognizes as prophets all those prophets who were mentioned in these Scriptures, including Abraham, Moses, David and Jesus.

With about 1 billion Muslims around the globe, Islam is the fastest-growing religion in the world. Every country in the world has at least a small Muslim community. There are now Muslims in nearly every town in the United States, with more substantial numbers in larger cities, especially in the East and Midwest and on the West Coast. In Canada, there are Muslims in every major city, with substantial numbers in the provinces of Ontario, Alberta and British Columbia.

U.S. Islamic centers and organizations: 2,000
U.S. membership: 7 million
(2001 data from the American Muslim Council)

For more information, contact:
Islamic Society of North America
P.O. Box 38
Plainfield, IN 46168

Canadian Islamic centers and organizations: 100
Canadian membership: 650,000
(2000 data from the Muslim World League)

110

For more information contact:

Islamic Society of North
    America–Canada
2200 South Sheridan Way
Mississauga, ON L5J 2M4
(905) 403-8406
www.isnacanada.com

Muslim World League
Canadian Office
2550 Argentia Road #220
Mississauga, ON L5N 5R1
(905) 542-1050
www.mwlcanada.org

2 · THE BASIC SERVICE

While Muslims are required to pray five times a day—daybreak, noon, midafternoon, sunset and evening—this can be done either in a mosque or wherever individual Muslims may be. Prayer, which is in Arabic, is preceded with *wadu* ("WAH-doo"), washing with water that cleanses the body (hands, mouth, face and feet) and spirit. Congregants then face Mecca and, depending on the time of day, do two to four prostrations (*raka'ah*, pronounced "RAH-kah"). Each *raka'ah* begins with the declaration, "God is most great," and consists of bows, prostrations and the recitation of fixed prayers. At the end of prayer, the *taslim* ("TAHS-lihm"), or "peace greeting," "Peace be upon all of you and the mercy and the blessings of God," is repeated twice.

On Friday, *jumma* ("JUH-mah"), the noon prayer, is a congregational prayer and is recited at a central mosque designated for that purpose.

In a mosque, men and women form separate lines for prayer, extending from one side of the mosque's main sanctuary to the other. The tight ranks symbolize unity and equality within the Muslim community. Each gender has its own line to maintain modesty and concentration during the physical movements of standing, bowing and prostration. Their separation does not indicate relative superiority or inferiority. This *jumma* lasts between 30 and 60 minutes.

APPROPRIATE ATTIRE

Men: Casual shirt and slacks. Head covering is not required.

Women: A dress or skirt and blouse are recommended. Clothing should cover arms and hems should reach below the knees. A scarf is required to cover the head. Women may wear open-toed shoes and/or modest jewelry.

There are no rules regarding colors of clothing, but openly wearing crosses, Stars of David, jewelry with the signs of the zodiac and pendants with faces or heads of animals or people is discouraged.

THE SANCTUARY

What are the major sections of the mosque?

The entrance: Where shoes are removed, since they are not worn inside a mosque.

A musallah ("muh-SAL-ah"), or prayer room: Where prayers are recited. Every *musallah* is oriented toward Mecca, which Muslims face during prayers. The prayer room is open and uncluttered to accommodate lines of worshipers who stand and bow in unison. There are no pews or chairs. Members of the congregation sit on the floor. Some mosques have a balcony in the *musallah* reserved for women. Other mosques accommodate men and women in the same *musallah*, or they may have totally separate areas for men and women.

The qiblah ("KIHB-lah"): The direction to which the imam, or prayer leader, faces while praying. In the United States, Muslims face the northeast toward Mecca; in Canada, Muslims face the southeast.

A mihrab ("MEE-rahb"), or niche that indicates which wall of the mosque faces toward Mecca: The *mihrab* is often decorated with Arabic calligraphy. Its curved shape helps reflect the voice of the imam, the prayer leader, back toward the congregation.

Facilities to perform wadu ("WAH-doo"), or washings with water of the hands, face and feet: These are done prior to prayers as a way to purify one's self before standing in front of God. *Wadu* facilities range from wash basins to specially designed areas with built-in benches, floor drains and faucets.

A multipurpose room: Used for seminars and lectures.

THE SERVICE

When should guests arrive and where should they sit? Arrive early. Some congregants arrive as much as 30 to 60 minutes before the service starts. Non-Muslim guests will be advised to sit separately from Muslims, since Islamic practice forbids them from joining the prayer line. Like the rest of the worshipers in the mosque, guests sit on the prayer rug on the floor.

If arriving late, are there times when a guest should *not* enter the service? No.

Are there times when a guest should *not* leave the service? Do not leave when congregational prayer is being conducted.

A congregational prayer is offered in a group. Muslims are encouraged to pray in groups in mosques, although many pray as individuals and families at home.

Who are the major officiants, leaders or participants and what do they do?
An imam ("EE-mahm"), who leads the prayers and delivers a sermon.
A muazzin ("MOO-ah-zin"), who calls the faithful to prayer.

What are the major ritual objects of the service? None.

What books are used? None, since prayers are memorized. (This means that praying individually requires learning the proper rituals in advance. Newcomers to the faith pray in groups and follow the lead of the imam.)

To indicate the order of the service: Periodic announcements are made by a *muazzin*, who calls the *Adhan* ("AHD-han") and the *Iqamah* ("IK-ah-mah"). The *Adhan*, which is aired through public loudspeakers, alerts people that the time of prayer has started. The *Iqamah* is intended to alert mosque worshipers that congregational prayer is about to begin.

GUEST BEHAVIOR DURING THE SERVICE

Will a guest who is not a Muslim be expected to do anything other than sit? No.

Are there any parts of the service in which a guest who is not a Muslim should *not* participate? No.

If not disruptive to the service, is it okay to:
Take pictures? No.
Use a flash? No.
Use a video camera? No.
Use a tape recorder? Yes.

(Note: Different Islamic centers have different policies regarding such matters as cameras and tape recorders. If you wish to use such equipment during the service, check in advance with an official of the mosque or center.)

Will contributions to the mosque be collected at the service? Some mosque leaders pass boxes to collect donations; others mount boxes in mosques for voluntary contributions. Non-Muslims are not expected to make a contribution, since that would be perceived as having imposed an obligation upon guests and, thus, would violate the traditional generosity shown toward guests in Islamic culture.

How much is it customary to contribute? This is entirely at the discretion of each person. Perhaps $1 to $10 maximum.

AFTER THE SERVICE

Is there usually a reception after the service? No.

Is it okay to leave early? Yes.

GENERAL GUIDELINES AND ADVICE

Guests will observe Muslims making two *raka'ah* of prayer upon entering the mosque. This is a way to "greet" and honor the mosque. A full *raka'ah* consists of recitations during one standing, one bowing, and two prostrating motions (separated by a short sitting). Each prayer time requires a specific number of *raka'ah*. For example, dawn prayer consists of two *raka'ah*, noon consists of four and sunset of three. Visiting non-Muslims should not perform *raka'ah*, since the ritual is reserved for Muslims.

Worshipers and guests must not talk when the imam delivers a sermon.

Women should cover their hair with a scarf before entering *musallah*, or the prayer area of a mosque. Some mosques have a separate area for women. When there is no separate room for women, they pray behind the men.

SPECIAL VOCABULARY

Key words or phrases that it might be helpful for a visitor to know:
Salat ("SAH-laht"): "Prayer."
As salaam alaikum (ahs SAH-lahm ah-LAY-koom"): "Peace be upon you." A common greeting between Muslims.
Wa alaikum salaam (wah ah-LAY-koom SAH-lahm"): "And upon you

the peace." A common response to the above greeting.

Salla allahu alayhi wa salaam ("SAH-lah ah-LAH-hoo ah-LAY-hee wah SAH-lahm"): "May the peace and blessings of Allah be upon him." This is said when any prophet of God is mentioned.

Allah subhana wa tala ("AH-lah SOOB-hah-nah wah TAH-lah"): "God, Who is highly glorified and honored."

Raka'ah ("RAH-kah"): A unit of prayer ritual that consists of motions and verbal recitations.

DOGMA AND IDEOLOGY

Muslims believe:

One becomes a Muslim by saying and believing the *shahadah* ("SHAH-hah-dah"): "There is no god but God and Muhammad is the messenger of God."

A Muslim prays five times a day. The prayers take 5 to 10 minutes. Muslims pray communally at noon on Friday. Muslims face Mecca during their prayers as a sign of unity. But they do not "pray" to Mecca; they pray to God.

A tax on assets is gathered by the community and distributed according to need. Called the *zakat*, it is generally 2$^{1}/_{2}$ percent of one's income.

Muslims abstain from food, drink and sexual activity from sunrise to sunset during the lunar month of Ramadan.

A Muslim must make the *hajj* ("hahj"), or pilgrimage to Mecca, at least once in his or her lifetime if physically and financially able. The hajj symbolizes unity and equality. Muslims of different races, wealth, status and gender gather in Mecca for hajj, and all are equal before God.

Some basic books to which a guest can refer to learn more about Islam:

Islam: A Short History by Karen Armstrong (New York: Modern Library, 2002).

Islam: The Straight Path by John L. Esposito (New York: Oxford University Press, 2004).

The Qur'an ("koo-RAHN"), of which there are several English translations. A good translation is by Yusuf Ali. This can be found in mosques and many bookstores.

The Qur'an and Sayings of Prophet Muhammad: Selections Annotated & Explained annotated by Sohaib N. Sultan; translation by Yusuf Ali, revised by Sohaib N. Sultan (Woodstock, Vt.: SkyLight Paths Publishing, 2007).

What You Will See Inside a Mosque by Aisha Karen Khan with photographs by Aaron Pepis (Woodstock, Vt.: SkyLight Paths Publishing, 2008).

3 · HOLY DAYS AND FESTIVALS

Ramadan ("RAH-mah-dahn"). Occurs during all of Ramadan, the ninth month of the Islamic calendar. (Since Muslims follow the lunar calendar, Ramadan starts about ten days earlier in the solar calendar every year.) From sunrise to sunset, all adult Muslims whose health permits are to abstain from food, drink, smoking and sexual activity. Ramadan is a time for reflection and spiritual discipline, to express gratitude for God's guidance and to atone for past sins. It is recommended that each Muslim read the entire Qur'an during this month.

The traditional greeting for this holiday is *"Ramadan mubarak"* ("RAH-mah-dahn moo-BAR-ahk"), meaning, "May God give you a blessed month." The traditional response is *"Ramadan karim"* ("RAH-mah-dahn KAH-reem"), meaning, "May God give you a generous month."

Id al-Fitr ("id AHL-fih-ter"). The Feast of the Breaking of the Fast, which is celebrated at the end of Ramadan to mark the completion of fasting. The holiday lasts for three days, during which family members gather to feast and exchange presents. In many Muslim countries, it is a national holiday. It is also a time for attending mosque and paying the special alms for the poor, *zakat al-fitr*, required by Islamic law.

The traditional greeting for this holiday is *"Id mubarak"* ("id moo-BAR-ahk"), which means "[May God make it a] blessed feast." The response is *"Id karim"* ("id KAH-reem"), which means "[May God make it a] kind feast."

Id al-Adha ("id uhl-AHD-hah"). Occurs two to three months after Ramadan and commemorates Abraham's obedience to God when he told him to sacrifice his son, Ishmael, and Ishmael's submission to the sacrifice. The holiday is marked by slaughtering animals to feed the poor.

The traditional greeting for this holiday is *"Id mubarak"* ("id moo-BAR-ahk"), which means "[May God make it] a blessed feast."

Lailat ul-Qadr ("LIE-laht ul-KAH-dur"). The last 10 days of Ramadan, during which special prayers are offered. This commemorates the "Night of Power" when the Prophet Muhammad first received God's revelation. Although the revelation occurred upon one particular night, it is celebrated during 10 days since the exact night is unknown. All

that is known is that the revelation occurred during the last 10 days of Ramadan. During *Lailat ul-Qadr*, Muslims sometimes seclude themselves in their mosque, leaving only when necessary. There is no traditional greeting for these days.

al-Isra Wal Miraj ("al-IZ-rah wahl MEE-rahj"), "The Night Journey and the Ascension," which is observed on the 27th day of Rajab, which is the seventh month of the Muslim lunar calendar. The holiday commemorates the night when the Prophet Muhammad is believed to have made a miraculous journey from Mecca to the Aqsa Mosque in Jerusalem, where he then traveled to the heavens, where God commanded him to initiate prayers five times each day. There is no traditional greeting for this holiday.

4 · LIFE CYCLE EVENTS

Birth Ceremony

The ceremony is called an *akikah* ("ah-KEE-kah"). A ceremony in itself, it usually lasts about 30 to 60 minutes. An *akikah* is very informal and is not universally practiced by Muslims. What transpires at it varies from culture to culture and, often, from home to home. Generally, it is simply a way to welcome a newborn infant.

BEFORE THE CEREMONY

Are guests usually invited by a formal invitation? Non-Muslims will usually receive an oral invitation, either over the telephone or in person.

For Muslims, the time and place of the event are usually posted in the mosque or announced after Friday prayers.

If not stated explicitly, should one assume that children are invited? Yes.

If one can't attend, what should one do? RSVP with regrets and send a gift. Usually cash is appropriate. While the range of the cash given as presents is wide, Muslims are taught to be generous.

APPROPRIATE ATTIRE

Men: Casual shirt and slacks. Head covering is not required.

Women: A dress or skirt and blouse are recommended. Clothing should cover the arms and hems should reach below the knees. A scarf is required to cover the head. Women may wear open-toed shoes and/or modest jewelry.

For both men and women, there are no rules regarding colors of clothing, but openly wearing crosses, Stars of David, jewelry with the signs of the zodiac and pendants with faces or heads of animals or people is discouraged.

GIFTS

Is a gift customarily expected? Yes. Usually cash is appropriate. While the range of the cash given as presents is wide, Muslims are taught to be generous.

Should gifts be brought to the ceremony? They can either be sent to the home of the parents or be brought to the ceremony. If cash is given, it is usually presented in an envelope, along with a card.

THE CEREMONY

Where will the ceremony take place? Either in the home of the parents of the child or in the general-purpose room of their mosque.

When should guests arrive and where should they sit? Arrive at the time called for the ceremony to begin. Sit wherever you wish. Men and women will sit in different parts of the room. They should inquire about where women go and where men go. In the United States, Muslims and their guests sit on chairs.

If arriving late, are there times when a guest should *not* enter the ceremony? No.

Are there times when a guest should *not* leave the ceremony? No.

Who are the major officiants, leaders or participants at the ceremony and what do they do? Possibly a family member, who may say some informal words about the newborn.

What books are used? None.

To indicate the order of the ceremony: An *akikah* is brief and informal. There is no need to indicate the order of the event.

Will a guest who is not a Muslim be expected to do anything other than sit? No.

**Are there any parts of the ceremony in which a guest who is not

a Muslim should *not* participate?
No.

If not disruptive to the ceremony, is it okay to:
Take pictures? No.
Use a flash? No.
Use a video camera? No.
Use a tape recorder? Yes.

(Note: Different Islamic centers have different policies regarding such matters as cameras and tape recorders. If you wish to use such equipment during the ceremony, check in advance with an official of the mosque or center.)

Will contributions to the mosque be collected at the ceremony? Some mosque leaders pass boxes to collect donations; others mount boxes in mosques for voluntary contributions. Non-Muslims are not expected to make a contribution, since that would be perceived as having imposed an obligation upon guests and, thus, would violate the traditional generosity shown toward guests in Islamic culture.

How much is customary to contribute? This is entirely at the discretion of each person. Perhaps $1 to $10 maximum.

AFTER THE CEREMONY

Is there usually a reception after the ceremony? There may be a reception. Such traditions differ from culture to culture and from mosque to mosque. If so, light food and beverages will be served, but no alcoholic beverages. There may be dancing and/or music, again depending on the particular mosque and the culture in which it is set.

Would it be considered impolite to neither eat nor drink? No.

Is there a grace or benediction before eating or drinking? No.

Is there a grace or benediction after eating or drinking? No.

Is there a traditional greeting for the family? Yes. It is *"Mabrook"* ("MAH-brook"). This means "Congratulations."

Is there a traditional form of address for clergy who may be at the reception? An imam may be directly addressed by the title of "Imam" or by his name.

Is it okay to leave early? Yes.

Initiation Ceremony

At the *"shahada"* ("SHAH-hah-dah") or "witnessing," a Muslim repeats the Islamic declaration of faith: "There is no deity but God, and Muhammad is the messenger of God." "Taking *shahada*," as the ritual is called, is a ceremony in itself. It is usually done at any age from the midteens upward. It must be witnessed by either two male Muslims or eight female Muslims. The *shahada* may last between 15 and 30 minutes.

BEFORE THE CEREMONY

Are guests usually invited by a formal invitation? The individual making the *shahada* will invite friends or family, either in person, by phone or by written invitation. Often, an announcement is made that certain individuals will make *shahada* at the end of a particular service.

If not stated explicitly, should one assume that children are invited? Yes.

If one can't attend, what should one do? RSVP with regrets. No gift is expected.

APPROPRIATE ATTIRE

Men: Casual shirt and slacks. Head covering is not required.

Women: A dress or skirt and blouse are recommended. Clothing should cover the arms and hems should reach below the knees. A scarf is required to cover the head. Women may wear open-toed shoes and/or modest jewelry.

For both men and women, there are no rules regarding colors of clothing, but openly wearing crosses, Stars of David, jewelry with the signs of the zodiac and pendants with faces or heads of animals or people is discouraged.

GIFTS

Is a gift customarily expected? No.

Should gifts be brought to the ceremony? See above.

THE CEREMONY

Where will the ceremony take place? Either in the main sanctuary or in a special room of a mosque or at the home of the person making the *shahada*.

When should guests arrive and where should they sit? Arrive early. Someone will advise guests where to sit.

If arriving late, are there times when a guest should *not* enter the ceremony? No.

Are there times when a guest should *not* leave the ceremony? No.

Who are the major officiants, leaders or participants at the ceremony and what do they do?
An imam, who leads the prayers and delivers a sermon.
A muezzin, who calls the faithful to prayer.

What books are used? None, since prayers are memorized. (This means that praying individually requires learning the proper rituals in advance. Newcomers to the faith pray in groups and follow the lead of the imam.)

To indicate the order of the ceremony: A *shahada* is brief and informal. No need to indicate the order of the event.

Will a guest who is not a Muslim be expected to do anything other than sit? No.

Are there any parts of the ceremony in which a guest who is not a Muslim should *not* participate? No.

If not disruptive to the ceremony, is it okay to:
Take pictures? Yes.
Use a flash? No.
Use a video camera? Yes.
Use a tape recorder? Yes.
    (Note: Different Islamic centers have different policies regarding such

matters as cameras and tape recorders. If you wish to use such equipment during the ceremony, check in advance with an official of the mosque or center.)

If the *shahada* is held in a mosque, will contributions to the mosque be collected at the service? There will not be a collection, but in some mosques, boxes are mounted on the wall for voluntary contributions. Non-Muslims are not expected to make a contribution, since that would be perceived as having imposed an obligation upon guests and, thus, would violate the traditional generosity shown toward guests in Islamic culture.

How much is it customary to contribute? This is entirely at the discretion of each person. Perhaps $1 to $10 maximum.

AFTER THE CEREMONY

Is there usually a reception after the ceremony? No.

Is there a traditional greeting for the family? Yes. It is *"Mabrook"* ("MAH-brook"). This means "Congratulations."

Is there a traditional form of address for clergy whom a guest may meet? An imam may be directly addressed by the title of "Imam" or by his name.

Marriage Ceremony

Marriage is incumbent on every Muslim man and woman unless they are financially or physically unable to be married. It is regarded as the norm for all and essential to the growth and stability of the family, which is the basic unit of society. Marriage is regarded as a sacred contract or covenant, not a sacrament, that legalizes sexual intercourse and the procreation of children.

The marriage ceremony usually lasts about 30 minutes, but can last more than one hour. It is a ceremony in itself.

BEFORE THE CEREMONY

Are guests usually invited by a formal invitation? Non-Muslims are usually invited orally, either over the telephone or in person. For Muslims, invitations may be posted in a mosque or announced after the noon prayers on Friday.

If not stated explicitly, should one assume that children are invited? Yes.

If one can't attend, what should one do? RSVP with regrets and send a gift, either money or whatever items one deems appropriate for the needs of the newlyweds.

APPROPRIATE ATTIRE

Men: Casual shirt and slacks. Head covering is not required.

Women: A dress or skirt and blouse are recommended. Clothing should cover the arms and hems should reach below the knees. A scarf is required to cover the head. Women may wear open-toed shoes and/or modest jewelry.

For both men and women, there are no rules regarding colors of clothing, but openly wearing crosses, Stars of David, jewelry with the signs of the zodiac and pendants with faces or heads of animals or people is discouraged.

GIFTS

Is a gift customarily expected? Yes, either money or whatever items one deems appropriate for the needs of the newlyweds.

Should gifts be brought to the ceremony? They can either be sent to the home of the newlyweds or be brought to the ceremony.

THE CEREMONY

Where will the ceremony take place? In a mosque.

When should guests arrive and where should they sit? Arrive at the time called for the wedding to start. Sit wherever you wish.

If arriving late, are there times when a guest should *not* enter the ceremony? No.

Are there times when a guest should *not* leave the ceremony? No.

Who are the major officiants, leaders or participants at the ceremony and what do they do?

An imam, or Islamic prayer leader, who usually delivers a sermon about marriage. This may be in Arabic if the newlyweds are Arabic-speaking or in English if they are English-speaking. Or it may be a mixture of both languages.

Two witnesses, who witness the oral and written contract entered into by the bride and groom.
The groom, who offers marriage to the bride.
The bride, who accepts the offer.

What books are used? None.

To indicate the order of the ceremony: Weddings are brief and informal. There is no need to indicate the order of the event.

Will a guest who is not a Muslim be expected to do anything other than sit? No.

Are there any parts of the ceremony in which a guest who is not a Muslim should *not* participate? No.

If not disruptive to the ceremony, is it okay to:
Take pictures? Yes.
Use a flash? Yes.
Use a video camera? Yes.
Use a tape recorder? Yes.
(Note: Different Islamic centers have different policies regarding such matters as cameras and tape recorders. If you wish to use such equipment during the ceremony, check in advance with an official of the mosque or center.)

Will contributions to the mosque be collected at the ceremony? There will not be a collection, but in some mosques, boxes are mounted on the wall for voluntary contributions. Non-Muslims are not expected to make a contribution, since that would be perceived as having imposed an obligation upon guests and, thus, would violate the traditional generosity shown toward guests in Islamic culture.

How much is it customary to contribute? This is entirely at the discretion of each person. Perhaps $1 to $10 maximum.

AFTER THE CEREMONY

Is there usually a reception after the ceremony? Yes. This is called a *waleemah* ("wah-LEEH-mah"). It may last two hours or more and can be held anywhere: in the mosque, a home, a catering hall or any other site. Beverages and such food as meat, rice, fruit, and sweets will be served. There will be no alcoholic beverages. There may be dancing and/or music, but not if the *waleemah* is held in a mosque.

Would it be considered impolite to neither eat nor drink? No.

Is there a grace or benediction before eating or drinking? No.

Is there a grace or benediction after eating or drinking? No.

Is there a traditional greeting for the family? *"Mabrook alaik"* ("MAH-brook ah-LAYK"), "Congratulations," if addressing a male. *"Mabrook alaiki"* ("MAH-brook ah-LAYK-ee"), "Congratulations," if addressing a female.

Is there a traditional form of address for clergy who may be at the reception? An imam may be directly addressed by the title of "Imam" or by his name.

Is it okay to leave early? Yes.

Funerals and Mourning

The Muslim view of the afterlife includes a universal belief in a final Day of Reckoning, when all people will be called upon to give account for their actions. The Qur'an describes the pleasures of heaven enjoyed by the righteous— as well as the torments of hell—in vivid, physical detail. Individual Muslims hold a range of differing opinions about how literally those descriptions are to be taken.

An Islamic funeral is a service in itself and usually lasts about 30 to 60 minutes. In some cases, it may last more than an hour.

BEFORE THE CEREMONY

How soon after the death does the funeral usually take place? Two to three days.

What should a non-Muslim do upon hearing of the death of a member of that faith? Call or visit the bereaved. If one visits, shake hands or hug and kiss the family members of the same gender, sit and talk quietly and offer some quiet prayer.

APPROPRIATE ATTIRE

Men: Casual shirt and slacks. Head covering is not required.

Women: A dress is recommended. Clothing should cover the arms and hems should reach below the knees. A scarf is required to cover the head.

For both men and women, there are no rules regarding colors of clothing, but openly wearing crosses, Stars of David, jewelry with the signs of the zodiac and pendants with faces or heads of animals or people is discouraged.

Dark, somber colors are advised.

GIFTS

Is it appropriate to send flowers or make a contribution? Send flowers after the funeral to the home of the bereaved.

Is it appropriate to send food? Yes.

THE CEREMONY

Where will the ceremony take place? At a funeral home or in the general-purpose room of the mosque.

When should guests arrive and where should they sit? Arrive at the time set for the funeral. An usher will advise guests on where to sit.

If arriving late, are there times when a guest should *not* enter the ceremony? No.

Will the bereaved family be present at the funeral home before the ceremony? No.

Is there a traditional greeting for the family? No. Just offer your condolences.

Will there be an open casket? Never.

Who are the major officiants at the ceremony and what do they do? *An imam*, who presides.

What books are used? The Qur'an.

To indicate the order of the ceremony: No directions are given during the service, which is intended to be as simple as possible.

Will a guest who is not a Muslim be expected to do anything other than sit? No.

Are there any parts of the ceremony in which a guest who is not a Muslim should *not* participate? No.

If not disruptive to the ceremony, is it okay to:
Take pictures? No.
Use a flash? No.
Use a video camera? No.
Use a tape recorder? No.

Will contributions to the mosque be collected at the ceremony? No.

THE INTERMENT

Should guests attend the interment? Yes.

Whom should one ask for directions? An imam.

What happens at the graveside? The *Janazah* prayers ("jah-NAH-zah") for the dead are recited and the deceased is buried. Muslims are never cremated.

Do guests who are not Muslims participate at the graveside ceremony? No, they are simply present.

COMFORTING THE BEREAVED

Is it appropriate to visit the home of the bereaved after the funeral? Yes. Visit any time during the days of mourning, which are religiously mandated not to exceed 40 days. The number of mourning days that one actually observes is individually set and can be determined by telephoning the home of the bereaved. When visiting the home of a mourner, talk quietly with the bereaved and other visitors. Often, visitors and mourners sit in silence while someone reads aloud from the Qur'an or a tape of a reading from the Qur'an is played.

Will there be a religious service at the home of the bereaved? No.

Will food be served? Possibly. Often, women in the local Muslim community prepare food for mourners and their guests.

How soon after the funeral will a mourner usually return to a normal work schedule? After a few days.

How soon after the funeral will a mourner usually return to a normal social schedule? There are no prescriptions in Islam about such matters. This is more culturally determined than religiously determined. Usually, women do not engage in normal social activities until 40 days after the death of a member of their immediate family. There are no norms for men.

Are there mourning customs to which a friend who is not a Muslim should be sensitive? Bereaved usually wear black, although this is a cultural norm and not a religious prescription.

Are there rituals for observing the anniversary of the death? No.

5 . HOME CELEBRATIONS

Not applicable to Islam.

12

Jehovah's Witnesses

1. HISTORY AND BELIEFS

The Jehovah's Witnesses are a worldwide faith known for their assertive proselytizing and expectations of an imminent apocalypse. They have drawn attention because of their refusal to celebrate Christmas, by their dedicated missionary work and by using Jehovah as the sole name of God.

Jehovah's Witnesses derive their name from the 43rd chapter of the Book of Isaiah, in which the gods of the nations are invited to bring forth their witnesses to prove their claimed cases of righteousness or to hear the witnesses for Jehovah's side and acknowledge the truth: "Ye are my witnesses, saith Jehovah, and my servants whom I have chosen; that ye may know and believe me, and understand that I am he; before me there was no God formed, neither shall there be after me. I, even I, am Jehovah; and besides me there is no savior" (Isaiah 43:10–11, American Standard Version of the Bible).

In the Bible, all faithful worshipers, such as Abel, Noah, Abraham and Jesus, were called "witnesses of God" (Hebrews 11:1–12:1; Revelation 3:14).

The faith was founded in western Pennsylvania in the early 1870s by Charles Taze Russell, who had organized a Bible study group to promote the basic teachings of the Bible. It was his desire to return to the teachings of first-century Christianity.

Jehovah's Witnesses believe that God demands unconditional obedience and that the infallible source of truth is the Bible, which is true in every detail. Jesus, who was the Son of God and was his first creation, was responsible for all the rest of God's creation on earth. While residing on earth, Jesus was entirely a man. After his death, he was raised by God to heaven and restored to a place second only to that of his Father, Jehovah.

The fulfillment of God's Kingdom will occur through the battle of Armageddon, the appearance of the Lord in the air, the thousand-year rule on earth of Christ (during which resurrection and judgment take place). This process began in 1914 and its completion will soon occur.

Members of the Church are expected to devote their primary loyalty and time to the movement, and not participate in politics or interfaith movements. They believe that all human laws that do not conflict with God's law should be obeyed. They also do not vote in civic elections or serve in the military. They respect each country's flag (or other national symbols), but do not salute it, since they believe this would be idolatry.

U.S. churches: 12,728
U.S. membership: 1.1 million
(data from the 2010 Yearbook of American and Canadian Churches*)*

For more information, contact:
Jehovah's Witnesses
25 Columbia Heights
Brooklyn, NY 11201
(718) 560-5000
www.watchtower.org

Canadian churches: 1,335
Canadian membership: 112,092
(data from the 2010 Yearbook of American and Canadian Churches*)*

For more information, contact:
Jehovah's Witnesses
Canadian Branch Office
Box 4100
Halton Hills, ON L7G 4Y4
(888) 301-4259

2 · THE BASIC SERVICE

Congregational meetings are highly instructional and primarily deal with Bible teachings, prophecy or counsel on Christian living. Some of these meetings are conducted as Bible studies with audience participation, usually using a magazine (such as *The Watchtower*) or a book published by the Jehovah's Witnesses' publishing house, the Watchtower Society. The person conducting the study may pose questions based on a paragraph that has been read aloud to the group.

Meetings last slightly more than one hour and are held on Sundays, with the times varying among congregations, and on two other days each week.

APPROPRIATE ATTIRE

Men: Jacket and tie are usually worn, although they are not required. No head covering is required.

Women: A dress or a skirt and blouse. Dress "modestly" and "sensibly." Hems need not reach below the knees nor must clothing cover the arms. Open-toed shoes and modest jewelry are permissible. No head covering is required.

There are no rules regarding colors of clothing.

THE SANCTUARY

What are the major sections of the meeting hall? Kingdom Halls, the name of Jehovah's Witnesses' meeting halls, are usually plain structures, inside and out. They resemble auditoriums more than churches or synagogues.

THE SERVICE

When should guests arrive and where should they sit? Arrive early. Sit wherever you wish.

If arriving late, are there times when a guest should *not* enter the service? No, but latecomers will be assisted by attendants to find an appropriate seat.

Are there times when a guest should *not* leave the service? No.

Who are the major officiants, leaders or participants and what do they do?

The Congregation Elders, who deliver talks on the Bible and lead Bible discussions with the congregants.

What are the major ritual objects of the service? None.

What books are used? The Old and New Testaments, primarily the New World Translation (New York: The Watchtower Bible and Tract Society of New York, 1961); *The Watchtower,* a semimonthly journal published by Jehovah's Witnesses headquarters in Brooklyn, N.Y.; and a hymnal, *Sing to Jehovah* (New York: The Watchtower Bible and Tract Society of New York, 2009).

To indicate the order of the service: Periodic announcements will be made by an elder in the congregation.

GUEST BEHAVIOR DURING THE SERVICE

Will a guest who is not a Jehovah's Witness be expected to do anything other than sit? It is entirely optional for a guest of another faith to stand and sing with the congregation and to answer questions during a discussion of the Bible. During prayer, guests may bow their heads reverently. Jehovah's Witnesses do not kneel during their congregational meetings.

Are there any parts of the service in which a guest who is not a Jehovah's Witness should *not* participate? No.

If not disruptive to the service, is it okay to:
Take pictures? Yes.
Use a flash? Yes.
Use a video camera? Yes.
Use a tape recorder? Yes.

(Note: Do not use the above equipment during prayer. Using a flash during the Bible talk would also be inappropriate.)

Will contributions to the church be collected at the service? No.

AFTER THE SERVICE

Is there usually a reception after the service? No.

Is there a traditional form of address for clergy whom a guest may meet? Either "Brother" or "Mr.," followed by last name.

GENERAL GUIDELINES AND ADVICE

None provided.

SPECIAL VOCABULARY

Key words or phrases that it might be helpful for a visitor to know:

Jehovah: The personal name of the one true God. From the Book of Psalms (83:18) in the King James Version of the Bible: "That men may know that Thou, whose name alone is Jehovah, art the most high over all the earth." Also from the New World Translation of Isaiah (42:8): "I am Jehovah. That is My name."

Hebrew Scriptures and *Christian Greek Scriptures:* The terms used, respectively, for the Old and New Testaments.

DOGMA AND IDEOLOGY

Jehovah's Witnesses believe:

The books of the Bible's Old and New Testaments are divinely inspired and historically accurate.

Jehovah created earth for humanity and settled the first human pair, Adam and Eve, in the Garden of Eden. If obedient to God, they had the prospect of living forever and expanding the paradise earthwide. With their sin, humanity lost this paradise. Yet, God's purpose for the earth will not fail. The means by which Jehovah will fulfill his purpose for earth is through the Kingdom of God with Jesus as King. This heavenly government will soon remove wickedness from the earth and convert it into a paradise wherein true worshipers will live forever. There will also be a resurrection of the dead into that Paradise.

The Kingdom of God began to rule invisibly in heaven in 1914 and after the wicked are destroyed will usher in the 1,000-year Reign of Christ (the Millennium) during which the earth and humanity will be helped to reach perfection and to live endlessly on earth.

A basic pamphlet to which a guest can refer to learn more about Jehovah's Witnesses:

What Does the Bible Really Teach? (Brooklyn, N.Y.: The Watchtower Bible and Tract Society of New York, 2005).

3 · HOLY DAYS AND FESTIVALS

The Memorial of Christ's Death, also called the Lord's Evening Meal. This special congregational meeting is held in each Kingdom Hall after sundown of the first evening of the Jewish holiday of Passover, which occurs in either March or April. (The date varies because the Hebrew calendar is lunar-based.) There is no traditional greeting for this one holiday observed by Jehovah's Witnesses.

4 · LIFE CYCLE EVENTS

Birth Ceremony

Not applicable to Jehovah's Witnesses.

Initiation Ceremony

Not applicable to Jehovah's Witnesses.

Marriage Ceremony

Jehovah's Witnesses view marriage as a sacred vow made before God. It seals a permanent union that can be broken only by infidelity or death. The marriage ceremony, which may last about 30 minutes, is a ceremony in itself.

BEFORE THE CEREMONY

Are guests usually invited by a formal invitation? Yes. An announcement is made in a Kingdom Hall issuing a general invitation to all members of the congregation. Guests who are not members of the congregation usually receive a written invitation.

If not stated explicitly, should one assume that children are invited? Yes.

If one can't attend, what should one do? Nothing is required if one is a member who has heard the invitation in a Kingdom Hall. If one has received a written invitation, RSVP with regrets.

APPROPRIATE ATTIRE

Men: A jacket and tie. No head covering is required.

Women: A dress or a skirt and blouse. Dress "modestly" and "sensibly." Hems need not reach below the knees nor must clothing cover the arms. Open-toed shoes and modest jewelry are permissible. No head covering is required.

There are no rules regarding colors of clothing.

GIFTS

Is a gift customarily expected? While gifts are surely not required, they are certainly appropriate. Cash, bonds or such household items as sheets, kitchenware or small appliances are customary.

Should gifts be brought to the ceremony? Either to the ceremony or to the reception afterward.

THE CEREMONY

Where will the ceremony take place? In the main auditorium of a Kingdom Hall where Bible lectures are normally given.

When should guests arrive and where should they sit? Arrive early to avoid causing a distraction. Attendants will seat guests. The front few rows are reserved for family.

If arriving late, are there times when a guest should *not* enter the ceremony? No, but usually attendants will seat late-arriving guests in such a way as not to create a disturbance.

Are there times when a guest should *not* leave the ceremony? No.

Who are the major officiants, leaders or participants at the ceremony and what do they do?
The Congregation Elder, who gives a Bible talk to the bride and groom and solemnizes the marriage.

What books are used? The Old and New Testaments, primarily the New World Translation (New York: The Watchtower Bible and Tract Society of New York, 1961).

To indicate the order of the ceremony: The officiating elder will make periodic announcements.

Will a guest who is not a Jehovah's Witness be expected to do anything other than sit? No.

Are there any parts of the ceremony in which a guest who is not a Jehovah's Witness should *not* participate? No.

If not disruptive to the ceremony, is it okay to:
Take pictures? Yes.
Use a flash? Yes.
Use a video camera? Yes.
Use a tape recorder? Yes.
(Note: Do not use the above equipment during prayer. Flash pictures should not be taken during the Bible talk, since this can be very distracting.)

Will contributions to the church be collected at the ceremony? No.

AFTER THE CEREMONY

Is there usually a reception after the ceremony? Yes. It may be held in homes or a catering hall. It is never held in the Kingdom Hall where the wedding took place. Usually, refreshments are served. The reception may last more than two hours.

Would it be considered impolite to neither eat nor drink? No.

Is there a grace or benediction before eating or drinking? Yes.

Is there a grace or benediction after eating or drinking? No.

Is there a traditional greeting for the family? Just offer your congratulations.

Is there a traditional form of address for clergy who may be at the reception? Either "Brother" or "Mr.," followed by last name.

Is it okay to leave early? Yes.

Funerals and Mourning

Jehovah's Witnesses believe that the dead are "conscious of nothing at all" and are asleep in the grave awaiting resurrection to life. While the majority will be raised to life in an earthly paradise, a small number—144,000—will be raised as immortal spirit creatures to rule with Christ in the heavenly Kingdom of God.

The funeral service, which is a ceremony in itself, may last about 15 to 30 minutes.

BEFORE THE CEREMONY

How soon after the death does the funeral usually take place? Usually within one week.

What should a non–Jehovah's Witness do upon hearing of the death of a member of that faith? Telephone or visit the bereaved to offer your condolences.

APPROPRIATE ATTIRE

Men: A jacket and tie. No head covering is required.

Women: A dress or a skirt and blouse. Dress "modestly" and "sensibly." Hems need not reach below the knees nor must clothing cover the arms. Open-toed shoes and modest jewelry are permissible. No head covering is required.

There are no rules regarding colors of clothing, but what is worn should respect the somberness of the occasion.

GIFTS

Is it appropriate to send flowers or make a contribution? Yes. Flowers may be sent to the home of the bereaved before or after the funeral or to the funeral home. Notice that contributions in memory of the deceased have been donated to a charity can be sent to the mourners' home before or after the funeral.

Is it appropriate to send food? Yes. This can be sent to the home of the bereaved before or after the funeral.

THE CEREMONY

Where will the ceremony take place? Either at a Kingdom Hall or in a funeral home.

When should guests arrive and where should they sit? Arrive early to avoid causing a distraction. Attendants will seat guests. The front few rows are reserved for family.

If arriving late, are there times when a guest should *not* enter the ceremony? No, but attendants will direct latecomers to seats.

Will the bereaved family be present at the Kingdom Hall or funeral home before the ceremony? Possibly.

Is there a traditional greeting for the family? No. Just offer your condolences.

Will there be an open casket? Possibly. This depends on the preference of the immediate family.

Is a guest expected to view the body? There are no such expectations.

What is appropriate behavior upon viewing the body? Look upon it somberly for a few moments.

Who are the major officiants at the ceremony and what do they do?
The Congregation Elder, who will deliver a talk from the Bible designed to comfort the bereaved.

What books are used? Usually no books are used by the congregation. Occasionally, a Bible, such as the New World Translation (New York: The Watchtower Bible and Tract Society of New York, 1961) or a songbook, such as *Sing Praises to Jehovah* (New York: The Watchtower Bible and Tract Society of New York, 1984) may be used.

To indicate the order of the ceremony: Directions are not necessary because of the brevity of the service, which is led entirely by the Congregation Elder.

Will a guest who is not a Jehovah's Witness be expected to do anything other than sit? No.

Are there any parts of the ceremony in which a guest who is not a Jehovah's Witness should *not* participate? No.

If not disruptive to the ceremony, is it okay to:

Take pictures? No.

Use a flash? No.

Use a video camera? No.

Use a tape recorder? Yes.

Will contributions to the church be collected at the ceremony? No.

THE INTERMENT

Should guests attend the interment? Such attendance is done at the discretion of the guest.

Whom should one ask for directions? The funeral director or his or her assistants.

What happens at the graveside? Brief comments on the Scriptures are followed by prayer.

Do guests who are not Jehovah's Witnesses participate at the graveside ceremony? No, they are simply present.

COMFORTING THE BEREAVED

Is it appropriate to visit the home of the bereaved after the funeral? Yes. The length of the visit depends on the circumstances. Discussing with the bereaved what you appreciated about the deceased is helpful.

Will there be a religious service at the home of the bereaved? No.

Will food be served? Possibly. This depends on the preference of the mourners.

How soon after the funeral will a mourner usually return to a normal work schedule? This depends on the preferences and the circumstances of the mourners. There is no set time for remaining away from work, although mourners are usually absent from work for at least a few days.

How soon after the funeral will a mourner usually return to a normal social schedule? This is entirely an individual matter and depends on the preferences and the circumstances of the mourners. There is no set time for abstaining from social activities.

Are there mourning customs to which a friend who is not a Jehovah's Witness should be sensitive? No.

Are there rituals for observing the anniversary of the death? No.

5 · HOME CELEBRATIONS

Not applicable to Jehovah's Witnesses.

13

Jewish

1. HISTORY AND BELIEFS

Judaism includes religious rituals and beliefs along with a code of ethical behavior. It also incorporates and reflects the ancient history of the Jews as a nation in its rituals, ceremonies and celebrations. Today, its adherents include people of every race and most nations.

The foundation of Judaism is the Torah, the first five books of the Bible (Genesis, Exodus, Leviticus, Numbers and Deuteronomy). According to the Torah, God made a covenant with the Jews, beginning with the three patriarchs: Abraham; his son Isaac; and his grandson Jacob, whose name God changed to "Israel." At a time when people worshiped many gods, the Jewish people, through this covenant, accepted the "One God" as the only God.

Central to this covenant is the concept of being "chosen" as a people, for as Moses tells his people in the Bible: "The Lord has chosen you to be a people for His own possession, out of all the peoples that are on the face of the earth" (Deuteronomy 14:2). Being "cho-sen" does not confer special privilege. It means that the Jewish people are obliged to bring God's message to the world.

As part of God's covenant with Abraham, his descendants were promised the area now known as Israel—the Promised Land—as their homeland. They took possession of it in approximately 1200 B.C.E. The conquering Romans destroyed Jerusalem and its Temple, which was the center of Jewish religious life, and drove the Jewish people from their land to end repeated rebellions. This began the period known as "the Diaspora," when the Jewish people were without a homeland. Many drifted to the northern and southern rim of the Mediterranean, while others emigrated eastward.

Jewish settlement in the American colonies began in 1654 in New Amsterdam (later called New York). Jewish immigration to Canada began in 1760, with the first synagogue being established in 1768. The modern Jewish state, Israel, was founded in 1948, three years after the end of the Holocaust in which 6 million Jews were killed.

Before the Diaspora, Judaism as

a religion evolved under a hereditary priesthood that officiated at the Temple in Jerusalem, and through the ethical and moral teachings of a series of prophets. Following the Temple's destruction, religious leadership passed from priests to *rabbis*—teachers and scholars. Today, the rabbinate includes both men and women in all movements except the Orthodox.

There are now four major Jewish religious movements in the United States and Canada. In terms of theology, Reform Judaism is at the liberal end, followed by Reconstructionist, Conservative and Orthodox—both modern and traditional (which includes several fundamentalist groups, such as the Hasidim).

Hebrew, the traditional language of Jewish worship, is used to varying degrees in the services or celebrations of each movement. Each also has its own version of the prayer book, and almost all include translations of the Hebrew material.

Reform Judaism, which began in the early 19th century in Germany, regards Judaism as an on-going process resulting from the relationship between God and the Jewish people over its history. It considers Torah divinely inspired and subject to individual interpretation based on study, and emphasizes the ethical and moral messages of the prophets to help create a just society.

Reconstructionism, founded in the 1930s, is the most recent of the Jewish movements. Here the essence of Judaism is defined as embodying an entire civilization and not only a religion. At the core of this civilization is a people who have the authority and the responsibility to "reconstruct" its contents from generation to generation.

Conservative Judaism began in the mid-19th century as a reaction to what its founders perceived to be Reform's radicalism. It teaches that while the Torah as a whole is binding and that much of Jewish law remains authoritative, nonetheless new ideas and practices have always influenced Jewish beliefs and rituals and this should continue today as well.

Orthodox Judaism teaches that Torah was divinely revealed to Moses at Mount Sinai and that the *halachah* ("hah-lah-KHAH"), the interpretative process of that law, is both divinely guided and authoritative. Thus, no law stemming from the Torah can be tampered with even if it displeases modern sensibilities. Orthodoxy often rejects more modern forms of Judaism as deviations from divine truths and authentic modes of Jewish life.

Houses of worship in the Orthodox, Conservative and Reconstructionist movement are typically called "synagogues." Usually, only a Reform house of worship is called a "temple."

U.S. synagogues/temples:
Over 2,500 total
Reform: 900
Conservative: 800
Reconstructionist: 101
Orthodox: 1,000

U.S. membership: Over 4 million
Reform: 1.8 million
Conservative: 1.6 million
Reconstructionist: 60,000
Orthodox: 600,000
   (data from each denomination's central office)

For more information, contact:

Union for Reform Judaism
633 Third Avenue
New York, NY 10017
(212) 650-4000
www.urj.org

United Synagogue of
   Conservative Judaism
820 Second Avenue
New York, NY 10017
(212) 533-7800
www.uscj.org

Jewish Reconstructionist Federation
Beit Devora
101 Greenwood Avenue, Suite 430
Jenkintown, PA 19046
(215) 885-5601
www.jrf.org
Reconstructionist Rabbinical College
rrc.www.edu

Union of Orthodox Jewish
   Congregations of America
11 Broadway
New York, NY 10004
(212) 563-4000
www.ou.org

Canadian synagogues/temples:
Over 248 total
Reform: 29
Conservative: 43
Reconstructionist: 3
Orthodox: 124

Canadian membership: Over
   365,000 total

Reform: 4,000
Conservative: Not available.
Reconstructionist: Not available.
Orthodox: Not available.
   (data from each denomination's central office)

For more information, contact:

Canadian Jewish Congress
(877) 823-8703 (Canada only)
www.cjc.ca

Canadian Council of
   Conservative Synagogues
842 Eglinton Avenue West
PO Box 85532
Toronto, ON 5MN 0A2
(647) 367-9351
www.canadianccs.ca

2 · THE BASIC SERVICE

According to Jewish tradition, communal prayer requires a *minyan* ("MIN-yahn"), a quorum of at least 10 persons over the age of 13. It takes place three times daily: in the early morning, at midday, and at sunset. Each communal prayer service takes about 15 to 30 minutes. If a Jewish person cannot join the communal prayer, he or she may pray alone, omitting from the service certain prayers that are said only when there is a minyan. Orthodox and some Conservative congregations only count males in the number of persons in the minyan.

Each service contains many common elements and some minor variations according to the time of day and the time of the month. The fullest Jewish service takes place on the Jewish Sabbath, or *Shabbat* ("shah-BAHT"), which begins at sunset on Friday and ends at nightfall on Saturday. All Orthodox and Conservative congregations have services on Friday evenings and Saturday mornings, as do most Reform and Reconstructionist congregations.

The major units of the service are the *Amidah* ("ah-mee-DAH"), a series of praises, thanks and petitions to God; and the *Sh'ma*, whose central phrase, "Hear O Israel, the Lord is our God, the Lord is One," is a declaration of faith, a pledge of allegiance and an affirmation of Judaism. Another key element is the public reading from the Torah scroll, the first five books of the Bible.

The Friday evening service may last 30 to 90 minutes and the Saturday morning service may last from 90 minutes to over three hours, depending on the congregation. Services are usually longer in Orthodox and Conservative congregations than in Reform or Reconstructionist. The amount of Hebrew used during the service varies with each congregation, but Reform congregations will use the least and Orthodox the most. Prayer books normally include translations or interpretations of the Hebrew material.

APPROPRIATE ATTIRE

Men: A jacket and tie are never inappropriate. In some Reform and Reconstructionist congregations, more informal attire may be appropriate on occasion.

A small head covering called a *yarmulke* ("YAHR-mihl-kah") or *kippah* ("keep-AH") is required in all Orthodox, Conservative and Reconstructionist congregations and in some Reform congregations. They will be available just before one enters the main sanctuary. If required in Reform congregations, a sign is usually posted to that effect.

Women: A dress, skirt and blouse, or a pants suit. In general, clothing should be modest, depending on the fashion and the locale.

In some Conservative synagogues, a hat or another head covering may be required. Open-toed shoes and modest jewelry are appropriate. In Orthodox congregations, clothing should cover the arms, hems should reach below the knees and heads should be covered with a hat or veil. On the Sabbath, do not carry a purse or similar accessory, since Jewish law prohibits labor, including carrying objects, on Shabbat.

Note: The *tallit* ("tah-LEET"), or prayer shawl, is worn by all Orthodox men, Conservative and Reconstructionist men and some women, and by some men and women in Reform congregations. Non-Jews should not wear the *tallit*.

Do not openly wear symbols of other faiths, such as a cross.

There are no rules regarding colors of clothing.

THE SANCTUARY

What are the major sections of the synagogue/temple?

The bimah ("BEE-mah"): The part of the sanctuary from where the service is led and where the rabbi and cantor stand and sit. Also called the pulpit. It is usually raised above the level where congregants sit and is at the front or in the middle of the sanctuary.

The ark: The cabinet on the pulpit where the Torah is kept.

The Torah reading table: The table on which the Torah is opened and read.

The rabbi's pulpit: Where the rabbi stands when delivering his or her sermon or when teaching and commenting on the service.

The eternal light: A lamp, either gas or electric, that burns continuously above and in front of the ark where the Torah is kept.

The mehitsah ("meh-HEET-sah"): A partition used in Orthodox congregations to separate the seating sections for men and women. In more traditional congregations, women are seated to the rear of the men or in a balcony above them. In others, they are seated in a section parallel to the men's. Some "modern" Orthodox congregations have eliminated the *mehitsah*, but men and women still sit separately.

THE SERVICE

When should guests arrive and where should they sit?
At events occurring on Saturday morning it is customary for guests who are not Jews to arrive at the scheduled time at Reform and Reconstructionist services.

For Orthodox or Conservative services, which tend to be longer, unless you want to participate in the entire service, ask your host the time you should arrive so you can be present for the specific event within the service for which you have been invited.

Sit wherever you wish, while respecting any separation of men and women, which occurs in all Orthodox congregations.

If arriving late, are there times when a guest should *not* enter the service?
Do not enter when the congregation is standing or during the rabbi's sermon. In most congregations, an usher will advise latecomers when to enter.

Are there times when a guest should *not* leave the service?
Don't leave when the congregation is standing, when the Torah is being taken out or returned to the ark, when the rabbi is speaking or when the specific ceremony during the service for which you have been invited is taking place.

Who are the major officiants, leaders or participants and what do they do?

The rabbi, who directs the service and teaches and preaches. (Any Jewish person over the age of 13 may lead a service; in an Orthodox congregation, this can only be a male.) In larger congregations, there may be a senior rabbi and one or more rabbis who are his or her assistants.

The cantor, who chants and sings parts of the service and leads the congregation in song.

The Torah reader, who reads or chants from the Torah.

The *gabbai* ("gab-BYE"), a layperson who oversees the honors of reading from the Torah and of saying blessings for the Torah reading.

The congregation's president, or his or her representative, who may welcome congregants and visitors from the *bimah* and make announcements about upcoming events and programs.

Note: In smaller congregations, the same person may have more than one role. For instance, the rabbi may also be the cantor.

What are the major ritual objects of the service?

The tallit, or prayer shawl, which is worn by all Orthodox men, Conservative and Reconstructionist men and some women, and by some men and women in Reform congregations. Non-Jews should not wear the *tallit*.

The Torah ("TOH-rah"), a scroll on which is handwritten the first five books of the Bible: Genesis, Exodus, Leviticus, Numbers and Deuteronomy.

The yad ("yahd"), a metal pointer used when reading the Torah because one is not supposed to touch the handwritten letters.

The menorah ("min-OHR-ah"), a seven-branched candelabra, which was part of the ancient Temple in Jerusalem and which is often placed on the *bimah* as an ornament.

The ark, the place in which a Torah scroll(s) is kept on the *bimah*.

Torah ornaments, such as a cover of fabric, a breastplate and crown of silver, which adorn the outside of the closed scroll.

Tefillin ("teh-FILL-in"), or phylacteries, two small black leather boxes containing four biblical passages which a male Jew from the age of 13 wears on the left arm and the head during morning services on weekdays. They are held in place with leather straps. They are not worn for Shabbat services or festivals.

What books are used? The *siddur,* ("SEE-door") or prayerbook, which varies among (and sometimes within) the various religious movements; and the *chumash* ("KOOH-mahsh"), which contains the first five books of the Bible (Genesis, Exodus, Leviticus, Numbers and Deuteronomy), and the traditional section from Prophets that is associated with each weekly Torah portion and is read after the public Torah reading (called the *haftarah,* "hahf-TOH-rah"). It also may contain editorial commentaries on the text.

To indicate the order of the service: In most congregations, the rabbi or another leader of the service will make periodic announcements. In some Orthodox congregations, it is generally assumed that those present know the order of the service and no announcements are made. In many Orthodox, Conservative and Reconstructionist congregations major portions of the service are read individually, often aloud, at the individual's own pace. As a result, the service may appear to be unorganized.

GUEST BEHAVIOR DURING THE SERVICE

Will a guest who is not Jewish be expected to do anything other

than sit? They are expected to stand with the congregation. It is optional for them to read prayers aloud and sing with congregants if this would not violate their religious beliefs. Kneeling is not part of any Jewish service.

Are there any parts of the service in which a guest who is not Jewish should *not* participate? In all Orthodox, Conservative and Reconstructionist and in most Reform congregations, non-Jews will not be called to read from the Torah or participate in any honors involving the Torah.

If not disruptive to the service, is it okay to:
Take pictures? No.
Use a flash? No.
Use a video camera? No.
Use a tape recorder? No.

Will contributions to the synagogue/temple be collected at the service? No.

AFTER THE SERVICE

Is there usually a reception after the service? Yes. This is called a *kiddush* ("kee-DOOSH") or an *oneg Shabbat* ("OH-neg shah-BAHT"). It may last 30 to 60 minutes. Usually served is such light food as coffee, tea, fruit, pastries or punch. Sometimes appetizer-type foods are served. Wait for a blessing to be said before eating or drinking. Wine and grape juice are provided in almost all congregations for the ceremonial blessing before drinking the "fruit of the vine." A blessing called *ha'motzi* ("hah-MOH-tsee") is recited before eating bread. In all Orthodox and some Conservative congregations,

ritual hand washing is done before eating or drinking.

All Orthodox and many Conservative and Reconstructionist congregations have a grace after meals called *birkat hamazon* ("beer-KAHT hah-mah-ZONE"). This is increasingly common in Reform ceremonies.

Is there a traditional form of address for clergy who may be at the reception? "Rabbi" or "Cantor."

Is it okay to leave early? Yes.

GENERAL GUIDELINES AND ADVICE

In Orthodox congregations, decorum in synagogue calls for no public display of physical affection between the sexes. Often, Orthodox men and women do not even shake each other's hands. On Shabbat, most Orthodox Jews do not drive, smoke, write, use the telephone, turn electricity on or off, cook, handle money or do work of any kind. Many Conservative and Reconstructionist and some Reform Jews will abstain from some of these activities.

SPECIAL VOCABULARY

Key words or phrases that it might be helpful for a visitor to know:
Torah ("TOH-rah"): Most commonly used to refer to the scroll of the Five Books of Moses (Genesis, Exodus, Leviticus, Numbers and Deuteronomy).
Aliyah ("ah-lee-YAH"): Literally "going up," it is the honor of being called to the *bimah* to participate in reading the Torah.

Sh'ma ("shih-MAH"): A central prayer of the worship service. Essentially a statement of faith that is derived from Deuteronomy, chapter 6: "Hear O Israel, the Lord is our God, the Lord is One."

Amidah ("ah-mee-DAH"): A series of praises, thanks and petitions to God. Recited by the entire congregation while standing, they are the central part of the prayer service.

Simcha ("SIHM-khah"): Means "to rejoice." May be used during a service to refer to a special happy event, such as a birth, a bar or bat mitzvah or a wedding.

Mazal tov ("MAH-zahl tohv"): Literally "Good luck," but used as "congratulations." Especially used at the occasion of a *simcha*.

DOGMA AND IDEOLOGY

There is no single official creed that all Jews accept.

Jews believe:

There is only one God, to whom prayer is directed, and with whom each person has a personal and direct relationship.

Congregational prayer and community are a cornerstone of faith.

The Torah is a guide to righteous living, as a continual source of revelation, although not all accept it literally.

Study of Torah is equivalent to prayer.

God is supreme over all and possesses absolute sovereignty.

People have free will and there is no original sin.

Righteousness is not limited to members of the Jewish faith.

They share a sense of community with and responsibility for Jews throughout the world.

Some basic books to which a guest can refer to learn more about Judaism:

Conservative Judaism: The New Century by Neil Gillman (West Orange, N.J.: Behrman House, Inc., 1993).

The Jewish Home: A Guide for Jewish Living by Daniel B. Syme (New York, URJ Press, 2003).

Jewish Spirituality: A Brief Introduction for Christians by Lawrence Kushner (Woodstock, Vt.: Jewish Lights Publishing, 2001).

The Rituals and Practices of a Jewish Life: A Handbook for Personal Spiritual Renewal by Rabbi Kerry M. Olitzky and Rabbi Daniel Judson (Woodstock, Vt.: Jewish Lights Publishing, 2002).

This Is My God: The Jewish Way of Life by Herman Wouk (New York: Back Bay Books, 1992).

What Is a Jew? by Morris N. Kertzer, revised by Lawrence A. Hoffman (New York: Touchstone, 1996).

What You Will See Inside a Synagogue by Rabbi Lawrence A. Hoffman and Dr. Ron Wolfson with photographs by Bill Aron (Woodstock, Vt.: SkyLight Paths Publishing, 2008).

3 · HOLY DAYS AND FESTIVALS

Jewish holy days and festivals celebrate historical events in the life of the Jewish people or are times that the Torah specifically sets aside for religious services. Noted below for each major holiday are those times when observant Jews are required to abstain from "work" on their days of observance. The definition of activities that constitute "work" varies, but all include transacting business.

A lunar-based religious calendar is used, so each new day starts at sunset. Sunday is the first day of the week. The Sabbath, the weekly seventh day of rest, begins at sunset on Friday and is observed until nightfall on Saturday. The coincidence of Jewish holidays with the solar-based Christian calendar varies as much as a month from year to year.

Rosh Hashanah ("rohsh hah-SHAH-nah"). The Jewish religious New Year, which also commemorates the creation of the world, traditionally counted as being approximately 5,800 years ago. Occurs on the first and second days of the Hebrew month of Tishrei and is observed on both days in Orthodox, Conservative and Reconstructionist congregations and on the first day only in Reform congregations. Usually occurs mid-September to mid-October. The greeting for Rosh Hashanah is "Happy New Year," in Hebrew *"Shana Tovah"* ("shah-NAH toh-VAH"). Almost all Jews abstain from work on their days of observance.

Yom Kippur ("yohm kee-POOR"). The Day of Atonement, on which one engages in reflection and prayer and formally repents for sins committed during the previous Hebrew year. Occurs on the 10th day of the Hebrew month of Tishrei, which usually falls in late September to mid-October. The greetings for Yom Kippur are "Have an easy fast" or "Happy New Year," in Hebrew *"Shana Tovah"* ("shah-NAH toh-VAH"). Jews 13 or older are required to abstain from work and fast (no liquids or food) from the sundown when Yom Kippur begins until nightfall of the following day.

Sukkot ("soo-KOTE"). The Feast of Booths. An eight-day harvest holiday. This usually occurs in early or mid-October. A traditional greeting is "Happy holiday," or, in Hebrew, *"Chag samayach"* ("hahg sah-MAY-ahk"). Orthodox Jews in particular abstain from work during the first two days and last two days of the holiday, as do many Conservative Jews, while Reconstructionist and Reform Jews may abstain from work on the first and last days only.

Chanukah ("HAH-noo-kah"). The Festival of Lights. Commemorates the victory in about 163 B.C.E. of the Maccabees over the Syrians who tried to eradicate Judaism. It is observed for the eight days beginning with the 25th day of the Hebrew month of Kislev. This is usually in early to mid-December. The traditional greeting is "Happy Chanukah" or, in Hebrew, *"Chanukah samayach"* ("HAH-noo-kah sah-MAY-ahk"). There are no requirements to abstain from work during Chanukah.

Purim ("POO-rim"). A celebration of deliverance from destruction. Marked by reading the Purim story from a *megillah* ("m'gee-LAH"), a scroll of the Book of Esther, and merry-making. Usually occurs in late February or early March. The traditional greeting is "Happy Holiday," in Hebrew, *"Chag samayach"* ("hahg sah-MAY-ack"); or "Happy Purim." There are no requirements to abstain from work on Purim.

Pesach ("PAY-sakh"). Passover. Celebrates the Jewish people's freedom from slavery in Egypt. Beginning with the 15th day of the Hebrew month of Nisan, it is observed for eight days by Orthodox, Conservative and Reconstructionist Jews and for seven days by Reform Jews. Almost all Jews abstain from eating bread and other foods made with yeast. Usually occurs in late March or early to mid-April. A traditional greeting is "Happy holiday," in Hebrew, "*Chag samayach*" ("hahg sah-MAY-ack"); or "Happy Passover." Orthodox Jews in particular abstain from work during the first two days and the last two days of the holiday, as do many Conservative Jews. Reconstructionist and Reform Jews may abstain from work on the first and last days only.

Shavuot ("shah-voo-OTE"). The Festival of Weeks. Commemorates the giving of the Torah at Mount Sinai, as well as the first fruits of the spring harvest. Occurs on the sixth and seventh of the Hebrew month of Sivan, which usually occurs in May or June. A traditional greeting is "Happy holiday," or in Hebrew, "*Chag samayach*" ("hahg sah-MAY-ahk"). Orthodox Jews in particular abstain from work during both days of this holiday, as do many Conservative Jews, while Reconstructionist and Reform Jews observe it for only one day.

4. LIFE CYCLE EVENTS

Birth Ceremony

In Hebrew, the ceremony is called a *brit* ("breet"), which literally means "covenant," and can apply to newborn males and females.

For boys, the *brit milah* ("breet mee-LAH"), or the "covenant of circumcision," occurs on the eighth day of a male child's life. This is a sign of the covenant between God and the Jewish people. The biblical roots of circumcision are in Genesis, which states that God told Abraham, "Every male among you shall be circumcised…, and that shall be the sign of the covenant between Me and you throughout the generations" (Genesis 17:10).

The circumcision may be performed at home, in a synagogue/temple or in a hospital. It requires removing the entire foreskin of the penis, a simple surgical technique that takes only a few seconds. The entire ceremony, including giving the child his Hebrew name, may take 15 to 60 minutes.

For girls, the naming ceremony is the *brit bat* ("breet baht"), the "covenant of the daughter," or the *brit hayyim* ("breet hy-YEEM"), the "covenant of life." It is held at home or at the synagogue/temple, usually during the Torah reading portion of the Sabbath or weekday service.

If a more creative or nontraditional baby-naming ceremony is held at home, it may take about 20 minutes.

BEFORE THE CEREMONY

Are guests usually invited by a formal invitation? They are usually invited by telephone or by written invitation.

If not stated explicitly, should one assume that children are invited? Yes.

If one can't attend, what should one do? RSVP with regrets and send a small gift appropriate for the child, such as clothing, a toy or baby equipment.

APPROPRIATE ATTIRE

Men: If the ceremony is at home, dress casually, although a jacket and tie may be appropriate. If at a synagogue/temple, a jacket and tie are appropriate.

A small head covering called a *yarmulke* ("YAHR-mihl-kah") or *kippah* ("keep-AH") is required in all Orthodox, Conservative and Reconstructionist congregations and in some Reform congregations, as well as in services in the homes of members of such congregations. They will be available just before one enters the main sanctuary or will be provided if the ceremony is at home. If required in a Reform congregation, a sign is usually posted to that effect.

Women: If the ceremony is at home, dress may be casual. If it is at a synagogue/temple, wear a dress, a skirt and blouse or a pants suit. Clothing should be modest, depending on the fashion and the locale. Open-toed shoes and jewelry are appropriate. In Orthodox congregations, clothing should cover the arms, hems should reach below the knees and heads should be covered with a hat or veil. On the Sabbath, do not carry a purse or similar accessory, since Jewish law prohibits labor, including carrying objects, on Shabbat.

Note: A traditional prayer shawl, a *tallit* ("tah-LEET"), may also be available at the entrance to the sanctuary. The *tallit* is worn by all Orthodox men, Conservative and Reconstructionist men and some women, and by some men and women in Reform congregations. Non-Jews should not wear the *tallit*.

Do not openly wear symbols of other faiths, such as a cross.

There are no rules regarding colors of clothing, but this is a festive time.

GIFTS

Is a gift customarily expected? Yes, often cash, U.S. or Israeli savings bonds, toys or children's clothing or baby equipment.

Should gifts be brought to the ceremony? Either to the synagogue/temple (if the ceremony is not on the Sabbath) or to the home.

THE CEREMONY

Where will the ceremony take place? At the child's home, or at a synagogue/temple.

When should guests arrive and where should they sit? Arrive early. Sit anywhere, except in the front row, which is usually reserved for close family members.

If arriving late, are there times when a guest should *not* enter the ceremony? Not for a *brit* at home. If the *brit* is at a synagogue/temple, ushers usually will tell latecomers when they can enter.

Are there times when a guest should *not* leave the ceremony? Not if the ceremony is at home. If at a synagogue/temple, do not leave when the congregation is standing, when the Torah is being taken out or returned to the ark, when the rabbi is speaking, or when the specific ceremony during the service for which you have been invited is taking place.

Who are the major officiants, leaders or participants at the ceremony and what do they do?

For a male's *brit milah*:

A mohel ("MOH-hail"), or specially trained ritual circumciser, who may also be a rabbi or physician.

A rabbi, who may also be the *mohel.*

The child's parents, who recite blessings and may hold the child during the ceremony.

The child's grandparents, who bring the child into the room where the ceremony is held.

The child's godparents, who hold the child during the actual circumcision and who must be members of the Jewish faith.

For a girl's naming ceremony:

A rabbi.

The child's parents, who recite blessings and may hold the child during the ceremony.

The child's grandparents, who bring the child into the room where the ceremony is held.

The child's godparents.

A cantor (if the ceremony is in a synagogue), who leads the congregation in song.

The Torah reader (if the ceremony is in a synagogue), who chants from the Torah.

The gabbai ("gab-BYE") (if the ceremony is in a synagogue), who oversees the honors of reading from the Torah.

What books are used? *The siddur* ("SEE-door"), or prayer book, or a ceremony specially prepared by the parents.

To indicate the order of the ceremony: The rabbi or another leader of the service will make periodic announcements.

Will a guest who is not Jewish be expected to do anything other than sit? They are expected to stand with the congregation. It is optional for them to read prayers aloud and sing with other guests if this would not violate their religious beliefs.

Are there any parts of the ceremony in which a guest who is not Jewish should *not* participate? In Orthodox, Conservative and Reconstructionist and in most Reform congregations, non-Jews will not be called to read from the Torah or participate in any honors involving the Torah.

If not disruptive to the ceremony, is it okay to:

Take pictures? Ask the rabbi and ask permission of the host.

Use a flash? Ask the rabbi and ask permission of the host.

Use a video camera? Ask the rabbi and ask permission of the host.

Use a tape recorder? Ask the rabbi and ask permission of the host.

Will contributions to the synagogue/temple be collected at the ceremony? No.

AFTER THE CEREMONY

Is there usually a reception after the ceremony? There is almost always a reception called a *kiddush* ("kee-DOOSH"). Usually served is such light food as coffee, tea, fruit, pastries or punch. Sometimes appetizer-type foods are served. Wine and grape juice are provided in almost all congregations for the ceremonial blessing before drinking the "fruit of the vine." There is no music or dancing.

If in the home, the reception may last up to two hours. If in a synagogue/temple, it may last 30 to 60 minutes.

Among Orthodox Jews, the reception may include a meal and possibly a brief sermon or discourse by the father, or some distinguished family member, guest or the rabbi. At the home of the infant's parents, a catering hall or the site of the *brit,* the reception may last one hour.

Would it be considered impolite to neither eat nor drink? No.

Is there a grace or benediction before eating or drinking? Yes. Wait for a blessing to be said before eating or drinking. A blessing is said before drinking wine or grape juice. A blessing called *ha'motzi* ("hah-MOH-tsee") is recited before eating bread. In all Orthodox and some Conservative congregations, ritual hand washing is done before eating or drinking.

Is there a grace or benediction after eating or drinking? All Orthodox and many Conservative and Reconstructionist congregations have a grace after meals called *birkat hamazon* ("beer-KAHT hah-mah-ZONE"). This is increasingly common in Reform ceremonies.

Is there a traditional greeting for the family? "Congratulations," or, in Hebrew, "*Mazal tov*" ("MAH-zahl tohv").

Is there a traditional form of address for clergy who may be at the reception? "Rabbi" or "Cantor." There is no special form of address for the *mohel.*

Is it okay to leave early? Yes.

Initiation Ceremony

These ceremonies mark an adolescent's entry into religious adulthood and responsibility, after which they are included in the *minyan* ("MIN-yahn") or quorum of 10 Jewish people (men or women in Reform, Reconstructionist and Conservative congregations; only men in Orthodox) needed to hold congregational prayers.

For a boy, *bar mitzvah* ("bahr MITS-vah"), or "son of the commandment," occurs upon reaching the age of 13, when, according to Jewish tradition, males are liable for their own transgressions and their fathers no longer bear this responsibility.

A *bat mitzvah* ("baht MITS-vah"), or "daughter of the commandment," is held at the age of 12 or 13. According to Jewish law, females attain religious adulthood and responsibility upon reaching 12 years and one day. There are no specific legal requirements in Judaism for a girl to participate in a ceremony marking this occasion, and bat mitzvah ceremonies began only in the 20th century.

In Orthodox, Conservative and Reconstructionist congregations, a boy publicly reads from the Torah for the first time at a bar mitzvah and a girl reads from the *haftarah* (a reading from Prophets) at a bat mitzvah. In a Reform congregation, both boys and girls publicly read from the Torah. In those Reform congregations where the haftarah is read, boys and girls also read from this text. He or she may also lead other parts of the service, and usually deliver a speech to the congregation on the significance of attaining religious adulthood.

A bar or bat mitzvah service is always part of a larger, basic service and is almost always on a Saturday morning.

Bar or bat mitzvah services usually last about one hour in Reform congregations and about two hours in Orthodox, Conservative and Reconstructionist congregations. The balance of the basic Sabbath service will add about an hour (or more) to the entire service.

BEFORE THE CEREMONY

Are guests usually invited by a formal invitation? Yes.

If not stated explicitly, should one assume that children are invited? No.

If one can't attend, what should one do? RSVP with your regrets and send a small gift or check ($25 to $100) for the bar/bat mitzvah boy or girl.

APPROPRIATE ATTIRE

Men: A jacket and tie are never inappropriate. At some times, more informal attire may be appropriate in some Reform and Reconstructionist congregations.

A small head covering called a *yarmulke* ("YAHR-mihl-kah") or *kippah* ("keep-AH") is required in all Orthodox, Conservative and Reconstructionist congregations and in some Reform congregations. They will be available just before one enters the main sanctuary. If required in Reform congregations, a sign is usually posted to that effect.

Women: A dress, a skirt and blouse or a pants suit. In general, clothing should be modest, depending on the fashion and the locale. Open-toed shoes and modest jewelry are appropriate. In some Conservative synagogues, a hat or another form of head covering may be required, especially if a woman ascends to the ark, where the Torah is kept, or to the pulpit. In Orthodox congregations, clothing should cover the arms, hems should reach below the knees and heads should be covered with a hat or veil. On the Sabbath, do not carry a purse or similar accessory, since Jewish law prohibits labor, including carrying objects, on Shabbat.

Note: A traditional prayer shawl, a *tallit* ("tah-LEET"), may also be available at the entrance to the sanctuary. The *tallit* is worn by all Orthodox men, Conservative and Reconstructionist men and some women, and by some men and women in Reform congregations. Non-Jews should not wear the *tallit*.

Do not openly wear symbols of other faiths, such as a cross.

There are no rules regarding colors of clothing, but this is a festive occasion.

GIFTS

Is a gift customarily expected? Yes. Customary gifts are cash or U.S. or Israeli savings bonds valued at $50 to $250, or books or ritual items of Judaica.

Should gifts be brought to the ceremony? Gifts should be sent to the child's home.

THE CEREMONY

Where will the ceremony take place? In the sanctuary of the synagogue/temple.

When should guests arrive and where should they sit? It is more customary for guests who are not Jews to arrive at the time called at Reform and Reconstructionist Saturday morning services than at Conservative and Orthodox services, which tend to be longer. Unless you want to participate in the entire sevice, ask your host the time you should arrive so you can be present for the specific event within the service for which you have been invited. Sit wherever you wish, while respecting any separation of men and women, which occurs in all Orthodox congregations.

If arriving late, are there times when a guest should *not* enter the ceremony? Do not enter when the congregation is standing or during the rabbi's sermon. In most congregations, an usher will advise latecomers when they can enter.

Are there times when a guest should *not* leave the ceremony? Yes, when the congregation is standing, when the Torah is being taken out or returned to the ark, when the rabbi is speaking, or when the specific ceremony during the service for which you have been invited is taking place.

Who are the major officiants, leaders or participants at the ceremony and what do they do?

The bar or bat mitzvah boy or girl.

The child's parents.

The rabbi, who directs the service and teaches and preaches. (Any Jewish person over the age of 13 may lead a service; in an Orthodox congregation, this can only be a male.) In larger congregations, there may be a senior rabbi and one or more rabbis who are his or her assistants.

The cantor, who chants and sings parts of the service and leads the congregation in song.

The Torah reader, who chants from the Torah.

The gabbai ("gab-BYE"), a layperson who oversees the honors of reading from the Torah and of saying blessings for the Torah reading.

The congregation's president, or his or her representative, who may welcome congregants and visitors from the *bimah* ("BEE-mah") and make announcements about upcoming events and programs.

Note: In smaller congregations, the same person may have more than one role. For instance, the rabbi may also be the cantor.

What books are used? The *siddur* ("SEE-door"), or prayerbook, which varies among (and sometimes within) the various religious movements; and the *chumash* ("KOOH-mahsh"), which contains the first five books of the Torah, also known as the Five Books of Moses: Genesis, Exodus, Leviticus, Numbers and Deuteronomy. It also contains a traditional section from Prophets that is associated with each Torah section and that is read after the Torah reading (which is called the *haftarah*, pronounced "hahf-TOH-rah") and may contain editorial commentaries on the text.

To indicate the order of the ceremony: In most congregations, the rabbi or another leader of the service will make periodic announcements. In some Orthodox congregations, it is generally assumed that those present know the order of the service and no announcements are made. In many Orthodox congregations major portions of the service are read individually, often aloud, at the individual's own pace. As a result, the service may appear to be unorganized.

Will a guest who is not Jewish be expected to do anything other than sit? They are expected to stand with the congregation. It is optional for them to read prayers aloud and to sing with congregants, if this would not violate their religious beliefs.

Are there any parts of the ceremony in which a guest who is not Jewish should *not* participate? In Orthodox, Conservative and Reconstructionist and in most Reform congregations, non-Jews are not called to read from the Torah or participate in any honors involving the Torah.

If not disruptive to the ceremony, is it okay to:

Take pictures? Not on Saturdays; possibly on other days. Ask your host.

Use a flash? Not on Saturdays; possibly on other days. Ask your host.

Use a video camera? Not on Saturdays; possibly on other days. Ask your host.

Use a tape recorder? Not on Saturdays; possibly on other days. Ask your host.

Will contributions to the synagogue/temple be collected at the ceremony? No.

AFTER THE CEREMONY

Is there usually a reception after the ceremony? There is usually a small, relatively brief (15 to 30 minutes) reception for the entire congregation and invited guests. This is called a *kiddush* ("kee-DOOSH") and almost always is held in a reception area of the synagogue/temple. Usually served is coffee, tea, fruit, pastries or punch. Sometimes appetizer-type foods are served. There may be wine and, in some congregations, whiskey.

For invited guests only, there may be a larger reception and celebration after the kiddush at which a full meal is served and at which there is music and dancing. This may be held in a reception room of the synagogue/temple, in a separate catering hall/hotel or at the home of the bar or bat mitzvah child. This meal and celebration may last three hours or more.

Would it be considered impolite to neither eat nor drink? No. In general, guests should not expect nonkosher food, such as pork or shellfish, or expect to mix dairy and meat products at the reception if it is *kosher* (observes the traditional Jewish dietary laws). All Orthodox receptions, most Conservative and Reconstructionist and some Reform receptions are kosher.

Is there a grace or benediction before eating or drinking? Yes. Wait for a blessing to be said before eating or drinking. A blessing is said before drinking wine or grape juice. A blessing called *ha'motzi* ("hah-MOH-tsee") is recited before eating bread. It might be led by a rabbi, cantor or layperson who is an honored guest. In all Orthodox and some Conservative congregations, ritual hand washing is done before eating or drinking.

Is there a grace or benediction after eating or drinking? All Orthodox and many Conservative and Reconstructionist congregations or households have a grace after meals called *birkat hamazon* ("beer-KAHT hah-mah-ZONE"). This is increasingly common in Reform ceremonies.

Is there a traditional greeting for the family? "Congratulations" or, in Hebrew, "*Mazal tov*" ("MAH-zahl tohv").

Is there a traditional form of address for clergy who may be at the reception? "Rabbi" or "Cantor."

Is it okay to leave early? Yes, but usually only after the main course has been served.

Marriage Ceremony

Judaism considers marriage a divine command, a sacred bond and a means of personal fulfillment. Marriage is deemed the natural and desirable state of every adult. The Hebrew word for marriage is *kiddushin* ("kee-doo-SHEEN"), which means "sanctification."

The *huppah* ("hoo-PAH"), or wedding canopy, under which the ceremony takes place, symbolizes the canopy of the heavens under which all life transpires. A glass, which the groom breaks underfoot after he and the bride have said their wedding vows, is an ancient tradition that has been interpreted in many ways, including commemorating at this time of great joy a moment of great sadness: the destruction of the Temple in Jerusalem in 70 C.E.

The wedding ceremony is always a ceremony in itself. It may take about 15 to 30 minutes.

BEFORE THE CEREMONY

Are guests usually invited by a formal invitation? Yes.

If not stated explicitly, should one assume that children are invited? No.

If one can't attend, what should one do? RSVP with regrets and send a gift.

APPROPRIATE ATTIRE

Men: Attire depends on the social formality of the event. A small head covering called a *yarmulke* ("YAHR-mil-kah") or *kippah* ("keep-AH") is required in all Orthodox, Conservative and Reconstructionist ceremonies and in some Reform ceremonies. They will be provided to guests.

Women: Attire depends on the social formality of the event. For most Orthodox ceremonies, clothing, such as a dress or skirt and blouse, should be modest and cover the arms, and hems should reach below the knees. Open-toed shoes and modest jewelry are appropriate. In some Orthodox and Conservative ceremonies, a head covering may be required.

Do not openly wear symbols of other faiths, such as a cross.

There are no rules regarding colors of clothing, but this is a very festive event.

GIFTS

Is a gift customarily expected? Yes. Appropriate are such household items as small appliances or sheets or towels. Money is also appropriate, with amounts between $50 and $300 recommended. The bride is often listed in the bridal registry at a local department store.

Should gifts be brought to the ceremony? No. Send them to the bride's home or to the reception.

THE CEREMONY

Where will the ceremony take place? Depending on the desires of the couple, it may be at a synagogue/temple, at a catering hall, at home or at any other location chosen by them.

When should guests arrive and where should they sit? It is customary to arrive at the time called. Ushers usually will be present to seat you. Otherwise, sit wherever you wish.

If arriving late, are there times when a guest should *not* enter the ceremony? Do not enter during the processional or recessional.

Are there times when a guest should *not* leave the ceremony? Not during the processional or recessional or while the officiant is blessing or addressing the couple.

Who are the major officiants, leaders or participants at the ceremony and what do they do?
The rabbi, who leads the ceremony.
The cantor, who sings during the ceremony or who may lead it instead of a rabbi.
The bride and groom.
Parents of the bride and groom and other members of the wedding party.

What books are used? None. There may be special material prepared by the bridal couple.

To indicate the order of the ceremony: There may be a program.

Will a guest who is not Jewish be expected to do anything other than sit? No.

Are there any parts of the ceremony in which a guest who is not Jewish should *not* participate? No.

If not disruptive to the ceremony, is it okay to:

Take pictures? Possibly. Ask your host.

Use a flash? Possibly. Ask your host.

Use a video camera? Possibly. Ask your host.

Use a tape recorder? Possibly. Ask your host.

Will contributions to the synagogue/temple be collected at the ceremony? No.

AFTER THE CEREMONY

Is there usually a reception after the ceremony? Weddings are times of great celebration. Often, a full meal is served at which there is music and dancing. This may be held in a reception room of the synagogue/temple, in a separate catering hall, at a hotel, or at another site. There may also be a light smorgasbord before the ceremony itself.

Guests should not expect to mix dairy and meat products at the reception if it is kosher (observes the traditional Jewish dietary laws). All Orthodox receptions, most Conservative and Reconstructionist and some Reform receptions are kosher.

Would it be considered impolite to neither eat nor drink? No.

Is there a grace or benediction before eating or drinking? Yes. Wait for a blessing to be said before eating or drinking. A benediction called *ha'-motzi* ("hah-MOH-tsee") is recited before eating bread. It might be said by a rabbi, cantor or a layperson who is an honored guest.

Is there a grace or benediction after eating or drinking? All Orthodox and many Conservative and Reconstructionist ceremonies have a grace after meals called *birkat hamazon* ("beer-KAHT hah-mah-ZONE"). This is increasingly common in Reform ceremonies.

Is there a traditional greeting for the family? "Congratulations," or, in Hebrew, "*Mazal tov*" ("MAH-zal tohv").

Is there a traditional form of address for clergy who may be at the reception? "Rabbi" or "cantor."

Is it okay to leave early? Yes, but usually only after the main course has been served.

Funerals and Mourning

A Jewish funeral will last between 15 and 60 minutes. It is a time of intense mourning and public grieving. It is a service in itself and is not part of a larger service.

The Reform movement rejects all notions of bodily resurrection and of a physical life after death. Instead, it believes in the immortality of every soul, which will eventually return to God. True immortality resides in memories treasured in this world by those who knew and loved the deceased.

The Reconstructionist movement does not believe in bodily resurrection. It believes that, upon death, the soul rejoins the universe.

The Conservative movement talks about the resurrection of the dead, but does not specify whether this will be a physical or a spiritual resurrection. The former would occur upon the coming of the Messiah; the latter would occur by those remaining on earth sensing and remembering the deceased.

Orthodox Jews believe in bodily resurrection and a physical life after death. This would occur upon the coming of the Messiah. In the meantime, there are rough equivalents to heaven and hell, with righteous souls enjoying the pleasures of *olam ha'bah* ("oh-LAHM hah-BAH"), "the world to come," which has a Garden of Eden–like quality; and the wicked suffering in the fiery pits of Gehenna ("geh-HEN-ah").

Traditional Jewish law forbids cremation, but cremation is allowed among Reform Jews.

BEFORE THE CEREMONY

How soon after the death does the funeral usually take place? The day after the death, unless there are extraordinary circumstances. In some Reform families, within two to three days after the death.

What should a non-Jew do upon hearing of the death of a member of that faith? Telephone or visit the bereaved at home and offer condolences and to help out in any way. Possibly bring food to their home. Especially for Orthodox families, make certain the food is kosher (conforms with traditional Jewish dietary laws). If particularly close with the bereaved, offer to take them to the funeral home to arrange details for the funeral.

APPROPRIATE ATTIRE

Men: A jacket and tie. A small head covering called a *yarmulke* ("YAHR-mil-kah") or *kippah* ("keep-AH") is required at Orthodox, Conservative and Reconstructionist funerals and at some Reform funerals. They will be available at the funeral home or synagogue/temple.

Women: A dress or a skirt and blouse. Clothing should be modest.

At some Conservative funerals, a hat or another form of head covering may be required. Open-toed shoes and modest jewelry are appropriate. For Orthodox funerals, clothing should cover the arms, hems should reach below the knees and heads should be covered with a hat or veil.

Do not openly wear symbols of other faiths, such as a cross.

Somber colors for clothing are recommended.

GIFTS

Is it appropriate to send flowers or make a contribution? Flowers are never appropriate for Orthodox, Conservative and Reconstructionist funerals, but are sometimes appropriate for Reform funerals. Contributions in memory of the deceased are customary. Small contributions are often given to a charity or cause favored by the deceased that may be listed in an obituary in a local newspaper; to a special fund established by the bereaved family; or to a Jewish organization, particularly the Jewish National Fund (42 East 69th Street, New York, N.Y. 10021; 888-563-0999; www.jnf.org), which plants trees in Israel, and will send the bereaved family a letter informing them that you have "planted a tree in Israel" in memory of the deceased.

Is it appropriate to send food? Yes, to the home of the bereaved after the funeral. Even if the family is not ritually observant, it is best if the food is kosher (conforms with traditional Jewish dietary laws) to avoid even the possibility of offending them.

THE CEREMONY

Where will the ceremony take place? Either at a synagogue/temple or at a funeral home.

When should guests arrive and where should they sit? Arrive on time. Ushers may be available to direct guests to seating.

If arriving late, are there times when a guest should *not* enter the ceremony? Do not enter during the processional or recessional, if they take place, or while eulogies are being delivered.

Will the bereaved family be present at the synagogue/temple or the funeral home before the ceremony? Yes, usually for no longer than one hour.

Is there a traditional greeting for the family? Offer condolences, such as "I'm sorry for your loss."

Will there be an open casket? Never.

Who are the major officiants at the ceremony and what do they do?

A rabbi, who officiates and delivers a eulogy.
A cantor, who sings.
Family members or friends, who may also deliver a eulogy or memorial.

What books are used? None. The service is led entirely by the rabbi, with no lay participation other than eulogies or memorials by relatives or friends.

To indicate the order of the ceremony: The officiating rabbi will make occasional announcements.

Will a guest who is not Jewish be expected to do anything other than sit? Guests are expected to stand with the other mourners.

Are there any parts of the ceremony in which a guest who is not Jewish should *not* participate? No.

If not disruptive to the ceremony, is it okay to:
Take pictures? No.
Use a flash? No.
Use a video camera? No.
Use a tape recorder? Possibly. Ask permission from a member of the deceased's immediate family.

Will contributions to the synagogue/temple be collected at the ceremony? No.

THE INTERMENT

Should guests attend the interment? It is expected only of family and close friends, not acquaintances.

Whom should one ask for directions? The funeral director.

What happens at the graveside?
The service will vary, depending as
much on the family's background as
on its religious affiliation. At the sim-
plest graveside service, the rabbi
recites prayers and leads the family in
the mourners' *kaddish* ("KAH-dish"),
the prayer for the deceased. At a traditional service, once the mourners
have arrived at the cemetery, there is a
slow procession to the grave itself,
with several pauses along the way.
After prayers and kaddish have been
recited, all present participate in filling in the grave by each putting one
spadeful of earth into it. As the closest
family members leave the gravesite,
they pass between two rows of relatives and friends.

**Do guests who are not Jews par-
ticipate at the graveside ceremony?** They participate in filling in
the grave, if this custom is followed.
Otherwise, they are simply present.

COMFORTING THE
BEREAVED

**Is it appropriate to visit the home
of the bereaved after the funeral?**
Yes. The family sits in mourning for
seven days after the funeral. This is
called the *shiva* period ("SHIH-vah").
Visits should last about 30 minutes.
They are usually made during the day-
time or early evening hours. After
expressing your condolences, it is customary to sit quietly or talk to other
callers, and wait to be spoken to by the
principal mourners.

There are no ritual objects at the
home of the bereaved, but some home
traditions during the mourning period
may include:

Covering mirrors in the home to con-
    centrate on mourning and not on
    vanity.
Burning a special memorial candle for
    seven days in memory of the
    deceased.
Immediate members of the family sit-
    ting on small chairs or boxes; wear-
    ing a black ribbon that has been cut
    and slippers or just socks rather than
    shoes; and, for men, not shaving.

All these symbolize mourners' lack
of interest in their comfort or how
they appear to others.

**Will there be a religious service at
the home of the bereaved?** Yes.
Twice a day, morning and evening.
These usually last about 10 to 20 minutes. Non-Jews should take a prayer
book when these are offered and may
silently read the English, if this does
not violate their religious beliefs. They
should stand when those present stand
during the brief service.

Will food be served? Probably.
Guests should not wait for a grace or
benediction before eating. Guests will
eat as they arrive, after expressing
their condolences to the breaved.

**How soon after the funeral will a
mourner usually return to a normal work schedule?** One week.

**How soon after the funeral will a
mourner usually return to a normal social schedule?** One month to
one year, depending on the deceased's
relation to the person as well as personal inclination.

**Are there mourning customs to
which a friend who is not Jewish
should be sensitive?** For eleven

months after the death of their parent or child, 30 days for other relatives, mourners who follow traditional practice will attend daily morning and/or evening services at synagogue/temple, where he (or she, too, in a more "modern" Orthodox household) participates in the service and, in particular, recites the mourners' *kaddish* ("KAH-dish"), the special prayer for the deceased.

Are there rituals for observing the anniversary of the death? The anniversary of the death is called a *yahrzeit* ("YAHR-tzite"), upon which the bereaved attends service at a synagogue/temple and lights at home a *yahrzeit* candle that burns for 24 hours. An "unveiling" of the tombstone usually takes place on approximately the first anniversary of the death and involves a simple ceremony at the gravesite. Attendance is by specific invitation only.

5 · HOME CELEBRATIONS

Passover Seder

When does it occur? In the springtime.

What is its significance? Passover commemorates the Jewish people's liberation from slavery in Egypt.

What is the proper greeting to the celebrants? "Happy Passover" or "Happy holiday," which in Hebrew is *"Chag samayach"* ("hahg sah-MAY-ahk").

BEFORE THE CEREMONY

Are guests usually invited by a formal invitation? Yes. They may receive a phone call, or be invited face-to-face.

If not stated explicitly, should one assume children are invited? No. Clarify this with your host.

If one can't attend, what should one do? Express regrets. Send flowers or special Passover candy.

APPROPRIATE ATTIRE

Men: Ask your host about attire. Some may prefer jacket and tie; others may request more informal attire. A small head covering called a *yarmulke* ("YAHR-mil-kah") or *kippah* ("keep-AH") is required at all Orthodox and most Conservative and Reconstructionist seders and at some Reform seders. If required, your host will provide them for you.

Women: Ask your host about attire. Some may prefer a dress or a skirt and blouse or a pants suit. Open-toed shoes and modest jewelry are appropriate.

Do not openly wear symbols of other faiths, such as a cross.

There are no rules regarding colors of clothing, but this is a festive occasion.

GIFTS

Is a gift customarily expected? This is entirely optional.

If one decides to give a gift, is a certain type of gift appropriate? Flowers for the seder table or special Passover candy are welcome.

THE CEREMONY

The Passover *seder* ("SAY-dihr") is a festive dinner at home at which the story of the Jewish people's liberation from slavery in Egypt, the Exodus, is told. Rituals precede and follow the meal. A seder is usually led by the head of the household, although everyone present participates.

Seders (including the meal) may take from 90 minutes to more than three hours, depending upon the detail in which the story is told and family customs. It is customary to arrive at the time called; this is a dinner, as well as a religious celebration.

What are the major ritual objects of the ceremony?
A seder plate, on which are symbols of various aspects of the Passover story.
Matzah ("MAH-tzah"), or flat, unleavened bread, similar to the bread made by the Jewish people as they fled Egypt.

What books are used? A *Haggadah* ("hah-GAH-dah"), a text in Hebrew and English that tells the Passover story and its meaning for each generation. There are hundreds of different versions of the Haggadah. Many focus on different elements of the holiday or interpret it from their own particular perspective, such as feminism or ecology, but all tell the basic story of the Exodus.

Will a guest who is not Jewish be expected to do anything other than sit? If asked to do so by the leader, they should read aloud English portions of the Haggadah.

Are there any parts of the ceremony in which a non-Jewish guest should *not* participate? No.

If not disruptive to the ceremony, is it okay to:
Take pictures? Probably; ask your host.
Use a flash? Probably; ask your host.
Use a video camera? Probably; ask your host.
Use a tape recorder? Probably; ask your host.

EATING AND DRINKING

Is a meal part of the celebration? Yes. It is usually served after the first part of the ritual portion of the seder.

Will there be alcoholic beverages? Wine is an integral part of the seder. Other alcoholic beverages may be served prior to or after the seder, depending upon the family's customs.

Would it be considered impolite not to eat? Yes, since the meal is central to the celebration.

Is there a grace or benediction before eating or drinking? Yes. Wait for a blessing before eating or drinking. There are usually several blessings over wine and different types of food. There is also a ritual washing of the hands.

Is there a grace or benediction after eating or drinking? Yes. This is called *birkat hamazon* ("beer-KAHT hah-mah-ZONE").

At the meal, will a guest be asked to say or do anything? If asked to do so by the leader, they should read aloud English portions of the Haggadah.

Will there be:
Dancing? No.
Music? Usually there is just singing. Guitar or piano may accompany the singing.

GENERAL GUIDELINES AND ADVICE

Listen to the seder leader for instructions about the meaning and the order of the seder and for what to do.

Shabbat Dinner

When does it occur? Friday evenings.

What is its significance? *Shabbat* ("shah-BAHT"), or the Sabbath, commemorates the day on which God rested after creating the world during the previous six days. The Jewish Sabbath begins at sunset on Friday and ends at nightfall on Saturday. The Shabbat dinner, which is held at home on Friday evening, is a family-oriented celebration of the Sabbath.

What is the proper greeting to the celebrants? *"Shabbat shalom"* ("shah-BAHT shah-LOME"), Hebrew for "Peaceful Sabbath."

BEFORE THE CEREMONY

Are guests usually invited by a formal invitation? Yes. They may receive a phone call or be invited face-to-face.

If not stated explicitly, should one assume that children are invited? Yes.

If one can't attend, what should one do? Express regrets.

APPROPRIATE ATTIRE

Men: Ask your hosts about attire. Some may prefer jacket and tie; others may prefer more informal attire. A small head covering called a *yarmulke* ("YAHR-mil-kah") or *kippah* ("keep-AH") is required during all Orthodox and most Conservative and Reconstructionist Shabbat dinners and at some Reform Shabbat dinners. If required, they will be provided.

Women: Ask your hosts about attire. Some may prefer a dress or a skirt and blouse or a pants suit. Open-toed shoes and modest jewelry are appropriate. In Orthodox homes, clothing should cover the arms, hems should reach below the knees. Do not carry a purse or similar accessory, since Jewish law prohibits labor, including carrying objects, on Shabbat.

Do not openly wear symbols of other faiths, such as a cross.

There are no rules regarding colors of clothing, but in some Orthodox homes, such bright colors as red or hot pink are not appropriate.

GIFTS

Is a gift customarily expected? This is entirely optional.

If one decides to give a gift, is a certain type of gift appropriate? Flowers or candy would be welcome.

THE CEREMONY

Welcoming the Sabbath is a joyous event and may include the following, although some may be done before guests arrive: Lighting the Sabbath candles and reciting the blessing over them; reciting *kiddush* ("kee-DOOSH"), a prayer accompanied by wine or grape juice before dinner; reciting *ha'motzi* ("hah-MOH-tsee"), the blessing over bread; parents blessing their children; songs to celebrate and welcome the Sabbath.

Depending on how many rituals are observed, they may take about five to 15 minutes.

The ceremony is usually led by the head of the household, although everyone present may participate. The Sabbath dinner is a celebration in itself and is not part of a larger service. Its duration will be that of a social dinner. Arrive at the time called, since this is a social dinner as well as a religious celebration.

What are the major ritual objects of the ceremony?

A kippah ("keep-AH"), or small head covering.

Sabbath candlesticks (two), for the ceremonial lighting of candles to welcome Shabbat and mark its beginning.

A kiddush ("kee-DOOSH") *cup,* for the ritual blessing over wine.

A loaf or two of challah ("HAH-lah"), specially prepared, braided Sabbath bread.

What books are used? A *siddur* ("SEE-door"), or prayer book, or an abbreviated version of it (called a *bencher* or *birkon*) that is just for this purpose.

Will a guest who is not Jewish be expected to do anything other than sit? Stand when other participants stand. If asked to do so by the leader, guests should read aloud English portions of the prayer book if these do not violate their religious beliefs.

Are there any parts of the ceremony in which a non-Jewish guest should *not* participate? No.

If not disruptive to the ceremony, is it okay to:

Take pictures? Not in Orthodox homes; possibly in others. Ask your host.

Use a flash? Not in Orthodox homes; possibly in others. Ask your host.

Use a video camera? Not in Orthodox homes; possibly in others. Ask your host.

Use a tape recorder? Not in Orthodox homes; possibly in others. Ask your host.

EATING AND DRINKING

Is a meal part of the celebration? Yes, an integral part.

Will there be alcoholic beverages? Wine is part of the Shabbat ritual. Other alcoholic beverages may be served, depending on the family's social customs.

Would it be considered impolite to neither eat nor drink? Yes, since the meal is central to the celebration.

Is there a grace or benediction before eating or drinking? Yes. Wait for a blessing to be said before eating or drinking. The blessing over bread is called *ha'motzi* ("hah-MOH-tsee"). In some homes, there is also a ritual washing of the hands.

Is there a grace or benediction after eating or drinking? Yes. This is called *birkat hamazon* ("beer-KAHT hah-mah-ZONE"). It will be said in all Orthodox homes and in some other Jewish homes.

At the meal, will a guest be asked to say or do anything? Stand when other participants stand. If asked to do so by the leader, guests should read aloud English portions of the prayer book and join in any singing, if these do not violate their religious beliefs.

Will there be:
Dancing? No.
Music? Usually there is just singing. Guitar or piano may accompany the singing, except in more ritually observant homes.

GENERAL GUIDELINES AND ADVICE

On Shabbat, most Orthodox Jews, and others who are more ritually observant, do not drive, smoke, write, use the telephone, turn electricity on or off, cook or handle money. It is expected that guests observe the same customs while visiting an Orthodox home.

Do not expect such foods as pork or shellfish or expect to mix dairy and meat products, since Orthodox and many other Jewish households "keep kosher" (observe the traditional Jewish dietary laws).

Orthodox men ordinarily do not shake the hands of women to whom they are not married, and Orthodox women ordinarily do not shake the hands of men to whom they are not married; nor is there public display of physical affection (such as kissing or hugging) between men and women who are not married to each other.

14

Lutheran

1. HISTORY AND BELIEFS

Lutherans trace their faith back to the German reformer Martin Luther (1483–1546), who sought to reform doctrines and practices of the Roman Catholic Church. Objecting to the Church's teachings that one is saved in part by doing good works, he maintained that, according to the Bible, one is made just in God's eyes only by trusting in Jesus' accomplishments for humanity. This is distinct from any good that one does.

Luther also objected to corruption among the clergy and advocated worship in the language of the people rather than in Latin. He favored a married, rather than a celibate, clergy.

Although the Church of Rome considered Luther disloyal and drove him out, later many priests and laity, especially in northern Germany, eventually agreed with Luther's teachings and revamped already existing churches around them.

German and Scandinavian immigrants brought the Lutheran faith to North America. By 1900, scores of small Lutheran church bodies were divided from one another by language, theology and the extent of their assimilation into North American society. Although still somewhat divided along ethnic lines, the main divisions today are between those who are theologically liberal and those who are theologically conservative.

In the United States, the two main Lutheran denominations are the Evangelical Lutheran Church in America and the Lutheran Church–Missouri Synod. The former was created by uniting many earlier churches; the latter, which is a national church despite its name, is more conservative theologically.

In Canada, the Evangelical Lutheran Church in Canada is comparable to the Evangelical Lutheran Church in America; while the Lutheran Church–Canada is the Canadian counterpart to the Lutheran Church–Missouri Synod, and relates closely to that body.

The Evangelical Lutheran Church in America:

U.S. churches: 10,396
U.S. membership: 4.6 million

159

The Lutheran Church–Missouri Synod:
U.S. churches: 6,123
U.S. membership: 2.3 million
(data from the 2010 Yearbook of American and Canadian Churches*)*

For more information, contact:
The Evangelical Lutheran Church
 in America
8765 West Higgins Road
Chicago, IL 60631
(773) 380-2700
info@elca.org
www.elca.org

The Lutheran Church–Missouri Synod
International Center
1333 South Kirkwood Road
St. Louis, MO 63122-7295
(314) 843-5267
infocenter@lcms.org
www.lcms.org

*The Evangelical Lutheran Church
 in Canada:*
Canadian churches: 623
Canadian membership: 175,000

Lutheran Church–Canada:
Canadian churches: 319
Canadian membership: 72,116
(data from the 2010 Yearbook of American and Canadian Churches*)*

For more information contact:
The Evangelical Lutheran Church
 in Canada
302–393 Portage Avenue
Winnipeg, MB R3B 3H6
(204) 984-9150

Lutheran Church–Canada
3074 Portage Avenue
Winnipeg, MB R3K 0Y2
(204) 895-3433
www.lutheranchurch.ca

2 · THE BASIC SERVICE

The basic worship service is a relatively simple formal liturgy that retains the traditional form of the mass with an emphasis on the preaching of God's word and celebration of the Lord's Supper. (The ritual commemorating the Lord's Supper is known as Holy Communion.) The service includes hymns, psalms, responsive readings, Bible readings, a sermon and, often, the Communion liturgy.

Lutherans believe that the Lord's Supper is a direct encounter with God, and that Jesus Christ's body and blood are present through the bread and wine of the Eucharist.

The service usually lasts less than one hour.

APPROPRIATE ATTIRE

Men: Jacket and tie or slightly more casual clothing. Varies from congregation to congregation. No head covering is required.

Women: Dress, skirt and blouse, or pants suit are acceptable. Open-toed shoes and modest jewelry are fine. Hems need not reach below the knees. No head covering is required.

In some congregations, "dressy" leisure clothes are acceptable for men and women, especially in summer. Shorts should never be worn.

There are no rules regarding colors of clothing.

THE SANCTUARY

What are the major sections of the church? The architecture of Lutheran churches varies from the most traditional gothic to avant-garde modern styles. These are the key areas in every church:

The narthex: The vestibule or entrance hall. This is at the end of the nave (see below) and opposite the altar area. Usually, the main outside door enters into the narthex.

The nave: Where congregants sit.

The choir loft: Where the choir sits.

The chancel: Includes the altar and pulpit and seating for clergy. The pastor conducts the worship from this area.

THE SERVICE

When should guests arrive and where should they sit? Although this standard varies by culture and community, it is generally appropriate to arrive a few minutes early to be seated, since services typically begin at the hour called. Usually, ushers will be available to assist you in finding a seat.

If arriving late, are there times when a guest should *not* enter the service? Do not enter during the spoken part of the service. Entry during songs is fine.

Are there times when a guest should *not* leave the service? Do not exit while any prayers are being recited or the sermon is being deliv-ered. Leaving during songs is fine. Almost everyone remains until the end. If you plan to leave by a certain time, sit near the rear of the church and leave quietly.

Who are the major officiants, leaders or participants and what do they do?

The pastor, who preaches, oversees others and administers sacraments.

Assisting ministers, who aid with prayers and administering certain sacraments.

The lector, who reads the scripture lessons.

An acolyte, who lights candles and assists with Communion and other tasks. This is usually a teenager.

The choir, which leads singing.

Ushers and greeters, who welcome guests, seat them and distribute books.

The music leader, who plays an organ and directs the choir.

What are the major ritual objects of the service?

The altar, which symbolizes the presence of God.

The pulpit, which the pastor uses for preaching.

The lectern, where scripture is read.

The baptismal font, which is used for baptizing. It is usually near the front of the church.

A cross or a crucifix (a cross with a representation of the body of Jesus Christ on it).

What books are used? A Bible and a hymnal, usually the *Lutheran Book of Worship* (Minneapolis, Minn.: Augsburg Fortress, 1978) and/or *Evangelical Lutheran Worship* (Minneapolis, Minn.: Augsburg Fortress, 2007) in the Evangelical Lutheran Church in America; or

The Lutheran Hymnal (St. Louis, Mo.: Concordia Publishing House, 2006) and/or *Lutheran Worship* (St. Louis, Mo.: Concordia Publishing House, 1982) in the Missouri Synod churches. Books will be found in the pews or chair racks, or will be handed out by the ushers.

To indicate the order of the service: There will be a program and/or the pastor or assisting minister will make periodic announcements.

GUEST BEHAVIOR DURING THE SERVICE

Will a guest who is not a Lutheran be expected to do anything other than sit? The level of participation depends on whether or not the guest is Christian. Christians will generally be expected to stand, kneel and sing with the congregation and read prayers aloud. Non-Christians are expected to stand with congregants, but not necessarily to kneel, sing or pray with them. Remaining seated when others are kneeling is fine.

Are there any parts of the service in which a non-Lutheran guest should *not* participate? Who is welcome to receive Holy Communion varies among Lutheran churches. The worship bulletin will usually state the policy for visitors.

If not disruptive to the service, is it okay to:
Take pictures? Only with prior permission from the pastor.
Use a flash? Only with prior permission from the pastor.
Use a video camera? Only with prior permission from the pastor.
Use a tape recorder? Only with prior permission from the pastor.

Will contributions to the church be collected at the service? Generally, contributions are collected by ushers passing an offering plate or basket among the seated congregation. It is the guest's choice whether or not to contribute.

How much is it customary to contribute? A donation (cash or check) of $1 to $10 is appropriate.

AFTER THE SERVICE

Is there usually a reception after the service? This will vary by location. Coffee and cookies may be served in a reception area or in the church basement. The reception may last about half an hour.

Is there a traditional form of address for clergy who may be at the reception? "Pastor" followed by last name.

Is it okay to leave early? Yes.

GENERAL GUIDELINES AND ADVICE

Guests have a special place of honor in the thinking of most congregations. You may be invited to sign a guest book or "friendship pad" or to introduce yourself.

Respect the dignity of the service. Although you need not stand when the congregation does, you may feel more comfortable doing so.

Do not hesitate to ask an usher or a "greeter" (who is often identified by a name tag) any questions about the service. Also, feel free to ask a worshiper in your pew for assistance in following the liturgy, should you have any difficulty.

A typical mistake guests sometimes make is to automatically stand and follow other worshipers who are in the same pew when they go to the altar to receive Holy Communion. Guests should remain in the pew and not go forward to receive Communion. Do not fear you will stand out: Others will be staying in the pews, also.

SPECIAL VOCABULARY

Key words or phrases that it might be helpful for a visitor to know:

Holy Communion: A rite through which Lutherans believe they receive Christ's body and blood as assurance that God has forgiven their sins.

Grace: The loving mercy that God shows us in Jesus Christ.

Alleluia (Hallelujah): From the Hebrew, "Praise ye the Lord!"

Lessons: Readings from the Bible (or Scripture), including the Old Testament, the Epistles (generally from one of the letters of St. Paul or another New Testament writer) and the Gospel (a reading from Matthew, Mark, Luke or John, the "biographers" of Jesus).

Creed: Statement of belief. Generally, one of the early Christian creeds is used, either the Apostles' Creed or the Nicene Creed.

DOGMA AND IDEOLOGY

Lutherans believe:

The Law of God, as found, for example, in the Ten Commandments, tells what God expects of us and how we are to live. The Law also shows us that we fall short of God's expectations and that we are disobedient to God.

The Gospel is the good news of how God remains faithful to his justice, which demands punishment for our disobedience (our sin); and to his love and mercy, which does not want to see any of us punished or separated from him because of our sin.

The good news (which is what "Gospel" means) is that the eternal Son of God, who is himself fully God, became a man in the person of Jesus of Nazareth, lived a life of perfect obedience that we cannot live, and suffered God's own punishment for our sin so we don't have to. Instead, we are freely forgiven through Jesus Christ and given eternal life with God as a free gift.

Some books to which a guest can refer to learn more about the Lutheran faith:

Lutheran Worship: History and Practice, edited by Fred L. Precht (St. Louis, Mo.: Concordia Publishing House, 1994).

The Lutherans in North America, edited by E. Clifford Nelson (Philadelphia: Fortress Press, 1980).

The Small Catechism by Martin Luther (St. Louis, Mo.: Concordia Publishing House, 2008).

These Evangelical Lutheran Churches of Ours by Kenn Ward (Winfield, B.C.: Wood Lake Books, 1994).

3 · HOLY DAYS AND FESTIVALS

Advent. Begins four weeks before Christmas. The purpose is to prepare for Christmas and to focus on Christ. There is no traditional greeting to Lutherans for Advent. Additional services are sometimes added to the church schedule.

Christmas. Occurs on the evening of December 24 and the day of December 25. Marks the birth and the incarnation of God as a man. The traditional greeting to Lutherans is "Merry Christmas" or "Blessed Christmas."

Lent. Begins on Ash Wednesday, which occurs six weeks before Easter. The purpose is to prepare for Easter. There is no traditional greeting to Lutherans for Lent. Between Lent and Easter, abstention from entertainment is encouraged, as is increased giving to the poor. Often, there are midweek worship services. Some churches sponsor a light soup supper once a week, with proceeds going toward combating world hunger and encouraging global peace. While traditionally, among many Christian denominations, Lent is a time of fasting or abstaining from certain foods, relatively few contemporary Lutherans now do this and such fasting is given little prominence by the Church.

Easter. Always falls on the Sunday after the first full moon that occurs on or after March 21. Celebrates the Resurrection of Jesus Christ. The traditional greeting to Lutherans is "Happy Easter." In worship services, the pastor may greet congregants with, "He is risen!" Congregants respond with "He is risen, indeed!"

Pentecost Sunday. The seventh Sunday after Easter. Celebrates the coming of the Holy Spirit, which is the empowering spirit of God in human life. This is often considered the birth of the Christian church. There is no traditional greeting for this holiday.

Reformation Day. Occurs on October 31. Reformation Sunday, the day on which Reformation Day is celebrated, is the Sunday before Reformation Day. Commemorates October 31, 1517, the day on which Martin Luther is said to have nailed 95 statements of belief (called the "95 Theses") on the door of the Castle Church in Wittenberg, Germany. This was then the practice for inviting scholarly debate. There is no traditional greeting for this holiday.

4 · LIFE CYCLE EVENTS

Birth Ceremony

Baptism is the one-time sacrament of initiation into the family of God, the Holy Christian Church. In the Lutheran Church, infants are baptized. (Also baptized are previously unbaptized youths or adults when they confess faith in Jesus Christ and ask to join the church.)

As a sacrament, baptism is a means by which God creates and strengthens faith and through which he assures the forgiveness of sins and the promise of eternal life with him. Baptism is done with water applied to the head of the person being initiated and in the name of the Father, the Son and the Holy Spirit (the three persons of God). It marks entry into Christian faith, not simply the birth of a child.

Typically, the baptism is part of a Sunday service. When this occurs, the service will be slightly longer than the "basic service" described above, which usually lasts less than an hour, and will focus on the baptism.

BEFORE THE CEREMONY

Are guests usually invited by a formal invitation? Guests are usually invited by a note or phone call.

If not stated explicitly, should one assume that children are invited? Yes.

If one can't attend, what should one do? Call the family to express congratulations or send a baptism card. These are available at most card shops.

APPROPRIATE ATTIRE

Men: Jacket and tie or slightly more casual clothing. Varies from congregation to congregation. No head covering is required.

Women: Dress, skirt and blouse, or pants suit are acceptable. Open-toed shoes and modest jewelry are fine. Hems need not reach below the knees. No head covering is required.

In some congregations, "dressy" leisure clothes are acceptable for men and women, especially in summer. Shorts should never be worn.

There are no rules regarding colors of clothing.

GIFTS

Is a gift customarily expected? Yes, clothing or toys for a newborn are most frequently given. Money is not appropriate.

Should gifts be brought to the ceremony? It is customary to bring a gift to the home following the ceremony.

THE CEREMONY

Where will the ceremony take place? Partly at the baptismal font in the main sanctuary of the church; partly near the altar.

When should guests arrive and where should they sit? Arrive a few minutes early to be seated, since services typically begin at the hour called. Ushers will help you find a seat.

If arriving late, are there times when a guest should *not* enter the ceremony? Do not enter during the spoken part of the service. Entry during songs is fine.

Are there times when a guest should *not* leave the ceremony? Almost everyone remains until the end. If you plan to leave by a certain time, sit near the rear of the church and leave quietly. Do not leave while any prayers are being recited or the sermon is being delivered. Departure during songs is advised.

Who are the major officiants, leaders or participants at the ceremony and what do they do?
The pastor, who presides and baptizes.
An assisting minister, who leads prayers and assists the pastor.
Ushers, who greet congregants and guests and assist in seating.
The sponsors, who answer questions and confess to the Christian faith on

behalf of the infant being baptized. (Parents may also serve this function.) Sponsors are not used at youth or adult baptisms, since those being baptized can speak for themselves.

What books are used? A Bible and a hymnal, usually the *Lutheran Book of Worship* (Minneapolis, Minn.: Augsburg Fortress, 1978) and/or *Evangelical Lutheran Worship* (Minneapolis, Minn.: Augsburg Fortress, 2007) in the Evangelical Lutheran Church in America; or *The Lutheran Hymnal* (St. Louis, Mo.: Concordia Publishing House, 2006) and/or *Lutheran Worship* (St. Louis, Mo.: Concordia Publishing House, 1982) in the Missouri Synod churches. Books will be found in the pews or chair racks, or will be handed out by the ushers.

To indicate the order of the ceremony: There will be a program and/or the pastor or assisting minister will make periodic announcements.

Will a guest who is not a Lutheran be expected to do anything other than sit? The level of participation depends on whether or not the guest is Christian. Christians will generally be expected to stand, kneel and sing with the congregation and read prayers aloud. Non-Christians are expected to stand with congregants, but not necessarily to kneel, sing or pray with them. Remaining seated when others are kneeling is fine.

Are there any parts of the ceremony in which a guest who is not a Lutheran should *not* participate? Who is welcome to receive Holy Communion varies among Lutheran churches. The worship bulletin will usually state the policy for visitors.

If not disruptive to the ceremony, is it okay to:
Take pictures? Only with prior permission from the pastor.
Use a flash? Only with prior permission from the pastor.
Use a video camera? Only with prior permission from the pastor.
Use a tape recorder? Only with prior permission from the pastor.

Will contributions to the church be collected at the ceremony? Generally, contributions are collected by ushers passing an offering plate or basket among the seated congregation. It is the guest's choice whether or not to contribute.

How much is it customary to contribute? A donation (cash or check) of $1 to $10 is appropriate.

AFTER THE CEREMONY

Is there usually a reception after the ceremony? There may be a reception after the ceremony at the home of the infant's parents. This may include a meal or refreshments and presenting gifts to the baptized. Since this is generally a family affair, you should behave as you would as a guest in someone's home.

Would it be considered impolite to neither eat nor drink? No.

Is there a grace or benediction before eating or drinking? No.

Is there a grace or benediction after eating or drinking? No.

Is there a traditional greeting for the family? Offer your congratulations.

Is there a traditional form of address for clergy who may be at

the reception? "Pastor" followed by last name.

Is it okay to leave early? Yes.

Initiation Ceremony

Confirmation is a church rite in which one who was previously baptized expresses his or her faith in Jesus Christ. The ceremony is an additional liturgy added to the "basic service." In it, confirmands come forward individually as their names are called and the pastor places his or her hands on the confirmand's head and prays God's blessing on that person. (Women are ordained as priests only in the Evangelical Lutheran Church in America, not in the Lutheran Church—Missouri Synod.) Generally, a special verse of Scripture, selected especially for that confirmand, is read.

Confirmation usually takes place in early adolescence and often in a group.

BEFORE THE CEREMONY

Are guests usually invited by a formal invitation? Yes.

If not stated explicitly, should one assume that children are invited? Yes.

If one can't attend, what should one do? Send a gift or call the family to express congratulations.

APPROPRIATE ATTIRE

Men: Jacket and tie or slightly more casual clothing. Varies from congregation to congregation. No head covering is required.

Women: Dress, skirt and blouse, or pants suit are acceptable. Open-toed shoes and modest jewelry are fine. Hems need not reach below the knees. No head covering is required.

In some congregations, "dressy" leisure clothes are acceptable for men and women, especially in summer. Shorts should never be worn.

There are no rules regarding colors of clothing.

GIFTS

Is a gift customarily expected? It is customary to present a gift at the confirmation of youths. It is appropriate to give money (between $20 and $50) or religious books and objects.

Should gifts be brought to the ceremony? The gift should be brought to the home after the service.

THE CEREMONY

Where will the ceremony take place? In the main sanctuary of the church.

When should guests arrive and where should they sit? Although this standard varies by culture and community, it is generally appropriate to arrive a few minutes early to be seated, since services typically begin at the hour called.

If arriving late, are there times when a guest should *not* enter the ceremony? Do not enter during prayers. Usually, ushers will help you find a seat.

Are there times when a guest should *not* leave the ceremony? Almost everyone remains until the end. If you plan to leave by a certain time, sit near the rear of the church and leave quietly. Do not leave while any prayers are being recited or the sermon is being delivered. Departure during songs is advised.

Who are the major officiants, leaders or participants at the ceremony and what do they do?

The pastor, who preaches, oversees others and administers sacraments.

The assisting ministers, who aid with prayers and certain sacraments.

Ushers and greeters, who welcome guests, seat them and distribute books.

The music leader, who plays an organ, directs the choir and leads singing.

The readers, who read lessons from Scripture.

What books are used? A Bible and a hymnal, usually the *Lutheran Book of Worship* (Minneapolis, Minn.: Augsburg Fortress, 1978) and/or *Evangelical Lutheran Worship* (Minneapolis, Minn.: Augsburg Fortress, 2007) in the Evangelical Lutheran Church in America; or *The Lutheran Hymnal* (St. Louis, Mo.: Concordia Publishing House, 2006) and/or *Lutheran Worship* (St. Louis, Mo.: Concordia Publishing House, 1982) in the Missouri Synod churches. Books will be found in the pews or chair racks, or will be handed out by the ushers.

To indicate the order of the ceremony: There will be a program and/or the pastor or assisting minister will make periodic announcements.

Will a guest who is not a Lutheran be expected to do anything other than sit? The level of participation depends on whether or not the guest is Christian. Christians will generally be expected to stand, kneel and sing with the congregation and read prayers aloud. Non-Christians are expected to stand with congregants, but not necessarily to kneel, sing or pray with them. Remaining seated when others are kneeling is fine.

Are there any parts of the ceremony in which a non-Lutheran should *not* participate? Who is welcome to receive Holy Communion varies among Lutheran churches. The worship bulletin will usually state the policy for visitors.

If not disruptive to the ceremony, is it okay to:

Take pictures? Only with prior permission from the pastor.

Use a flash? Only with prior permission from the pastor.

Use a video camera? Only with prior permission from the pastor.

Use a tape recorder? Only with prior permission from the pastor.

Will contributions to the church be collected at the ceremony? Generally, contributions are collected by ushers passing an offering plate or basket among the seated congregation. It is the guest's choice whether or not to contribute.

How much is it customary to contribute? A donation (cash or check) of $1 to $10 is appropriate.

AFTER THE CEREMONY

Is there usually a reception after the ceremony? There may be a reception at the church in the fellowship hall. Generally, individual families plan receptions in their homes for invited guests. There will probably be light refreshments or a meal. If at home, alcoholic beverages may be served.

If it is held at the church, the reception may last about 30 minutes. If in a home or restaurant, it usually lasts at least two hours.

Would it be considered impolite to neither eat nor drink? No.

Is there a grace or benediction before eating or drinking? Guests should wait for the saying of grace or an invocation before eating.

Is there a grace or benediction after eating or drinking? There may be a benediction after the meal.

Is there a traditional greeting for the family? It is proper to congratulate the confirmand and his or her family.

Is there a traditional form of address for clergy who may be at the reception? "Pastor" followed by last name.

Is it okay to leave early? Yes.

Marriage Ceremony

A church wedding is an act of worship, not a civil service. In the service, the couple profess their love for and their commitment to each other before God and ask his blessing on their marriage. The same decorum exercised in any worship service should be exercised in the wedding service.

The ceremony may either be a service in itself or be part of the Holy Communion service. The bridal party will proceed in, then the pastor will read appropriate lessons from the Bible and ask the bride and groom about their lifelong commitment to one another. The pastor will deliver a brief homily, wedding vows and rings will be exchanged, and the pastor will pronounce the couple husband and wife.

If the ceremony is a service by itself, it will last 15 to 30 minutes. If part of the celebration of Holy Communion and also depending on the music selected, it will last around half an hour.

BEFORE THE CEREMONY

Are guests usually invited by a formal invitation? Yes.

If not stated explicitly, should one assume that children are invited? Yes.

If one can't attend, what should one do? Reply in writing or call and send a gift.

APPROPRIATE ATTIRE

Local social norms prevail, although weddings tend to be somewhat formal.

Men: Jacket and tie. No head covering required.

Women: Dress, skirt and blouse, or pants suit are acceptable. Open-toed shoes and modest jewelry are fine. Hems need not reach the knees. No head covering required.

There are no rules regarding colors of clothing.

GIFTS

Is a gift customarily expected? Yes. Appropriate gifts are such household items as appliances, dishes, towels or blankets. The bride is often listed in the bridal registry at a local department store.

Should gifts be brought to the ceremony? If you are also invited to the reception afterward, gifts are more often brought to the reception and placed on the gift table there.

THE CEREMONY

Where will the ceremony take place? In the main sanctuary of the house of worship. The bridal party will stand near the altar in the chancel, the area in front of the sanctuary, which includes the altar and pulpit and seating for clergy.

When should guests arrive and where should they sit? It is appropriate to arrive before the time called for the ceremony. An usher will tell you where to sit.

If arriving late, are there times when a guest should *not* enter the ceremony? Do not enter during the processional or recessional or during prayer.

Are there times when a guest should *not* leave the ceremony? Do not leave during the processional or recessional or during prayer.

Who are the major officiants, leaders or participants at the ceremony and what do they do? *The pastor*, who presides.

What books are used? A hymnal may be used.

To indicate the order of the ceremony: There will be a program.

Will a guest who is not a Lutheran be expected to do anything other than sit? Guests are not expected to do anything other than sit and enjoy.

Are there any parts of the ceremony in which a guest who is not a Lutheran should *not* participate? Who is welcome to receive Holy Communion varies among Lutheran churches. The worship bulletin will usually state the policy for visitors.

If not disruptive to the ceremony, is it okay to:
Take pictures? Only with prior permission from the pastor.
Use a flash? Only with prior permission from the pastor.
Use a video camera? Only with prior permission from the pastor.
Use a tape recorder? Only with prior permission from the pastor.

Will contributions to the church be collected at the ceremony? No.

AFTER THE CEREMONY

Is there usually a reception after the ceremony? Customs vary locally and by individual preference. However, there will generally be a reception in the church, at home or in a catering hall. Depending on local custom, there may be music and dancing. The menu will vary from light refreshments and cake to a full meal. Alcoholic beverages may be served if the reception is held outside the church.

If the reception is held at a church, it will be less than 30 minutes. If at a home or restaurant, it will usually last at least two hours.

Would it be considered impolite to neither eat nor drink? Yes. If you have dietary restrictions, inform your host or hostess in advance.

Is there a grace or benediction before eating or drinking? Guests should wait for the saying of grace or an invocation before eating.

Is there a grace or benediction after eating or drinking? No.

Is there a traditional greeting for the family? Congratulate the new couple and their parents.

Is there a traditional form of address for clergy who may be at the reception? "Pastor" followed by last name.

Is it okay to leave early? Yes.

Funerals and Mourning

For Lutherans, death is not the end of life, but the beginning of new life. While Lutherans will grieve, they do not mourn as do those who have no hope of ever seeing the deceased again or without the sure hope that those who die in faith in Jesus Christ are assured eternal life with God.

The funeral is usually a service in itself. The pastor presides. Pallbearers carry or push the casket on rollers into the funeral home or church sanctuary. The service will rarely last more than 30 minutes. All attending are expected to remain to the end.

BEFORE THE CEREMONY

How soon after the death does the funeral usually take place? There is no set period during which the funeral should occur, but it usually takes place within three days after death.

What should a non-Lutheran do upon hearing of the death of a member of that faith? Call the bereaved, visit or send a note to express your sympathy at their loss. Express your care and love for the bereaved.

APPROPRIATE ATTIRE

Men: Jacket and tie. No head covering is required.

Women: A dress or skirt and blouse are acceptable. Open-toed shoes and modest jewelry are fine. Hems need not reach the knees. No head covering is required.

Local social customs govern, but conservative clothing and dark, somber colors are recommended.

GIFTS

Is it appropriate to send flowers or make a contribution? It is appropriate to send flowers unless the family expresses otherwise. Send them to the deceased's home or to the funeral home where the funeral will be held.

It is also appropriate to make a donation in the form of a "memorial" in memory of the deceased. The family will often announce, either through the funeral home or in the funeral worship folder, the preferred charity or church for memorial contributions. Memorials are often mailed or hand-delivered to the funeral home or church office. There is no standard amount to be donated.

Is it appropriate to send food? You may want to send food to the home of the bereaved for the family and their guests.

THE CEREMONY

Where will the ceremony take place? Typically, in the church of the deceased, although it may be at a funeral home.

When should guests arrive and where should they sit? It is customary to arrive early enough to be seated when the service begins. Someone will tell you where and when to sit.

If arriving late, are there times when a guest should *not* enter the ceremony? Do not enter during the procession or prayer.

Will the bereaved family be present at the church or funeral home before the ceremony? If there is a visitation at the funeral home the night before the funeral, you can attend and express your sorrow and regret.

Is there a traditional greeting for the family? Just offer your condolences.

Will there be an open casket? Possibly.

Is a guest expected to view the body? This is optional.

What is appropriate behavior upon viewing the body? Stand quietly and then move on.

Who are the major officiants at the ceremony and what do they do? *The pastor*, who presides.

What books are used? A hymnal, usually the *Lutheran Book of Worship* (Minneapolis, Minn.: Augsburg Fortress, 1978) and/or *Evangelical Lutheran Worship* (Minneapolis, Minn.: Augsburg Fortress, 2007) in the Evangelical Lutheran Church in America; or *The Lutheran Hymnal* (St. Louis, Mo.: Concordia Publishing House, 2006) and/or *Lutheran Worship* (St. Louis, Mo.: Concordia Publishing House, 1982) in the Missouri Synod churches.

To indicate the order of the ceremony: There will be a program or the pastor will make periodic announcements.

Will a guest who is not a Lutheran be expected to do anything other than sit? The level of participation depends on whether or not the guest is Christian. Christians will generally be expected to stand, kneel and sing with the congregation and read prayers aloud. Non-Christians are expected to stand with congregants, but not necessarily to kneel, sing or pray with them. Remaining seated when others are kneeling is fine.

Are there any parts of the ceremony in which a guest who is not a Lutheran should *not* participate?

Who is welcome to receive Holy Communion varies among Lutheran churches. The worship bulletin will usually state the policy for visitors.

If not disruptive to the ceremony, it is okay to:

Take pictures? Only with prior permission from the pastor.

Use a flash? Only with prior permission from the pastor.

Use a video camera? Only with prior permission from the pastor.

Use a tape recorder? Only with prior permission from the pastor.

Will contributions to the church be collected at the ceremony? No.

THE INTERMENT

Should guests attend the interment? Yes.

Whom should one ask for directions? Either join the funeral procession or ask the funeral director for directions.

What happens at the graveside? The casket is carried to the grave. Prayers and readings are offered. The pastor blesses the earth placed on the casket and blesses those gathered at the graveside.

Do guests who are not Lutherans participate at the graveside service? If this does not conflict with their own religious beliefs, they recite the Lord's Prayer and join in these responses to other prayers: "The Lord be with you" and "And also with you."

COMFORTING THE BEREAVED

Is it appropriate to visit the home of the bereaved after the funeral? Yes, more than once is appropriate. Share in the conversation and refreshments.

Will there be a religious service at the home of the bereaved? No.

Will food be served? Possibly. If food is served, wait for the saying of grace before eating. It would be impolite not to eat, unless you have dietary restrictions. (If so, mention these to your host or hostess.) There may be alcoholic beverages, depending on the family's custom.

How soon after the funeral will a mourner usually return to a normal work schedule? Bereaved often stay home from work for several days.

How soon after the funeral will a mourner usually return to a normal social schedule? Not for several weeks after the funeral.

Are there mourning customs to which a friend who is not a Lutheran should be sensitive? No.

Are there rituals for observing the anniversary of the death? While there are no specific rituals, some congregations remember the first-year anniversary in prayers in church.

5. HOME CELEBRATIONS

Not applicable to Lutherans.

15

Mennonite/Amish

1. HISTORY AND BELIEFS

There are nearly 20 organized groups of Mennonites in North America. They vary in lifestyle and religious practice, but all originate from the same 16th-century Anabaptist movement in Europe. The Anabaptist movement began when a small group of religious reformers claimed Protestant reformers were not sufficiently "radical." They also differed with mainstream Protestants on the timing of baptism. Protestants called for baptism of infants, while Anabaptists mandated that one should be baptized after reaching an "age of accountability," which usually begins with early adolescence and confers the ability to profess belief for one's self.

The name "Mennonite" is derived from that of the 16th-century Dutch Anabaptist leader Menno Simons. Originally a Roman Catholic priest, Simons became convinced of the falsity of traditional Catholic doctrine and practice of his time, but hesitated at breaking with the Church. He joined the Anabaptists, who were then being persecuted. Grateful for his leadership, the group later adopt-

ed a variation on his name.

Over the years, Mennonites have maintained cultural traditions and religious beliefs in differing ways. While this has led to the formation of various Mennonite groups, they hold certain beliefs in common. Among these are that one should emulate Jesus in everyday living and behavior; that the Bible is the inspired word of God; and that Jesus taught the way of peace. Mennonite faith cannot easily be labeled a liberal or a conservative Christian denomination. Rather, it is an alternative to mainstream religion, one that emphasizes evangelism, peace and justice, and that focuses on a holistic approach to Christ's way of personal salvation, while maintaining concern for the physical as well as the spiritual needs of others.

The one over-arching Mennonite belief that differs from all Christian denominations (except for the Society of Friends, or "Quakers," and the Church of the Brethren) is the Church's stand on war and violence. In principle, Mennonites have always been conscientious objectors to war, although individual members have opted for non-

174

combatant roles and even military service. More recently, the broadest emphasis has been placed on "non-violence" so it includes such issues as abortion and capital punishment.

Mennonites began emigrating to North America from Switzerland in the mid-17th century, spreading westward from Pennsylvania and concentrating in rural colonies where they practiced their faith and Swiss culture.

In a second spurt of Mennonite emigration in the late 19th century, Mennonites of Dutch, German and Swiss ancestry who had settled in Ukraine fled Czarist efforts to conscript them into the Russian army. They settled primarily in the Midwestern areas of the United States and Canada. Third and fourth waves of emigration followed both world wars.

An emphasis on missionary work in this century has helped the Church develop so much into an international institution that now more than one-third of adult Mennonites are nonwhites. Mennonites combine a keen sense of evangelism with a theology of relief and material aid to people in want. For over 75 years, the Mennonite Central Committee, a relief agency operating around the world, has helped the needy and addressed issues of peace and justice.

The Amish, or the Amish-Mennonite, as they are more properly known, originated from a disagreement among European Mennonites regarding "shunning," a practice that had been adopted by the Dutch

Mennonites in 1632. Shunning demanded avoiding a fellow Mennonite who had transgressed. In the late 17th century, a Swiss Mennonite, Jacob Ammann, became concerned over laxity in the Swiss and Alsatian Mennonite communities when a woman who had admitted speaking a falsehood was not shunned. Ammann also rejected a prevalent belief that the souls would be saved of those who were sincerely sympathetic to the Mennonite, but did not join the faith. And he urged simplicity and uniformity as a guard against pride. This included the admonition that men not trim their beards. Today, the Amish call for simplicity extends to not using motorized vehicles, partly because of concerns that they could take Amish too far from their own community.

The group that eventually coalesced around Ammann and his teachings called themselves "Amish" in his honor. The first Amish arrived in North America around 1727, but a congregation was not formed until 1749 in Berks County, Pennsylvania. By the mid-19th century, there were significant Amish communities in Lancaster and Chester counties in Pennsylvania and in Holmes County, Ohio, as well as in Waterloo County, Ontario, Canada.

The largest Mennonite and Amish denominations in the United States are the Mennonite Church, USA, with 964 churches and over 100,000 members; and the Old Order Amish Church, widely known for its resistance to modern technology, which has 898 churches and almost 81,000 members.

Smaller, more traditional denominations include the Beachy Amish Mennonite (211 churches; 12,062 members); the Fellowship of Evangelical Bible Churches (19 churches; 2,197 members); and the Reformed Mennonite Church (8 churches; 270 members).

The largest Mennonite and Amish denominations in Canada include the Mennonite Church Canada, with 225 churches and 32,000 members; the General Conference of the Mennonite Brethren Churches–Canada, with 207 churches and 28,368 members; and various Russian Mennonite immigrant groups numbering 20,164 members.

Smaller, more traditional denominations include Old Order Mennonite (5,763 members); Beachy Amish and Old Order Amish (1,612 members); Mennonite Church (independent and unaffiliated groups, 2,187 members).

U.S. churches: 2,100
U.S. membership: 201,521
   (data from the 2005 and 2010 Yearbook of American and Canadian Churches*)*

For more information, contact:
The Beachy Amish Mennonite Church
7809 South Herren Road
Partridge, KS 67566
(620) 567-2286

The General Conference of
   Mennonite Brethren
4812 East Butler Avenue
Fresno, CA 93727
(209) 452-1713

Mennonite Church USA
722 Main Street
Newton, KS 67114
(316) 283-5100
www.mennoniteusa.org

The Old Order Amish Church
4324 SR 39
Millersburg, OH 44654
(330) 893-2883

Canadian churches: Not available.
Canadian membership: Not available.

For more information, contact:

Mennonite Church Canada
600 Shaftesbury Boulevard
Winnipeg, MB R3P 0M4
(204) 888-6781
www.mennonitechurch.ca

Canadian Conference of Mennonite
   Brethren Churches
1310 Taylor Avenue
Winnipeg, MB R3M 3Z6
(204) 669-6575
www.mbconf.ca

Evangelical Mennonite Conference
   of Canada
440 Main Street
Steinbach, MB R5G 1Z5
(204) 326-6401
www.emconf.ca

Evangelical Mennonite Mission
   Conference
Box 52059 Niakwa P.O.
Winnipeg, MB R2M 5P9
(204) 253-7929
www.emmc.ca

2 · THE BASIC SERVICE

To Mennonites and Amish, worship is a time to pray, to praise God, to sing hymns and to read or listen to the word of God as read from the Bible. Worship is considered to be a "corporate event"—the coming together of a body of believers focused on Christ and living a Christ-like life each day. It is also a time for personal spiritual fulfillment.

The length of Sunday morning worship services varies. Beachy Amish services may last two and one-half hours, while General Conference Mennonite churches services last 30 to 60 minutes and General Conference of Mennonite Brethren services last slightly more than one hour.

APPROPRIATE ATTIRE

Men: Expected attire varies. In more conservative denominations, such as the Beachy Amish Mennonite, a suit jacket is worn, but without a tie. In other denominations, casual attire is acceptable, but those attending the church for the first time are advised to wear a jacket and tie. In the General Conference of Mennonite Brethren, a jacket and tie or slightly more casual attire is acceptable.

In no denomination is a head covering required.

Women: Expected attire varies. In more conservative denominations, such as the Beachy Amish Mennonite, women are expected to wear dresses that cover their arms and have hems that reach below their knees. Neither open-toed shoes nor modest jewelry are permissible. Church members cover their heads, but visitors are not expected to do so.

In less conservative denominations, such as the General Conference of Mennonite Brethren, women may wear dresses, a skirt and blouse or a pants suit or more casual attire, although those attending the church for the first time are advised to dress somewhat conservatively. Clothing need not cover the arms nor hems reach below the knees. Open-toed shoes and modest jewelry are permissible. No head covering is required.

Dark, solid colors are advised for more conservative denominations, such as the Beachy Amish Mennonite. For the services of less conservative groups, there are no rules regarding colors of clothing.

THE SANCTUARY

What are the major sections of the church?

The sanctuary: Where the congregation gathers for worship.

The pulpit: Where lay and religious leaders speak to the congregation.

Choir loft or seats: May be either on the raised area in front of the congregation or in another location in the sanctuary.

THE SERVICE

When should guests arrive and where should they sit? Arrive shortly before the time for which the service has been called. Beachy Amish Mennonite churches always start their services at 9:30 A.M. on Sunday mornings. Other denominations begin worship at various times, so the visitor should check the time in advance with the church or with a friend who is Mennonite.

In most Mennonite denominations, ushers will usually advise congregants and guests where to sit. Beachy Amish do not have ushers.

If arriving late, are there times when a guest should *not* enter the service? Do not enter during Scripture readings or while prayers are being said. It may be best for tardy congregants and guests to enter while a hymn is being sung.

Are there times when a guest should *not* leave the service? No.

Who are the major officiants, leaders or participants and what do they do?
Preachers or pastors, who read Scripture, lead prayers, make announcements and deliver the sermon.
Musicians or song leaders, who direct the choir or lead hymn singing.
Lay church members, who have been asked in advance of the service to read Scripture or to sing.

What are the major ritual objects of the service?
The Communion table, from which Communion is served.
A Bible, which often lies open on the Communion table.

What books are used? In each denomination, various translations of the Bible are used.

Various hymnals are also used throughout the denominations. The Mennonite Church USA, Mennonite Church Canada, and the Church of the Brethren use *Hymnal: A Worship Book* (Newton, Kans.: Faith and Life Press, 1992). The Mennonite Brethren Church uses *Worship Together* (Fresno, Calif.: Board of Faith and Life, General Conference of Mennonite Brethren Churches, 1995).

A church bulletin may also be used that includes prayers, responses or hymns.

To indicate the order of the service: A program may be distributed or the pastor may make periodic announcements.

GUEST BEHAVIOR DURING THE SERVICE

Will a guest who is neither Mennonite nor Amish be expected to do anything other than sit? In all but the most conservative Churches, a visitor would rarely do wrong by remaining seated when congregants stand or kneel, although the latter is rare in most congregations. However, if it does not violate their religious beliefs, the guest would be more in place by standing when others stand. Also, it is optional for guests to sing and read prayers aloud with the congregants.

Are there any parts of the service in which a guest who is neither Mennonite nor Amish should *not* participate? Communion is not offered to guests who are not Christian.

If not disruptive to the service, is it okay to:

Take pictures? Not in more conservative denominations, such as the Beachy Amish Mennonite. Possibly (but only with prior permission of the pastor) in less conservative denominations, such as the General Conference of Mennonite Brethren.

Use a flash? No.

Use a video camera? Not in more conservative denominations, such as the Beachy Amish Mennonite. Possibly (but only with prior permission of the pastor) in less conservative denominations, such as the General Conference of Mennonite Brethren.

Use a tape recorder? Possibly (but only with prior permission of the pastor) in all Mennonite churches.

Will contributions to the church be collected at the service? Collections will be taken in the churches of most Mennonite denominations, but not in those of the General Conference of Mennonite Brethren.

How much is it customary to contribute? Guests are not expected to contribute, but should they choose to do so, $1 to $10 is appropriate.

AFTER THE SERVICE

Is there usually a reception after the service? Most denominations do not have a reception after the service. No alcoholic beverages are served at these. Grace over the food is usually recited before the meal, which may last between 30 and 60 minutes.

Churches belonging to the General Conference of Mennonite Brethren usually have a "coffee time" after the service at which coffee and rolls are served. This may last about 30 minutes.

Is there a traditional form of address for clergy whom a guest may meet? "Pastor."

Is it okay to leave early? Yes.

GENERAL GUIDELINES AND ADVICE

Guests are always welcome and should feel free to ask church members or a pastor about the congregants' faith and religious practice.

SPECIAL VOCABULARY

Key words or phrases that it might be helpful for a visitor to know:

Holy Communion: A rite through which Mennonites and Amish believe they receive Christ's body and blood as assurance that God has forgiven their sins.

Lessons: Readings from the Bible (or "Scripture"), including the Old Testament (the Hebrew scriptures, written before the birth of Jesus); the Epistles (generally from one of the letters of St. Paul or another New Testament writer); and the Gospel (a reading from Matthew, Mark, Luke or John, the "biographers" of Jesus).

DOGMA AND IDEOLOGY

Mennonites and Amish believe:

Jesus Christ is central to worship and to everyday living, which should emulate Christ's example.

The Bible is the inspired word of God.

Church membership is voluntary, with adult baptism upon one declaring his or her faith.

Jesus Christ taught the way of peace, and one should not serve in the military.

Basic books to which a guest can refer to learn more about Mennonites and Amish:

Building on the Rock: A Biblical Vision of Being Church Together from an Anabaptist Mennonite Perspective by Walfred J. Fahrer (Eugene, Ore.: Wipf and Stock Publishers, 2005).

Family Matters: Discovering the Mennonite Brethren by Lynn Jost and Connie Faber (Winnipeg, Manitoba: Kindred Productions, 2002).

An Introduction to Mennonite History: A Popular History of the Anabaptists and the Mennonites by Cornelius J. Dyck (Scottsdale, Pa.: Herald Press, 1993).

Smith's Story of the Mennonites by C. Henry Smith (Eugene, Ore.: Wipf and Stock Publishers, 2005.).

3 · HOLY DAYS AND FESTIVALS

Christmas. Always falls on December 25. Celebrates the birth of Christ. Many congregations observe Christmas Eve, which falls on December 24, with a worship service that may include singing, reenactments of the Nativity scene in Bethlehem, and a reading of the Christmas story from the Bible. The traditional greeting is "Merry Christmas."

Ash Wednesday. Occurs 40 days before Easter. Commemorates the beginning of Lent, which is a season for preparation and penitence before Easter itself. There is no traditional greeting for this holiday.

Easter. Always falls on the Sunday after the first full moon that occurs on or after the spring equinox of March 21. Commemorates the death and resurrection of Jesus. The traditional greeting is "Happy Easter."

Pentecost. Occurs 50 days after Easter because this is when the Holy Ghost (the spirit of Jesus) descended on His followers. Celebrates the power of the Holy Spirit and its manifestation in the early Christian church. There is no traditional greeting for this holiday.

4 · LIFE CYCLE EVENTS

Birth Ceremony

Smaller, more conservative denominations (such as the Beachy Amish Mennonite) do not have a formal celebration for the birth of a child. Some larger Mennonite denominations, such as the General Conference of Mennonite Brethren, have a "child consecration," which is held when a child is an infant or a toddler.

During the consecration, which is part of a regular Sunday worship service, the pastor blesses the child and his or her parents, and congregants respond to an oral invitation to help raise the child in a Christian environment. The ceremony itself lasts only two or three minutes.

BEFORE THE CEREMONY

Are guests usually invited by a formal invitation? No. The consecration is usually announced at the previous Sunday's worship service.

If not stated explicitly, should one assume that children are invited? Yes.

If one can't attend, what should one do? Verbally give your best wishes to the new parents.

APPROPRIATE ATTIRE

Men: Expected attire varies. Generally in those denominations that have a child consecration, casual attire is acceptable, but those attending the church for the first time are advised to wear a jacket and tie. No head covering is required regardless of a specific denomination's degree of conservatism.

Women: Expected attire varies. Generally in those denominations that have a child consecration, women may wear a dress, a skirt and blouse or a pants suit or more casual attire, although those attending the church for the first time are advised to dress conservatively. Clothing need not cover the arms nor hems reach below the knees. Open-toed shoes and modest jewelry are permissible. No head covering is required.

Generally in those denominations that have a child consecration, there are no rules regarding colors of clothing.

GIFTS

Is a gift customarily expected? No.

THE CEREMONY

Where will the ceremony take place? In the church's sanctuary.

When should guests arrive and where should they sit? Arrive shortly before the time for which the service has been called. Ushers will usually advise congregants and guests where to sit.

If arriving late, are there times when a guest should *not* enter the ceremony? Do not enter during the invocation. It may be best for tardy congregants and guests to enter while a hymn is being sung.

Are there times when a guest should *not* leave the ceremony? No.

Who are the major officiants, leaders or participants at the ceremony and what do they do?
The pastor, who blesses the child and parents, and asks congregants to help raise the child in a Christian environment.
The child, parents and occasionally siblings.

What books are used? In each denomination, various translations of the Bible are used.

Various hymnals are also used throughout the denominations. The Mennonite Church USA, Mennonite Church Canada, and the Church of the Brethren use *Hymnal: A Worship Book* (Newton, Kans.: Faith and Life Press, 1992). The Mennonite Brethren Church uses *Worship Together* (Fresno, Calif.: Board of Faith and Life, General Conference of Mennonite Brethren Churches, 1995).

A church bulletin may also be used that includes prayers, responses or hymns.

To indicate the order of the ceremony: Ushers will distribute a program.

Will a guest who is neither Mennonite nor Amish be expected to do anything other than sit? In all but the most conservative churches, a visitor would rarely do wrong by remaining seated when congregants stand or kneel, although the latter is rare in most congregations. However, if it does not violate their religious beliefs, the guest would be more in place by standing when others stand. Also, it is optional for guests to sing and read prayers aloud with the congregants.

Are there any parts of the ceremony in which a guest who is neither Mennonite nor Amish should *not* participate? Communion is not offered to guests who are not Christian.

If not disruptive to the ceremony, is it okay to:

Take pictures? Not in more conservative denominations, such as the Beachy Amish Mennonite. Possibly (but only with prior permission of the pastor) in less conservative denominations, such as the General Conference of Mennonite Brethren.

Use a flash? No.

Use a video camera? Not in more conservative denominations, such as the Beachy Amish Mennonite. Possibly (but only with prior permission of the pastor) in less conservative denominations, such as the General Conference of Mennonite Brethren.

Use a tape recorder? Possibly (but only with prior permission of the pastor) in all Mennonite churches.

Will contributions to the church be collected at the ceremony? There will be no collection at the child consecration itself, but there will be one during the worship service which includes the consecration in the churches of most Mennonite denominations, but not in those of the General Conference of Mennonite Brethren.

How much is it customary to contribute? Guests are not expected to contribute, but should they choose to do so, $1 to $10 is appropriate.

AFTER THE CEREMONY

Is there usually a reception after the ceremony? No.

Is there a traditional greeting for the family? "Congratulations."

Is there a traditional form of address for clergy whom a guest may meet? "Pastor."

Initiation Ceremony

In most denominations, a baptism is held for males and females who are in their early adolescence. In the General Conference of Mennonite Brethren, baptism may occur anytime from the onset of early adolescence into adulthood.

During the ceremony, candidates express their commitment to Christ, and kneel while a pastor sprinkles or pours water on their heads. Candidates may be baptized either individually or, if an adolescent, with their Sunday School classmates. The baptism may be either a service in itself or part of a Sunday worship service. The baptism may last 15 to 30 minutes.

BEFORE THE CEREMONY

Are guests usually invited by a formal invitation? No. The baptismal candidate and/or his or her family may verbally invite friends and extended family.

If not stated explicitly, should one assume that children are invited? Yes.

If one can't attend, what should one do? Verbally RSVP with best wishes.

APPROPRIATE ATTIRE

Men: Expected attire varies with the denomination and with the setting of the baptism. If the baptism is performed outdoors, wear casual clothing (although jeans and T-shirts are frowned upon).

If the baptism is performed indoors by a more conservative denomination (such as the Beachy Amish Mennonite), a suit jacket is worn, but not a tie. If it is performed indoors as part of worship by other denominations (such as the General Conference of Mennonite Brethren), casual attire appropriate for worship is acceptable, but those attending the church for the first time are advised to dress conservatively in a jacket and tie.

In no denomination is a head covering required.

Women: Expected attire varies. If the baptism is performed outdoors, wear casual clothing (although jeans and T-shirts are frowned upon).

If the baptism is performed indoors by a more conservative denomination (such as the Beachy Amish Mennonite), women are expected to wear dresses that cover their arms and have hems that reach below their knees. Neither open-toed shoes nor modest jewelry are permissible. Church members cover their heads, but visitors are not expected to do so.

If the baptism is performed indoors as part of worship by other denominations (such as the General Conference of Mennonite Brethren), women may wear a dress, a skirt and blouse or a pants suit or more casual attire, although those attending the church for their first time are advised to dress conservatively. Clothing need not cover their arms nor hems reach below the knees. Open-toed shoes and modest jewelry are permissible. No head covering is required.

Dark, solid colors are advised for more conservative denominations, such as the Beachy Amish Mennonite. For less conservative denominations, there are no rules regarding colors of clothing.

GIFTS

Is a gift customarily expected? No.

THE CEREMONY

Where will the ceremony take place? Either outdoors or in the church's sanctuary.

When should guests arrive and where should they sit? Arrive shortly before the time for which the worship or baptism service has been called. If the baptism is being held indoors, ushers will usually advise congregants and guests where to sit.

If arriving late, are there times when a guest should *not* enter the ceremony? Do not enter while Scriptures are being read, prayers are being recited or during the invocation to worship. It may be best for tardy congregants and guests to enter while a hymn is being sung.

Are there times when a guest should *not* leave the ceremony? No.

Who are the major officiants, leaders or participants at the ceremony and what do they do?
The pastor, who baptizes the candidate.
The candidate.

What books are used? In each denomination, various translations of the Bible are used.

Various hymnals are also used throughout the denominations. The Mennonite Church USA, Mennonite Church Canada, and the Church of the Brethren use *Hymnal: A Worship Book* (Newton, Kans.: Faith and Life Press, 1992). The Mennonite Brethren Church uses *Worship Together* (Fresno, Calif.: Board of Faith and Life, General Conference of Mennonite Brethren Churches, 1995).

To indicate the order of the ceremony: A program will be distributed.

Will a guest who is neither Mennonite nor Amish be expected to do anything other than sit? In all but the most conservative churches, a visitor would rarely do wrong by remaining seated when congregants stand or kneel, although the latter is rare in most congregations. However, if it does not violate their religious beliefs, the guest would be more in place by standing when others stand. Also, it is optional for guests to sing and read prayers aloud with the congregants.

Are there any parts of the ceremony in which a guest who is neither Mennonite nor Amish should *not* participate? No.

If not disruptive to the ceremony, is it okay to:
Take pictures? Possibly, but only with prior permission of the pastor.
Use a flash? Possibly, but only with prior permission of the pastor.
Use a video camera? Possibly, but only with prior permission of the pastor.
Use a tape recorder? Possibly, but only with prior permission of the pastor.

Will contributions to the church be collected at the ceremony? There will be no collection at the baptism itself, but there will be one if it is part of a Sunday worship service in the churches of most Mennonite denominations, but not in those of the General Conference of Mennonite Brethren.

How much is it customary to contribute? Guests are not expected to contribute, but should they choose to do so, $1 to $10 is appropriate.

AFTER THE CEREMONY

Is there usually a reception after the ceremony? Yes, although no food is served. It is usually held in the same building or the same outdoor site as the baptismal ceremony. If held indoors, those who have just been baptized gather at the back of the sanctuary to be greeted by well-wishers. The reception may last about 30 minutes.

Is there a traditional greeting for the family? No. Just offer your congratulations.

Is there a traditional form of address for clergy whom a guest may meet? "Pastor."

Is it okay to leave early? Yes.

Marriage Ceremony

Mennonites and Amish believe that marriage was instituted by God for companionship, procreation and the nurturing of children. Those who marry should share a common Christian commitment. Divorce constitutes a basic violation of God's will.

A Mennonite or Amish wedding is an act of worship in which the couple profess their love for and their commitment to each other before God and ask his blessing on their wedding. The same decorum exercised in any worship service should be exercised in the wedding service.

During the ceremony, the wedding party progresses in, then the pastor reads appropriate lessons from the Bible and asks the bride and groom about their commitment to one another. The pastor delivers a brief homily, wedding vows and rings are exchanged, and the couple are pronounced man and wife.

The wedding is often a ceremony unto itself but may be part of a broader worship service. It usually lasts about 30 to 60 minutes, although some may last more than one hour.

BEFORE THE CEREMONY

Are guests usually invited by a formal invitation? Yes.

If not stated explicitly, should one assume that children are invited? No.

If one can't attend, what should one do? RSVP with regrets and send a gift. (Note: Gifts are not expected at weddings of the General Conference of Mennonite Brethren.)

APPROPRIATE ATTIRE

Men: In more conservative denominations, such as the Beachy Amish Mennonite, a suit jacket coat is worn, but without a tie. In other denominations, such as the General Conference of Mennonite Brethren, a jacket and tie are worn. No head covering is required.

Women: In more conservative denominations, such as the Beachy Amish Mennonite, women are expected to wear dresses that cover their arms and have hems that reach below their knees. Neither open-toed shoes nor modest jewelry are permissible. Church members cover their heads, but visitors are not expected to do so.

In less conservative denominations, such as the General Conference of Mennonite Brethren, women may wear a dress or a skirt and blouse. Clothing need not cover women's arms nor hems reach below the knees. Open-toed shoes and modest jewelry are permissible. No head covering is required.

Dark, solid colors are advised for more conservative denominations, such as the Beachy Amish Mennonite. For less conservative denominations, there are no rules regarding colors of clothing.

GIFTS

Is a gift customarily expected? Gifts are not expected at weddings in the General Conference of Mennonite Brethren. They are generally expected at weddings of other Mennonite denominations. Items for setting up a household are appropriate.

Should gifts be brought to the ceremony? Yes.

THE CEREMONY

Where will the ceremony take place? In the main sanctuary of the church.

When should guests arrive and where should they sit? Arrive shortly before the time for which the ceremony has been called. Ushers will advise guests where to sit.

If arriving late, are there times when a guest should *not* enter the ceremony? Do not enter during the procession of the wedding party or while prayers are being recited.

Are there times when a guest should *not* leave the ceremony? No.

Who are the major officiants, leaders or participants at the ceremony and what do they do?
The bishop or pastor, depending on the denomination, who performs the wedding ceremony.
The bride and groom and their parents.
Musicians and/or song leaders.

What books are used? In each denomination, various translations of the Bible are used.

Various hymnals are also used throughout the denominations. The Mennonite Church USA, Mennonite Church Canada, and the Church of the Brethren use *Hymnal: A Worship Book* (Newton, Kans.: Faith and Life Press, 1992). The Mennonite Brethren Church uses *Worship Together* (Fresno, Calif.: Board of Faith and Life, General Conference of Mennonite Brethren Churches, 1995).

To indicate the order of the ceremony: A program will be distributed.

Will a guest who is neither Mennonite nor Amish be expected to do anything other than sit? Guests are expected to stand with congregants when they arise. If it does not violate their religious beliefs, it is optional for them to sing and read prayers aloud with the congregants.

Are there any parts of the ceremony in which a guest who is neither Mennonite nor Amish should *not* participate? If the wedding is part of a broader worship service at which Communion is offered, it is not given to guests who are not Christian.

If not disruptive to the ceremony, is it okay to:

Take pictures? Not allowed in most denominations. Possibly (but only with prior permission of the pastor) in the General Conference of Mennonite Brethren.

Use a flash? Not allowed in most denominations. Possibly (but only with prior permission of the pastor) in the General Conference of Mennonite Brethren.

Use a video camera? Not allowed in most denominations. Possibly (but only with prior permission of the pastor) in the General Conference of Mennonite Brethren.

Use a tape recorder? Not allowed in most denominations. Possibly (but only with prior permission of the pastor) in the General Conference of Mennonite Brethren.

Will contributions to the church be collected at the ceremony? No.

AFTER THE CEREMONY

Is there usually a reception after the ceremony? Yes. This is usually held in the same building as the wedding ceremony. Refreshments may range from sandwiches, nuts and beverages to a full meal. Almost always, cake and ice cream are served. There will be no alcoholic beverages. There will be no dancing, although musicians may play background music after weddings of some less conservative denominations. The reception may last from 30 minutes to more than two hours.

Would it be considered impolite to neither eat nor drink? No.

Is there a grace or benediction before eating or drinking? Possibly.

Is there a grace or benediction after eating or drinking? No.

Is there a traditional greeting for the family? "Congratulations" or "Best wishes."

Is there a traditional form of address for clergy who may be at the reception? "Pastor."

Is it okay to leave early? Yes.

Funerals and Mourning

Mennonites and Amish regard death as part of God's plan. Those who die as believers will share in the resurrection and be with Christ forever. The righteous will inherit the Kingdom of God; the unrighteous shall suffer the anguish of eternal hell. At the resurrection, Christ will create a new heaven and a new earth in which righteousness will reign.

A funeral or memorial service in a Mennonite or Amish church celebrates the life of the deceased and their passing into eternal spiritual life after death.

The funeral service may last between 30 and 90 minutes.

BEFORE THE CEREMONY

How soon after the death does the funeral usually take place? Two to three days.

What should a non-Mennonite or non-Amish do upon hearing of the death of a member of that faith? In most denominations, one may telephone or visit the bereaved or send them a card or letter to express condolences and concern for the family. Depending on one's relationship with the bereaved, one may also personally visit them.

APPROPRIATE ATTIRE

Men: In more conservative denominations, such as the Beachy Amish Mennonite, a suit jacket is worn, but without a tie. In other denominations, such as the General Conference of Mennonite Brethren, a suit or a jacket and tie are worn.

No Mennonite denomination requires a head covering.

Women: In more conservative denominations, such as the Beachy Amish Mennonite, women are expected to wear dresses that cover their arms and have hems that reach below their knees. Neither open-toed shoes nor modest jewelry are permissible. Church members cover their heads, but visitors are not expected to do so.

In less conservative denominations, such as the General Conference of Mennonite Brethren, women may wear a dress or a skirt and blouse. Clothing need not cover women's arms nor hems reach below the knees. Open-toed shoes and modest jewelry are permissible. No head covering is required.

Dark, somber, solid colors are advised for all denominations.

GIFTS

Is it appropriate to send flowers or make a contribution? Do not send flowers to bereaved who belong to more conservative denominations, such as the Beachy Amish Mennonite Church. For funerals in other Mennonite denominations, flowers are appropriate. These may be sent to the home of the bereaved upon hearing of the death or to the church where the funeral will be held. Contributions may be made in memory of the deceased to a cause designated by the bereaved family.

Is it appropriate to send food? Food may be sent to the home of the bereaved upon hearing of the death or after the funeral. It is recommended to send prepared foods that can be refrigerated until needed.

THE CEREMONY

Where will the ceremony take place? Usually in the main sanctuary of the church; sometimes in a funeral home.

When should guests arrive and where should they sit? Arrive shortly before the time for which the funeral has been called. Ushers will advise guests where to sit.

If arriving late, are there times when a guest should *not* enter the ceremony? Do not enter while prayers are being recited.

Will the bereaved family be present at the church or funeral home before the ceremony? No.

Is there a traditional greeting for the family? Express your concern by using such phrases as "My condolences to you" or "I want to express my sympathy to you."

Will there be an open casket? Often in some Mennonite or Amish denominations. Rarely in the General Conference of Mennonite Brethren.

Is a guest expected to view the body? Usually.

What is appropriate behavior upon viewing the body? Pause in front of the casket or walk slowly past it, then sit in the sanctuary where the funeral will be held.

Who are the major officiants at the ceremony and what do they do?
The pastor, who presides.
The song leader and/or musicians, who lead or provide music.

What books are used? Various translations of the Bible are used.

In each denomination, various hymnals are used. The Mennonite Church USA, Mennonite Church Canada, and the Church of the Brethren use *Hymnal: A Worship Book* (Newton, Kans.: Faith and Life Press, 1992). The Mennonite Brethren Church uses *Worship Together* (Fresno, Calif.: Board of Faith and Life, General Conference of Mennonite Brethren Churches, 1995).

To indicate the order of the ceremony: A program may be provided. If not, periodic announcements will be made by the pastor.

Will a guest who is neither Mennonite nor Amish be expected to do anything other than sit? Guests who do not belong to these Churches are expected to stand with congregants when they arise. If it does not violate their religious beliefs, it is optional for them to sing and read prayers aloud with the congregants.

Are there any parts of the ceremony in which a guest who is neither Mennonite nor Amish should *not* participate? No.

If not disruptive to the ceremony, is it okay to:
Take pictures? No.
Use a flash? No.
Use a video camera? No.
Use a tape recorder? No.

Will contributions to the church be collected at the ceremony? No.

THE INTERMENT

Should guests attend the interment? This is entirely optional. Often, the interment is intended only for family and close friends, and sometimes only for family.

Whom should one ask for directions? An usher.

What happens at the graveside? The pastor recites some opening words and a brief sermon, Scripture is read, and the casket is lowered into the ground and covered.

Do guests who are neither Mennonite nor Amish participate at the graveside ceremony? No, they are simply present.

COMFORTING THE BEREAVED

Is it appropriate to visit the home of the bereaved after the funeral? Yes, for anywhere from five to 20 minutes. It is appropriate to inquire about how the family is doing during this time of grief. Unless one is a close friend or a family member, it is advised to avoid asking for details about the illness and the death of the deceased.

Will there be a religious service at the home of the bereaved? No.

Will food be served? Possibly, but no alcoholic beverages.

How soon after the funeral will a mourner usually return to a normal work schedule? The Church has no set ritual, but it is common for bereaved to be absent from work for a few days to a whole week after the funeral.

How soon after the funeral will a mourner usually return to a normal social schedule? The Church has no set ritual, but it is common for bereaved to abstain from socializing from a few days to a whole week after the funeral.

Are there mourning customs to which a friend who is neither Mennonite nor Amish should be sensitive? No.

Are there rituals for observing the anniversary of the death? Cards remembering the deceased are appreciated upon the one-year anniversary of the death.

5 · HOME CELEBRATIONS

Not applicable to Mennonites or Amish.

16

Methodist

1. HISTORY AND BELIEFS

The Methodist movement began in 18th-century England under the preaching of John Wesley, an Anglican priest who was a prodigious evangelical preacher, writer and organizer. While a student at Oxford University, he and his brother, Charles, led the Holy Club of devout students, whom scoffers called the "Methodists."

Wesley's teachings affirmed the freedom of human will as promoted by grace. He saw each person's depth of sin matched by the height of sanctification to which the Holy Spirit, the empowering spirit of God, can lead persons of faith.

Although Wesley remained an Anglican and disavowed attempts to form a new church, Methodism eventually became another church body. During a conference in Baltimore, Maryland, in 1784, the Methodist Church was founded as an ecclesiastical organization and the first Methodist bishop in the United States was elected.

The Methodist movement was first represented in Canada by Laurence Coughlan, who began to preach in Newfoundland in 1766. It wasn't until 1884, however, that the Methodist Church was formed in Canada, from the merger of the Methodist Episcopal Church and smaller Methodist bodies with the Wesleyan Methodist Church, the Conference of Eastern British America and the New Connexion Church, which had united in 1874. The Free Methodists, entering from the United States in 1876, were few in number and have remained separate.

In the 19th century, strong missionary programs helped plant Methodism abroad. Methodist missionaries from America followed their British colleagues to India and Africa, where they founded new churches. Americans and Canadians also founded churches in East Asia, Latin America and continental Europe.

Local Methodist churches are called "charges." Their ministers are appointed by the bishop at an annual conference, and each church elects its own administrative board, which initiates planning and sets local goals and policies.

There are about 125 Methodist denominations around the globe and 14 separate Methodist bodies in the United States. Of these, the United Methodist Church is numerically the largest.

In Canada, the Methodist Church ceased to exist as a separate denomination in 1925, when it joined with Congregationalists and the majority of Presbyterian churches to form the United Church of Canada. The Free Methodist Church in Canada, which was incorporated in 1927 and which gained full autonomy from the U.S. parent denomination in 1990, remains intact.

U.S. churches: 34,136
U.S. membership: 7.9 million
(data from the 2010 Yearbook of American and Canadian Churches)

For more information, contact:
The United Methodist Church
InfoServ, United Methodist
  Information Service
PO Box 320
Nashville, TN 37202-0320
infoserv@umcom.org
www.umc.org

Canadian churches: 149
Canadian membership: 7,603
(data from the 2010 Yearbook of American and Canadian Churches)

For more information, contact:
Free Methodist Church in Canada
4315 Village Centre Court
Mississauga, ON L4Z 1S2
(905) 848-2600
www.fmc-canada.org

2 · THE BASIC SERVICE

To Methodists, worship is a congregation's encounter and communion with God and with one another in God's name. It includes praise and prayer, Scripture read-ings, a sermon and sometimes Holy Communion. Most Methodist services last about one hour.

APPROPRIATE ATTIRE

Men: Jacket and tie. No head covering is required.

Women: A dress. The arms do not necessarily have to be covered nor do hems have to be below the knees. Open-toed shoes and modest jewelry are permissible. No head covering is required.

There are no rules regarding colors of clothing.

THE SANCTUARY

What are the major sections of the church?
The platform or chancel: A raised section at the front of the church. This is where the leaders and the choir function.
The nave: Where congregants sit on pews.

THE SERVICE

When should guests arrive and where should they sit? Arrive at the time for which the service has been called. An usher will indicate where to sit. There are usually no restrictions on where to sit.

If arriving late, are there times when a guest should *not* enter the service? Yes. Ushers will seat you when appropriate.

Are there times when a guest should *not* leave the service? No.

Who are the major officiants, leaders or participants and what do they do?

The pastor, who presides, preaches and celebrates Communion.

The associate pastor or the assisting layperson, who aids the senior pastor in leading the service.

The choir or soloists, who sing hymns and psalms.

What are the major ritual objects of the service?

Bread, which is eaten during Holy Communion and signifies the body of Jesus Christ.

Grape juice, which the pastor presents to congregants to drink during Holy Communion and which signifies the blood of Jesus Christ.

What books are used? The United Methodist Hymnal (Nashville, Tenn.: United Methodist Publishing House, 1989); *The Faith We Sing* (2000), a supplement to the *Hymnal*; and a Bible. United Methodists have no official Bible translation, although the New Revised Standard Version (which is printed by several publishers) is the most commonly used translation.

To indicate the order of the service: A program will be provided and periodic announcements will be made by the pastor or another leader.

GUEST BEHAVIOR DURING THE SERVICE

Will a guest who is not a Methodist be expected to do anything other than sit? Standing and kneeling with the congregation and reading prayers aloud and singing with congregants are all optional. Guests are welcome to participate if this does not compromise their personal beliefs.

Are there any parts of the service in which a guest who is not a Methodist should *not* participate?
Yes. Methodists invite all to receive Holy Communion, but guests should be aware that partaking of Communion is regarded as an act of identification with Christianity. Feel free to remain seated as others go forward for Communion. Likewise, if Communion bread and cups are passed among the pews, feel free to pass them along without partaking.

If not disruptive to the service, is it okay to:

Take pictures? Possibly. Ask ushers.

Use a flash? Possibly. Ask ushers.

Use a video camera? Possibly. Ask ushers.

Use a tape recorder? Possibly. Ask ushers.

Will contributions to the church be collected at the service? Yes. The offering plate will be passed through the congregation during the service. This usually occurs immediately before or after the sermon.

How much is it customary to contribute? The customary offering is from $1 to $10.

AFTER THE SERVICE

Is there usually a reception after the service? Yes, in the church's reception area. It usually lasts less than 30 minutes, and pastry, coffee and tea are ordinarily served.

It is not considered impolite to neither eat nor drink. There is no grace or benediction before or after eating or drinking.

Is there a traditional form of address for clergy who may be at the reception? "Reverend" or "Pastor."

Is it okay to leave early? Yes.

GENERAL GUIDELINES AND ADVICE

The chief potential for mistake occurs during Holy Communion. Feel free not to partake if you cannot in good conscience do so. But Christian guests should also be aware that the Methodist Church never refuses Communion to anyone.

The cups at Holy Communion always contain grape juice, not wine. Children, as well as adults, are welcome to partake.

SPECIAL VOCABULARY

None provided.

DOGMA AND IDEOLOGY

Methodists believe:

The doctrine of the Trinity: God is the Father, the Son (embodied by Jesus Christ), and the Holy Spirit (the empowering spirit of God).

In the natural sinfulness of humanity.

In humanity's fall from grace and the need for individual repentance.

In freedom of will.

In practice, Methodists are highly diverse in their beliefs and tend to emphasize right living more than orthodoxy of belief.

A basic book to which a guest can refer to learn more about the Methodist Church: *Worshiping with United Methodists* by Hoyt L. Hickman (Nashville, Tenn.: Abingdon Press, 2007).

3 · HOLY DAYS AND FESTIVALS

Advent. Begins four weeks before Christmas. The purpose is to prepare for Christmas and to focus on Christ. There is no traditional greeting for Advent.

Christmas. Occurs on the evening of December 24 and the day of December 25. Marks the birth and the incarnation of God as a man. The traditional greeting is "Merry Christmas."

Lent. Begins on Ash Wednesday, which occurs six weeks before Easter. The purpose is to prepare for Easter. Between Lent and Easter, fasting and abstention from entertainment are encouraged, as is increased giving to the poor. Often, there are midweek worship services. There are no traditional greetings for this holiday.

Easter. Always falls on the Sunday after the first full moon that occurs on or after March 21. Celebrates the Resurrection of Jesus Christ. The traditional greeting to Methodists is "Happy Easter."

Pentecost Sunday. The seventh Sunday after Easter. Celebrates the coming of the Holy Spirit, which is the empowering spirit of God in human life. This is often considered the birth of the Christian church. There are no traditional greetings for this holiday.

4 · LIFE CYCLE EVENTS

Birth Ceremony

Baptism initiates an infant into Christianity. It is administered once to each person, usually during infancy. The major ritual object used during the ceremony is a baptismal font, which holds the baptismal water. The pastor sprinkles or pours water on the person's head or immerses the person in water. This signifies the washing away of sins. God is invoked to strengthen this new Christian, and the congregation, as well as the parents and godparents, pledge to nurture him or her in the Christian faith and life.

Baptism is part of the larger weekly congregational Sunday morning service, which usually lasts about an hour.

BEFORE THE CEREMONY

Are guests usually invited by a formal invitation? Yes.

If not stated explicitly, should one assume that children are invited? Yes.

If one can't attend, what should one do? Any one of these is appropriate: Send flowers or a gift or telephone the parents with your congratulations and your regrets that you can't attend.

APPROPRIATE ATTIRE

Men: Jacket and tie. No head covering is required.

Women: A dress. The arms do not necessarily have to be covered nor do hems have to be below the knees. Open-toed shoes and modest jewelry are permissible. No head covering is required.

There are no rules regarding colors of clothing.

GIFTS

Is a gift customarily expected? No, but it is appropriate. Gifts such as savings bonds or baby clothes or toys are commonly given.

Should gifts be brought to the ceremony? Usually gifts can be brought to the reception.

THE CEREMONY

Where will the ceremony take place? In the parents' church.

When should guests arrive and where should they sit? Arrive at the time for which the service has been called. Ushers will indicate where to sit. There are usually no restrictions on where to sit.

If arriving late, are there times when a guest should *not* enter the ceremony? Yes. Ushers will seat you when appropriate.

Are there times when a guest should *not* leave the ceremony? No.

Who are the major officiants, leaders or participants in the ceremony and what do they do?
The pastor, who will baptize the child.

What books are used? *The United Methodist Hymnal* (Nashville, Tenn.: United Methodist Publishing House, 1989); *The Faith We Sing* (2000), a supplement to the *Hymnal*; and a Bible. United Methodists have no official Bible translation, although the New Revised Standard Version (which is printed by several publishers) is the most commonly used translation.

To indicate the order of the ceremony: A program will be provided and periodic announcements will be made by the pastor or his or her assistant.

Will a guest who is not a Methodist be expected to do anything other than sit? Standing and kneeling with the congregation and reading prayers aloud and singing with congregants are all optional. Guests are welcome to participate if this does not compromise their personal beliefs.

Are there any parts of the ceremony in which a guest who is not a Methodist should *not* participate? Yes. Methodists invite all to receive Holy Communion, but guests should be aware that partaking of Communion is regarded as an act of identification with Christianity. Feel free to remain seated as others go forward for Communion. Likewise, if Communion bread and cups are passed among the pews, feel free to pass them along without partaking. Christian guests should be aware that the Methodist Church never refuses Communion to anyone. The cups at Holy Communion always contain grape juice, not wine. Children, as well as adults, are welcome to partake.

If not disruptive to the ceremony, is it okay to:
Take pictures? Possibly. Ask ushers.
Use a flash? Possibly. Ask ushers.
Use a video camera? Possibly. Ask ushers.
Use a tape recorder? Possibly. Ask ushers.

Will contributions to the church be collected at the ceremony? Yes. The offering plate will be passed through the congregation during the service. This usually occurs immediately before or after the sermon.

How much is it customary to contribute? The customary offering is from $1 to $10.

AFTER THE CEREMONY

Is there usually a reception after the ceremony? There is often a reception lasting about 30 minutes in the church's reception area. Pastry, coffee and tea are ordinarily served.

Would it be considered impolite to neither eat nor drink? No.

Is there a grace or benediction before eating or drinking? No.

Is there a grace or benediction after eating or drinking? No.

Is there a traditional greeting for the family? No. Just offer your congratulations.

Is there a traditional form of address for clergy who may be at the reception? "Reverend" or "Pastor."

Is it okay to leave early? Yes.

Initiation Ceremony

Confirmation is conferred on an early adolescent. It is a Methodist's first profession of faith. The candidates affirm for themselves the Christian faith and church into which they were baptized (usually as infants).

Teens participate in the ceremony with members of their confirmation class. The 15-minute ceremony is part of a larger Sunday morning service, which lasts about an hour.

BEFORE THE CEREMONY

Are guests usually invited by a formal invitation? No.

If not stated explicitly, should one assume that children are invited? Yes.

If one can't attend, what should one do? Either of these is appropriate: Send flowers or a gift or telephone the parents with your congratulations and your regrets that you can't attend.

APPROPRIATE ATTIRE

Men: Jacket and tie. No head covering is required.

Women: A dress. The arms do not necessarily have to be covered nor do hems have to be below the knees. Open-toed shoes and modest jewelry are permissible. No head covering is required.

There are no rules regarding colors of clothing.

GIFTS

Is a gift customarily expected? No.

THE CEREMONY

Where will the ceremony take place? Usually at the front of the main sanctuary of the church.

When should guests arrive and where should they sit? Arrive at the time for which the service has been called. An usher will indicate where to sit. There are usually no restrictions on where to sit.

If arriving late, are there times when a guest should *not* enter the ceremony? Yes. Ushers will seat you when appropriate.

Are there times when a guest should *not* leave the ceremony? No.

Who are the major officiants, leaders or participants at the ceremony and what do they do? *The pastor*, who confirms the teen.

What books are used? *The United Methodist Hymnal* (Nashville, Tenn.: United Methodist Publishing House, 1989); *The Faith We Sing* (2000), a supplement to the *Hymnal*; and a Bible. United Methodists have no official Bible translation, although the New Revised Standard Version (which is printed by several publishers) is the most commonly used translation.

To indicate the order of the ceremony: A program will be provided, and periodic announcements will be made by the pastor or his assistant.

Will a guest who is not a Methodist be expected to do anything other than sit? Standing and kneeling with the congregation and reading prayers aloud and singing with congregants are all optional. Guests are welcome to participate if this does not compromise their personal beliefs.

Are there any parts of the ceremony in which a guest who is not a Methodist should *not* participate? Yes. Methodists invite all to receive Holy Communion, but guests should be aware that partaking of Communion is regarded as an act of identification with Christianity. Feel free to remain seated as others go forward for Communion. Likewise, if Communion bread and cups are passed among the pews, feel free to pass them along without partaking. Christian guests should be aware that the Methodist Church never refuses Communion to anyone. The cups at Holy Communion always contain grape juice, not wine. Children, as well as adults, are welcome to partake.

If not disruptive to the ceremony, is it okay to:
Take pictures? Possibly. Ask ushers.
Use a flash? Possibly. Ask ushers.
Use a video camera? Possibly. Ask ushers.
Use a tape recorder? Possibly. Ask ushers.

Will contributions to the church be collected at the ceremony? Yes. The offering plate will be passed through the congregation during the service. This usually occurs immediately before or after the sermon.

How much is it customary to contribute? The customary offering is from $1 to $10.

AFTER THE CEREMONY

Is there usually a reception after the ceremony? There is often a reception lasting about 30 minutes in the church's reception area. Pastry, coffee and tea are ordinarily served.

Would it be considered impolite to neither eat nor drink? No.

Is there a grace or benediction before eating or drinking? No.

Is there a grace or benediction after eating or drinking? No.

Is there a traditional greeting for the family? No. Just offer your congratulations.

Is there a traditional form of address for clergy who may be at the reception? "Reverend" or "Pastor."

Is it okay to leave early? Yes.

Marriage Ceremony

Marriage is the uniting of a man and a woman in a union that is intended—and that is pledged—to be lifelong. The marriage ceremony is a service in itself. It may last between 15 and 30 minutes.

BEFORE THE CEREMONY

Are guests usually invited by a formal invitation? Yes.

If not stated explicitly, should one assume that children are invited? No.

If one can't attend, what should one do? RSVP with your regrets and send a gift.

APPROPRIATE ATTIRE

Men: Jacket and tie. No head covering is required.

Women: A dress. The arms do not necessarily have to be covered nor do hems have to be below the knees. Open-toed shoes and modest jewelry are permissible. No head covering is required.

There are no rules regarding colors of clothing.

GIFTS

Is a gift ordinarily expected? Yes. Such gifts as small appliances, sheets, towels or other household gifts are appropriate.

Should gifts be brought to the ceremony? No, send them to the home of the newlyweds.

THE CEREMONY

Where will the ceremony take place? Usually in the main sanctuary of a church.

When should guests arrive and where should they sit? Arrive early. Depending on the setting, ushers may show guests where to sit.

If arriving late, are there times when a guest should *not* enter the ceremony? Ushers will assist latecomers.

Are there times when a guest should *not* leave the ceremony? No.

Who are the major officiants, leaders or participants at the ceremony and what do they do?
The pastor, who officiates.
The bride and groom.
The wedding party.

What books are used? Possibly a hymnal.

To indicate the order of the ceremony: A program will be provided.

Will a guest who is not a Methodist be expected to do anything other than sit? Standing and kneeling with the congregation and reading prayers aloud and singing with congregants are all optional. Guests are welcome to participate if this does not compromise their personal beliefs.

Are there any parts of the ceremony in which a guest who is not a Methodist should *not* participate? Yes. Holy Communion may be offered at the service. Methodists invite all to receive Holy Communion, but guests should be aware that partaking of Communion is regarded as an act of identification with Christianity. Feel free to remain seated as others go forward for Communion. Likewise, if Communion bread and cups are passed among the pews, feel free to pass them along without partaking.

If not disruptive to the ceremony, is it okay to:
Take pictures? Possibly. Ask ushers.
Use a flash? Possibly. Ask ushers.
Use a video camera? Possibly. Ask ushers.
Use a tape recorder? Possibly. Ask ushers.

Will contributions to the church be collected at the ceremony? No.

AFTER THE CEREMONY

Is there usually a reception after the ceremony? There is often a reception that may last one to two hours. It may be at a home, a catering facility or in the same building as the ceremony. Ordinarily, food and beverages are served and there is dancing and music. Alcoholic beverages may be served.

Would it be considered impolite to neither eat nor drink? No.

Is there a grace or benediction before eating or drinking? No.

Is there a grace or benediction after eating or drinking? No.

Is there a traditional greeting for the family? No. Just offer your congratulations.

Is there a traditional form of address for clergy who may be at the reception? "Reverend" or "Pastor."

Is it okay to leave early? Yes, but usually only after toasts have been made and the wedding cake has been served.

Funerals and Mourning

The United Methodist Church affirms that life is eternal and that, in faith, one can look forward to life with God after death.

United Methodists have diverse beliefs about afterlife and are generally content to look forward to it as a glorious mystery. Funerals have as their purposes: (1) expressing grief and comforting one another in our bereavement, (2) celebrating the life of the deceased, and (3) affirming faith in life with God after death. Which of these is most emphasized at the funeral depends on the circumstances of the death and the extent of the faith of the deceased.

BEFORE THE CEREMONY

How soon after the death will the funeral usually take place? Usually within two to three days.

What should a non-Methodist do upon hearing of the death of a member of that faith? Telephone or visit the bereaved.

APPROPRIATE ATTIRE

Men: Jacket and tie. No head covering is required.

Women: A dress. Open-toed shoes and modest jewelry are permissible. No head covering is required.

There are no rules regarding colors of clothing, but somber, dark colors are recommended for men and women.

GIFTS

Is it appropriate to send flowers or make a contribution? Yes. Send flowers to the home of the bereaved. Contributions are also optional. The recommended charity may be mentioned in the deceased's obituary.

Is it appropriate to send food? Yes. Send it to the home of the bereaved.

THE CEREMONY

Where will the ceremony take place? At a church or funeral home.

When should guests arrive and where should they sit? Arrive early. Ushers will advise where to sit.

If arriving late, are there times when a guest should *not* enter the ceremony? No.

Will the bereaved family be present at the church or funeral home before the ceremony? Possibly.

Is there a traditional greeting for the family? Simply express your condolences.

Will there be an open casket? Usually.

Is a guest expected to view the body? This is entirely optional.

What is appropriate behavior upon viewing the body? Silent prayer.

Who are the major officiants at the ceremony and what do they do? *A pastor*, who officiates.

To indicate the order of the ceremony: A program will be provided.

Will a guest who is not a Methodist be expected to do anything other than sit? No.

Are there any parts of the service in which a guest who is not a Methodist should *not* participate? No.

If not disruptive to the ceremony, is it okay to:
Take pictures? No.

Use a flash? No.
Use a video camera? No.
Use a tape recorder? No.

Will contributions to the church be collected at the ceremony? No.

THE INTERMENT

Should guests attend the interment? Yes.

Whom should one ask for directions? The funeral director.

What happens at the graveside? Prayers are recited by the pastor and the body is committed to the ground. If there has been a cremation, which is done privately before the service, the ashes are either buried or put in a vault. Military or fraternal rites may be part of the graveside service.

Do guests who are not Methodists participate at the graveside ceremony? No. They are simply present.

COMFORTING THE BEREAVED

Is it appropriate to visit the home of the bereaved after the funeral? Yes, at any mutually convenient time. How long one stays depends on your closeness to the bereaved. Typically, one stays about 30 to 45 minutes.

Will there be a religious service at the home of the bereaved? No.

Will food be served? No.

How soon after the funeral will a mourner usually return to a normal work schedule? This is entirely at the discretion of the bereaved.

How soon after the funeral will a mourner usually return to a normal social schedule? This is entirely at the discretion of the bereaved.

Are there mourning customs to which a friend who is not a Methodist should be sensitive? No.

Are there rituals for observing the anniversary of the death? There may be a service commemorating the deceased.

5. HOME CELEBRATIONS

Not applicable to Methodists.

17

Mormon
(Church of Jesus Christ
of Latter-day Saints)

1. HISTORY AND BELIEFS

The Church of Jesus Christ of Latter-day Saints, the largest indigenous American religious group, was founded by Joseph Smith in the early 19th century. Living in upstate New York, Smith had a vision in 1820 in which God and Jesus Christ appeared to him. Three years later, the angel Moroni told him of the location of gold tablets containing God's revelations. In 1830, Smith published a translation of these revelations entitled *The Book of Mormon*. He soon became the "seer, translator, prophet and apostle" of a group committed to restoring the church established centuries before by Christ.

Latter-day Saints stressed the coming of Christ's Kingdom to earth and encouraged others to adhere to the teachings of the Savior.

Smith's group moved first to Ohio, and then to Missouri, where violence ensued prompted by their polygamy and their antislavery stance. Persecution forced the group to move to Illinois, where they built their own city and named it Nauvoo. In 1844, while imprisoned for destroying an opposition printing press, Smith was killed by a mob that attacked the jail.

Schisms erupted amid the subsequent leadership vacuum and concern over polygamy, a practice that Smith had said in 1843 had come to him in a vision and that became Church doctrine in 1852. Most Latter-day Saints followed the leadership of Brigham Young, who led them into the Great Salt Lake area of what is now Utah. Latter-day Saints are headquartered there to this day.

While many Latter-day Saints' beliefs are similar to orthodox Christian ideas, Smith uniquely taught that God, although omniscient, has a material body. He taught that through repentance and baptism by immersion, anyone can gain entrance to Christ's earthly kingdom. Through "proxies" who receive baptism in a Latter-day Saints' temple, the dead may also share in the highest of postmortal rewards or blessings.

The Church teaches that men and women are equal in the eyes of the Lord and that they cannot achieve the highest eternal rewards without each other.

The charge given by Jesus to Matthew, "Go ye unto all the world" to share the teachings of his gospel, motivates the Church's more than 52,000 full-time missionaries around the world. Most are college-age males who serve for two years at their own expense. Their success has led to the Church's currently having more than 28,500 congregations in 160 nations and territories around the world.

In addition to churches, where worship services are conducted, temples are located around the world. These are closed on Sundays, but open every other day of the week for marriages and other sacred ordinances. Only faithful members of the Church may enter a temple.

U.S. churches and temples: 13,363
U.S. membership: 6 million
(data from the 2010 Yearbook of American and Canadian Churches)

For more information, contact:

The Church of Jesus Christ of
    Latter-day Saints
50 E. North Temple Street
Salt Lake City, UT 84150
(801) 240-1000
www.lds.org
www.newsroomlds.org

Canadian churches and temples: 481
Canadian membership: 178,102
(data from the 2010 Yearbook of American and Canadian Churches)

For more information, contact:

The Church of Jesus Christ of
    Latter-day Saints
1185 Eglinton Avenue
Box 116
North York, ON M3C 3C6
(416) 431-7891

2 · THE BASIC SERVICE

The basic service is called a "sacrament meeting." It includes an opening song sung by the congregation; an opening prayer assigned in advance and offered from the pulpit by a lay member of the congregation; a "sacramental song" sung by the congregation; "sacramental prayers" recited by a young (usually 16- to 18-year-old) lay priest on the bread and the water of Communion and upon their distribution among congregants by teenagers on trays and in individual cups; brief talks by one or more youths of the congregation on a subject of their choice related to the Gospels; a sermon, often delivered by a lay member of the congregation; a closing song by the congregation; and a benediction or closing prayer offered by a congregant.

The sacrament represents a reminder of the crucifixion and of the atonement of Jesus for the sins of humanity. It also renews the covenants congregants made when they were baptized into the Church.

The service usually lasts slightly over an hour.

APPROPRIATE ATTIRE

Men: A suit or sport jacket and tie. No head covering required.

Women: A dress or a skirt and blouse. No head covering required, but the overall fashion statement should be conservative and dignified. Hems should be near the knees. Open-toed shoes and modest jewelry are permissible.

Modest and dignified clothing is appreciated.

THE SANCTUARY

What are the major sections of the church?

The chapel: Where the worship service is held.
The choir loft: From which the choir sings.
The pulpit: Where the lay priests officiate.
The pews: Where congregants sit.

THE SERVICE

When should guests arrive and where should they sit? Arrive early and sit where you wish.

If arriving late, are there times when a guest should *not* enter the service? Do not enter during Communion.

Are there times when a guest should *not* leave the service? Do not leave during Communion unless absolutely necessary.

Who are the major officiants, leaders or participants and what do they do?

A bishop, who presides over the service.
Two bishop's counselors, assistants to the bishop. The bishop and his two counselors take weekly turns conducting the worship service.

What are the major ritual objects of the service? The bread and water of the Sacrament (the Communion), which are passed among congregants in trays and individual cups.

What books are used? The King James Version of the Bible and *The Book of Mormon, The Doctrine and Covenants, The Hymns of the Church of Jesus Christ of Latter-day Saints,* and *The Pearl of Great Price* (Salt Lake City, Utah: Church of Jesus Christ of Latter-day Saints). The Bible and other scriptures are used only by those conducting the service, but congregants may refer to their personal copies of the scriptures to follow along, if they wish.

To indicate the order of the service: A program may be distributed.

GUEST BEHAVIOR DURING THE SERVICE

Will a guest who is not a Latter-day Saint be expected to do anything other than sit? Guests of other faiths are invited to sing and pray with the congregation, but they are not expected to do so, especially if participating would violate their own religious beliefs. One of the few times the congregation stands during the service is midway through the service during the singing of the "Rest Hymn." Again, guests are invited to stand, but are not obligated to do so.

Are there any parts of the service in which a guest who is not a Latter-day Saint should *not* participate? No, although it is one's personal choice whether to receive the Sacrament.

If not disruptive to the service, is it okay to:
Take pictures? No.
Use a flash? No.
Use a video camera? No.
Use a tape recorder? No.

Will contributions to the church be collected at the service? No.

AFTER THE SERVICE

Is there usually a reception after the service? No.

Is there a traditional form of address for clergy whom a guest may meet? The chief officiant is referred to as "Bishop," followed by his last name. His counselors are addressed as "Brother," followed by their last names.

GENERAL GUIDELINES AND ADVICE

There is no kneeling at Latter-day Saint services.

SPECIAL VOCABULARY

Key words or phrases that it might be helpful for a visitor to know:
Sacrament: The Communion of bread and water.
"Brother" and *"Sister":* Terms for fellow members of the Church.

DOGMA AND IDEOLOGY

Mormons believe:
The Godhead is composed of God the Father; his son, Jesus Christ; and the Holy Ghost. They are considered one in purpose, but are separate in being.

Revelation from God did not cease nearly 2,000 years ago with the crucifixion of Jesus Christ. Rather, it has continued through the centuries through various living prophets. The presidents of the Church are considered to be prophets in the same sense that Moses and other biblical leaders were also prophets.

The Book of Mormon is divinely inspired scripture, as is the Holy Bible. They are used side by side in Church curricula.

The Word of Wisdom, a health code divinely revealed in 1833, forbids the use of tobacco, alcoholic beverages, tea and coffee, and emphasizes a healthy diet and physical and spiritual fitness.

The biblical principle of tithing, or donating 10 percent of one's income to the church, is adhered to by faithful members.

A professional clergy is not needed. Instead, churches are led and staffed by lay members without financial compensation.

Some basic books to which a guest can refer to learn more:
The Book of Mormon (Salt Lake City, Utah: Church of Jesus Christ of Latter-day Saints).
The Doctrine and Covenants (Salt Lake City, Utah: Church of Jesus Christ of Latter-day Saints).
The Pearl of Great Price (Salt Lake City, Utah: Church of Jesus Christ of Latter-day Saints).

Our Search for Happiness: An Invitation to Understand the Church of Jesus Christ of Latter-day Saints by M. Russell Ballard (Salt Lake City, Utah: Deseret Book, 1995).

The Book of Mormon: Annotated and Explained annotated by Jana Riess (Woodstock, Vt.: SkyLight Paths Publishing, 2005).

3. HOLY DAYS AND FESTIVALS

Christmas. Always falls on December 25. Celebrates the birth of Christ. A traditional greeting for this holiday is "Merry Christmas."

Easter. Usually occurs in April. Commemorates the death and Resurrection of Jesus. Always falls on the Sunday after the first full moon that occurs on or after the spring equinox of March 21. There is no traditional greeting for this holiday.

4. LIFE CYCLE EVENTS

Birth Ceremony

The ceremony for the blessing and naming of a newborn infant is part of a regular worship service on the first Sunday of the month. The ceremony, which is the same for males and females, consists of a brief blessing. The worship service of which the blessing is a part lasts slightly more than one hour.

BEFORE THE CEREMONY

Are guests usually invited by a formal invitation? Invitations are usually fairly informal and often given verbally.

If not stated explicitly, should one assume that children are invited? Yes.

If one can't attend, what should one do? RSVP with regrets.

APPROPRIATE ATTIRE

Men: A suit or sport jacket and tie. No head covering required.

Women: A dress or a skirt and blouse. No head covering required, but the overall fashion statement should be conservative and dignified. Hems should be near the knees. Open-toed shoes and modest jewelry are permissible.

Modest and dignified clothing is appreciated.

GIFTS

Is a gift customarily expected? No.

Should gifts be brought to the ceremony? See above.

THE CEREMONY

Where will the ceremony take place? In the parents' church.

When should guests arrive and where should they sit? Arrive early and sit wherever you wish.

If arriving late, are there times when a guest should *not* enter the ceremony? Do not enter during Communion.

Are there times when a guest should *not* leave the ceremony? Do not leave during Communion.

Who are the major officiants, leaders or participants at the ceremony and what do they do?

The child's father, a lay leader or another designated holder of the priesthood, who blesses the child.

A bishop, who presides over the service.

Two bishop's counselors, assistants to the bishop.

What books are used? No books are used for the blessing itself. Used for the rest of the worship service, of which the blessing is a part, are the King James Version of the Bible and *The Hymns of the Church of Jesus Christ of Latter-day Saints, The Book of Mormon, The Doctrine and Covenants* and *The Pearl of Great Price* (Salt Lake City, Utah: Church of Jesus Christ of Latter-day Saints). The Bible and other scriptures are used only by those conducting the service, but congregants may refer to their personal copies of the scriptures to follow along, if they wish.

To indicate the order of the ceremony: A program may be distributed.

Will a guest who is not a Latter-day Saint be expected to do anything other than sit? Guests of other faiths are invited to sing and pray with the congregation, but they are not expected to do so, especially if participating would violate their own religious beliefs. One of the few times the congregation stands during the service is midway through the service during the singing of the "Rest Hymn." Again, guests are invited to stand, but are not obligated to do so.

Are there any parts of the ceremony in which a guest who is not a Latter-day Saint should *not* participate? No, although it is one's personal choice whether to receive the Sacrament.

If not disruptive to the ceremony, is it okay to:
Take pictures? No.
Use a flash? No.
Use a video camera? No.
Use a tape recorder? No.

Will contributions to the church be collected at the ceremony? No.

AFTER THE CEREMONY

Is there usually a reception after the ceremony? No.

Is there a traditional form of address for clergy whom a guest may meet? The chief officiant is referred to as "Bishop," followed by his last name. His counselors are addressed as "Brother," followed by their last names.

Initiation Ceremony

Baptism follows the biblical example of immersion and is for the remission of one's sins. Since young children are incapable of sin, they are not baptized until the age of eight, which is considered the age of moral accountability. The baptismal ceremony may be for an individual child or for a group of children or for an adult convert. The ceremony lasts about 15 to 30 minutes.

At the first worship service after the baptism, the individual is "confirmed" as a member of the Church by the laying on of hands by a member of the lay priesthood.

BEFORE THE CEREMONY

Are guests usually invited by a formal invitation? Invitations are usually issued verbally.

If not stated explicitly, should one assume that children are invited? Yes.

If one can't attend, what should one do? RSVP with regrets.

APPROPRIATE ATTIRE

Men: A suit or sport jacket and tie. No head covering required.

Women: A dress or a skirt and blouse. No head covering required, but the overall fashion statement should be conservative and dignified. Open-toed shoes and modest jewelry are permissible.

Modest and dignified clothing is appreciated.

GIFTS

Is a gift customarily expected? No.

Should gifts be brought to the ceremony? See above.

THE CEREMONY

Where will the ceremony take place? There is a service in the chapel or in the baptismal font room of the church, then guests, family and the child proceed to the baptistery for the baptism itself.

When should guests arrive and where should they sit? Arrive at the time for which the ceremony has been called and sit wherever you wish.

If arriving late, are there times when a guest should *not* enter the ceremony? No.

Are there times when a guest should *not* leave the ceremony? No, but since the service is relatively brief, all present are expected to remain for its duration.

Who are the major officiants, leaders or participants at the ceremony and what do they do?
A presiding officer, usually (but not necessarily) a bishop, who presides over the service.
The father or a lay priest, who performs the baptismal immersion.
Other lay members, who deliver the invocation and benediction and deliver a brief talk.

What books are used? No texts are distributed, although speakers may refer to the Scriptures.

To indicate the order of the ceremony: A program may be distributed.

Will a guest who is not a Latter-day Saint be expected to do anything other than sit? No.

Are there any parts of the ceremony in which a guest who is not a Latter-day Saint should *not* participate? No.

If not disruptive to the ceremony, is it okay to:
Take pictures? No.

Use a flash? No.
Use a video camera? No.
Use a tape recorder? No.

Will contributions to the church be collected at the ceremony? No.

AFTER THE CEREMONY

Is there usually a reception after the ceremony? Depending on the family, there may be a reception at their home or elsewhere. If so, light food may be served, but no alcoholic beverages.

Would it be considered impolite to neither eat nor drink? No.

Is there a grace or benediction before eating or drinking? Possibly. Tradition calls for a prayer of thanks for the food.

Is there a grace or benediction after eating or drinking? No.

Is there a traditional greeting for the family? Just offer your congratulations.

Is there a traditional form of address for clergy who may be at the reception? A bishop is referred to as "Bishop," followed by his last name. Other officiants are addressed as "Brother," followed by their last names.

Is it okay to leave early? Yes.

Marriage Ceremony

Reflecting the Church's emphasis on strong family solidarity and the potential for eternal family relationships, Latter-day Saints believe that marriage performed in a Church temple need not end at death, but, instead, has the potential of continuing forever. Also reflecting Church interpretations of the "strict morality" taught by Jesus are proscriptions against adultery and prescriptions for absolute fidelity during marriage.

BEFORE THE CEREMONY

Are guests usually invited by a formal invitation? Yes.

If not stated explicitly, should one assume that children are invited? Children do not attend a marriage ceremony performed in the temples, but they may be invited to a ceremony performed in a church or a civil ceremony performed elsewhere.

If one can't attend, what should one do? RSVP with regrets.

APPROPRIATE ATTIRE

Men: A suit or sport jacket and tie. No head covering required.

Women: A dress or a skirt and blouse. No head covering required, but the overall fashion statement should be conservative and dignified. Hems should be near the knees. Open-toed shoes and modest jewelry are permissible.

Modest and dignified clothing is appreciated.

GIFTS

Is a gift customarily expected? The option to present a gift (and the nature of the gift) is left to the invited individual.

Should gifts be brought to the ceremony? Gifts are traditionally presented at postnuptial receptions.

THE CEREMONY

Where will the ceremony take place? Members of the Church are encouraged to be married in one of its temples, which are located around the world. A temple, which is different from a local church building where worship services are conducted, is closed on Sundays, but open every other day of the week for marriages and other sacred ordinances.

Only faithful members of the Church may enter a temple. Guests invited to the temple marriage ceremony must present a "temple recommend" issued by their bishop to indicate that they are, indeed, faithful members.

A couple may also choose to be married in a local church meetinghouse, a home or another location.

When should guests arrive and where should they sit? Arrive at the time for which the service is called and sit wherever you wish.

If arriving late, are there times when a guest should *not* enter the ceremony? No.

Are there times when a guest should *not* leave the ceremony? Leaving early is discouraged.

Who are the major officiants, leaders or participants at the ceremony and what do they do? Authorized clergy perform the ceremony.

What books are used? Possibly Scriptures.

Will a guest who is not a Latter-day Saint be expected to do anything other than sit? No.

Are there any parts of the ceremony in which a guest who is not a Latter-day Saint should *not* participate? All guests only observe the ceremony.

If not disruptive to the ceremony, is it okay to:
Take pictures? No.
Use a flash? No.
Use a video camera? No.
Use a tape recorder? No.

Will contributions to the church be collected at the ceremony? No.

AFTER THE CEREMONY

Is there usually a reception after the ceremony? There is usually a reception, but where it is held and what is done there is the personal choice of the bride and groom. Traditionally, it is an open-house type of affair.

Would it be considered impolite to neither eat nor drink? No.

Is there a grace or benediction before eating or drinking? Possibly. This is the choice of the hosts.

Is there a grace or benediction after eating or drinking? No.

Is there a traditional greeting for the family? No. Just offer your congratulations.

Is there a traditional form of address for clergy who may be at the reception? A bishop is referred to as "Bishop," followed by his last name. His counselors are addressed as "Brother," followed by their last names.

Is it okay to leave early? Yes, since at the traditional open-house type of reception guests stay as long as they feel is appropriate.

Funerals and Mourning

Latter-day Saints believe that all who have ever lived on earth are literally the spiritual children of God and resided with him in a premortal existence. The same with those who will ever live on earth. Through the Resurrection of Jesus, all will be resurrected and through atonement and obedience to his gospel, all have the opportunity for salvation.

A Latter-day Saint funeral is a service in itself. The length of the service varies according to the program outlined by the family, but it usually lasts about 60 to 90 minutes.

BEFORE THE CEREMONY

How soon after the death does the funeral usually take place? There is no set limit, although typically it occurs within one week after the death. The timing of the funeral is solely the choice of the immediate family and depends on circumstances.

What should someone who is not a Latter-day Saint do upon hearing of the death of a member of that faith? Visit, telephone or write to the family, expressing your condolences and offering your assistance, if needed.

APPROPRIATE ATTIRE

Men: A suit or sport jacket and tie. No head covering required.

Women: A dress, suit or a skirt and blouse. No head covering required, but the overall fashion statement should be conservative and dignified. Hems should be near the knees. Open-toed shoes and modest jewelry are permissible.

Modest and dignified clothing is appreciated.

GIFTS

Is it appropriate to send flowers or make a contribution? It is appropriate, but not expected to do either. These may be sent before or after the funeral, to the funeral itself (which may be held in a church or a funeral home) or to the home of the bereaved.

Is it appropriate to send food? Food for the bereaved family members is usually prepared and organized by the women's organization of the local congregation.

THE CEREMONY

Where will the ceremony take place? Either in a church or in a funeral home or at the graveside.

When should guests arrive and where should they sit? Arrive at the time for which the service has been called. Sit wherever you wish.

If arriving late, are there times when a guest should *not* enter the ceremony? No.

Will the bereaved family be present at the church or the funeral home before the ceremony? Usually.

Is there a traditional greeting for the family? No. Just offer your condolences.

Will there be an open casket? Sometimes. This is done at the choice of the family.

Is a guest expected to view the body? Viewing is entirely optional.

What is appropriate behavior upon viewing the body? Observe it with dignity and reverence.

Who are the major officiants at the ceremony and what do they do?
The officer of the church who conducts the service. This person is chosen by the family, but is typically the bishop of the congregation to which the deceased belonged.
Speakers who deliver eulogies.

What books are used? Speakers will use Scriptures. Hymn books may be used by the congregation.

To indicate the order of the ceremony: A program may be distributed.

Will a guest who is not a Latter-day Saint be expected to do anything other than sit? No.

Are there any parts of the ceremony in which a guest who is not a Latter-day Saint should *not* participate? No.

If not disruptive to the ceremony, is it okay to:
Take pictures? No.
Use a flash? No.
Use a video camera? No.
Use a tape recorder? Possibly, if it can be done with discretion.

Will contributions to the church be collected at the ceremony? No.

THE INTERMENT

Should guests attend the interment? Yes, unless it is a private interment, which is rare. If the burial is private, attendance is only by invitation.

Whom should one ask for directions? The director of the funeral home or the person who officiated at the service may give directions from the pulpit. Also, the printed program may have directions.

What happens at the graveside? The grave is dedicated in a prayer offered by a lay priest, who is usually (but not necessarily) a member of the family of the deceased. Then the deceased is buried.

Do guests who are not Latter-day Saints participate at the graveside ceremony? No, they are simply present.

COMFORTING THE BEREAVED

Is it appropriate to visit the home of the bereaved after the funeral? Yes, if one wishes to do so.

Will there be a religious service at the home of the bereaved? No.

Will food be served? There may be light food, but no alcoholic beverages. At the choice of the hosts, a grace or benediction may be said before eating.

How soon after the funeral will a mourner usually return to a normal work schedule? There is no set time. Absence from work is at the discretion of the mourner.

How soon after the funeral will a mourner usually return to a normal social schedule? There is no set time. Absence from social events is at the discretion of the mourner.

Are there mourning customs to which a friend who is not a Latter-day Saint should be sensitive? No.

Are there rituals for observing the anniversary of the death? No.

5 · HOME CELEBRATIONS

Latter-day Saints observe a Family Home Evening one night each week. This is usually held on Mondays, but may be held on any other day. The intention is to cement family ties and cohesion. Usually attending are family members, but occasionally guests may be invited.

While there are no set activities, a Family Home Evening may include conversation, reading and singing together, taking walks or engaging in other recreational pursuits, playing games or praying together.

18

Native American/First Nations

Native American/First Nations religion does not exist as a single, readily identifiable faith. (In practice, few Native Peoples use the word *religion* to describe their traditional ceremonies and practices. The term is used here to help those outside the community relate in some way to the understandings and "the way of life" of aboriginal/indigenous peoples.) Indigenous Americans (whom United States law recognizes as American Indians and Alaska Natives) and First Nations peoples in Canada have diverse and rich religious traditions. Although it is impossible to generalize about the diverse ceremonial practices of Native Americans/First Nations peoples, some suggestions regarding respectful behavior at their religious ceremonies can be made based on the beliefs and values that are the foundation of their deeply spiritual worldviews.

Because these beliefs and values are intimately related to Native people's sense of the sacred, they directly influence what would count as respectful and appropriate behavior for those invited to attend most Native American/First Nations religious ceremonies. Since even those who are well-intentioned are often not aware of these beliefs and values, they may behave in ways that Native Peoples interpret as disrespectful toward their religious ceremonies and practices. Diverse religious traditions explain why those who have briefly visited—or actually lived—with Native Peoples report that they have encountered a people who are deeply connected to the sacred.

According to the 2000 United States census, American Indian and Alaska Native populations total approximately 2.4 million. Although this is roughly one percent of the total population of the United States, the more than 500 nations of the Native Peoples represent approximately 90 percent of the ethnic diversity in the United States. Among Native Peoples, there are nine major language families with almost 200 distinct dialects. From a constitutional viewpoint, the First Americans are citizens of their own various nations as well as of the United States.

Many First Nations people in Canada do not consider themselves to be "American" nor, for that matter, citizens of Canada. They see themselves as people of First Nations communities such as

Whata First Nations, or Shawanaga First Nations, or Peepeekisis First Nations. *Indian* is a term specifically used by the government of Canada to define certain aboriginal people mentioned in the Indian Act of 1867 and excludes many people of aboriginal ancestry. There are 53 aboriginal languages in Canada, including Inuit and Metis languages.

If you consider the geographic and cultural diversity of the five largest tribal groups in the United States alone—the Cherokee in North Carolina and Oklahoma, the Navajo in Arizona and New Mexico, the Chippewa of the Northern and Great Lakes regions, the Sioux (which include the Lakota, Dakota and Nakota) spread across the northern plains, and the Choctaw in Mississippi and Oklahoma—you begin to grasp why it is impossible to generalize about the cultural practices and, specifically, the religious ceremonies and practices of Native American/First Nations peoples.

1. HISTORY AND BELIEFS

Over the last 500 years, Native Peoples have endured what they consider to be almost constant disrespect. Recognizing this unpleasant legacy will help those desiring to visit Native American religious ceremonies understand why many Native Peoples are wary about sharing the most important elements of their identity with those who do not share their faith.

In 1879, for instance, the Carlisle Indian Boarding School was created in Carlisle, Pennsylvania. This was the first of what would eventually be dozens of off-reservation boarding schools designed to "solve" the "Indian Problem." In the late 1870s, the federal government assumed that the "Indian Problem" could be eradicated by education built around creating institutions dedicated to the complete cultural assimilation of Native American boys and girls and erasing their beliefs, values and culture. Similar policies were enacted by the federal government of Canada.

Not surprisingly, given the centrality of the sacred to Native culture and identity, completely eradicating their indigenous religious and spiritual traditions was deemed a prerequisite for successful "education." Christian clergy often ran these schools, since "civilizing" these children meant converting them to Christianity.

Understanding just this small part of the history of Native Peoples when attending their religious events and ceremonies can help you appreciate the intrinsically communitarian and private nature of their religious practices.

Native American/First Nations religion is primarily about experience, not about theology or doctrine. It is simultaneously a personal and a profoundly communal experience. The nearly universal rule among Native Peoples that explains this is that ceremonies, customs and various cultural traditions, which are all ways of exercising spirituality, are, at their core, *community* activities for community members. Religious experience is profoundly shaped by one's membership and involvement in a community and one's life at a specific geographic place in relation to the whole of Creation.

Native spirituality denies the dichotomies common to Western religions.

The Western dualisms of supernatural versus natural, spiritual versus earthly/worldly, sacred versus profane and heaven versus hell do not easily fit with Native spirituality. Unlike religious traditions that see life on earth filled primarily with evil, toil and suffering, Native spirituality perceives the world as deeply endowed with the sacred power of the Creator.

Native languages, oral traditions, symbols, ceremonial objects and ceremonial practices speak directly to the recognition that humans are surrounded by the spiritual power of the Creator. Traditional prayers and ceremonies embody the widely held belief that we are imbued with one small part of the spirit of our Creator.

For Native peoples, the entire natural world is full of the sacred.

Each living part of Creation, and especially the places important to each tribe or village, serves as but one entrance into the power of the sacred. With this recognition of the complexity of Creation and the Creator's power comes the obvious realization that humans are but one part of the natural world, and not necessarily a privileged part or even the only "persons" inhabiting the earth.

Consequently, the high degree of religious diversity among Native Peoples reflects another widely shared element in traditional Native religious practices.

Native religious activities are almost universally attached to specific places.

These sacred sites mark the appropriate place for the enactment of certain ceremonies and religious activities. Even Native Peoples who experienced painful removal and relocation from their indigenous homelands in the 18th and 19th centuries found sacred sites in places new to them where their religious traditions could be carried out.

Most Native sacred sites are not analogous to a church, a temple or a shrine, which are consecrated as sacred by humans and built from blueprints, plans and drawings. Instead, Native ceremonial sites are often located on the land where specific tribes identify their spiritual center.

The places Native Peoples identify as their respective homelands and the communities that exist there are at the center of their religious experience. At the most fundamental level, the rich spirituality of Native peoples is literally "grounded" in their experience of the natural world as the cathedral of their Creator.

Native religious traditions are profoundly holistic.

Native faiths or teachings often refer to Creation itself as a complex web of life or a sacred circle in which all aspects of the natural world connect to each other. Because of this, humanity, in most Native worldviews, does not hold a privileged place above the rest of

Creation, but is understood to be only a small part of Creation.

In many Native worldviews, many "persons" other than humans inhabit the world. Native Peoples attribute the qualities of power, consciousness and volition generally identified with the Western view of personhood to many living things. Consequently, Native Peoples perceive the environment to be inhabited with four-legged "persons" that swim in the water or winged "persons" that fly. To the Native way of thinking, these "persons" are also part of the moral and political community. Most importantly, they are also part of the spiritual community. In Native thought, to recognize that the earth is sacred is also to acknowledge all the "members" of our many respective communities.

The holistic nature of Native worldviews and spirituality gives a centrality to the idea of balance in one's life and in the world. Living in a good, healthy, beautiful way requires one to recognize that growth and success are achieved by integrating psychological, physical and spiritual well-being.

Native religious traditions openly acknowledge the existence of unseen powers.

Forces and mysteries exist that Native Peoples experience and recognize, but cannot see or fully understand or comprehend. These sacred powers are not mysteries that need to be solved, but exist because humanity cannot know and understand everything about Creation or the Creator.

Native religions have no tradition of proselytizing.

Spiritual leaders and wisdom keepers do not undertake missionary activities. Their dependence on experience and on understanding the diversity of the circle of life makes it perfectly acceptable—and, perhaps to them, inevitable—that people from different places will have different religions. Consequently, Native Peoples were always confused by other people who insisted they be just like them. This appreciation for the biological and cultural diversity of Mother Earth and her children explains Native respect for people's different ways of honoring the Creator and Creation. It also explains why Native people are often wary of those so interested in their traditions when the Creator gave all human beings a knowledge of the sacred.

2 · ETIQUETTE SUGGESTIONS

Invitations are rarely given to strangers or outsiders to attend Native religious ceremonies and observances. In fact, it is usually preferred that one be a stranger to Native religious practices unless an invitation has been extended to attend a particular ceremony.

This statement may seem harsh unless you remember that Native Peoples primarily view their ceremonies as personal experiences shaped by an essentially community-based ceremony or ritual. It is, therefore, improbable that you would arrive as an outsider at a Native religious ceremony. Indigenous custom and habit generally frown on outsiders, even polite ones, from attending what is First Peoples' most precious way of identifying themselves as a people. The personal and communal nature of religious experience, combined with the lack of any mission to convert others or share traditions with those from outside one's Native community, means that it is best for you to respectfully keep your distance, unless specifically invited by a Native person to attend a ceremony.

Once invited, you will find hosts who are warm and open and who will give you as much information as is required to respectfully observe a ceremony. In addition, you will discover that Native people are very forgiving of slight breaches of etiquette, especially since, given the nature of the ceremonies, there is little expectation that visitors have prior knowledge of what they are observing and the specific behavior expected of them.

GENERAL GUIDELINES AND ADVICE

Here are some general guidelines:

- Pay attention. Be quiet. Listen.
- Once a ceremony or service begins, refrain from asking questions.
- Forget your ego and self-consciousness. These have no place in Native religious ceremonies. As human beings, we are all simultaneously beautiful and pitiful. Elders often use the latter term as an expression of our humility in the presence of the sacred. It speaks to the First Peoples' acknowledgment that man is just one small part of Creation.
- Worship takes many forms.
- Inquire beforehand about how you should dress for a specific religious event, since it may take place outside, given Native people's attachment to nature and sacred sites. Weather conditions and the climate in general should always be taken into consideration when choosing attire for a particular ceremony or ritual.
- Be prepared to sit and stand for long periods of time. Ceremonies often require both.
- Be prepared to stay awhile at the ceremony. Ceremonies take as long as they need to take. Do not look at your watch. Ceremonies may last more than a few hours; sometimes they continue for several days.
- Before the ceremony begins, inquire about the appropriateness of coming and going during the course of the ceremony.
- Generally, contributions are not collected at Native ceremonies. In many situations in Canada, it is customary to give tobacco to the leader of the ceremony. It indicates respect and that you have come in humility and in need of teaching and prayer.
- Do not worry about doing the "wrong thing." Native people are very forgiving of your unfamiliarity with their faith and spiritual rituals.
- The best forms of address to use for religious or tribal leaders are "Mr.," followed by that person's last name. Do not use any of the stereotypical terms that have been promulgated by entertainment media, such as "Chief" or "Medicine Man."
- Try to limit your questions to a very practical nature and focus them on your behavior. Many Native people find it rude to be asked about the

meaning of everything that will be done at a ceremony, or all the sacred objects that will be used or the nature of symbolism invoked. In Native religious traditions, experience is the greatest teacher. Meaning may not easily lend itself to a verbal or theological explanation. Again, your host or hostess will generally give you as much information as he or she feels you need.

QUESTIONS TO ASK

Here are some questions you might ask your hosts:

- When should I arrive?
- Where should I sit?
- If arriving late, are there times when I should not enter the service or ceremony?
- Are there times when I should not leave the service or ceremony?
- Who are the major officiants, leaders or participants at a service or ceremony and what do they do?
- What are the major ritual objects of a service or ceremony?
- What books, if any, are used?
- Are any announcements given to tribal members and/or their guests to indicate the order of the service or ceremony?
- Will a guest who is not a Native person be expected to do anything other than sit?
- Are there any parts of the service or ceremony in which someone who is not a Native person should not participate?
- If not disruptive to the service or ceremony, is it okay to:
  - Take pictures?
  - Use a flash?
  - Use a video camera?
  - Use a tape recorder?
- Is there usually a reception after the service or ceremony?
- Is there a traditional form of address for religious or tribal leaders?
- Is it okay to leave early?

SPECIAL VOCABULARY

A few key words or phrases that it might be helpful for a visitor to know and that will help you appreciate the diversity of ceremonial practice:

Blessingway Ceremony: A ceremonial chant that recounts the Navajo Creation story and that is usually recited over two nights. It is performed to maintain a positive or healthy environment and to prevent imbalance or disharmony.

Faith: Native Peoples would not say that their spirituality is based on "faith," as that word is commonly used. Native spirituality is grounded in experiencing the sacred in the natural world.

Potlatch Ceremony: A diverse, complex series of ceremonies practiced by the Native Peoples of the northwest coast of North America. Its central function is to maintain balance and harmony among one's community. It generally consists of a community feast during which the host, typically a family, presents gifts to guests and also reenacts the family's oral history from mythic times to the present.

Religion: Traditionally, Native Peoples do not think of their spirituality as a religion embodied in formal doctrine or theology. Rather, they understand their spirituality as embodying a way of life. It is the very manner in which one lives. From a Native standpoint, religion might be thought of as the awareness of the sacred in our lives and the acknowledgment of it through ceremony, custom and habit.

The Sacred: As opposed to a conception of god or deity, for which many Native languages have no specific word, "the sacred" broadly captures the experience of the divine in this world.

Sacred Circle: A symbolic representation of many Native Peoples' conception of the world and life. It captures ecological cycles of life and death and represents one's journey along the path of life.

Sacred Sites: Sites that Native Peoples recognize as being imbued with a specific or special aspect of the sacred.

Stomp Dances: A common style of dance with tribes originally from the southeastern United States. The primary rhythm is provided by singing, the use of gourds rattled by men, and turtle shells that are filled with pebbles and tied to women's legs.

Sun Dance Ceremony: The most important annual religious ceremony for about 30 Plains tribes. Its meaning varies somewhat from tribe to tribe, but it is basically a test of courage and a demonstration of personal sacrifice. During the three-day ceremony, men undergo "piercing." This means they are suspended from a sacred pole by skewers of wood inserted into their chests.

Sweat Lodge Ceremony: A ceremony common to many Native peoples. Its functions and use vary from tribe to tribe, but it generally provides purification and healing and restores balance in one's life.

Wisdom Keepers: Also known as Elders. Living repositories of Native traditional wisdom, ceremonial practices and customs. The title does not necessarily imply age, since it is earned through extensive training and practice.

Some basic books to which a guest can refer to learn more about Native American beliefs:

God Is Red: A Native View of Religion by Vine Deloria Jr. (Golden, Colo.: Fulcrum Publishing, 2003).

Native American Religions and Cultures of North America: Anthropology of the Sacred edited by Lawrence E. Sullivan (New York: Continuum, 2000).

Native Religions of North America by Ake Hultkrantz (San Francisco: HarperCollins, 1987; reissued in 1998 by Waveland Press).

Native American Stories of the Sacred: Annotated and Explained retold by Evan T. Pritchard (Woodstock, Vt.: SkyLight Paths Publishing, 2005).

3 · SEASONAL CEREMONIES

In addition to the life cycle ceremonies noted below, Native American/First Nations religions also have seasonal ceremonies throughout the year. These are invariably tied to cycles of nature. Native Americans in the Southwest, for example, observe the Green Corn Ceremony. This marks the full ripening of the late corn crop, which is usually in July or August. The ceremony is essentially a purification and renewal ceremony. Renewal is represented through the ripening of the corn and the promise of another year's bounty. Purification occurs at three levels: throughout all Creation, throughout society, and within each individual.

The indigenous peoples of the Southwest closely guard the details of the Green Corn Ceremony, which is not open to those from outside the local Native American community.

Another ceremony tied to the seasons is the Hopis' Soyalangw Ceremony. This highly secretive ceremony is held at the winter solstice and involves the highest Hopi priests. It marks the beginning of a new year and stresses the importance of renewal and the maintenance of balance throughout all Creation. It also emphasizes that each person understand his or her proper place within Creation.

Non-invited guests cannot witness a Soyalangw Ceremony, since it is held inside a *kiva,* a ceremonial lodge. But public dances linked to the ceremony are held after the ritual is concluded. Visitors might see these were they to journey to a Hopi village. While the dances are related to the Soyalangw Ceremony, they are widely perceived as "social dances" and are enveloped by fewer restrictions and more informal protocol than other Hopi ceremonies.

In the Canadian context, there are many ceremonies that are sacred and secret. Anyone who is allowed to participate should do so with a quiet, humble, respectful attitude.

4 · LIFE CYCLE EVENTS

Birth Ceremonies

While Native American birth ceremonies vary widely, three specific tribal traditions show some similarities.

ZUNI

On the eighth day of its new life, a Zuni baby's head is washed by the women of the father's clan and the infant is "introduced" to the world at sunrise. Corn meal is placed in the infant's hand and more corn meal is sprinkled to the east to acknowledge the rising sun. The paternal grandmother offers what serves as both a prayer and an introduction for the new infant. In part, this prayer asks the sun father to help the infant start the road of life in a good way.

OMAHA

Traditionally, the Omaha Indians also "introduce" their infants to the universe on the eighth day of their new lives. In the Omaha religious tradition, the child benefits from being introduced to the entirety of Creation. This includes the natural elements and the "beings" on which fragile human life heavily depends. In this ceremony, a spiritual elder stands at the door of the dwelling where the newborn lives and asks all the parts and beings of Creation to take notice of the infant and to help make the infant's future path of life smooth.

NAVAJO

Among the Navajo, special care is taken of the child before birth. Expecting parents are instructed not to attend certain ceremonies and funerals for fear that harm could come to the unborn child. Before birth, a Blessingway Ceremony is often performed for the mother and soon-to-be-born infant. This ceremony includes one of the central ceremonial chants of the Navajo religious tradition. The Blessingway Ceremony and chant, which is performed over two nights and often referred to as a "no sleep chant," recounts the events of Navajo Creation and invokes the sense of harmony and balance that pervades Creation. This chant is often used to help people when there is a sense of imbalance in one's life or an illness. For an impending birth, this ceremony and chant are performed to ensure the health and safety of mother and child.

Among the Navajo, a rather unique celebration is held when an infant gives its first laugh. This jubilant celebration involves a "give-away" sponsored by the person who first saw or helped the infant laugh. In this celebration, a meal is usually given by the sponsor (on the reservation, a sheep may be butchered for this meal) to guests and simple, not necessarily extravagant gifts are given by the sponsor to each guest. The celebration marks the first time the infant is allowed to wear jewelry. In Navajo traditions, this celebration is crucial because it is believed the infant will grow up to be selfish if the "give-away" is not held.

Although each of these birth ceremonies slightly varies, they also have much in common. Each marks the proper start of the child down the path of life by ensuring that he or she is introduced to the sacred in a manner that will result in a healthy, harmonious and balanced life.

Sharing a meal is a traditional part of each of these ceremonies. A polite guest will always stay and enjoy this meal with the hosts. The meal and the conversation and fellowship during it are expressions of the good relations with others that the infant will experience as he or she embarks on his or her own path in life. Most parents will accept gifts for their children at these ceremonies. It is advisable that such practical gifts as clothing or a blanket be presented, although toys are also appropriate.

However, in the case of the Navajo, as indicated above, pretty "materialistic" items would not be given to the child until after the infant laughs and a "give-away" is held.

At any Native Peoples ceremony that welcomes a newborn, the child's parents and grandparents can be greeted with "Congratulations."

Initiation Ceremonies

Although complex, strictly prescribed ceremonial practices once marked the onset of puberty for

Native boys and girls, many of these ceremonies are no longer performed. Modern life and its schedules and routines implictly discourage the observance of most of these elaborate ceremonies, which lasted over several days and, in some cases, several months.

The coming-of-age religious ceremonies that continue today are most often given for girls when they begin menstruation. These ceremonies often involve a young girl going into seclusion for several days during her first menstrual period and being instructed by her mother, grandmothers and aunts about the value and power of womanhood. While earlier Native religious traditions often allowed little or no interaction with the larger community during this sacred event in a young woman's life, today's tribes, notably the Navajo and Apache, that continue to ceremonially mark this event allow everyone to share in this coming-of-age ceremony. Among the Navajo and the Apache, these ceremonies last four days. While the young woman undergoes her instructions separate from the larger community, feasting and socializing occur for those celebrating the event.

At any of these Native Peoples coming-of-age ceremonies, the child and her parents can be greeted with "Congratulations," plus a statement that reflects your pride in the young teen's achievement.

Marriage Ceremonies

As with each of the above circle-of-life ceremonies, one of the central functions of the marriage ceremony is to impress upon the participants (in this case, the bride and groom) the importance of the new stage of life they are entering. The marriage ceremony both celebrates the event and prepares the new husband and wife to begin their journey together in a good way.

Traditionally, marriage ceremonies have always been community celebrations, although they have also been modernized in some ways. As Nico Strange Owl-Raben explained in an article about her Cheyenne wedding in a 1991 issue of *Native Peoples* magazine,

> I use the word "tradition" carefully. Tradition is not a stagnant thing. It is always changing and adapting. My wedding could not have been like my grandmother's. It was not possible. I have heard about the changes in my grandmother's generation and I have seen what happened in my mother's. Now my generation is experiencing change. My wedding incorporated tradition so that we could have a blend.

Consequently, contemporary Native wedding ceremonies often combine old and new ways. For instance, Ms. Strange Owl-Raben's Cheyenne wedding combined traditional Cheyenne attire, custom and symbolism with some modern societal conventions. The ceremony was held outside amid a semicircle of tipis that had been erected in a northern Rocky Mountain alpine meadow—a cathedral, of sorts, in Native worldviews. In keeping with Cheyenne tradition, the bride's wedding dress was made of buckskin by the bride's mother and maternal aunts. The groom, a non-Cheyenne, wore a business suit. The bride entered the ceremony riding a horse led by her father in a procession led by her mother. After a judge performed a civil marriage ceremony, a traditional Cheyenne ceremony that consisted of a simple blessing was offered by Richard Tall Bull, a Southern Cheyenne Wisdom Keeper or Elder.

The blessing was the center of the traditional Cheyenne ceremony. After completing the prayer, Mr. Tall Bull burned sacred cedar and fanned the smoke over the couple and then fanned it into the sky with a sacred eagle feather. This manner of offering prayers is widely shared by Native Peoples throughout North America. Cedar, sweet grass, sage and tobacco are often burned as sacraments when prayers are offered, and the eagle feather is an almost universally shared sacred ceremonial item among Native Peoples. The power of the feather is closely associated with the power of the eagle, and the right to possess and use it is earned.

Another aspect of the traditional Cheyenne marriage ceremony is the strict traditions regarding relationships between the future wife and husband and their respective in-laws. In the Cheyenne tradition, the new husband should not interact with his new mother-in-law and her sisters (his wife's maternal aunts). By custom, they are to live as if they are "invisible" to each other. To a non-Native, this might appear rude. But in Cheyenne traditions, such conduct is deemed to be a way to ensure familial harmony.

Many Native Peoples have similar practices. Although it would be impolite for a guest to directly inquire about this behavior, careful observation will usually reveal whether the "invisibility" between certain persons is part of the customs of the Native Peoples you are visiting.

After the formal marriage ceremony, as in most religious faiths, a celebratory meal follows. Presents are welcomed by the newly married couple and are generally of a very practical nature, such as blankets, dishes, pots, pans and small household items. (In the case of Ms. Strange Owl-Raben's wedding, her mother gave the couple a traditional gift of a tipi, a dwelling that is central to living the Cheyenne way of life even today. Of course, the gift of a tipi would be fitting for plains tribes, but of little utility to any of the tribes of the Southwest or Southeast where tipis are not used.)

At a Native American/First Nations wedding ceremony, the bride and groom can be greeted with "Congratulations," plus a wish that they enjoy a happy and fruitful life together.

Funerals and Mourning

Many Native Peoples believe that death is the beginning of another journey, into the next world. Since one's spirit often needs help to make this journey, strict rules often govern the behavior of the living relatives of the deceased to ensure their loved one a good start in his or her journey to the other world. Some Potawatomi continue their ancient tradition of setting a place for the spirit of the deceased person at a funeral feast, in order for the spirit of the deceased to partake of the "spirit" food.

Among the Yuchi, who are politically recognized as part of the Creek Nation of Oklahoma and number less than 1,000, Christian burial customs are occasionally interwoven with Yuchi traditions. These may include placing such items as a hunting rifle, a blanket, some tobacco and other personal items in an adult male's coffin before interment. This reflects the Yuchi belief that one's journey in an afterlife is not significantly different from our present life.

At a Native funeral, express your sympathy and empathy to the bereaved. While Native beliefs assert that death is not necessarily the termination of life, the bereaved still mourn the absence from this life of the one who has died.

Many tribes restrict what bereaved relatives can eat and/or what kinds of activities they can engage in after the death of a loved one. This represents a sacrifice by the living for those who have moved on in the circle of life.

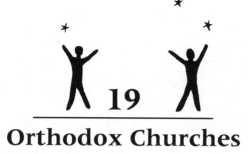

19

Orthodox Churches

(Includes the Antiochian Orthodox Church, the Carpatho-Russian Orthodox Church, the Greek Orthodox Church, the Orthodox Church in North America [also known as the Russian Orthodox Church], the Romanian Orthodox Church, the Serbian Orthodox Church, and the Ukrainian Orthodox Church. An entire chapter was devoted to Greek Orthodoxy in the first volume of How to Be a Perfect Stranger, *since it is the Orthodox denomination with the largest membership in the United States.)*

1 • HISTORY AND BELIEFS

The Orthodox Church, or the Eastern half of the Christian church, became independent in 1054 C.E. In that year the Great Schism occurred, causing a complete breakdown in communication and relations between the Roman Catholic Church, based in Rome, and the Orthodox Church, based in Constantinople. When the patriarchs of the various Orthodox churches meet, they are presided over by the Patriarch of Constantinople (present-day Istanbul), who is considered to be the "first among equals."

The term *Orthodox* is used to reflect adherents' belief that they believe and worship God correctly. Essentially, Orthodox Christians consider their beliefs similar to those of other Christian traditions, but believe that the balance and integrity of the teachings of Jesus' 12 apostles have been preserved inviolate by their Church.

Orthodoxy holds that the eternal truths of God's saving revelation in Jesus Christ are preserved in the living tradition of the Church under the guidance and inspiration of the Holy Spirit, which is the empowering spirit of God and the particular endowment of the Church. While the Holy Scriptures are the written testimony of God's revelation, Holy Tradition is the all-encompassing experience of the Church under the guidance and direction of the Holy Spirit.

Orthodox churches are hierarchical and self-governing. They are also called "Eastern" because they stem from countries that shared the Christian heritage of the eastern part of the Roman and Byzantine

Empire. They completely agree on matters of faith, despite a diversity of culture, language and the lands in which they flowered before arriving in North America.

Orthodox churches in North America today include:

• The American Carpatho-Russian Orthodox Greek Catholic Church, a self-governing diocese formalized in 1938 whose founders came from present-day Slovakia.

• The Antiochian Orthodox Christian Archdiocese of North America, an Arabic-language church whose first parish in North America was founded in Brooklyn in 1895. The Church in Antioch traces its origins to the days of the apostles Peter and Paul, and to the Syrian city of Antioch in which the Book of Acts says the followers of Jesus Christ were first called "Christians."

• The Greek Orthodox Archdiocese of America, which is under the jurisdiction of the Ecumenical Patriarchate of Constantinople in Istanbul.

• The Orthodox Church in America, which was given full, independent status by the Russian Orthodox Church in 1970. It is composed of ethnic Russians, Bulgarians, Albanians and Romanians.

• The Romanian Orthodox Church in America, which was founded in 1929 and was granted ecclesiastical autonomy in 1950 from the Church in Romania.

• The Serbian Orthodox Church in the U.S.A. and Canada, which was created in 1921 and whose patriarchal seat is in Belgrade, Serbia.

• The Ukrainian Orthodox Church of

America, which was organized in 1928; and the Ukrainian Orthodox Church of Canada, which was organized in 1918 and is the largest Ukrainian Orthodox Church beyond the borders of Ukraine.

U.S. churches:

Antiochian Orthodox: 256
Carpatho-Russian Orthodox: 80
Greek Orthodox: 560
Romanian Orthodox: 32
Russian Orthodox (also known as the Orthodox Church in America, or the OCA): 737
Serbian Orthodox: 68
Ukrainian Orthodox: 118

U.S. membership:

Antiochian Orthodox: 430,000
Carpatho-Russian Orthodox: 13,721
Greek Orthodox: 1.5 million
Romanian Orthodox: 9,700
Russian Orthodox (also known as the Orthodox Church in America, or the OCA): Not available.
Serbian Orthodox: 67,000
Ukrainian Orthodox: 50,000
  (data from the 2010 Yearbook of American and Canadian Churches)

For more information, contact:

The American Carpatho-Russian
    Orthodox Diocese of the USA
312 Garfield Street
Johnstown, PA 15906
(814) 539-4207
www.acrod.org

The Antiochian Orthodox Christian
    Archdiocese of North America
358 Mountain Road
Englewood, NJ 07631
(201) 871-1355
www.antiochian.org

The Greek Orthodox Archdiocese
of America
8-10 East 79th Street
New York, NY 10021
(212) 570-3500
www.goarch.org

The Orthodox Church in America
P.O. Box 675
Syosset, NY 11791-0675
(516) 922-0550
www.oca.org

The Romanian Orthodox Church in
America
5410 North Newland Avenue
Chicago, IL 60656
(773) 774-1677
www.romarch.org

The Serbian Orthodox Church
in the U.S.A. and Canada
St. Sava Monastery
P.O. Box 519
Libertyville, IL 60048
(847) 367-0698
serbianorthodoxchurch.com

The Ukrainian Orthodox Church
of the U.S.A.
P.O. Box 495
South Bound Brook, NJ 08880
(732) 356-0090
www.uocofusa.org

Canadian churches:
Antiochan Orthodox: 18
Greek Orthodox: 76
Romanian Orthodox: 26
*Russian Orthodox (also known
as the Orthodox Church
in America):* 68
Serbian Orthodox: 26
Ukrainian Orthodox: 273

Canadian membership:
Antiochan Orthodox: 130,000

Greek Orthodox: 350,000
Romanian Orthodox: 8,200
*Russian Orthodox (also known as the
Orthodox Church in America):* 10,000
Serbian Orthodox: 235,000
Ukrainian Orthodox: 32,000
(data from the 2010 Yearbook of Ameri-
can and Canadian Churches*)*

For more information, contact:

The Antiochian Orthodox Christian
Archdiocese of North America
358 Mountain Road
Englewood, NJ 07631
(201) 871-1355
www.antiochian.org

Greek Orthodox Metropolis of
Toronto (Canada)
86 Overlea Boulevard
Toronto, ON M4H 1C6
(416) 429-5757
www.gocanada.org

The Orthodox Church in America
(Archdiocese of Canada)
P.O. Box 179
Spencerville, ON K0E 1X0
(613) 925-5226
www.archdiocese.ca

Serbian Orthodox Church in the
U.S.A. and Canada
Diocese of Canada
7470 McNiven Road, R.R. 3
Campbellville, ON L0P 1B0
(905) 878-0043

Ukrainian Orthodox Church of
Canada
Office of the Consistory
9 Saint Johns Avenue
Winnipeg, MB R2W 1G8
(204) 586-3093
www.uocc.ca

2 · THE BASIC SERVICE

In the Orthodox churches, the purpose of worship and theology is mystical union with God. The liturgy is not a private performance by a priest, since he cannot perform the liturgy alone, but a joint act of laity and clergy. The language of prayer alludes to the majesty and transcendence of God, while also conveying God's presence.

A regular part of Orthodox services is the burning of incense by a priest or bishop. The rising smoke from the incense represents prayers being carried to heaven.

Eucharistic services take place every Sunday and every major feast day. They usually last from one and a half to two hours.

APPROPRIATE ATTIRE

Men: A jacket and tie. More casual clothing is permissible in the summer, although jeans are discouraged. No head covering is required.

Women: A dress or a skirt and blouse. Clothing should cover the arms and hems should reach below the knees. A head covering is not required. Open-toed shoes and modest jewelry may be worn. Shorts, tank tops and sneakers should not be worn.

There are no rules regarding colors of clothing.

THE SANCTUARY

What are the major sections of the church?

The vestibule: The main entrance.

The nave: Where one woships and participates in the service.

The sanctuary: Where the priest or bishop stands.

THE SERVICE

When should guests arrive and where should they sit? It is customary to arrive either early or at the time for which the service has been called. In most Orthodox churches, ushers will advise guests where to sit.

If arriving late, are there times when a guest should *not* enter the service? Do not enter during Scripture readings and priestly blessings.

Are there times when a guest should *not* leave the service? No.

Who are the major officiants, leaders or participants and what do they do?

A bishop, who is the chief celebrant.

A priest, who may be the chief celebrant or the assistant to the bishop.

The deacon, subdeacon and altar server, all of whom assist the bishop or priest.

Acolytes, altar boys who assist the adult officiants.

What are the major ritual objects of the service?

Icons, two-dimensional artistic images of saints or of events in the life of Christ.

A gold-covered book containing the four Gospels from the New Testament.

Censer, an incense holder. Smoke from the incense represents prayers being carried to heaven.

Chalice, a gold cup. Held by a priest or bishop; contains the Holy Eucharist, the bread and wine, which, after being consecrated by the Holy Spirit through the bishop or priest, become mystically changed into the body and blood of Christ.

What books are used? The American Carpatho-Russian Orthodox Diocese uses *The Divine Liturgy of St. John Chrysostom* (Johnstown, Pa.: American Carpatho-Russian Orthodox Diocese, 1988); and the *Come to Me Prayer Book* (Johnstown, Pa.: American Carpatho-Russian Orthodox Diocese, 1986).

The Antiochian Orthodox Church uses *The Service Book* (Englewood, N.J.: Antiochian Archdiocese, 2006); *The Orthodox Study Bible* (Nashville, Tenn.: Thomas Nelson Publishers, 2008); and *The Liturgikon* (Englewood, N.J.: Antiochian Archdiocese, 1994).

The Romanian Orthodox Episcopate of America uses *Divine & Holy Liturgy for Orthodox Christians* (Grass Lake, Mich.: Romanian Orthodox Episcopate of America, 1975) and *Unison Liturgical Responses* (Grass Lake, Mich.: Romanian Orthodox Episcopate of America, 1977).

The Orthodox Church in America uses *Divine Liturgy* (New York: The Orthodox Church in America, 1967).

Several books may be used in the Greek Orthodox, Serbian Orthodox and Ukrainian Orthodox Churches, such as *The Divine Liturgy of St. John Chrysostom* (Brookline, Mass.: Holy Cross Orthodox Press, 1985).

To indicate the order of the service: A program will be distributed or, most often, guests follow a liturgy service book that is in the pews.

GUEST BEHAVIOR DURING THE SERVICE

Will a guest who is not a member of an Orthodox church be expected to do anything other than sit? Yes. Stand when the congregants rise. Kneeling with them is appropriate only if it does not violate a visitor's own religious beliefs. Otherwise, visitors may sit when congregants kneel. Reading prayers aloud and singing with the congregants are optional.

Are there any parts of the service in which a guest who is not a member of an Orthodox church should *not* participate? Do not participate in Holy Communion. This is the high point of the service. It occurs after a priest or bishop advances toward the congregation from the altar, holds up the chalice and says, "With fear of God, with faith and with love, draw ye near." Congregants then go forward to receive Communion.

If not disruptive to the service, is it okay to:

Take pictures? Yes, but only with prior permission of a church official.

Use a flash? Yes, but only with prior permission of a church official.

Use a video camera? Yes, but only with prior permission of a church official.

Use a tape recorder? Yes, but only with prior permission of a church official.

Will contributions to the church be collected at the service? Yes. Trays are passed through the congregation at the end of the service.

How much is it customary to contribute? Contributions are entirely optional. While the amount of the contribution is at the discretion of congregants or visitors and the various Orthodox churches do not feel comfortable recommending specific amounts to guests, contributions between $1 and $10 are common.

AFTER THE SERVICE

Is there usually a reception after the service? A 30- to 60-minute reception is usually held in a room or hall adjoining the church. Light food, such as coffee and pastry, is ordinarily served. No alcoholic beverages are served at this reception in Orthodox churches (although alcohol may be served on special occasions at receptions or banquets). In the Orthodox Church in America, also known as the Russian Orthodox Church, there will be a prayer of blessing before eating or drinking.

Is there a traditional form of address for clergy who may be at the reception? "Father."

Is it okay to leave early? Yes.

GENERAL GUIDELINES AND ADVICE

Many Orthodox churches have books or pamphlets in each pew that explain the service and that follow it, word for word. Also, since about 50 percent of each Orthodox service is in English, guests who are not Orthodox should not anticipate a service that is predominantly in another language.

SPECIAL VOCABULARY

Key words or phrases that it might be helpful for a visitor to know:

Theotokos ("Thee-oh-TOH-kohs"): "Mother of God."

Prokimenon ("Proh-KEE-min-non"): "Offertory."

Proskomen ("PROS-koh-men"): "Let us attend."

Dynamis ("THEE-nah-mees"): "With greater power."

DOGMA AND IDEOLOGY

Members of Orthodox churches believe:

In the Holy Trinity (the Father, the Son and the Holy Spirit).

That after consecration, the Eucharist, the ritual meal of bread and wine that occurs during the service, is the body and blood of Christ. This is in contrast to some Christian denominations that consider the Eucharist to be symbolic.

That the final authority for the Church is not vested in the pope.

Some basic books to which a guest can refer to learn more about Orthodox churches:

The Liturgikon by the Antiochian Archdiocese (Englewood, N.J.: Antiochian Archdiocese, 1994).

Orthodox Christian Catechism, 2 vols., edited by Duane Pederson (Hollywood, Calif.: Orthodox Christian Prison Ministry, 1996).

The Orthodox Church by Timothy Ware (London: Penguin Books, 1993).

The Orthodox Faith: An Elementary Handbook on the Orthodox Church, 4 vols., by Thomas Hopko (New York: Department of Religious Education of the Orthodox Church in America, 1972–1976).

These four volumes are being made available at no charge, in HTML format, on the web at the Orthodox Church in America website, www.oca.org.

For those who might like hard copy, the series is available from St. Vladimir's Seminary Bookstore (www.svspress.com), either as a set or as individual volumes.

3 · HOLY DAYS AND FESTIVALS

Elevation of the Cross. Observed on September 14. Marks the finding of the true cross by the Empress Helena, the mother of Emperor Constantine, in the fourth century. This is a strict fast day. There is no traditional greeting for this holiday.

Nativity of Christ. A one-week celebration that begins December 25. Marks the birth of Jesus Christ. Orthodox church members traditionally greet each other with "Christ is born!" The response is "Glorify him!" Non-Orthodox can greet church members with "Merry Christmas!"

Theophany of Our Lord. A one-week celebration beginning January 6. Marks the baptism of Jesus Christ. Church members traditionally greet each other with "Glory to Jesus Christ!" The response is "Glory Forever!" Non-Orthodox can greet members with a smile and a handshake.

Annunciation. March 25. Marks the conception of Jesus Christ within the Virgin Mary. There are no traditional greetings for this holiday. Although this holiday usually occurs during Lent, a 40-day fast during which one abstains from eating fish, meat and dairy products, church members may eat fish on this day.

Palm Sunday. Date of observance varies, although it usually occurs in April and is always the Sunday before Easter. Marks the entrance of Jesus Christ into Jerusalem. Although Palm Sunday occurs during Lent, a 40-day fast during which one abstains from eating fish, meat and dairy products, members of Orthodox churches may eat fish on this day.

Easter, also called Pascha ("PAS-ka"). Date of observance varies, but it usually occurs in April. Observes the Resurrection of Jesus Christ after his crucifixion. The traditional greeting among church members is "Christ is risen!" The response to this is "Truly he is risen!" Those who do not belong to the Orthodox Church can greet Church members with "Happy Easter."

4 · LIFE CYCLE EVENTS

Birth Ceremony

The ceremony marking the birth of a child is the same for a male and a female infant. It marks initiation into the Church, forgiveness of sins and the beginning of the Christian life. Through baptism, one dies with Christ so he or she may rise with Christ.

The Antiochian Orthodox Church refers to this service as "Churching."

The baptism service incorporates Chrismation (known in other

Christian denominations as confirmation), Baptism and First Communion. During the baptism, the child is fully immersed three times in a baptismal font, and then anointed (or "chrismated") with oil on the forehead, chest, hands, neck, back and feet. The Communion emphasizes the fullness of participation in the sacramental life of the church. During it, the child is given the body and blood of Jesus Christ, which is known as the Eucharist, and which is bread and wine that have been consecrated by the Holy Spirit at a divine liturgy conducted by a priest or bishop.

In the Antiochian Orthodox Church, the ceremony may be celebrated as part of the Sunday Divine Liturgy. In most Orthodox churches, Baptism/Chrismation is a ceremony in itself.

BEFORE THE CEREMONY

Are guests usually invited by a formal invitation? Yes, usually either by a written invitation or over the telephone.

If not stated explicitly, should one assume that children are invited? Yes.

If one can't attend, what should one do? Telephone your regrets to the family, send a gift and visit the family soon after the ceremony.

APPROPRIATE ATTIRE

Men: A jacket and tie. More casual clothing is permissible in the summer, although jeans are discouraged. No head covering is required.

Women: A dress or a skirt and blouse. Clothing should cover the arms and hems should reach below the knee. A head covering is not required. Open-toed shoes and modest jewelry may be worn. Shorts, tank tops and sneakers should not be worn.

There are no rules regarding colors of clothing.

GIFTS

Is a gift customarily expected? Yes. If one chooses to give a gift, either cash or baby clothes are appropriate.

Should gifts be brought to the ceremony? Yes.

THE CEREMONY

Where will the ceremony take place? Most often in the main vestibule of the parents' house of worship.

When should guests arrive and where should they sit? Arrive early. Usually those present stand during the ceremony, since it does not take place in the main sanctuary.

If arriving late, are there times when a guest should *not* enter the ceremony? Do not enter during Scripture readings and priestly blessings.

Are there times when a guest should *not* leave the ceremony? No.

Who are the major officiants, leaders or participants at the ceremony and what do they do?

A bishop, who is the chief celebrant.

A priest, who may be the chief celebrant or the assistant to the bishop, and who baptizes and confirms the child.

The deacon, subdeacon and altar server, all of whom assist the bishop or priest.

What books are used? The American Carpatho-Russian Church and the Antiochian Orthodox Church use *The Service Book* (Englewood, N.J.: Antiochian Archdiocese, 2006) and *The Orthodox Study Bible* (Nashville, Tenn.: Thomas Nelson Publishers, 2008).

The Romanian Orthodox Episcopate of America uses *Holy Baptism* (Grass Lake, Mich.: Romanian Orthodox Episcopate of America, 1993).

The Orthodox Church in America uses the *Baptismal Service Book* (New York: The Orthodox Church in America, 1967).

Several books may be used in the Greek Orthodox, Serbian Orthodox and Ukrainian Orthodox Churches, such as *The Divine Liturgy of St. John Chrysostom* (Brookline, Mass.: Holy Cross Orthodox Press, 1985).

To indicate the order of the ceremony: A program may be distributed.

Will a guest who is not a member of an Orthodox church be expected to do anything other than stand with those present? No. Reading prayers aloud and singing with the congregants are optional. If the Baptism/ Chrismation is part of the Sunday Divine Liturgy (as it may be in the Antiochian Orthodox Church), then guests may kneel with congregants only if it does not violate their own religious beliefs. Otherwise, visitors may sit when congregants kneel. Guests are expected to stand with the congregants.

Are there any parts of the ceremony in which a guest who is not a member of an Orthodox church should *not* participate? If the Baptism/Chrismation is part of the Sunday Divine Liturgy, when Holy Communion is offered, then those who are not Orthodox should not participate. This is the high point of the service and occurs after a priest or bishop advances toward the congregation from the altar, holds up the chalice and says, "With fear of God, with faith and with love, draw ye near." Congregants then go forward to receive Communion.

If not disruptive to the ceremony, is it okay to:

Take pictures? Yes, but only with prior permission of a church official.

Use a flash? Yes, but only with prior permission of a church official.

Use a video camera? Yes, but only with prior permission of a church official.

Use a tape recorder? Yes, but only with prior permission of a church official.

Will contributions to the church be collected at the ceremony? No, unless the Baptism/Chrismation is part of the Sunday Divine Liturgy. Then, trays are passed through the congregation at the end of the service.

How much is it customary to contribute? Contributions are entirely optional. While the amount of the contribution is at the discretion of congregants or visitors and the various Orthodox churches do not feel comfortable recommending specific amounts to guests, contributions between $1 and $10 are common.

AFTER THE CEREMONY

Is there usually a reception after the ceremony? Yes. This may last from 30 minutes to two hours and may be held in the same building as the ceremony, at the parents' home or at a catering hall. A meal will be served, often accompanied by alcoholic beverages.

Would it be considered impolite to neither eat nor drink? No.

Is there a grace or benediction before eating or drinking? Yes. An invocation is recited to bless the food.

Is there a grace or benediction after eating or drinking? Yes.

Is there a traditional greeting for the family? Guests who are not members of an Orthodox church can just offer their congratulations. Parents who belong to the Antiochian Orthodox Church are often greeted with the phrase "A blessed Churching" or "A blessed baptism," although the traditional greeting for all occasions in the Church is "Mabbrook" ("MAB-brook"), which means "Blessings." For other Orthodox churches, there is no traditional greeting.

Is there a traditional form of address for clergy who may be at the reception? Yes. It is "Father."

Is it okay to leave early? Yes.

Initiation Ceremony

In most Orthodox churches, baptism around the age of one to three months serves as one's initiation into the church. But in the Anti-ochian Orthodox Church, a 15- to 30-minute ceremony is done with pre-adolescents in an individual ceremony (not with a class of others).

BEFORE THE CEREMONY

Are guests usually invited by a formal invitation? Yes.

If not stated explicitly, should one assume that children are invited? Yes, in most Orthodox churches.

If one can't attend, what should one do? Telephone your regrets to the family and send a gift to the child. Visit the family at another time.

APPROPRIATE ATTIRE

Men: A jacket and tie. More casual clothing is permissible in the summer, although jeans are discouraged. No head covering is required.

Women: A dress or a skirt and blouse. Clothing should cover the arms and hems should reach below the knee. A head covering is not required. Open-toed shoes and modest jewelry may be worn. Shorts, tank tops and sneakers should not be worn.

There are no rules regarding colors of clothing.

GIFTS

Is a gift customarily expected? Yes. Either cash or clothes are appropriate.

Should gifts be brought to the ceremony? Yes.

THE CEREMONY

Where will the ceremony take place? In the baptismal area of the family's house of worship.

When should guests arrive and where should they sit? Arrive early. An usher will advise guests where to sit.

If arriving late, are there times when a guest should *not* enter the ceremony? Do not enter during Scripture readings and priestly blessings.

Are there times when a guest should *not* leave the ceremony? No.

Who are the major officiants, leaders or participants at the ceremony and what do they do?
A bishop, who is the chief celebrant.
A priest, who may be the chief celebrant or the assistant to the bishop.
The deacon, subdeacon and altar server, all of whom assist the bishop or priest.

What books are used? *The Service Book* (Englewood, N.J.: Antiochian Archdiocese, 2006) and *The Orthodox Study Bible* (Nashville, Tenn.: Thomas Nelson Publishers, 2008).

To indicate the order of the ceremony: A program will be distributed to congregants and guests.

Will a guest who is not a member of an Orthodox church be expected to do anything other than sit? Stand when the congregants arise. Kneeling with them is appropriate only if it does not violate a visitor's own religious beliefs. Otherwise, visitors may sit when congregants kneel. Reading prayers aloud and singing with the congregants are optional.

Are there any parts of the ceremony in which a guest who is not a member of an Orthodox church should *not* participate? Yes. Holy Communion. This is the high point of the ceremony. It occurs after a priest or bishop advances toward the congregation from the altar, holds up the chalice and says, "With fear of God, with faith and with love, draw ye near." Congregants then go forward to receive Communion.

If not disruptive to the ceremony, is it okay to:
Take pictures? Yes, but only with prior permission of a church official.
Use a flash? Yes, but only with prior permission of a church official.
Use a video camera? Yes, but only with prior permission of a church official.
Use a tape recorder? Yes, but only with prior permission of a church official.

Will contributions to the church be collected at the ceremony? Yes. Trays are passed through the congregation at the end of the ceremony.

How much is it customary to contribute? Contributions are entirely optional. While the amount of the contribution is at the discretion of congregants or visitors and the various Orthodox churches do not feel comfortable recommending specific amounts to guests, contributions between $1 and $10 are common.

AFTER THE CEREMONY

Is there usually a reception after the ceremony? Members of the church often hold a reception after the ceremony. This may last from 30 minutes to two hours and may be held in the same building as the ceremony, at a catering hall or at the parents' home. A meal will be served, often accompanied by alcoholic beverages.

Would it be considered impolite to neither eat nor drink? No.

Is there a grace or benediction before eating or drinking? Yes. An invocation is recited to bless the food.

Is there a grace or benediction after eating or drinking? Yes.

Is there a traditional greeting for the family? Just offer your congratulations. A traditional greeting for all occasions in the Antiochian Orthodox Church is "Mabbrook" ("MAB-brook"), which means "Blessings."

Is there a traditional form of address for clergy who may be at the reception? "Father."

Is it okay to leave early? Yes.

Marriage Ceremony

To Orthodox Christians, marriage is a sacrament of union between man and woman, who enter it to be mutually complemented and to propagate the human race. In the Orthodox churches, rings are blessed and the bride and groom each wear a crown during the ceremony to symbolize sacrifices made in marriage, the priestly nature of marriage and the fact that the bride and groom are now heads of their creation.

The 45- to 60-minute marriage ceremony is a ceremony in itself and not part of a larger service.

BEFORE THE CEREMONY

Are guests usually invited by a formal invitation? Yes.

If not stated explicitly, should one assume that children are invited? No.

If one can't attend, what should one do? RSVP with regrets and send a gift.

APPROPRIATE ATTIRE

Men: A jacket and tie. No head covering is required.

Women: A dress or a skirt and blouse. Clothing should cover the arms and hems should reach below the knee. A head covering is not required. Open-toed shoes and modest jewelry may be worn.

There are no rules regarding colors of clothing.

GIFTS

Is a gift customarily expected? Yes. Customarily, this may be cash or household goods.

Should gifts be brought to the ceremony? Bring the gift to the ceremony or the reception or send it to the home of the newlyweds.

THE CEREMONY

Where will the ceremony take place? In the main sanctuary of the church chosen by the celebrants and their family.

When should guests arrive and where should they sit? It is customary to arrive either early or at the time for which the ceremony has been called. Ushers will advise guests on where to sit.

If arriving late, are there times when a guest should *not* enter the ceremony? Do not enter during Scripture readings and priestly blessings.

Are there times when a guest should *not* leave the ceremony? No.

Who are the major officiants, leaders or participants at the ceremony and what do they do?
A bishop, who is the chief celebrant.
A priest, who may be the chief celebrant or the assistant to the bishop.
The deacon, subdeacon and altar server, all of whom assist the bishop or priest.
The bride and groom.

What books are used? In most Orthodox churches, only officiating bishops and priests use a text at a marriage ceremony.

To indicate the order of the ceremony: A program will be distributed to congregants and guests.

Will a guest who is not a member of an Orthodox church be expected to do anything other than sit? Stand when the congregants arise. Kneeling with them is appropriate only if it does not violate a visitor's own religious beliefs. Otherwise, visitors may sit when congregants kneel. Reading prayers aloud and singing with the congregants are optional.

Are there any parts of the ceremony in which a guest who is not a member of an Orthodox church should *not* participate? No.

If not disruptive to the ceremony, is it okay to:
Take pictures? Yes, but only with prior permission of a church official.
Use a flash? Yes, but only with prior permission of a church official.
Use a video camera? Yes, but only with prior permission of a church official.
Use a tape recorder? Yes, but only with prior permission of a church official.

Will contributions to the church be collected at the ceremony? No.

AFTER THE CEREMONY

Is there usually a reception after the ceremony? Yes. This may last from one to four hours and may be held in the same building as the ceremony, at a catering hall or at the bride's parents' home. A meal will be served, often accompanied by alcoholic beverages.

Would it be considered impolite to neither eat nor drink? No.

Is there a grace or benediction before eating or drinking? Yes.

Is there a grace or benediction after eating or drinking? No.

Is there a traditional greeting for the family? In the Antiochian Orthodox Church, the traditional greeting for all occasions is "Mabbrook" ("MAB-brook"), which means "Blessings."

In the Romanian Orthodox Church, the traditional greeting is "La multi ani!" ("Lah MOOLTZ AH-nee"), which means "Many years!"

In other Orthodox churches, "Congratulations" is appropriate.

Is there a traditional form of address for clergy who may be at the reception? "Father."

Is it okay to leave early? Yes.

Funerals and Mourning

Orthodox churches believe that death is the separation of the soul (the spiritual dimension of each human being) from the body (the physical dimension of each human being). Upon death, we immediately begin to experience a foretaste of heaven and hell. This experience, known as the partial judgment, is based on the general character of our lives regarding behavior, character and communion with God.

At some unknown time in the future, the churches teach, Jesus Christ will return and inaugurate a new era in which his kingdom will be established. The final judgment will then occur. In our resurrected existence, we will either live eternally in heaven in communion with God, or live eternally in hell and out of communion with God.

The 30- to 60-minute funeral ceremony is not part of a larger service, although in the American Carpatho-Russian Church, the Eucharistic liturgy (essentially the Sunday morning worship service) is often celebrated in addition to the funeral service. This is done at the discretion of the bereaved family and may cause the entire ceremony to last up to 90 minutes.

BEFORE THE CEREMONY

How soon after the death does the funeral usually take place? Usually within two to three days.

What should a non-Orthodox do upon hearing of the death of a member of that faith? It is appropriate to visit or telephone the bereaved at their home before the funeral to express condolences and recall the life of the deceased. When visiting a bereaved family before the service, a traditional greeting to a member of the Antiochian Orthodox Church is "May his [or her] memory be eternal."

APPROPRIATE ATTIRE

Men: A jacket and tie. No head covering is required.

Women: A dress or a skirt and blouse. Clothing should cover the arms and hems should reach below the knee. A head covering is not required. Open-toed shoes and modest jewelry may be worn.

Somber, dark colors are recommended for both men and women.

GIFTS

Is it appropriate to send flowers or make a contribution? It is appropriate to send flowers to the funeral home before the funeral. It is also appropriate to make a contribution in the memory of the deceased either to his or her church or to a fund or charity designated by the family of the deceased.

Is it appropriate to send food? Yes. This is ordinarily sent to the home of the bereaved either upon initially hearing about the death or after the funeral.

THE CEREMONY

Where will the ceremony take place? Either at a funeral home or at the house of worship of the deceased.

When should guests arrive and where should they sit? Arrive early or at the time for which the ceremony has been called. Ushers will advise guests where to sit.

If arriving late, are there times when a guest should *not* enter the ceremony? No.

Will the bereaved family be present at the church or funeral home before the ceremony? Yes.

Is there a traditional greeting for the family? In the Antiochian Orthodox Church, a traditional greeting is "May God give you the strength to bear your loss." In other Orthodox churches, express your condolences.

Will there be an open casket? Yes.

Is a guest expected to view the body? This is optional.

What is appropriate behavior upon viewing the body? Stand briefly in front of the casket and offer a silent prayer. A Christian might also cross himself or herself and kiss the cross or icon resting on the casket.

Who are the major officiants at the ceremony and what do they do?
A bishop, who is the chief celebrant.
A priest, who may be the chief celebrant or the assistant to the bishop.
The deacon, subdeacon and altar server, all of whom assist the bishop or priest.

What books are used? In most Orthodox churches, only officiating bishops and priests use a text at a funeral ceremony.

To indicate the order of the ceremony: A program will be distributed.

Will a guest who is not a member of an Orthodox church be expected to do anything other than sit? Stand when the congregants arise. Kneeling with them is appropriate only if it does not violate a visitor's own religious beliefs. Otherwise, visitors may sit when congregants kneel. Reading prayers aloud and singing with the congregants are optional.

Are there any parts of the ceremony in which a guest who is not a member of an Orthodox church should *not* participate? No, unless the Eucharistic liturgy is celebrated. In that case, guests who are not Orthodox do not partake in Holy Communion. This is the high point of the ceremony. It occurs after a priest or bishop advances toward the congregation from the altar, holds up the chalice and says, "With fear of God, with faith and with love, draw ye near." Congregants then go forward to receive Communion.

If not disruptive to the ceremony, is it okay to:

Take pictures? No.

Use a flash? No.

Use a video camera? No.

Use a tape recorder? No.

Will contributions to the church be collected at the ceremony? No.

THE INTERMENT

Should guests attend the interment? This is entirely optional.

Whom should one ask for directions? Ask the funeral director or a family member.

What happens at the graveside? There will be a brief prayer ceremony, followed by the officiating priest or bishop usually putting soil on top of the casket so it forms the shape of a cross, and then each person present placing one flower on the casket or spreading soil on the casket. The flowers usually come from those sent to the church for the funeral and then conveyed to the cemetery with the casket. There will be no cremation, since this is not permitted in Orthodox churches.

Do guests who are not members of an Orthodox church participate at the graveside ceremony? No. They are simply present.

COMFORTING THE BEREAVED

Is it appropriate to visit the home of the bereaved after the funeral? Yes. The tradition in the Orthodox Church in America is to briefly visit the bereaved the same day as the funeral. Religious objects that a visitor may see at such a visit are icons, two-dimensional artistic images of saints; a lighted candle; and burning incense.

Will there be a religious service at the home of the bereaved? No.

Will food be served? A Meal of Mercy is often given in the church hall, a restaurant or the home of the deceased shortly after the burial. At the homes of members of the Antiochian Orthodox Church, usually coffee, pastries and/or fruit are served.

How soon after the funeral will a mourner usually return to a normal work schedule? The bereaved usually stays home from work for one week.

How soon after the funeral will a mourner usually return to a normal social schedule? The bereaved usually avoids social gatherings for two months. In some cases, especially that of widows, the bereaved may avoid such occasions for a full year after the loss of the deceased.

Are there mourning customs to which a friend who is not a member of an Orthodox church should be sensitive? Mourners usually avoid social gatherings for the first 40 days after the death. They may also wear only black clothing during this same period.

Are there rituals for observing the anniversary of the death? A memorial service is held on the Sunday closest to the 40th day after the death. Subsequent memorial services are held on the anniversary of the death.

5 · HOME CELEBRATIONS

The Home Blessing

When does it occur? Either on January 6, the Epiphany, which is the traditional date for having one's home blessed annually, or shortly after moving into a new home.

What is its significance? Holy water, which is sprinkled in each room, is used to sanctify the home, just as Jesus' baptism sanctified the waters of the River Jordan and all creation.

What is the proper greeting to the celebrants? "Congratulations" or "May God grant you many years!"

BEFORE THE CEREMONY

Are guests usually invited by a formal invitation? Either by telephone or by a written invitation.

If not stated explicitly, should one assume children are invited? No.

If one can't attend, what should one do? Telephone the celebrants with your regrets.

APPROPRIATE ATTIRE

Men: A jacket and tie or more casual clothing (except jeans) is appropriate. A head covering is not required.

Women: A dress or a skirt and blouse or a pants suit. It is not required that clothing cover the arms or that hems extend below the knees or to cover one's head.

Open-toed shoes and modest jewelry may be worn. A head covering is not required.

There are no rules regarding colors of clothing.

GIFTS

Is a gift customarily expected? This is entirely optional.

If one decides to give a gift, is a certain type of gift appropriate? The usual sort of housewarming gift, which should be brought to the house when you arrive.

THE CEREMONY

The home blessing ceremony lasts between 15 and 30 minutes. The major officiant is the priest, who blesses the home.

What are the major ritual objects of the ceremony?
The cross, which represents Christ's victory over death through his Resurrection.
Water, which is a vehicle for sanctification.
A basil flower, which is used to sprinkle water in the air in the configuration of a cross in each room throughout the house as the priest recites blessings.
A candle, which symbolizes that Christ is the Light of the world.

What books are used? Prayer books may be distributed.

Will a guest who is not a member of an Orthodox church be expected to do anything other than sit? Stand when the celebrants rise.

Are there any parts of the ceremony in which a guest who is not a member of an Orthodox church should *not* participate? No.

If not disruptive to the ceremony, is it okay to:
Take pictures? Yes.
Use a flash? Yes.
Use a video camera? Yes.
Use a tape recorder? Yes.

EATING AND DRINKING

Is a meal part of the celebration?
Possibly. If so, it is served after the ceremony.

Will there be alcoholic beverages?
Possibly.

Would it be considered impolite to neither eat nor drink? No.

Is there a grace or benediction before eating or drinking? Yes. An invocation is recited to bless the food.

Is there a grace or benediction after eating or drinking? No.

At the meal, will a guest be asked to say or do anything?
No.

Will there be:
Dancing? No.
Music? No.

GENERAL GUIDELINES AND ADVICE

None provided.

20

Pentecostal Church of God

1 • HISTORY AND BELIEFS

The Pentecostal Church of God was founded in Chicago in 1919 by a group of participants in the then-current Pentecostal revival movement in the United States. Many people involved in the movement spontaneously spoke "in tongues" (or in a language unknown to those speaking it) and claims were made of divine healing that saved lives. Since many of these experiences were associated with the coming of the Holy Spirit (the empowering quality of God) on the Day of Pentecost, participants in the revival were called Pentecostals.

The group that met in Chicago was convinced that a formal Pentecostal church was necessary because many smaller, new, independent Pentecostal houses of worship had become the targets of small-time crooks and con men. They deemed their fledgling Pentecostal Church of God to be indispensable for the Pentecostal revival to continue to thrive.

Pentecostals tenaciously believe in their direct access to God the Father, and believe prayer can manifest miracles. Worship services are demonstrative and energetic and are often marked by congregants speaking "in tongues." These are languages unknown to the speaker. Such speaking is interpreted as meaning that one is the recipient of the Holy Spirit. Alcohol and tobacco are prohibited to Church members.

The Pentecostal Church of God has a combination of representative and congregational forms of government. While local churches are self-governing and elect their own ministers and local leaders, they are also expected to harmoniously function with the Church's district and general organization. The bylaws of local churches cannot conflict with the Church's district or general bylaws. Each minister is accountable to his or her district board in matters of faith and conduct.

The Church's biennial general convention is its highest legislative body. Policy is made and governed by the Church's general executive board.

The Church's World Missions Department has ministers in 60 countries and maintains schools in most of these nations, as well. In addition, the Church's Indian Mission Department makes outreach to Native Americans.

Although the Pentecostal Church of God is not present within Canada, the broader Pentecostal tradition is well represented by the Pentecostal Assemblies of Canada and the Pentecostal Assemblies of Newfoundland, which have a combined total of 1,240 churches, 258,000 members, and offices in Mississauga, Ontario, and St. John's, Newfoundland, respectively.

U.S. churches: 1,134
U.S. membership: 98,579
   (*data from the* 2010 Yearbook of American and Canadian Churches)

For more information, contact:

The Pentecostal Church of God
4901 Pennsylvania
P.O. Box 850
Joplin, MO 64802
(417) 624-7050
www.pcg.org

2 · THE BASIC SERVICE

Worship in the Pentecostal Church of God is marked by spontaneity and freedom of expression, and especially by exuberant prayer, music and Scripture reading and "speaking in tongues." "Tongues" are used in three ways: praying, praising and giving messages from God through the Holy Spirit. "Praying in tongues" means that one is able to pray according to the will of God without the interference of one's natural desire. "Praising in tongues" lets the worshiper be free to express love for God without the inhibitions of natural language. This is the outward manifestation of the presence of the Holy Spirit.

Also, "messages in tongues" may be given during a service. According to Scripture, these "messages" should be interpreted by one who has the gift to make such an interpretation so they can edify the entire congregation.

The Lord's Supper (which certain other Christian denominations call Communion) may be offered at a worship service. The frequency of its observance by an individual church is at the discretion of each congregation.

Most churches have services Sunday morning and evening and Wednesday night. The Sunday morning service and the Wednesday night service may last between 60 and 90 minutes. The Sunday evening service may last for two to three hours.

APPROPRIATE ATTIRE

Men: A jacket and tie, or more casual attire, such as slacks and an informal shirt. No head covering is required.

Women: A dress or a skirt and blouse or other casual attire. Halters and shorts are frowned upon. Clothing need not cover the arms and hems need not reach below the knees. Open-toed shoes and modest jewelry are permissible. No head covering is required.

There are no rules regarding colors of clothing.

THE SANCTUARY

What are the major sections of the church?

The foyer: Where congregants and guests are greeted upon arrival by ushers or greeters.

The auditorium: Where congregants and guests are seated.

The platform or pulpit: Where the service leaders lead prayer, sing, read Scriptures and preach.

THE SERVICE

When should guests arrive and where should they sit? Arrive shortly before the time for which the service has been called. Sit wherever you wish.

If arriving late, are there times when a guest should *not* enter the service? Do not enter during prayers.

Are there times when a guest should *not* leave the service? Do not leave during prayers.

Who are the major officiants, leaders or participants and what do they do?

The minister, who is in charge of the service and delivers a sermon.

The worship leader, who leads singing and worship.

Associates, who make announcements and help the worship leader.

What are the major ritual objects of the service? There are none. Most churches have little, if any, adornment and usually lack statues and stained glass windows. The cross is the most commonly displayed symbol.

What books are used? Several translations of the Old and New Testaments are used throughout the Church. The most commonly used is the King James translation.

An overhead projector may be used to project the words of choruses to songs being sung by congregants.

To indicate the order of the service: Programs may be distributed or periodic announcements may be made by the minister.

GUEST BEHAVIOR DURING THE SERVICE

Will a guest who is not a member of the Pentecostal Church of God be expected to do anything other than sit? It is expected for guests to stand with the congregants. It is entirely optional for guests to sing with the congregants. Kneeling is seldom done during a service, although individual congregants may kneel at the end of the service in front of the altar. This is done entirely at their volition. Should there be kneeling during the service, guests may remain seated.

Are there any parts of the service in which a guest who is not a member of the Pentecostal Church of God should *not* participate? Non-Christians should not participate in the Lord's Supper, which is a memorial to the death and Resurrection of Jesus Christ. It is intended only for believers in Christ.

If not disruptive to the service, is it okay to:

Take pictures? Yes, but only with prior permission of the minister.

Use a flash? Rarely is this allowed—and only with prior permission of the minister—since it may distract from the service.

Use a video camera? Rarely is this allowed, and only with prior permission of the minister.

Use a tape recorder? Yes.

Will contributions to the church be collected at the service? Yes.

How much is it customary to contribute? If one chooses to give, a contribution between $1 and $10 is appropriate, although any contribution is appreciated.

AFTER THE SERVICE

Is there usually a reception after the service? No.

Is there a traditional form of address for clergy whom a guest may meet? "Pastor," "Minister" or "Brother."

GENERAL GUIDELINES AND ADVICE

None provided.

SPECIAL VOCABULARY

Key words or phrases that it might be helpful for a visitor to know:

Anointing with oil: An ancient Christian practice in which the sick are anointed with oil in the name of the Lord. This may be done either at the bedside of an ill person or at a Wednesday or Sunday worship service when the sick are asked to come forward to be anointed.

Foot washing: Commemorates Christ's washing of his disciples' feet at the Last Supper. Individual churches determine the form and the frequency with which they will practice foot washing. For the ritual, men and women are in separate rooms and each gender washes the feet of other members of the same gender. Depending on their church's tradition, they may wash the feet of just one individual or of all those present. Many churches never have a foot-washing service.

Lifting up of hands: Holding up one's hands during prayer and praise in anticipation of receiving the presence and power of the Holy Spirit.

The rapture: The "catching away" of believers by the Lord upon the return of Jesus Christ.

Regeneration: When a person has fully accepted Jesus Christ as his or her savior. Also known as "born again."

Salvation: The time when one's sins are forgiven by God and one enters into a genuine relationship with the divine.

Sanctification: Pentecostal doctrine in which holiness is considered to be a progressive work of God's grace beginning with regeneration.

DOGMA AND IDEOLOGY

Members of the Pentecostal Church of God believe:

The Old and New Testaments are the inspired Word of God.

God is a trinity in unity, consisting of the Father, the Son and the Holy Spirit (which is also known as the Holy Ghost).

Jesus Christ was born of a virgin birth, lived a sinless life, performed miracles, atoned for the sins of others on the cross and was resurrected bodily to be at the right hand of God the Father.

Regeneration by the Holy Spirit is absolutely essential for the salvation of the lost and sinful.

Baptism by water is through immersion, is a direct commandment of the Lord and is only for believers. Baptism symbolizes one's identification with Christ's death, burial and Resurrection.

Atoning for one's sins provides for divine healing.

The Lord's Supper is a commandment of Christ, and is a memorial to his death and Resurrection. It is for believers in Christ only.

Jesus Christ will bodily return to reign on earth for one thousand years and, according to Church literature, "to resurrect the dead and to catch away the living saints to meet him in the air." This is often referred to as the rapture. Teachings on the rapture are found in 1 Thessalonians (4:16–17). At the rapture, only believers in Christ will be resurrected to eternal life. The resurrection of sinners will occur seven years later, when they will face eternal damnation.

It is "unwise" to teach that Christ will return at a certain time or date.

Basic books to which a guest can refer to learn more about the Pentecostal Church of God:

The New International Dictionary of Pentecostal and Charismatic Movements edited by Stanley M. Burgess and Eduard M. van der Maas (Grand Rapids, Mich.: Zondervan Publishing House, 2002).

3 · HOLY DAYS AND FESTIVALS

Christmas. Celebrated on December 25. Marks the birth of Jesus Christ. Church members and non-Church members can greet each other with "Merry Christmas!"

Good Friday. The date of observance varies, although it usually occurs in April and is always the Friday before Easter. Marks the crucifixion of Christ in Jerusalem. There is no traditional greeting for this holiday.

Easter. The date of observance varies, but it usually occurs in April and is always on the Sunday after the first full moon that occurs on or after the spring equinox of March 21. Commemorates the Resurrection of Jesus Christ after his crucifixion. The traditional greeting is "Happy Easter."

Pentecost. Occurs 50 days after Easter because this is when the Holy Spirit descended on Christ's apostles. Celebrates the power of the Holy Spirit and its manifestation in the early Christian church. There is no traditional greeting for this holiday.

4 · LIFE CYCLE EVENTS

Birth Ceremony

This ceremony, which is called a dedication, is based on the biblical account of Jesus calling young children to him and blessing them. The Church does not believe that the dedication constitutes salvation, but rather that it lets the child's parents publicly commit themselves to their intention to raise the child in the teachings of Jesus.

During the dedication, which is for infants or young children, the minister asks the parents to pledge to live in such a way that, at an early age, their child will be a Christian. They respond with "We do." Some ministers also charge the congregation to help the parents by role-modeling Christian living for the child.

The dedication, which is the same for males and females, usually lasts about three to five minutes. It is part of a larger service (usually a Sunday morning worship service) that lasts about 60 to 90 minutes.

BEFORE THE CEREMONY

Are guests usually invited by a formal invitation? No.

If not stated explicitly, should one assume that children are invited? Yes.

If one can't attend, what should one do? RSVP orally with regrets.

APPROPRIATE ATTIRE

Men: A jacket and tie or more casual attire, such as slacks and an informal shirt. No head covering is required.

Women: A dress or a skirt and blouse or other casual attire. Halters and shorts are frowned upon. Clothing need not cover the arms and hems need not reach below the knees. Open-toed shoes and modest jewelry are permissible. No head covering is required.

There are no rules regarding colors of clothing.

GIFTS

Is a gift customarily expected? No.

Should gifts be brought to the ceremony? See above.

THE CEREMONY

Where will the ceremony take place? In the main auditorium of the church.

When should guests arrive and where should they sit? Arrive shortly before the time for which the ceremony has been called. Sit wherever you wish.

If arriving late, are there times when a guest should *not* enter the ceremony? Do not enter during prayers.

Are there times when a guest should *not* leave the ceremony? Do not leave during prayers.

Who are the major officiants, leaders or participants at the ceremony and what do they do?
The minister, who leads the prayer of dedication and makes comments about the infant.
The child's parents.
The child.

What books are used? A Bible and a hymnal are used. Several translations of the Old and New Testaments are used throughout the Church. The most commonly used is the King James translation.

An overhead projector may be used to project the words of choruses to songs being sung by congregants.

To indicate the order of the ceremony: Periodic announcements will be made by the minister.

Will a guest who is not a member of the Pentecostal Church of God be expected to do anything other than sit? It is expected for guests to stand with the congregants. It is entirely optional for guests to sing with the congregants. Kneeling is seldom done during a service, although individual congregants may kneel at the end of the service in front of the altar. This is done entirely at their volition. Should there be kneeling during the service, guests may remain seated.

Are there any parts of the ceremony in which a guest who is not a member of the Pentecostal Church of God should *not* participate? Non-Christians should not participate in the Lord's Supper, which is a memorial to the death and Resurrection of Jesus Christ. It is intended only for believers in Christ.

If not disruptive to the ceremony, is it okay to:
Take pictures? Yes, but only with prior permission of the minister.
Use a flash? Rarely is this allowed—and only with prior permission of the minister—since it may distract from the ceremony.
Use a video camera? Rarely is this allowed, and only with prior permission of the minister.
Use a tape recorder? Yes.

Will contributions to the church be collected at the ceremony? Contributions will not be collected at the dedication itself, but they will be collected during the rest of the worship service.

How much is it customary to contribute? If one chooses to give, a contribution between $1 and $10 is appropriate; however, any contribution is appreciated.

AFTER THE CEREMONY

Is there usually a reception after the ceremony? No.

Is there a traditional greeting for the family? "Congratulations."

Is there a traditional form of address for clergy whom a guest may meet? "Minister," "Pastor" or "Brother."

Initiation Ceremony

This ceremony, which is the same for males and females, is called a baptism. During it, those who have accepted Christ as their savior are fully immersed in the baptismal waters.

Baptism is necessary because all people are born in a sinful condition. It is considered to be an outward expression of an inward spiritual work, and a public testimony of the death of the individual's sinful nature and of one's new birth in the spirit of Jesus. It endows believers with the power to witness and serve others, a dedication to the work of God, a more intense love for Jesus, and certain spiritual gifts. Baptism, which is performed once for any individual, can occur at any time during one's life. It always occurs after one has accepted Jesus Christ as his or her savior and after one has reached the age of accountability and knows right from wrong.

The baptismal ceremony is usually part of a regular Sunday morning or evening church service. The baptism itself may last about 15 to 30 minutes, depending on the number of persons being baptized.

BEFORE THE CEREMONY

Are guests usually invited by a formal invitation? They are usually invited informally and orally.

If not stated explicitly, should one assume that children are invited? Yes.

If one can't attend, what should one do? RSVP orally with regrets.

APPROPRIATE ATTIRE

Men: A jacket and tie or more casual attire, such as slacks and an informal shirt. No head covering is required.

Women: A dress or a skirt and blouse or other casual attire. Halters and shorts are frowned upon. Clothing need not cover the arms and hems need not reach below the knees. Open-toed shoes and modest jewelry are permissible. No head covering is required.

There are no rules regarding colors of clothing.

GIFTS

Is a gift customarily expected? No.

Should gifts be brought to the ceremony? See above.

THE CEREMONY

Where will the ceremony take place? In the main auditorium of the church.

When should guests arrive and where should they sit? Arrive shortly before the time for which the service has been called. Sit wherever you wish.

If arriving late, are there times when a guest should *not* enter the ceremony? Do not enter during prayers.

Are there times when a guest should *not* leave the ceremony? Do not leave during prayers.

Who are the major officiants, leaders or participants at the ceremony and what do they do?
The minister, who performs the baptism.

What books are used? A Bible and a hymnal are used. Several translations of the Old and New Testaments are used throughout the Church. The most commonly used is the King James translation.

An overhead projector may be used to project the words of choruses to songs being sung by congregants.

To indicate the order of the ceremony: Periodic announcements may be made by the minister or whoever is leading the ceremony.

Will a guest who is not a member of the Pentecostal Church of God be expected to do anything other than sit? It is expected for guests to stand with the congregants. It is entirely optional for guests to sing with the congregants. Kneeling is seldom done during the ceremony, although individual congregants may kneel at the end of the service directly in front of the altar. This is done entirely at their volition. Should there be kneeling during the service, guests may remain seated.

Are there any parts of the ceremony in which a guest who is not a member of the Pentecostal Church of God should *not* participate? Non-Christians should not participate in the Lord's Supper, which is a memorial to the death and Resurrection of Jesus Christ. It is intended only for believers in Christ.

If not disruptive to the ceremony, is it okay to:

Take pictures? Yes, but only with prior permission of the minister.

Use a flash? Yes, but only with prior permission of the minister.

Use a video camera? Yes, but only with prior permission of the minister.

Use a tape recorder? Yes.

Will contributions to the church be collected at the ceremony? Contributions will not be collected at the baptism itself, but they will be collected during the rest of the worship service.

How much is it customary to contribute? If one chooses to give, a contribution between $1 and $10 is appropriate; however, any contribution is appreciated.

AFTER THE CEREMONY

Is there usually a reception after the ceremony? No.

Is there a traditional greeting for the family? "Congratulations."

Is there a traditional form of address for clergy whom a guest may meet after the ceremony? "Minister," "Pastor" or "Brother."

Marriage Ceremony

The Pentecostal Church of God teaches that the family was the first institution ordained by God in the Garden of Eden. The basis for a family is marriage between a man and a woman. Marriage, which is not to be entered into lightly, is said to be "until death do us part."

The marriage ceremony is a ceremony in itself and may last 30 to 60 minutes.

BEFORE THE CEREMONY

Are guests usually invited by a formal invitation? Yes.

If not stated explicitly, should one assume that children are invited? Yes.

If one can't attend, what should one do? RSVP by card or letter with regrets and send a gift.

APPROPRIATE ATTIRE

Men: A jacket and tie or more casual attire, but not jeans or T-shirts. No head covering is required.

Women: A dress or a skirt and blouse. Clothing need not cover the arms and hems need not reach below the knees. Open-toed shoes and modest jewelry are permissible. No head covering is required.

There are no rules regarding colors of clothing.

GIFTS

Is a gift customarily expected? Yes. Cash, savings bonds or small household items are most frequently given.

Should gifts be brought to the ceremony? Gifts may either be brought to the ceremony or the reception afterward or be sent to the home of the newlyweds.

THE CEREMONY

Where will the ceremony take place? In the sanctuary of the church.

When should guests arrive and where should they sit? Arrive shortly before the time for which the ceremony has been called. Ushers will usually advise guests where to sit. Usually, the groom's family and friends sit on one side of the aisle and the bride's family and friends on the other.

If arriving late, are there times when a guest should *not* enter the ceremony? Do not enter during the processional or recessional of the wedding party.

Are there times when a guest should *not* leave the ceremony? Do not leave during the processional or recessional of the wedding party.

Who are the major officiants, leaders or participants at the ceremony and what do they do?
The minister, who officiates.
The bride and groom and members of the wedding party.

What books are used? No books are used by the guests.

To indicate the order of the ceremony: A program is sometimes distributed. If not, periodic announcements are made by the minister.

Will a guest who is not a member of the Pentecostal Church of God be expected to do anything other than sit? Guests of other faiths are expected to stand when other guests arise during the ceremony.

Are there any parts of the ceremony in which a guest who is not a member of the Pentecostal Church of God should *not* participate? No.

If not disruptive to the ceremony, is it okay to:
Take pictures? Yes, but only with prior permission of the minister.
Use a flash? Yes, but only with prior permission of the minister.
Use a video camera? Yes, but only with prior permission of the minister.
Use a tape recorder? Yes.

Will contributions to the church be collected at the ceremony? No.

AFTER THE CEREMONY

Is there usually a reception after the ceremony? Yes. It may be in the same building where the wedding ceremony was held or in a catering hall. Receptions usually include light food, such as finger foods, cake, mints, nuts and punch. There will be no alcoholic beverages or dancing, although there might be music. The reception may last 30 to 60 minutes.

Would it be considered impolite to neither eat nor drink? No.

Is there a grace or benediction before eating or drinking? No.

Is there a grace or benediction after eating or drinking? No.

Is there a traditional greeting for the family? Just offer your congratulations.

Is there a traditional form of address for clergy who may be at the reception? "Pastor," "Minister" or "Brother."

Is it okay to leave early? Yes.

Funerals and Mourning

Members of the Pentecostal Church of God believe that all Christians who have died will one day rise from their graves and meet the Lord "in the air." Meanwhile, Christians who are still alive will be caught up with those who have risen from their graves and will also be with the Lord. All who have thus joined with God will live forever.

A Pentecostal Church of God funeral usually begins with singing, Scripture reading or prayer. This is followed with hymns, prayer and worship to God, and a sermon and eulogy by the minister.

A ceremony in itself, the funeral ceremony lasts about 30 to 60 minutes.

BEFORE THE CEREMONY

How soon after the death does the funeral usually take place? Within two to three days.

What should someone who is not a member of the Pentecostal Church of God do upon hearing of the death of a member of that faith? Telephone or visit the bereaved to offer condolences and sympathies and offer to assist in any way possible.

APPROPRIATE ATTIRE

Men: A jacket and tie. No head covering is required.

Women: A dress or a skirt and blouse. Clothing need not cover the arms and hems need not reach below the knees. Open-toed shoes and modest jewelry are permissible. No head covering is required.

Dark, somber colors for clothing are advised.

GIFTS

Is it appropriate to send flowers or make a contribution? Flowers may be sent to the funeral home or church where the funeral ceremony is held. Contributions may be sent to a memorial fund determined by the bereaved.

Is it appropriate to send food? Yes. Send or take it yourself to the home of the bereaved.

THE CEREMONY

Where will the ceremony take place? Either in a church or in a funeral home.

When should guests arrive and where should they sit? Arrive at the time for which the ceremony has been scheduled. Ushers usually advise guests where to sit.

If arriving late, are there times when a guest should *not* enter the ceremony? No.

Will the bereaved family be present at the church or funeral home before the ceremony? Yes.

Is there a traditional greeting for the family? Just offer your condolences.

Will there be an open casket? Possibly. This varies with local custom.

Is a guest expected to view the body? This is optional.

What is appropriate behavior upon viewing the body? Look into the casket while walking slowly past it, then follow the instructions of the funeral director.

Who are the major officiants at the ceremony and what do they do?
The minister, who delivers a brief sermon and tribute to the deceased.
Musicians, who sing two or three songs.

What books are used? No books are used by mourners or guests.

To indicate the order of the ceremony: Either a program will be distributed or the minister will make the necessary announcements.

Will a guest who is not a member of the Pentecostal Church of God be expected to do anything other than sit? Guests of other faiths are expected to stand when other guests arise during the ceremony. While there is usually no kneeling during a funeral ceremony, if there is kneeling, guests of other faiths may remain seated.

Are there any parts of the ceremony in which a guest who is not a member of the Pentecostal Church of God should *not* participate? No.

If not disruptive to the ceremony, is it okay to:
Take pictures? No.
Use a flash? No.
Use a video camera? No.
Use a tape recorder? Yes.

Will contributions to the church be collected at the ceremony? No.

THE INTERMENT

Should guests attend the interment? Attendance is optional.

Whom should one ask for directions? An usher or the funeral director or just follow the funeral procession.

What happens at the graveside? There is usually a prayer and Scripture readings, and sometimes a song. The casket is committed to the ground.

Do guests who are not members of the Pentecostal Church of God participate at the graveside ceremony? No, they are simply present.

COMFORTING THE BEREAVED

Is it appropriate to visit the home of the bereaved after the funeral? Yes, if one knows the family well.

Will there be a religious service at the home of the bereaved? No.

Will food be served? Possibly, but no alcoholic beverages.

How soon after the funeral will a mourner usually return to a normal work schedule? A few days, depending upon individual preference. The Church has no set tradition.

How soon after the funeral will a mourner usually return to a nor- **mal social schedule?** This is entirely the choice of the bereaved, since the Church has no set tradition. It is often determined by local cultural traditions.

Are there mourning customs to which a friend who is not a member of the Pentecostal Church of God should be sensitive? No.

Are there rituals for observing the anniversary of the death? No.

5 · HOME CELEBRATIONS

Not applicable to the Pentecostal Church of God.

Presbyterian

1 • HISTORY AND BELIEFS

The Presbyterian Church was founded on the ideals of the Protestant Reformation and based on the concept of democratic rule under the authority of God. John Calvin (1509–1564) is the father of Presbyterianism.

All Presbyterians are required to trust in Christ as their forgiving savior, promise to follow Christ and his example for living, and commit themselves to attend church and to become involved in its work. They believe in the Holy Spirit (the empowering presence of God) speaking through the Bible, and in the sanctity of life.

Presbyterian theology emphasizes the majesty of God, who is conceived not just as truth or beauty, but also as intention, purpose, energy and will. The human counterpart of this is understanding the Christian life as the embodiment of the purposes of God and the working out of these purposes in one's life. Because of this, Presbyterians include many social activists, and those who try to shape and influence culture and history.

The Presbyterian Church (USA) was formed when the Presbyterian Church in the United States merged in 1983 with the United Presbyterian Church in the United States of America. The consolidation ended a schism that occurred during the Civil War when Southern Presbyterians broke away from the Presbyterian Church in the United States of America to create the Presbyterian Church in the Confederate States. Today's Presbyterian Church is the result of at least 10 different denominational mergers over the last 250 years and is strongly ecumenical in outlook.

The Presbyterian Church in Canada was formed in 1875 by the union of four branches of Presbyterianism that had been established as Europeans settled the country. The church experienced remarkable growth during the next 50 years, reaching almost 1.5 million members, the largest church in the country of 8.7 million people. Presbyterians had initiated discussions with the Methodist and Congregationalist churches, leading to the formation of the United Church of Canada in 1925. But a third of Presbyterians were not satisfied with the final plans and stayed out of the new denomination.

U.S. churches: 10,751
U.S. membership: 2.8 million
(data from the 2010 Yearbook of American and Canadian Churches*)*

For more information, contact:
The Presbyterian Church (USA)
100 Witherspoon Street
Louisville, KY 40202
(888) 728-7228
www.pcusa.org

Canadian churches: 933
Canadian membership: 178,482
(data from the 2010 Yearbook of American and Canadian Churches*)*

For more information, contact:
The Presbyterian Church in Canada
50 Wynford Drive
Toronto, ON M3C 1J7
(416) 441-1111
www.presbyterian.ca

2 · THE BASIC SERVICE

There are four main components to a basic worship service, plus one specific to worship service in Canada:

The Gathering, which includes the call to worship, the opening prayer, hymns of praise and confession and pardons.

The Word, which includes readings from the Bible (either the Old or New Testament, or both), psalms and hymns, a sermon and a baptism if one is scheduled for that day.

The Response (in Canada), which usually includes prayers and the gathering of people's offerings.

The Eucharist, or Communion, which represents the Last Supper of Jesus Christ and his subsequent Resurrection.

The Sending, which includes hymns, psalms and a blessing.

The service usually lasts about one hour.

APPROPRIATE ATTIRE

Men: Jacket and tie or, at the discretion of the individual, more casual clothing. No head covering is required.

Women: Dress or a skirt and blouse or, at the discretion of the individual, more casual clothing. Open-toed shoes and modest jewelry permitted. Hems need not reach the knees nor need arms be covered. No head covering is required.

There are no rules regarding colors of clothing.

THE SANCTUARY

What are the major sections of the church?

The narthex: The vestibule or entrance hall. This is at the end of the nave (see below) and opposite the altar area. Usually, the main outside door enters into the narthex.

The nave: Where congregants sit.

The chancel: Includes the altar and pulpit and seating for clergy. The pastor conducts the worship from this area.

THE SERVICE

When should guests arrive and where should they sit? It is customary to arrive at the time called. Sit wherever you like.

If arriving late, are there times when a guest should *not* enter the service? If you arrive late, take your cues from an usher, who will seat you.

Are there times when a guest should *not* leave the service? Unless it's an emergency, do not leave the service until it is over.

Who are the major officiants, leaders or participants and what do they do?

The pastor, or minister (in Canada), who preaches and leads the service.

A lay leader or worship leader, who is present in some churches to assist the pastor.

What are the major ritual objects of the service?

Bread and wine, which are consecrated into the body and blood of Jesus Christ.

The paten and chalice, which, respectively, hold the consecrated bread and the wine.

The Communion table, where the chalice and paten are placed.

A cross without the body of Christ resting on it. The absence of Christ represents his Resurrection.

An open Bible on a lectern. Its openness symbolizes that the Old and New Testaments are the primary source of Scripture and of faith for Presbyterians.

What books are used? In the United States, the two main books in the service are a hymnal and a Bible. Since there are no prescribed editions of either, hymnals and the version of the Bible may differ from one congregation to another. The most recent edition of the Old and New Testaments recommended for Presbyterians is the New Revised Standard Version, which is printed by several publishers. The most recent hymnal is the *Presbyterian Hymnal* (Louisville, Ky.: Westminster/John Knox Press, 1990). No individual Presbyterian or individual Presbyterian church is required to use these.

In Canada, the two main books in worship are *The Book of Praise* and the Bible. *The Book of Praise* contains the hymns sung by the congregation. There is also growing use of a Psalter (1997) that allows for the Psalms to be read or (in very few churches) chanted.

To indicate the order of the service: A program or bulletin will be distributed and the pastor or minister will announce the service.

GUEST BEHAVIOR DURING THE SERVICE

Will a guest who is not a Presbyterian be expected to do anything other than sit? Nothing is "expected" of guests. If they wish, they may stand, sing and pray with the congregation if this does not compromise their own religious beliefs.

Are there any parts of the service in which a guest who is not a Presbyterian should *not* participate? No.

If not disruptive to the service, is it okay to:
Take pictures? No.
Use a flash? No.
Use a video camera? No.
Use a tape recorder? No.

Will contributions to the church be collected at the service? Yes, but guests are not expected to contribute.

How much is it customary to contribute? Between $1 and $10.

AFTER THE SERVICE

Is there usually a reception after the service? Often, there is a reception in the reception area that may last 30 minutes. Coffee is sometimes served. More substantial fare should not be expected. Alcohol will not be served. There is no benediction or grace before beginning.

Is there a traditional form of address for clergy who may be at the reception? "Reverend," followed by the pastor's last name. In Canada, simply "Mr." or "Ms." followed by the minister's last name. Not "Reverend."

Is it okay to leave early? Yes.

GENERAL GUIDELINES AND ADVICE

Nothing is "expected" of guests. They may stand, sing and pray with the congregation if this does not compromise their own religious beliefs. This is their choice.

SPECIAL VOCABULARY

None provided.

DOGMA AND IDEOLOGY

Presbyterians believe:

God alone is the Lord of conscience. This fundamental tenet of Presbyterianism refers to the belief that no temporal religious authority—no clergy—intercedes between each person and God, that the primary relationship is between each person and God.

God is revealed in Jesus Christ.

The Bible (both the Old and New Testaments) is the authoritative witness to God in Christ; God is incarnate in Jesus, and the Bible is the authoritative account of his life.

Clergy and laypersons are peers in the Church.

The Church is guided by a constitution and doctrinal statements that have the force of Church law. The constitution, which was the model for the constitution of the United States, addresses religious practice; the doctrinal statements address belief.

Some basic books to which a guest can refer to learn more about Presbyterianism:

A Brief History of the Presbyterians, by James H. Smylie (Louisville, Ky.: Geneva Press, 1996).

This Presbyterian Church of Ours, by John Congram (Winfield, B.C.: Wood Lake Books, 1995).

3 · HOLY DAYS AND FESTIVALS

Advent. Begins four weeks before Christmas. The purpose is to prepare for Christmas and to focus on Christ. There is no traditional greeting for Advent.

Christmas. Occurs on the evening of December 24 and the day of December 25. Marks the birth and the incarnation of God as a man.

The traditional greeting is "Merry Christmas."

Lent. Begins on Ash Wednesday, which occurs six weeks before Easter. The purpose is to prepare for Easter. There is no traditional greeting for Lent. Between Lent and Easter, abstention from entertainment is encouraged, as is increased giving to the poor. Often, there are midweek worship services. Very few Presbyterians fast during Lent.

Easter. Always falls on the Sunday after the first full moon that occurs on or after the spring equinox on March 21. Celebrates the Resurrection of Jesus Christ. The traditional greeting is "Happy Easter!" In worship services, the pastor may greet congregants with "He is risen!" Congregants respond with "He is risen, indeed!"

Pentecost Sunday. The seventh Sunday after Easter. Celebrates the coming of the Holy Spirit, which is the empowering spirit of God in human life. This is often considered the birth of the Christian church. There is no traditional greeting for this holiday.

4 · LIFE CYCLE EVENTS

Birth Ceremony

Baptism is usually the celebration of the birth of an infant into the Church, although it can occur anytime from birth onward through adulthood. The ceremony is usually integrated into a regular church service and may last about 15 minutes.

In the Presbyterian Church, baptism is administered only once.

The Church teaches that baptism "initiates us into the Church, bestows the promise of God's grace upon us, assures us that God forgives our sins, calls us to a life of Christian service and fulfillment."

A Presbyterian baptism has five parts:

"Presentation," in which the parents or guardians of the child bring the child forward for baptism. This happens immediately after the sermon.

"Profession of Faith and Promise," in which parents and the entire congregation promise to love and care for the newly baptized.

"Thanksgiving and Prayer," in which the congregation stands and offers God a prayer of praise and thanks.

The actual "Washing with Water," in which the minister addresses the infant by his or her new official name and says, "I baptize you in the name of the Father, and of the Son, and of the Holy Spirit." The minister then pours or sprinkles water over the child's head, or dips or immerses him or her in water.

The newly baptized infant is welcomed into the congregation and proclaimed a member of God's family.

BEFORE THE CEREMONY

Are guests usually invited by a formal invitation? Guests of other faiths are usually invited by a phone call.

If not stated explicitly, should one assume that children are invited? Yes.

If one can't attend, what should one do? RSVP with regrets. No present is expected.

APPROPRIATE ATTIRE

Men: Jacket and tie or, at the discretion of the individual, more casual clothing. No head covering is required.

Women: Dress or a skirt and blouse or, at the discretion of the individual, more casual clothing. Open-toed shoes and modest jewelry permitted. Hems need not reach the knees nor need arms be covered. No head covering is required.

There are no rules regarding colors of clothing.

GIFTS

Is a gift customarily expected? No.

THE CEREMONY

Where will the ceremony take place? In the main sanctuary of the church.

When should guests arrive and where should they sit? It is customary to arrive at the time called. Sit wherever you like.

If arriving late, are there times when a guest should *not* enter the ceremony? If you arrive late, take your cues from an usher, who will seat you.

Are there times when a guest should *not* leave the ceremony? Unless it's an emergency, do not leave the service until it is over.

Who are the major officiants, leaders or participants at the ceremony and what do they do?

The pastor or minister, who leads the service and performs the actual baptism.

An elder, who is a layperson elected and ordained by church members to exercise leadership of the church. He or she presents the child to the pastor for baptism and asks the parents and the congregation a series of questions that address their commitment to nurture the person being baptized and to help him or her follow Christ.

The parents, who present the child to the elder and answer his or her questions.

What books are used? In the United States, the two main books in the service are a hymnal and a Bible. Since there are no prescribed editions of either, hymnals and the version of the Bible may differ from one congregation to another. The most recent edition of the Old and New Testaments recommended for Presbyterians is the New Revised Standard Version, which is printed by several publishers. The most recent hymnal is the *Presbyterian Hymnal* (Louisville, Ky.: Westminster/John Knox Press, 1990). No individual Presbyterian or individual Presbyterian church is required to use these.

In Canada, the two main books in worship are *The Book of Praise* and the Bible. *The Book of Praise* contains the hymns sung by the congregation. There is also growing use of a Psalter (1997) that allows for the Psalms to be read or (in very few churches) chanted.

To indicate the order of the ceremony: A program or bulletin will be distributed and the pastor or minister will announce the service.

Will a guest who is not a Presbyterian be expected to do anything other than sit? Nothing is "expected" of guests. If they wish, they may stand, sing and pray with the congregation, if this does not compromise their own religious beliefs.

Guests who are Christian may take Communion with the congregation, if their faith permits it.

Are there any parts of the ceremony in which a guest who is not a Presbyterian should *not* participate? Guests need not participate in the "Profession of Faith and Promise," in which the entire congregation promises to love and care for the newly baptized; and the "Thanksgiving and Prayer," in which the congregation stands and offers God a prayer of praise and thanks.

If not disruptive to the ceremony, is it okay to:
Take pictures? No.
Use a flash? No.
Use a video camera? No.
Use a tape recorder? No.

Will contributions to the church be collected at the ceremony? Yes, but guests are not expected to contribute.

How much is it customary to contribute? Between $1 and $10.

AFTER THE CEREMONY

Is there usually a reception after the ceremony? No.

Is there a traditional form of address for clergy whom a guest may meet? "Reverend," followed by the pastor's last name. In Canada, simply "Mr." or "Ms." followed by the minister's last name. Not "Reverend."

Initiation Ceremony

The confirmation ceremony initiates one into the Church and may last 15 to 30 minutes. The participant is usually a preadolescent or early adolescent. The ceremony may be performed with an individual or with a class or others who are also being confirmed.

During the ceremony, there are a series of questions and answers between the pastor and the confirmands. These are formulaic. If the participants have not been baptized, this is done at the confirmation.

BEFORE THE CEREMONY

Are guests usually invited by a formal invitation? Guests of other faiths are usually invited by a phone call.

If not stated explicitly, should one assume that children are invited? Yes.

If one can't attend, what should one do? RSVP with regrets. A present is not expected.

APPROPRIATE ATTIRE

Men: Jacket and tie or, at the discretion of the individual, more casual clothing. No head covering is required.

Women: Dress or a skirt and blouse or, at the discretion of the individual, more casual clothing. Open-toed shoes and modest jewelry permitted. Hems need not reach the knees nor need arms be covered. No head covering is required.

There are no rules regarding colors of clothing.

GIFTS

Is a gift customarily expected? No.

THE CEREMONY

Where will the ceremony take place? In the main sanctuary of the church.

When should guests arrive and where should they sit? It is customary to arrive at the time called. Sit wherever you like.

If arriving late, are there times when a guest should *not* enter the ceremony? If you arrive late, take your cues from an usher, who will seat you.

Are there times when a guest should *not* leave the ceremony? Unless it's an emergency, do not leave the service until it is over.

Who are the major officiants, leaders or participants at the ceremony and what do they do?
The pastor, who leads the service.
An elder, who is a layperson elected and ordained by church members to exercise leadership of the church.

What books are used? In the United States, the two main books in the service are a hymnal and a Bible. Since there are no prescribed editions of either, hymnals and the version of the Bible may differ from one congregation to another. The most recent edition of the Old and New Testaments recommended for Presbyterians is the New Revised Standard Version, which is printed by several publishers. The most recent hymnal is the *Presbyterian Hymnal* (Louisville, Ky.: Westminster/John Knox Press, 1990). No individual Presbyterian or individual Presbyterian church is required to use these.

In Canada, the two main books in worship are *The Book of Praise* and the Bible. *The Book of Praise* contains the hymns sung by the congregation. There is also growing use of a Psalter (1997) that allows for the Psalms to be read or (in very few churches) chanted.

To indicate the order of the ceremony: A program or bulletin will be distributed and the pastor or minister will announce the service.

Will a guest who is not a Presbyterian be expected to do anything other than sit? Nothing is "expected" of guests. If they wish, they may stand, sing and pray with the congregation, if this does not compromise their own religious beliefs.

Are there any parts of the ceremony in which a guest who is not a Presbyterian should *not* participate? No.

If not disruptive to the ceremony, is it okay to:
Take pictures? No.
Use a flash? No.
Use a video camera? No.
Use a tape recorder? No.

Will contributions to the church be collected at the ceremony? Yes, but guests are not expected to contribute.

How much is it customary to contribute? Between $1 and $10.

AFTER THE CEREMONY

Is there usually a reception after the ceremony? Often, there is a reception in the reception area that may last 30 minutes. Coffee is sometimes served. More substantial fare should not be expected. Alcohol will not be served.

Would it be considered impolite to neither eat nor drink? No.

Is there a grace or benediction before eating or drinking? No.

Is there a grace or benediction after eating or drinking? No.

Is there a traditional greeting for the family? No. Just offer your congratulations.

Is there a traditional form of address for clergy who may be at the reception? "Reverend," followed by the pastor's last name. In Canada, simply "Mr." or "Ms." followed by the minister's last name. Not "Reverend."

Is it okay to leave early? Yes.

Marriage Ceremony

Presbyterians consider the marital relationship to be sacred, but the wedding ceremony is not a sacrament. For Presbyterians, there are only two sacraments: baptism and Communion.

The wedding ceremony varies widely, but generally follows the order of worship used by the church during Sunday services, with the addition of exchanging rings and vows. The wedding ceremony takes 30 to 60 minutes.

BEFORE THE CEREMONY

Are guests usually invited by a formal invitation? Yes.

If not stated explicitly, should one assume that children are invited? No.

If one can't attend, what should one do? RSVP with regrets and send a gift or card.

APPROPRIATE ATTIRE

Men: Jacket and tie or, at the discretion of the individual, more casual clothing. No head covering is required.

Women: Dress or a skirt and blouse or, at the discretion of the individual, more casual clothing. Open-toed shoes and modest jewelry permitted. Hems need not reach the knees nor need arms be covered. No head covering is required.

There are no rules regarding colors of clothing.

GIFTS

Is a gift customarily expected? Yes, usually such gifts as household items (towels, sheets, small appliances) are appropriate.

Should gifts be brought to the ceremony? Gifts should be sent to the home of the newlyweds or brought to the reception.

THE CEREMONY

Where will the ceremony take place? In the church.

When should guests arrive and where should they sit? Arrive on time. An usher will show guests where to sit.

If arriving late, are there times when a guest should *not* enter the ceremony? Follow the usher's cues for entering the service. Do not enter during the procession or recession of the wedding party.

Are there times when a guest should *not* leave the ceremony? Do not leave during the procession or recession of the wedding party.

Who are the major officiants, leaders or participants at the ceremony and what do they do?

The pastor or minister, who leads the service.

The bride and groom and the members of the wedding party.

What books are used? In the United States, the two main books in the service are a hymnal and a Bible. Since there are no prescribed editions of either, hymnals and the version of the Bible may differ from one congregation to another. The most recent edition of the Old and New Testaments recommended for Presbyterians is the New Revised Standard Version, which is printed by several publishers. The most recent hymnal is the *Presbyterian Hymnal* (Louisville, Ky.: Westminster/John Knox Press, 1990). No individual Presbyterian or individual Presbyterian church is required to use these.

In Canada, the two main books in worship are *The Book of Praise* and the Bible. *The Book of Praise* contains the hymns sung by the congregation. There is also growing use of a Psalter (1997) that allows for the Psalms to be read or (in very few churches) chanted.

To indicate the order of the ceremony: The pastor or minister will make announcements as the service proceeds. A printed program or bulletin for the service may be distributed.

Will a guest who is not a Presbyterian be expected to do anything other than sit? Nothing is "expected" of guests. If they wish, they may stand, sing and pray with the congregation, if this does not compromise their own religious beliefs.

Are there any parts of the ceremony in which a guest who is not a Presbyterian should *not* participate? No.

If not disruptive to the ceremony, is it okay to:
Take pictures? Yes.
Use a flash? No.
Use a video camera? Yes.
Use a tape recorder? Yes.

Will contributions to the church be collected at the ceremony? No.

AFTER THE CEREMONY

Is there usually a reception after the ceremony? There is usually a one- to two-hour reception, with eating, drinking and toasting. Alcoholic beverages will probably be served. There may also be dancing and music.

It may be in a church hall, a catering facility or another place chosen by the bride and groom.

Would it be considered impolite to neither eat nor drink? No.

Is there a grace or benediction before eating or drinking? Depends on local preferences.

Is there a grace or benediction after eating or drinking? No.

Is there a traditional greeting for the family? Just offer your congratulations to the bride and groom and their immediate family.

Is there a traditional form of address for clergy who may be at the reception? "Reverend," followed by the pastor's last name. In Canada, simply "Mr." or "Ms." followed by the minister's last name. Not "Reverend."

Is it okay to leave early? Depends on local preferences.

Funerals and Mourning

Presbyterians believe that in heaven the souls of the faithful are reunited with God in a warm and loving relationship. They also believe that it is not for humans to judge the fate of the unfaithful.

The funeral follows the order of Sunday worship, with prayers added both for the deceased and for those assembled. Scripture texts that are used convey assurances of eternal life. The funeral usually lasts about 30 to 60 minutes.

BEFORE THE CEREMONY

How soon after the death does the funeral usually take place? Usually within two to three days.

What should a non-Presbyterian do upon hearing of the death of a member of that faith? Telephone the bereaved to offer your condolences. Whether one visits the home of the bereaved varies with the mourners' preference and predisposition. Those who are known to be more "open" would probably welcome visitors. Those who are more private might prefer no visitors. One can certainly call the bereaved to get a sense of their preference.

APPROPRIATE ATTIRE

Men: Jacket and tie. No head covering is required.

Women: Dresses or skirt and blouse. Open-toed shoes and modest jewelry permitted. Hems need not reach the knees nor need arms be covered. No head covering is required.

There are no rules regarding colors of clothing, but dark, somber colors are recommended.

GIFTS

Is it appropriate to send flowers or make a contribution? Flowers are appreciated. They may be sent to the bereaved or to the funeral home before the funeral upon hearing the news of the death or shortly thereafter. Other contributions are not customary, although the family may suggest contributions to charity in lieu of flowers.

Is it appropriate to send food? Yes, to the home of the bereaved after the funeral.

THE CEREMONY

Where will the ceremony take place? At a church or a funeral home.

When should guests arrive and where should they sit? Arrive on time. Sit wherever you wish.

If arriving late, are there times when a guest should *not* enter the ceremony? If you arrive late, wait to be seated.

Will the bereaved family be present at the church or the funeral home before the ceremony? It is not customary for the family to be publicly present before the service.

Is there a traditional greeting for the family? Just offer your condolences.

Will there be an open casket? Rarely.

Is a guest expected to view the body? This is the individual's choice to make.

What is appropriate behavior upon viewing the body? Silent prayer.

Who are the major officiants at the ceremony and what do they do? *The pastor or minister*, who officiates.

What books are used? In the United States, the two main books in the service are a hymnal and a Bible. Since there are no prescribed editions of either, hymnals and the version of the Bible may differ from one congregation to another. The most recent edition of the Old and New Testaments recommended for Presbyterians is the New Revised Standard Version, which is printed by several publishers. The most recent hymnal is the *Presbyterian Hymnal* (Louisville, Ky.: Westminster/John Knox Press, 1990). No individual Presbyterian or individual Presbyterian church is required to use these.

In Canada, the two main books in worship are *The Book of Praise* and the Bible. *The Book of Praise* contains the hymns sung by the congregation. There is also growing use of a Psalter (1997) that allows for the Psalms to be read or (in very few churches) chanted.

To indicate the order of the ceremony: A program or bulletin will be distributed and the pastor or minister will announce the service.

Will a guest who is not a Presbyterian be expected to do anything other than sit? Guests are not expected to do or say anything at the funeral.

Are there any parts of the ceremony in which a guest who is not a Presbyterian should *not* participate? No.

If not disruptive to the ceremony, is it okay to:
Take pictures? No.
Use a flash? No.
Use a video camera? No.
Use a tape recorder? No.

Will contributions to the church be collected at the ceremony? No.

THE INTERMENT

Should guests attend the interment? Yes.

Whom should one ask for directions? The ushers.

What happens at the graveside? The officiating pastor or minister recites prayers. The graveside service may last 10 to 15 minutes.

Do guests who are not Presbyterians participate at the graveside service? No. They are simply present.

COMFORTING THE BEREAVED

Is it appropriate to visit the home of the bereaved after the funeral? This depends on the preferences of the bereaved. There is no set tradition. Frequently, mourners welcome visitors at their home after the funeral. This imparts a sense of community to the grieving process. Other mourners may prefer solitude and privacy.

Will there be a religious service at the home of the bereaved? No.

Will food be served? Possibly. This is at the discretion of the hosts.

How soon after the funeral will a mourner usually return to a normal work schedule? This is left to the discretion of the mourner, but is usually about a week.

How soon after the funeral will a mourner usually return to a normal social schedule? This is left to the discretion of the mourner, but is usually about a week.

Are there mourning customs to which a friend who is not Presbyterian should be sensitive? No.

Are there rituals for observing the anniversary of the death? No.

5 · HOME CELEBRATIONS

Not applicable to Presbyterians.

22

Quaker
(Religious Society of Friends)

1. HISTORY AND BELIEFS

The name Quaker was originally a nickname for the Children of Light or the Friends of Truth, as they called themselves. Members of the group were said to tremble or quake with religious zeal, and the nickname stuck. In time, they came to be known simply as "Friends."

The central Quaker conviction is that the saving knowledge and power of God are present as divine influences in each person through what has been variously called the "inner light," the "light of the eternal Christ within" or "the Seed within." Many affirm their acceptance of Jesus as their personal savior. Others conceive of the inward guide as a universal spirit that was in Jesus in abundant nature and is in everyone to some degree.

This reliance on the spirit within was a direct challenge to religions that relied on outward authority, such as Catholicism or mainstream Protestantism. Largely because of this, Quakers were persecuted from the time they were founded in England in the 1650s. This tapered off about four decades later, and the English Quakers continued to grow and establish Quaker meetings, or congregations, in many parts of the world, especially in the British colonies in North America.

Quakers do not have ordained ministers and do not celebrate outward Christian sacraments. They seek, instead, an inward reality and contend that all life is sacramental.

Belief in the "inner light" present in every person also accounts for the distinctive nature of unprogrammed Quaker worship, in which the congregation is silent except when individuals are moved to speak. This conviction also motivates Quaker confidence in working for the Kingdom of God in this world and their emphasis over the years on nonviolence and peace, abolishing slavery, relieving suffering, improving housing, educational and employment opportunities, reforming prisons, and eliminating prejudice and discrimination against minorities and the underprivileged.

Quakers are strongly opposed to war and conscription and seek to remove the causes of war and conflict. While a few Quakers have accepted the draft and fought in wars, most declare themselves to be conscientious objectors. A small minority are draft resisters, and refuse to register or in any way cooperate with the military system.

U.S. meetings, or congregations: 1,200

U.S. membership: 104,000
(data from the 2010 Yearbook of American and Canadian Churches*)*

For more information, contact:
The Friends World Committee for Consultation
Section of the Americas
1506 Race Street
Philadelphia, PA 19102
(215) 241-7250
www.fwccworld.org

Canadian meetings or worship groups: Not available
Canadian membership: 1,176
(data from Canadian Yearly Meeting Report, 2009*)*

For more information, contact:
Canadian Yearly Meeting
Religious Society of Friends (Quakers)
91A Fourth Avenue
Ottawa, ON K1S 2L1
(613) 235-8553
(888) 296-3222
www.quaker.ca

2 · THE BASIC SERVICE

There are two types of Quaker "meetings," or worship events: "unprogrammed" and "programmed." Unprogrammed meetings are held in the traditional manner of the Friends on the basis of silence. Worshipers sit and wait for divine guidance and inspiration. If so moved, they then speak. If so inspired, people may also sing. Either is called "vocal ministry."

Programmed meetings are planned in advance and may include hymn singing, vocal prayer, Bible reading, silent worship and a sermon. In many cases, worship is led by a pastor, who is generally paid and is responsible for other pastoral services in the meeting.

Either form of meeting usually lasts an hour.

APPROPRIATE ATTIRE

Men: Jackets and ties are more often worn by older Friends; more casual clothes are usually worn by younger Friends, especially those around college age or below. In general, the emphasis at Quaker meetings is on casual attire. No head covering is required.

Women: A skirt and blouse or pants suit. Open-toed shoes and modest jewelry are permissible. More casual clothes are usually worn by younger Friends, especially those around college age or below. In general, the emphasis at Quaker meetings is on casual attire. No head covering is required.

There are no rules regarding colors of clothing.

THE SANCTUARY

What are the major sections of the meetinghouse? Aside from the facing bench, where the elders traditionally sat, there is no undifferentiated section in the meetinghouse. In most meetinghouses, the facing bench has now been integrated into the rest of the seating, although raised benches on the side of the meetinghouse may remain. In Canada, many small meetings are held in members' homes.

An elder is a spiritually sensitive person appointed by the monthly meeting to assist the recorded ministers in their work and to share with them discernment and spiritual concern for members of the meeting. In Canada, where the term *elder* is rarely used, a meeting of Ministry and Counsel is appointed by the monthly meeting to oversee its spiritual life and to coordinate pastoral care for its members.

THE SERVICE

When should guests arrive and where should they sit? It is customary to arrive early. There are no restrictions on where to sit.

If arriving late, are there times when a guest should *not* enter the service? If someone is offering a vocal ministry, wait until he or she has finished.

Are there times when a guest should *not* leave the service? Ordinarily, no one leaves the meeting. If it is necessary to do so, do not leave when someone is offering vocal ministry.

Who are the major officiants, leaders or participants and what do they do? Two members of the meeting, who often belong to a worship and ministry committee (or a committee with a similar function),

will close the service by shaking hands with each other. This prompts all those attending to shake hands with those near them. This is often followed by introducing visitors and making announcements, and then by a coffee hour.

What are the major ritual objects of the service? There are none.

What books are used? In unprogrammed meetings, there is no collective oral or silent reading during the service. Bibles and hymnals may be available, as well as *Faith and Practice*, published by each yearly meeting, which is the overarching body that includes various monthly meetings, or congregations, in a specific geographic area. This book sets out the belief and the way of doing business of the yearly meeting.

Sometimes *Faith and Practice* is called *The Discipline*.

To indicate the order of the service: In unprogrammed meetings, no announcements are made or programs provided. The "order" of the service is spontaneous and determined by who is present and what, if anything, they are moved to say. However, brochures that explain Quaker services may be available in the meetinghouse.

Some programmed meetings provide written programs, in addition to general brochures about Friends' worship and belief.

GUEST BEHAVIOR DURING THE SERVICE

Will a guest who is not a Quaker be expected to do anything other than sit? No. Those attending an unprogrammed meeting for worship simply sit expectantly unless they are moved to speak or offer a prayer or message that comes out of the silence. All present, Quaker and non-Quaker, are welcome to give such "vocal ministry."

Are there any parts of the service in which a guest who is not a Quaker should *not* participate? No.

If not disruptive to the service, is it okay to:

Take pictures? No.

Use a flash? No.

Use a video camera? No.

Use a tape recorder? Possibly. Ask permission in advance from the meeting contact (clerk, pastor, secretary—whomever you can reach by phoning the meeting).

Will contributions to the meeting be collected at the service? Possibly, depending on the meetinghouse and its practices. Contribution envelopes may be next to the facing bench where the elders sit or at the table, usually in the front hallway of a meetinghouse, where literature and brochures about Friends are placed.

How much is it customary to contribute? Give as you feel led. Often, $1 to $10 is sufficient.

AFTER THE SERVICE

Is there usually a reception after the service? Yes, usually somewhere in the meeting building. It may last about 30 to 60 minutes. Usually, cookies, coffee and tea are served.

It is not considered impolite to neither eat nor drink. There is no grace or benediction before or after eating or drinking except before a full meal, when there is a blessing or silent grace.

Is there a traditional form of address for clergy who may be at the reception? Quakers have no ordained clergy; pastors and ministers do not have a traditional form of address.

Is it okay to leave early? Yes.

GENERAL GUIDELINES AND ADVICE

If a visitor is moved to offer a vocal ministry, the person should first consider his or her motivation for speaking. Those who speak should be mindful about how long they speak and respect the need for an interval of time for worshipers to receive and consider the previous message from another worshiper.

Do not speak unless deeply moved and certain that your message is one that needs to be shared with those present. Do not feel that you need to respond to a previous message. The messages offered at Quaker worship do not constitute a discussion.

SPECIAL VOCABULARY

None provided.

DOGMA AND IDEOLOGY

Quakers believe:

"Meeting," or worship, is held in the presence of God and no intermediary is needed between individual worshipers and God.

God can speak to—and potentially through—each person.

The true sacraments are experiences of inner spiritual grace, not outward material symbols of that grace. For Quakers, all of life's activities have sacred potential.

Some basic books to which a guest can refer to learn more about the Religious Society of Friends:

Friends for 350 Years: The History and Beliefs of the Society of Friends Since George Fox Started the Quaker Movement by Howard Brinton, with historical update and page and line notes by Margaret Hope Bacon (Wallingford, Pa.: Pendle Hill, 2002).

Guide to Quaker Practice by Howard Brinton (Wallingford, Pa.: Pendle Hill).

Introduction from Quaker Spirituality by Douglas Steere (Philadelphia Yearly Meeting, 1988).

One Explorer's Glossary of Quaker Terms by Warren Smith, edited by Mae Smith Bixby, revised by Deborah Haines (Philadelphia: Quaker Press of Friends General Conference, 2002).

Quaker Spirituality: Selected Writings, edited by Emile Griffin and Douglas V. Steere (New York: HarperCollins, 2005).

Three periodicals would also be useful: *Friends Journal,* an independent monthly magazine, is available from its offices at 1216 Arch St., Philadelphia, PA 19107; www.friendsjournal.org. *Quaker Life* is published 10 times yearly by the Friends United Meeting, 101 Quaker Hill Drive, Richmond, IN 47374; www.fum.org/QL. In Canada, *The Canadian Friend,* the bimonthly magazine of

the Canadian Yearly Meeting, is available from the Yearly Meeting Office at 91A Fourth Ave., Ottawa, ON K1S 2L1; www.quaker.ca/Publications.

3. HOLY DAYS AND FESTIVALS

Friends believe that every day is a holy day and that no one day is to be celebrated more than any other. Nevertheless, some Christmas and Easter celebrations do occasionally occur among Quakers through the influence of other Christian denominations. As with those denominations, Christmas, which always falls on December 25, celebrates the birth of Christ; and Easter, which usually occurs in April, commemorates the death and Resurrection of Jesus. Easter always falls on the Sunday after the first full moon that occurs on or after the spring equinox of March 21.

As with other Christian faiths, the traditional greetings among Quakers for these holidays are "Merry Christmas" and "Happy Easter."

4. LIFE CYCLE EVENTS

Birth Ceremony

While some Quaker meetings may hold a special or called meeting for worship to celebrate the birth of a child, there is generally no accepted way to commemorate a birth.

What transpires at a special, or called, meeting is the same as at an ordinary meeting. It is just convened, in this instance, for the purpose of celebrating the birth of a child.

Meetings usually last about an hour.

BEFORE THE CEREMONY

Are guests usually invited by a formal invitation? Possibly. If no invitation is extended to the meeting as a whole, then there is a formal invitation.

If not stated explicitly, should one assume that children are invited? Yes.

If one can't attend, what should one do? If there is a formal invitation, RSVP with your regrets.

APPROPRIATE ATTIRE

Men: Jackets and ties are more often worn by older Friends; more casual clothes are usually worn by younger Friends, especially those around college age or below. In general, the emphasis at Quaker meetings is on casual attire. No head covering is required.

Women: A skirt and blouse or pants suit. Open-toed shoes and modest jewelry are permissible. More casual clothes are usually worn by younger Friends, especially those around college age or below. In general, the emphasis at Quaker meetings is on casual attire. No head covering is required.

There are no rules regarding colors of clothing.

GIFTS

Is a gift customarily expected? Only if one is formally invited. There is no Quaker expectation about how much should be spent on a gift. Many Friends prefer to give educational presents to youngsters rather than toys designed to generate children's interest in such media programming as Saturday morning cartoons.

Should gifts be brought to the ceremony? They can be brought either to the ceremony or to the reception.

THE CEREMONY

Where will the ceremony take place? In the meetinghouse or the home of the parents.

When should guests arrive and where should they sit? It is customary to arrive early. There are no restrictions on where to sit.

If arriving late, are there times when a guest should *not* enter the ceremony? If someone is offering a vocal ministry, wait until he or she has finished.

Are there times when a guest should *not* leave the ceremony? Ordinarily, no one leaves the meeting. If it is necessary to do so, do not leave when someone is offering vocal ministry.

Who are the major officiants, leaders or participants at the ceremony and what do they do?
The family and child, who are the center of attention. Those present at the meeting may comment about the child or the family.

What books are used? Possibly a Bible or a hymnal.

To indicate the order of the ceremony: Probably nothing will be provided.

Will a guest who is not a Quaker be expected to do anything other than sit? No. Those attending an unprogrammed meeting for worship simply sit expectantly unless they are moved to speak or offer a prayer or message that comes out of the silence. All pres-ent, Quaker and non-Quaker, are welcome to give such "vocal ministry."

Are there any parts of the ceremony in which a guest who is not a Quaker should *not* participate? No.

If not disruptive to the ceremony, is it okay to:
Take pictures? No.
Use a flash? No.
Use a video camera? No.
Use a tape recorder? No.

Will contributions to the meeting be collected at the ceremony? Probably not.

AFTER THE CEREMONY

Is there usually a reception after the ceremony? There is usually a reception at which food is served. The reception may last 30 to 60 minutes.

Would it be considered impolite to neither eat nor drink? No.

Is there a grace or benediction before eating or drinking? If the meeting is serving a full meal, there will probably be a blessing or silent grace. If there is only light food, there will not be a blessing.

Is there a grace or benediction after eating or drinking? Not usually.

Is there a traditional greeting for the family? No. Simply offer your best wishes.

Is there a traditional form of address for clergy who may be at the reception? Quakers have no ordained clergy; pastors and ministers do not have a traditional form of address.

Is it okay to leave early? Yes.

Initiation Ceremony

Quakers have no special celebration initiating an adolescent into the faith. Some meetings may present a young Friend who is between 13 and 16 years old with a Bible or a copy of his or her yearly meeting's *Faith and Practice*. This is usually done privately or at First Day School, the Quaker term for Sunday school.

Marriage Ceremony

From its beginnings, the Religious Society of Friends has stressed the belief that marriage is a binding relationship entered into in the presence of God and of witnessing friends. Before this public commitment is made on the day of the wedding, the proposed marriage has already received the approval of the monthly meeting, which is given after careful consideration by an appointed committee.

A Quaker marriage ceremony has the form of a regular meeting, or worship service, but during it the bride and groom exchange vows and sign a marriage certificate. The certificate, which is a religious document, is read aloud, and then the meeting continues. There is also a legal marriage certificate that is witnessed by two members of the meeting's oversight committee.

There are two types of Quaker meetings: "unprogrammed" and "programmed." Unprogrammed meetings are held in the traditional manner of the Friends on the basis of silence. Worshipers sit and wait for divine guidance and inspiration. If so moved, they then speak to the group. This is called "vocal ministry."

Programmed meetings are planned in advance and usually include hymn singing, vocal prayers, Bible reading, silent worship and a sermon. In many cases, worship is led by a pastor, who is generally paid and is responsible for some other pastoral services in the meeting.

The marriage ceremony may last 30 to 60 minutes.

BEFORE THE CEREMONY

Are guests usually invited by a formal invitation? Yes.

If not stated explicitly, should one assume that children are invited? Yes.

If one can't attend, what should one do? RSVP with your regrets. Possibly send a gift.

APPROPRIATE ATTIRE

Men: Jacket and tie or more informal clothing. Varies with each ceremony. No head covering is required.

Women: A dress or a skirt and blouse or a pants suit. Open-toed shoes and modest jewelry are permissible. Varies with each ceremony. No head covering is required.

There are no rules regarding colors of clothing.

GIFTS

Is a gift customarily expected? Yes—anything the giver deems appropriate or that is requested by the newlyweds. Some couples may suggest that contributions be given to a certain charity or cause; others may register with a bridal registry.

Should gifts be brought to the ceremony? Usually they are sent to the home of the newlyweds.

THE CEREMONY

Where will the ceremony take place? Depending on the wishes of the bride and groom, it may be in their meetinghouse or in a home or outdoors.

When should guests arrive and where should they sit? Arrive early. Ushers will probably advise guests on where to sit. The front rows tend to be reserved for immediate members of the two families.

If arriving late, are there times when a guest should *not* enter the ceremo-

ny? If someone is offering a vocal ministry, wait until he or she has finished.

Are there times when a guest should *not* leave the ceremony? It is inappropriate to leave, especially during vocal ministry.

Who are the major officiants, leaders or participants and what do they do?
Members of the meeting or friends or relatives of the bride and groom, who will:
Bring the wedding certificate to the couple, who are usually at the front of the room.
Be appointed by the oversight committee in consultation with the couple to read the wedding certificate aloud to the guests.
Be asked by the oversight committee in consultation with the couple to briefly explain the procedure of the ceremony to those assembled.
Close the meeting. This is usually done by those at the front of the room (who had explained the purpose of marriage) shaking each other's hands. This is followed by guests shaking hands with those near them.

What books are used? A Bible or a hymnal.

To indicate the order of the ceremony: A verbal explanation of the service is usually sufficient.

Will a guest who is not a Quaker be expected to do anything other than sit? No, but guests are welcome to speak if moved to do so. All present should sign the marriage certificate afterward. This is usually placed in the meeting room and can be signed after the close of worship.

Are there any parts of the ceremony in which a guest who is not a Quaker should *not* participate? No.

If not disruptive to the ceremony, is it okay to:
Take pictures? No.
Use a flash? No.
Use a video camera? No.
Use a tape recorder? Possibly. Ask permission from the couple.
(Photos and videos are usually taken after the ceremony.)

Will contributions to the meeting be collected at the ceremony? No.

AFTER THE CEREMONY

Is there usually a reception after the ceremony? There is often a reception that may last one to two hours. It may be at a home, at a catering facility or at any other site chosen by the family. The extent of the food that is served varies from wedding to wedding. Some may have light food and beverages. Others may have a sit-down meal. Still others may have a potluck meal. Often, no alcohol is served, mostly because there was a Quaker tradition during most of the 19th century and the first half of the 20th century advising Friends to abstain from drinking alcohol.

Depending on the newlyweds' preferences, there may be music and/or dancing.

Would it be considered impolite to neither eat nor drink? No.

Is there a grace or benediction before eating or drinking? There may be a silent or spoken grace if the reception is a "sit-down" affair.

Is there a grace or benediction after eating or drinking? No.

Is there a traditional greeting for the family? Offer your congratulations.

Is there a traditional form of address for clergy who may be at the reception? No.

Is it okay to leave early? Yes, but usually only after the wedding cake is cut and served.

Funerals and Mourning

There are many Quaker attitudes about the possibility of life after death, since the Society of Friends is a religious body without creeds. Friends' beliefs about afterlife can be divided into three main areas:

There is no individual survival, but the good (and possibly the evil, also) that we do lives on in the lives of those who come after us.

The human spirit survives. This belief is not linked to the traditional duality of heaven and hell or to any theory of redemption by a savior figure. Instead, it sees survival after death as a continuation of this life, but with the possibility of progressing from one stage to another. Some Quakers also believe in rebirth or reincarnation.

An approach closer to the traditional Christian belief that accepts heaven and hell as places where souls go after the death of the physical body. One's destiny depends on the life led while on earth.

A Quaker funeral, or memorial meeting, is either "unprogrammed" or "programmed." Unprogrammed meetings are held in the traditional manner of the Friends on the basis of silence. Worshipers sit and wait for divine guidance and inspiration. If so moved, they then speak to the group. This is called "vocal ministry."

Programmed meetings are planned in advance and usually include hymn singing, vocal prayers, Bible reading, silent worship and a sermon. In many cases, worship is led by a pastor, who is generally paid and is responsible for some other pastoral services in the meeting.

Either form of meeting usually lasts an hour.

BEFORE THE CEREMONY

How soon after death does the funeral usually take place? This varies with the individual family. Scheduling the memorial service or meeting mostly depends on its convenience to the most people, since it is independent of the actual burial, which may take place within two to three days after death.

What should a non-Quaker do upon hearing of the death of a member of that faith? Telephone, visit or send letters of sympathy to the bereaved. There is no specific "ritual" for calling or expressing sympathy to someone who is mourning.

APPROPRIATE ATTIRE

Men: Jacket and tie. No head covering is required.

Women: A dress or skirt and blouse. Clothing should be modest.

Open-toed shoes and modest jewelry are permissible. No head covering is required.

There are no rules regarding colors of clothing, but dark, somber colors are recommended.

GIFTS

Is it appropriate to send flowers or make a contribution? Both are appropriate. Frequently, obituary notices in local newspapers will list specific charities to which contributions can be made in memory of the deceased.

Is it appropriate to send food? Close friends and neighbors may bring food to the home of the bereaved.

THE CEREMONY

Where will the ceremony take place? Usually in a Quaker meetinghouse, sometimes in a funeral home, and very rarely in a home.

When should guests arrive and where should they sit? Arrive early. Usually ushers will advise guests on where to sit.

If arriving late, are there times when a guest should *not* enter the ceremony? Do not enter when anyone is speaking.

Will the bereaved family be present at the meetinghouse or funeral home before the ceremony? No.

Is there a traditional greeting for the family? No.

Will there be an open casket? Very rarely.

Is a guest expected to view the body? This is entirely optional.

What is appropriate behavior upon viewing the body? Silence.

Who are the major officiants at the ceremony and what do they do? A person appointed by a meeting's oversight committee may explain Quaker custom at a memorial meeting to the non-Quakers present. This person may close the meeting at the appropriate time with a handshake to those seated nearby.

What books are used? The Bible or a hymnal.

To indicate the order of the ceremony: A program may be distributed that includes an obituary.

Will a guest who is not a Quaker be expected to do anything other than sit? No, especially since most Quakers simply sit during the service unless they are moved to speak or offer a prayer or message that comes out of the silence. All present, Quaker and non-Quaker, are welcome to speak if moved to do so.

Are there any parts of the ceremony in which a guest who is not a Quaker should *not* participate? No.

If not disruptive to the ceremony, is it okay to:
Take pictures? No.
Use a flash? No.
Use a video camera? No.
Use a tape recorder? Yes. This is often done, but it is still important to get permission from the family.

Will contributions to the meeting be collected at the ceremony? No.

THE INTERMENT

Should guests attend the interment? No. Usually only close family members attend.

What happens at the graveside? The body is committed to the ground. If there has been a cremation, the ashes are either buried or put in a vault. Sometimes, the ashes are scattered.

Do guests who are not Quakers participate at the graveside ceremony? No. They are simply present.

COMFORTING THE BEREAVED

Is it appropriate to visit the home of the bereaved after the funeral? Yes, although there is no specific "ritual" for calling or expressing sympathy to someone who is mourning. Nor is there a "ritual" that guides the behavior of the mourners.

Will there be a religious service at the home of the bereaved? No.

Will food be served? Possibly.

How soon after the funeral will a mourner usually return to a normal work schedule? This varies according to one's personal needs. There is no doctrine on mourning.

How soon after the funeral will a mourner usually return to a normal social schedule? This varies according to one's personal needs. The Quaker emphasis is to resume the fabric of one's life.

Are there rituals for observing the anniversary of the death? No.

5. HOME CELEBRATIONS

Not applicable to Quakers.

23

Reformed Church in America/Canada

1 • HISTORY AND BELIEFS

The Reformed Church began in the 1500s in Europe when groups of Christians who were opposed to any authority or practice that they believed could not be supported by a careful study of the Bible set themselves apart from the established Roman Church of the time. These Reformers adhered to the basic teachings of the early Christian church, but they also wrote new teachings, such as the Heidelberg Catechism, which was first published in 1563 and is still a standard that guides the life and religious witness of the Reformed Church in America.

The tone of the Heidelberg Catechism is mild, gentle and devotional, and celebrates the comfort that one can derive from Jesus Christ in life and in death. The Reformed Church in America requires every minister to cover the contents of the Heidelberg Catechism once every four years in his or her preaching.

The Reform movement's first church in America was the Reformed Dutch Church, which was founded in 1628 in New Amsterdam (now New York City). Not until 1764 was there a Reformed Church in the British colonies that used the English language. Starting with the American Revolution, the Dutch influence in the Church waned as the number of congregants of Scottish, German and English extraction increased. Finally, in 1867, the Church changed its name to the Reformed Church in America.

The Canadian branch of the denomination, which consists of 40 churches, is called the Reformed Church in Canada. (The Reform tradition is also represented in Canada by the Christian Reformed Church of North America, which has 250 churches, a membership of 51,500 and offices in Burlington, Ontario.)

Each of the Reformed Church's local congregations is governed by a "consistory," which is comprised of the church's pastor and elected elders and deacons. Each church belongs to a "classis," which oversees the congregations within its particular jurisdiction. Each classis sends representatives to its regional synod, of which there are seven in the United States and one in Canada. It also sends representatives to the General Synod, which meets annually to set direction and policy for the Church as a whole.

U.S. and Canadian churches: 933
U.S. and Canadian membership:
260,120
(data from the 2010 Yearbook of American and Canadian Churches*)*

For more information, contact:
The Reformed Church in America
475 Riverside Drive, 18th Floor
New York, NY 10115
(800) 968-6065
helpline@rca.org
www.rca.org

2 · THE BASIC SERVICE

Worship in the Reformed Church strongly emphasizes the Church's belief that the officiating minister is not an intermediary between congregants and God and that he or she does not offer worship for the congregation. Because of that, worship in the Church offers fixed formulas for the Sunday service because, as a Reformed minister has written, "it would rather trust the wisdom of the church in its long history than the erratic cleverness of any one person."

But the Church also offers individual ministers and churches a measure of freedom: For ordinary Sunday services, full and complete models for worship are provided. A church may—or may not—use them, but they serve as guides for what ought to be used.

Sunday morning worship generally has three components:
The Approach to God, in which congregants confess that they are not worthy to be in God's presence and so seek forgiveness in Jesus Christ.
The Word of God, in which congregants hear the Word as found in the Scriptures, preaching and the sacraments.
The Response to God's Word, in which congregants offer prayers and gratitude for God's work in the world.

Sunday worship also includes the Lord's Supper, which is also known as Holy Communion. Reformed Church congregations believe that Christ is spiritually present at Communion.

The service usually lasts about one hour.

APPROPRIATE ATTIRE

Men: A jacket and tie would never be out of place, although many congregations welcome more casual attire if chosen with discretion and taste as appropriate for a worship service. No head covering is required.

Women: A dress or a skirt and blouse or a pants suit, although many congregations welcome more casual attire if chosen with discretion and taste as appropriate for a worship service. Clothing need not cover the arms and hems need not reach below the knees. Open-toed shoes and modest jewelry are permissible. No head covering is required.

There are no rules regarding colors of clothing.

THE SANCTUARY

What are the major sections of the church?
The narthex or foyer: Where worshipers are greeted.
The sanctuary: Where congregants and guests sit.
The chancel: A raised section at the front of the sanctuary for a Communion table, a pulpit and a lectern and where ministers and other worship leaders sit.

THE SERVICE

When should guests arrive and where should they sit? Arrive about five to ten minutes before the scheduled start of the service. In many churches, ushers will advise guests where to sit.

If arriving late, are there times when a guest should *not* enter the service? Do not enter while prayers are being recited, during the reading of Scriptures or during the sermon.

Are there times when a guest should *not* leave the service? Do not leave while prayers are being recited, during the reading of Scriptures or during the sermon. If possible, do not leave except for an emergency.

Who are the major officiants, leaders or participants and what do they do?
The pastor, who is the primary leader of the service. He or she preaches a sermon and presides over the Communion and baptism.
Lay leaders, who may greet congregants and guests, make announcements about church activities and lead prayers.

What are the major ritual objects of the service?
Candles, which remind worshipers of God's illuminating presence.
Bread and wine or grape juice, which are served to worshipers during the Lord's Supper, which is also known as Communion. Most Reformed Church congregations believe that Christ is spiritually present at Communion. Unlike certain other Christian churches, they do not believe that the bread and wine or grape juice are transubstantiated into the actual body and blood of Christ.
A Bible, which is on the lectern or pulpit and which worship leaders read during the service.
The baptismal font, which contains water used during services that include baptisms.
A cross, which reminds worshipers of the suffering, death and Resurrection of Christ. The cross does not have on it the "body" of Christ since its emphasis is on his Resurrection.

What books are used? The Reformed Church in America uses the New Revised Standard Version of the Bible. A variety of hymnals are used in the Reformed Church. The Church plans to issue a new edition of its own hymnal, which will be forthcoming in 2013.

To indicate the order of the service: A program will be distributed and the pastor or lay leader will make periodic announcements.

GUEST BEHAVIOR DURING THE SERVICE

Will a guest who is not a member of the Reformed Church be expected to do anything other than sit? Guests are expected to join congregants when they stand during the service. It is entirely optional for them to read prayers aloud and sing with the congregation. In most congregations that belong to the Reformed Church, congregants do not kneel. In those churches where kneeling occurs, it is optional for guests to join in. Those guests who do not kneel should remain seated.

Are there any parts of the service in which a guest who is not a member of the Reformed Church should *not* participate? Non-Christian guests should not participate in Communion and in the Confession of Faith, which is the Apostle's Creed recited during Communion.

If not disruptive to the service, is it okay to:
Take pictures? No.
Use a flash? No.
Use a video camera? No.
Use a tape recorder? No.

Will contributions to the church be collected at the service? Yes. Ushers pass offering plates through the congregation during the service.

How much is it customary to contribute? It is entirely optional for guests to contribute. If they choose to do so, contributions between $1 and $20 are appropriate.

AFTER THE SERVICE

Is there usually a reception after the service? Yes. Most churches serve such light foods as coffee, tea, juice and pastry. No alcoholic beverages will be served. If a meal is served, which is not a frequent occurrence, grace may be said before eating. The reception may be in the church's narthex or fellowship hall and may last about 30 minutes.

Is there a traditional form of address for clergy who may be at the reception? "Pastor" or "Reverend."

Is it okay to leave early? Yes.

GENERAL GUIDELINES AND ADVICE

Take your cues from those around you. Do not remain standing when congregants have reseated themselves. Refrain from talking during services. Most churches offer a nursery or child care for young children.

SPECIAL VOCABULARY

Key words or phrases that it might be helpful for a visitor to know:
"And also with you." The proper response if someone says, "The peace of God be with you."

DOGMA AND IDEOLOGY

Members of the Reformed Church believe:
In the Trinitarian concept of the Divinity. This consists of the Father, the

Son (Jesus) and the Holy Spirit (the empowering spirit of God).

Each person who believes and trusts in Jesus has their sins forgiven, is endowed with "courage in the struggle for justice and peace," and is granted "eternal life in Your realm which has no end."

The Bible is the Word of God and the final authority for faith and practice.

God is at work in all walks of life and in all activities of each person. Hence, the Church does not hesitate to call government, business or any other authority to responsibility to the Lord.

Each person is called by God to service in the Church and to service in the community in whatever vocation he or she may have.

A basic booklet and some pamphlets to which a guest can refer to learn more about the Reformed Church:

Our Reformed Church by Howard G. Hageman, revised and updated by Gregg Mast (copyright Reformed Church Press).

A Three-Minute Tour of the Reformed Church in America

Are You Looking for a Church Home?

These may be obtained from Faith Alive Christian Resources, www.faithaliveresources.org.

3. HOLY DAYS AND FESTIVALS

Advent. Begins four weeks before Christmas. The purpose is to prepare for Christmas and to focus on Christ. There is no traditional greeting for Advent.

Christmas. Occurs on the evening of December 24 and the day of December 25. Marks the birth and the incarnation of God as a man. The traditional greeting is "Merry Christmas."

Lent. Begins on Ash Wednesday, which occurs six weeks before Easter. The purpose is to prepare for Easter and to reflect upon Christ. There is no traditional greeting for Lent. Between Lent and Easter, abstention from entertainment is encouraged, as is increased giving to the poor. Often, there are midweek worship services. A few members of the Reformed Church engage in a moderate fast (abstaining from certain foods) during Lent.

Easter. Always falls on the Sunday after the first full moon that occurs on or after March 21. Celebrates the Resurrection of Jesus Christ. The traditional greeting is "Happy Easter." In worship services, the pastor may greet congregants with, "He is risen." Congregants respond with "He is risen, indeed."

Pentecost Sunday. The seventh Sunday after Easter. Celebrates the coming of the Holy Spirit, which is the empowering spirit of God in human life. This is often considered the birth of the Christian church. There is no traditional greeting for this holiday.

4. LIFE CYCLE EVENTS

Birth Ceremony

The baptism ceremony is the same for males and females. Baptism can actually occur anytime from birth onward through adulthood. The ceremony is usually integrated into a regular church service and may last about 15 minutes.

In the Reformed Church, baptism is administered only once. Baptism initiates an individual into the Church and bestows God's grace upon that person. During the ceremony, the pastor pours or sprinkles water over the person's head. Another method of baptism that is used occasionally is "immersion," in which the person being baptized is lowered into the water and raised up again.

Baptism is almost always part of a larger Sunday morning service. The baptism itself may last about 15 minutes, while the entire service may last about one hour.

BEFORE THE CEREMONY

Are guests usually invited by a formal invitation? Invitations are usually oral.

If not stated explicitly, should one assume that children are invited? Yes.

If one can't attend, what should one do? RSVP with regrets. Gifts are not expected.

APPROPRIATE ATTIRE

Men: A jacket and tie would never be out of place, although many congregations welcome more casual attire if chosen with discretion and taste as appropriate for a worship service. No head covering is required.

Women: A dress or a skirt and blouse or a pants suit, although many congregations welcome more casual attire if chosen with discretion and taste as appropriate for a worship service. Clothing need not cover the arms and hems need not reach below the knees. Open-toed shoes and modest jewelry are permissible. No head covering is required.

There are no rules regarding colors of clothing.

GIFTS

Is a gift customarily expected? No.

THE CEREMONY

Where will the ceremony take place? Almost always in the church's main sanctuary. Only occasionally does a baptism occur at the parents' home or outdoors.

When should guests arrive and where should they sit? Arrive about five to ten minutes before the scheduled start of the service. In many churches, ushers will advise guests where to sit.

If arriving late, are there times when a guest should *not* enter the ceremony? Do not enter while prayers are being recited, during the reading of Scriptures or during the sermon.

Are there times when a guest should *not* leave the ceremony? Do not leave while prayers are being recited, during the reading of Scriptures, or during the sermon. If possible, do not leave except for an emergency.

Who are the major officiants, leaders or participants at the ceremony and what do they do?

The pastor, who is the primary leader of the service and presides over the baptism.

The child being baptized.

The child's parents, who present the child and pledge to raise him or her in Christ's faith.

The congregation, which welcomes the person being baptized into the community of faith.

What books are used? The Reformed Church in America uses the New Revised Standard Version of the Bible. A variety of hymnals are used in the Reformed Church. The Church plans to issue a new edition of its own hymnal, which will be forthcoming in 2013.

To indicate the order of the ceremony: A program will be distributed and the pastor will make periodic announcements.

Will a guest who is not a member of the Reformed Church be expected to do anything other than sit? Upon request of the family of the person being baptized, a guest may be asked to stand at the front of the sanctuary as a sponsor, a family member or a friend. If so, consult the family or the pastor for instructions. Ordinarily, guests are expected to join congregants when they stand during the service. It is entirely optional for them to read prayers aloud and sing with the congregation. In most congregations that belong to the Reformed Church, congregants do not kneel. In those churches where kneeling occurs, it is optional for guests to join in. Those guests who do not kneel should remain seated.

Are there any parts of the ceremony in which a guest who is not a member of the Reformed Church should *not* participate? Nonmembers should not participate with congregants when they recite the "vows of the congregation," in which they pledge to help guide the person being baptized to lead a Christian life.

If not disruptive to the ceremony, is it okay to:
Take pictures? No.
Use a flash? No.
Use a video camera? No.
Use a tape recorder? No.

Will contributions to the church be collected at the ceremony? Yes. Ushers pass offering plates through the congregation during the service.

How much is it customary to contribute? It is entirely optional for guests to contribute. If they choose to do so, contributions between $1 and $20 are appropriate.

AFTER THE CEREMONY

Is there usually a reception after the ceremony? No.

Is there a traditional greeting for the family? No. Just offer your congratulations.

Is there a traditional form of address for clergy whom a guest may meet? "Pastor" or "Reverend."

Initiation Ceremony

Confirmation is celebrated for teenagers who were baptized as infants. It offers a teen who was baptized the opportunity to publicly assent to the baptismal promises and celebrates the affirmation of baptism in the life of the individual. One is usually confirmed with other teens who have been in the same confirmation class.

The confirmation is usually part of the regular Sunday worship service. It may last about 15 minutes, although the entire service may last about an hour.

BEFORE THE CEREMONY

Are guests usually invited by a formal invitation? Invitations are usually issued orally.

If not stated explicitly, should one assume that children are invited? Yes.

If one can't attend, what should one do? RSVP with regrets. Gifts are not expected.

APPROPRIATE ATTIRE

Men: A jacket and tie would never be out of place, although many congregations welcome more casual attire if chosen with discretion and taste as appropriate for a worship service. No head covering is required.

Women: A dress or a skirt and blouse or a pants suit, although many congregations welcome more casual attire if chosen with discretion and taste as appropriate for a worship service. Clothing need not cover the arms and hems need not reach below the knees. Open-toed shoes and modest jewelry are permissible. No head covering is required.

There are no rules regarding colors of clothing.

GIFTS

Is a gift customarily expected? No.

THE CEREMONY

Where will the ceremony take place? In the church's main sanctuary.

When should guests arrive and where should they sit? Arrive about five to ten minutes before the scheduled start of the service. In many churches, ushers will advise guests where to sit.

If arriving late, are there times when a guest should *not* enter the ceremony? Do not enter while prayers are being recited, during the reading of Scriptures or during the sermon.

Are there times when a guest should *not* leave the ceremony? Do not leave while prayers are being recited, during the reading of Scriptures or during the sermon. If possible, do not leave except for an emergency.

Who are the major officiants, leaders or participants at the cere-

mony and what do they do?

The confirmand(s), the person(s) being confirmed.

The pastor, who is the primary leader of the service. He or she preaches a sermon and presides over the Communion and baptism.

What books are used? The Reformed Church in America uses the New Revised Standard Version of the Bible. A variety of hymnals are used in the Reformed Church. The Church plans to issue a new edition of its own hymnal, which will be forthcoming in 2013.

To indicate the order of the ceremony: A program will be distributed and the pastor will make periodic announcements.

Will a guest who is not a member of the Reformed Church be expected to do anything other than sit? If the family or the confirmand has specifically asked you to join them while standing in front of the congregation, then do so. Ordinarily, guests are expected to join congregants when they stand during the service. It is entirely optional for them to read prayers aloud and sing with the congregation. In most churches belonging to the Reformed Church, congregants do not kneel. In those churches where kneeling occurs, it is optional for guests to join in. Those guests who do not kneel should remain seated.

Are there any parts of the ceremony in which a guest who is not a member of the Reformed Church should *not* participate? No.

If not disruptive to the ceremony, is it okay to:
Take pictures? No.

Use a flash? No.
Use a video camera? No.
Use a tape recorder? No.

Will contributions to the church be collected at the ceremony? Yes. Ushers pass offering plates through the congregation during the service.

How much is it customary to contribute? It is entirely optional for guests to contribute. If they choose to do so, contributions between $1 and $20 are appropriate.

AFTER THE CEREMONY

Is there usually a reception after the ceremony? No, but there may be a receiving line in the church at which guests and congregants are greeted.

Is there a traditional greeting for the family? No. Just offer your congratulations.

Is there a traditional form of address for clergy whom a guest may meet? "Pastor" or "Reverend."

Marriage Ceremony

The Reformed Church teaches that the essence of marriage is a covenanted commitment that has its foundation in the faithfulness of God's love. The Church does not consider a wedding to be a sacrament, although the marital relationship is considered to be sacred.

The marriage ceremony is the occasion on which two people unite as husband and wife in the mutual exchange of marriage vows and wedding rings. The presiding official represents the Church and gives the marriage the Church's blessing. The congregation joins in affirming the marriage and in offering support and thanksgiving for the new family.

Usually, the wedding is a ceremony unto itself. Only rarely is it part of a regular Sunday worship service. It may last about 30 minutes.

BEFORE THE CEREMONY

Are guests usually invited by a formal invitation? Yes.

If not stated explicitly, should one assume that children are invited? Yes, although this may not apply to infants or toddlers.

If one can't attend, what should one do? RSVP with regrets and send a gift.

APPROPRIATE ATTIRE

Men: A jacket and tie. No head covering is required.

Women: A dress or a skirt and blouse. Clothing need not cover the arms and hems need not reach below the knees. Open-toed shoes and modest jewelry are permissible. No head covering is required.

There are no rules regarding colors of clothing.

GIFTS

Is a gift customarily expected? Yes. Cash or household items (such as sheets, kitchenware or small appliances) are appropriate.

Should gifts be brought to the ceremony? Gifts may be brought to the ceremony or to the reception that follows the ceremony. They may also be sent to the home of the newlyweds.

THE CEREMONY

Where will the ceremony take place? In the church's main sanctuary.

When should guests arrive and where should they sit? Arrive shortly before the time for which the wedding has been scheduled. Usually, ushers will advise guests where to sit.

If arriving late, are there times when a guest should *not* enter the ceremony? Do not enter during the processional or recessional of the wedding party or during the recitation of wedding vows. Follow the ushers' guidance for entering the ceremony.

Are there times when a guest should *not* leave the ceremony?
Do not leave during the processional or recessional of the wedding party or during the recitation of wedding vows.

Follow the ushers' guidance for leaving the ceremony.

Who are the major officiants, leaders or participants at the ceremony and what do they do?
The pastor, who presides over the ceremony.
The bride and groom and members of the wedding party.

What books are used? The Reformed Church in America uses the New Revised Standard Version of the Bible. A variety of hymnals are used in the Reformed Church. The Church plans to issue a new edition of its own hymnal, which will be forthcoming in 2013.

To indicate the order of the ceremony: The pastor will make periodic announcements.

Will a guest who is not a member of the Reformed Church be expected to do anything other than sit? Guests are expected to join congregants when they stand during the ceremony.

Are there any parts of the ceremony in which a guest who is not a member of the Reformed Church should *not* participate? No.

If not disruptive to the ceremony, is it okay to:
Take pictures? No.
Use a flash? No.
Use a video camera? No.
Use a tape recorder? No.

Will contributions to the church be collected at the ceremony? No.

AFTER THE CEREMONY

Is there usually a reception after the ceremony? Yes. It may be in a catering hall, a restaurant or a church reception hall, or at a home. There is usually a reception line and frequently a full meal is served. If the reception is not in the church, there may be alcoholic beverages and/or music and dancing. The presence of alcoholic beverages depends on family practice and choice. The reception may last one to two hours.

Would it be considered impolite to neither eat nor drink? No.

Is there a grace or benediction before eating or drinking? Grace may be said if a full meal is served.

Is there a grace or benediction after eating or drinking? No.

Is there a traditional greeting for the family? Just offer your congratulations.

Is there a traditional form of address for clergy who may be at the reception? "Pastor" or "Reverend."

Is it okay to leave early? Yes.

Funerals and Mourning

A funeral service is a time of comfort and hope for the bereaved. The hope of Church members is summarized by Jesus' words from John 11:25–26, "I am the resurrection and the life, says the Lord; whoever believes in Me, though he die, yet shall he live; and whoever lives and believes in Me shall never die."

The Reformed Church believes that to be absent from the body is to be present with the Lord.

The funeral is a service in itself. It lasts about 20 to 30 minutes.

BEFORE THE CEREMONY

How soon after the death does the funeral usually take place? Two to three days.

What should someone who is not a member of the Reformed Church do upon hearing of the death of a member of that faith? Telephone or visit the bereaved family or send a card to the bereaved to express your condolences.

APPROPRIATE ATTIRE

Men: A jacket and tie. No head covering is required.

Women: A dress or a skirt and blouse. Clothing need not cover the arms and hems need not reach below the knees. Open-toed shoes and modest jewelry are permissible. No head covering is required.

Dark, somber colors of clothing are advised. Bright, flashy tones are strongly discouraged.

GIFTS

Is it appropriate to send flowers or make a contribution? Flowers may be sent to the home of the bereaved upon hearing of the death or after the funeral, or they may be sent to the church or funeral home where the funeral ceremony will be held. Contributions to a church or organization designated by the family may be made after the funeral.

Is it appropriate to send food? Yes. This may be sent to the home of the bereaved.

THE CEREMONY

Where will the ceremony take place? Either in a church or a funeral home.

When should guests arrive and where should they sit? Arrive a few minutes before the time for which the ceremony has been scheduled. Sit wherever you wish, unless a specially marked section has been reserved for immediate family.

If arriving late, are there times when a guest should *not* enter the ceremony? Do not enter during prayers, the sermon or the eulogy. Follow ushers' guidance about entering the ceremony.

Will the bereaved family be present at the church or funeral home before the ceremony? Sometimes.

Is there a traditional greeting for the family? No. Just offer your condolences.

Will there be an open casket? Rarely. This depends on local customs and the preference of the family. "Viewing" time is sometimes scheduled in the days or hours before the funeral. "Viewing" may also be offered during or at the end of the funeral service itself.

Is a guest expected to view the body? This is entirely optional. If there is a "viewing" at the funeral and you do not wish to participate, excuse yourself from the line that forms to pass the casket. If you happen to be in the line that passes the casket and you do not wish to view the body, simply avert your eyes.

What is appropriate behavior upon viewing the body? View it silently and somberly. Do not touch it or place any flowers or memorabilia in the casket.

Who are the major officiants at the ceremony and what do they do?
A pastor, who officiates and delivers the sermon.
Possibly a family member or a close friend, who may also deliver a eulogy.

What books are used? No books are used by the bereaved or guests.

To indicate the order of the ceremony: Usually a program will be distributed; sometimes the pastor will make periodic announcements.

Will a guest who is not a member of the Reformed Church be expected to do anything other than sit? No. It is entirely optional for guests to read prayers aloud or to sing, stand or kneel when those present do so. In most funerals officiated by the Reformed Church, congregants do not kneel. In those churches where kneeling occurs, those guests who do not kneel should remain seated.

Are there any parts of the ceremony in which a guest who is not a member of the Reformed Church should *not* participate?
No.

If not disruptive to the ceremony, is it okay to:
Take pictures? No.
Use a flash? No.
Use a video camera? No.
Use a tape recorder? No.

Will contributions to the church be collected at the ceremony? No.

THE INTERMENT

Should guests attend the interment? This is entirely optional and is usually at the discretion of the guest, unless the minister announces at the funeral ceremony that the interment is only for family members.

Whom should one ask for directions? The funeral director.

What happens at the graveside? Scriptures are read, prayers are recited and the casket is placed in the ground.

Do guests who are not members of the Reformed Church participate at the graveside ceremony? No, they are simply present.

COMFORTING THE BEREAVED

Is it appropriate to visit the home of the bereaved after the funeral? Often, there is a reception at the church or home of the bereaved after the funeral. If not, visiting a few days after the funeral is appropriate. It is recommended that the length of the visit be fairly brief, such as 15 to 20 minutes.

Will there be a religious service at the home of the bereaved? Seldom is this done.

Will food be served? No.

How soon after the funeral will a mourner usually return to a normal social schedule? The Reformed Church does not specify the number of days that one should formally be in mourning. Local, ethnic and cultural customs are more relevant than any particular religious tradition of the Church.

Are there mourning customs to which a friend who is not a member of the Reformed Church should be sensitive? No. Local, ethnic and cultural customs are more relevant than any particular religious tradition of the Church.

Are there rituals for observing the anniversary of the death? No. Local, ethnic and cultural customs are more relevant than any particular religious tradition of the Church.

5 · HOME CELEBRATIONS

Not applicable to the Reformed Church.

24

Roman Catholic

1. HISTORY AND BELIEFS

The term *catholic* was first applied around 100 C.E. to the Christian church, which was then one entity. It meant being geographically universal, continuous with the Christian past and transcending language, race and nation. The test of catholicity was communion with the universal church and with the See of Rome.

After the Eastern and Western wings of the Church divided in 1054 C.E., *catholic* was more usually used to refer to the Church in the West under the spiritual leadership of the Holy See based in Rome. (This is commonly known as the Vatican.) Since the 16th century, "Roman Catholic" has meant the religious body that acknowledges the pope's authority and the Vatican as the center of ecclesiastical unity.

In the 19th century, the Church became increasingly centralized in Rome. In 1870, Vatican Council I declared that the pope has jurisdictional primacy over the entire Church, and that under certain circumstances, he is infallible in proclaiming doctrines of faith and morals.

In Roman Catholic teaching, revelation is summed up in Jesus Christ, who commanded his apostles to teach the Gospel. To preserve the living Gospel, the apostles appointed bishops as their successors. Roman Catholics believe in the unity of God, who is understood as God the Father, God (Jesus Christ) the Son and God the Holy Spirit. Catholicism teaches that original sin—Adam and Eve's expulsion from the Garden of Eden for disobeying God—alienated humanity from God, but did not totally corrupt man and woman, and that grace can fully make a sinner just.

Catholics especially venerate Mary, the mother of Jesus. Catholics believe that Mary was conceived without original sin, and that she was a virgin when Jesus was conceived.

Roman Catholicism has over 1.1 billion members in more than 2,000 dioceses around the world.

U.S. churches: 18,674
U.S. membership: 68.1 million
(data from the 2010 Yearbook of American and Canadian Churches)

For more information, contact:

The United States Conference of
  Catholic Bishops
3211 Fourth Street, Northeast
Washington, DC 20017-1194
(202) 541-3000
www.usccb.org

Canadian churches: 5,109
Canadian membership: 13 million
   (*data from the* 2010 Yearbook of American and Canadian Churches)

For more information, contact:
Canadian Conference of
   Catholic Bishops
2500 Don Reid Drive
Ottawa, ON K1H 2J2
(613) 241-9461
www.cccb.ca

2 · THE BASIC SERVICE

Sunday Mass lasts about one hour. It consists of two principal divisions called the "Liturgy of the Word," which features the proclamation of the Word of God, and the Eucharistic Liturgy, which focuses on Jesus' sacrifice on behalf of humanity through the Crucifixion.

During the Liturgy of the Word, passages from the Bible are read. The first is usually from Hebrew Scriptures (the Old Testament), the second and the third from the New Testament. Also, the presiding priest delivers a homily, an explanation of some point in the readings. He and the congregants together recite "the creed," a profession of their faith, and "the prayers of the faithful," which are prayers of petition concerning the needs of the church, the salvation of the world, public figures, individuals in need, and the local community.

During the Eucharistic Liturgy, bread and wine are transubstantiated through consecration into the body and blood of Jesus Christ, and the priest administers Communion (portions of the bread and wine) to congregants.

Hymns are sung at various points throughout the service.

APPROPRIATE ATTIRE

Men: Jacket and tie. No head covering required.

Women: Dress or a skirt and blouse or a pants suit. Jewelry and open-toed shoes are acceptable. Clothing should be modest, depending on the fashion and the locale. No head covering required.

There are no rules regarding colors of clothing.

THE SANCTUARY

What are the major sections of the church?

The sanctuary: The part of the church where the altar is located and where priests lead congregants in prayer. It is set off from the body of the church by a distinctive structural feature, such as an elevation above the floor level, or by ornamentation. It is usually at the front of the church, but may be centrally located.

The pulpit or lectern: The stand at which scriptural lessons and psalm responses are read and the word of God is preached.

Seating for congregants: Seats and kneeling benches, usually in front and/or to the side of the altar.

Statues: Images of Jesus, the Virgin Mary, Catholic saints and persons from the Old Testament. Generally, there is only one statue of any individual saint in a church.

Baptistery: The place for administering baptism. Some churches have baptisteries adjoining or near their entrance. This position indicates that through baptism, one is initiated, or "enters," the church. Contemporary practice favors placing the baptistery near the sanctuary and altar, or using a portable font in the same position. This emphasizes the relationship of baptism to the Eucharist, and the celebration of the death and Resurrection of Jesus Christ.

The confessional room: A boothlike structure in which priests hear confession of sins from penitents. There are separate compartments for each, and a grating or screen between them. Since the Second Vatican Council in the mid-1960s, there has been a trend in the United States to replace or supplement confessional booths with small reconciliation rooms that are arranged so priest and penitent can converse face-to-face.

Holy water fonts: Receptacles, usually at a church's entrance, containing holy water for Roman Catholics to use. It is customary for them, upon entering a church, to dip their first two fingers into a font and with them to make a sign of the cross. (Guests need not do this.)

Sanctuary lamp: A lamp that is kept burning continuously before a tabernacle in which the blessed sacrament is reserved, as a sign of the presence of Christ.

THE SERVICE

When should guests arrive and where should they sit? It is customary to arrive at the time called. Once you enter the sanctuary, sit wherever you like.

If arriving late, are there times when a guest should *not* enter the service? No.

Are there times when a guest should *not* leave the service? Unless it's an emergency, do not leave the service until it is over.

Who are the major officiants, leaders or participants and what do they do?

The priest, who reads the Gospel, comments upon it and offers the sacrifice, also known as the Eucharist, or Communion.

The lector, who reads the first two readings from the Scriptures to congregants. Can also lead prayers.

What are the major ritual objects of the service?

Bread and wine, which are transubstantiated through consecration into the body and blood of Jesus Christ.

The paten and chalice, which, respectively, hold the consecrated bread and wine. Gold coating is required of the interior parts of sacred vessels.

Candles, used for symbolic purposes. They represent Christ, the light and life of grace, at liturgical functions. Made of beeswax.

What books are used? The New American Bible (or another authorized translation) or a lectionary that contains selections from the Bible, and a prayer book, which is also called a missal.

To indicate the order of the service: Periodic announcements may be made by the lector or priest. Also, the basic outline of the service is usually provided in a printed program and hymns may be announced by a display located near the front of the sanctuary.

GUEST BEHAVIOR DURING THE SERVICE

Will a guest who is not a Catholic be expected to do anything other than sit? Yes. They are also expected to stand. It is optional for them to kneel with the congregation, read prayers aloud and sing with congregants.

Are there any parts of the service in which a guest who is not a Catholic should *not* participate? Such guests should not receive Communion or say any prayers contradictory to the beliefs of their own faith.

If not disruptive to the service, is it okay to:
Take pictures? Yes. Verify beforehand with the priest or usher.
Use a flash? No. Verify beforehand with the priest or usher.
Use a video camera? Yes. Verify beforehand with the priest or usher.
Use a tape recorder? Yes. Verify beforehand with the priest or usher.

Will contributions to the church be collected at the service? Yes, but guests are not expected to contribute.

How much is it customary to contribute? From $1 to $10.

AFTER THE SERVICE

Is there usually a reception after the service? Sometimes there is a 30- to 60-minute reception in the parish hall adjoining the sanctuary. Depending on the parish, light food may be served. It is not considered impolite to neither eat nor drink. Do not eat until a blessing is recited. Benedictions are also said after the reception.

Is there a traditional form of address for clergy who may be at the reception? "Father" if greeting a priest. "Your excellency" if greeting a bishop. "Your eminence" if greeting a cardinal.

Is it okay to leave early? Yes.

GENERAL GUIDELINES AND ADVICE

None provided.

SPECIAL VOCABULARY

None provided.

DOGMA AND IDEOLOGY

Roman Catholics believe:
Worship is directed toward God alone.
All revelation is summed up in Jesus Christ, who was both human and divine and commanded his twelve apostles to preach the Gospel.
The pope has primacy of jurisdiction over the Church. He and the body of bishops have infallibility when addressing religious issues.
The Eucharist (or Communion) is the center of church life. The Mass is considered to make present Christ's one sacrifice of death and Resurrection. During it, Christ is said to be present through the transubstantiation of the bread and wine of the Eucharist.

Some basic books to which a guest can refer to learn more about the Roman Catholic Church: *The Catechism of the Catholic Church* (New York:

Doubleday, 2003); and *What You Will See Inside a Catholic Church* (Woodstock, Vt.: SkyLight Paths, 2002), also available in Spanish.

3 · HOLY DAYS AND FESTIVALS

Christmas. Always falls on December 25. Celebrates the birth of Christ.

Easter. Commemorates the death and Resurrection of Jesus. Always falls on the Sunday after the first full moon that occurs on or after the spring equinox of March 21.

Pentecost. Occurs 50 days after Easter because this is when the Holy Ghost (the spirit of Jesus) descended on his apostles. Celebrates the power of the Holy Spirit and its manifestation in the early Christian church.

Ash Wednesday. Occurs 40 days before Easter. Commemorates the beginning of Lent, which is a season for preparation and penitence before Easter itself.

Maundy/Holy Thursday. Falls four days before Easter. Commemorates the institution of the Eucharist (also known as Communion) and Jesus' subsequent arrest and trial.

Good Friday. Three days before Easter. Commemorates the crucifixion, death and burial of Jesus.

4 · LIFE CYCLE EVENTS

Birth Ceremony

Baptism is the sacrament of spiritual regeneration by which a person, usually a six- to eight-week-old infant, is incorporated into Christ and made a member of his Mystical Body, given grace and cleansed of original sin. The virtues of faith, hope and charity are given with grace. The sacrament confers a character on the soul and can only be received once.

The baptismal ceremony is sometimes part of a larger service, usually a Mass. (For details on the Mass, see "The Basic Service" section above.) During the ceremony, a bishop, priest or deacon pours water on the forehead of the person being baptized and says, "I baptize you in the name of the Father and of the Son and of the Holy Spirit."

Catholics must first be baptized before they can receive other sacraments from their church.

BEFORE THE CEREMONY

Are guests usually invited by a formal invitation? Yes.

If not stated explicitly, should one assume that children are invited? Yes.

If one can't attend, what should one do? RSVP with regrets and send a gift.

APPROPRIATE ATTIRE

Men: Jacket and tie or more relaxed clothing. No head covering required.

Women: Dress or a skirt and blouse or a pants suit. Jewelry and open-toed shoes are acceptable. Clothing should be modest, depending on the fashion and the locale. No head covering required.

There are no rules regarding colors of clothing.

GIFTS

Is a gift customarily expected? Yes, the value of which depends solely on your socioeconomic level.

Should gifts be brought to the ceremony? Bring them to the reception afterward.

THE CEREMONY

Where will the ceremony take place? In the baptistery, which is usually near or adjoins the church entrance. Contemporary practice favors placing the baptistery near the sanctuary and altar, or using a portable font in the same position. This emphasizes the relationship of baptism to Communion and, thus, to the celebration of the death and Resurrection of Jesus Christ.

When should guests arrive and where should they sit? Arrive on time. Sit wherever you wish.

If arriving late, are there times when a guest should *not* enter the ceremony? No.

Are there times when a guest should *not* leave the ceremony? Do not leave before the service ends.

Who are the major officiants, leaders or participants at the ceremony and what do they do?

A priest, who will baptize the child.

What books are used? The main books are the hymnal, the New American Bible (or another authorized translation) or a lectionary that contains selections from the Bible, and a prayer book, which is also called a missal.

To indicate the order of the ceremony: Periodic announcements will be made by the lector or pastor. Also, the basic outline of the service is usually provided in a printed program and prayers will be announced by a display located near the front of the sanctuary.

Will a guest who is not a Catholic be expected to do anything other than sit? Guests are expected to stand with the congregation. It is optional for them to kneel, read prayers aloud and sing with the congregation.

Are there any parts of the ceremony in which a guest who is not a Catholic should *not* participate? Such guests should not receive Communion or say any prayers contradictory to the beliefs of their own faith.

If not disruptive to the ceremony, is it okay to:
Take pictures? Yes. Verify beforehand with the priest or usher.
Use a flash? No. Verify beforehand with the priest or usher.
Use a video camera? Yes. Verify beforehand with the priest or usher.
Use a tape recorder? Yes. Verify beforehand with the priest or usher.

Will contributions to the church be collected at the ceremony? No.

AFTER THE CEREMONY

Is there usually a reception after the ceremony? Yes, usually at the home of the baptized child. Food will be served. Alcoholic beverages may be served. There may be music and dancing. The reception may last one to two hours.

Would it be considered impolite to neither eat nor drink? No.

Is there a grace or benediction before eating or drinking? Yes.

Is there a grace or benediction after eating or drinking? Sometimes.

Is there a traditional greeting for the family? No, just offer your congratulations.

Is there a traditional form of address for clergy who may be at the reception? "Father" if greeting a priest. "Your excellency" if greeting a bishop. "Your eminence" if greeting a cardinal.

Is it okay to leave early? Yes.

Initiation Ceremony

Confirmation is the sacrament by which a baptized early adolescent is endowed with the fullness of baptismal grace, is united more intimately with the church, is enriched with the special power of the Holy Spirit, and is committed to be an authentic witness to Christ in word and action.

Those being confirmed often receive the sacrament with their entire confirmation class. The ceremony is sometimes part of a larger service. It will last slightly more than one hour.

Confirmation may occur between the ages of seven and 18, depending on the policy of the local diocese.

BEFORE THE CEREMONY

Are guests usually invited by a formal invitation? Yes.

If not stated explicitly, should one assume that children are invited? Yes.

If one can't attend, what should one do? RSVP with regrets and send a gift.

APPROPRIATE ATTIRE

Men: Jacket and tie or more relaxed clothing. No head covering required.

Women: Dress or a skirt and blouse or a pants suit. Jewelry and open-toed shoes are acceptable. Clothing should be modest, depending on the fashion and the locale. No head covering required.

There are no rules regarding colors of clothing.

GIFTS

Is a gift customarily expected? Yes. Often money is appropriate. The exact amount is totally discretionary.

Should gifts be brought to the ceremony? Bring them to the reception afterward.

THE CEREMONY

Where will the ceremony take place? In the main sanctuary of the confirmand's church.

When should guests arrive and where should they sit? It is customary to arrive at the time called. Sit wherever you wish.

If arriving late, are there times when a guest should *not* enter the ceremony? No.

Are there times when a guest should *not* leave the ceremony? Guests should remain until the ceremony ends.

Who are the major officiants, leaders or participants at the ceremony and what do they do?
The bishop, who anoints each confirmand with oil on the forehead.

What books are used? The main books are the hymnal, the New American Bible (or another authorized translation) or a lectionary that contains selections from the Bible, and a prayer book, which is also called a missal.

To indicate the order of the ceremony: Periodic announcements may be made by the lector or pastor. Also, the basic outline of the service is usually provided in a printed program and prayers will be announced by a display located near the front of the sanctuary.

Will a guest who is not a Catholic be expected to do anything other than sit? Guests are expected to stand with the congregation. It is optional for them to kneel, read prayers aloud or sing with the congregation.

Are there any parts of the ceremony in which a guest who is not a Catholic should *not* participate? Yes. Anything that implies a statement of faith that would violate their own beliefs.

If not disruptive to the ceremony, is it okay to:
Take pictures? Yes. Verify beforehand with the priest or usher.
Use a flash? No. Verify beforehand with the priest or usher.
Use a video camera? Yes. Verify beforehand with the priest or usher.
Use a tape recorder? Yes. Verify beforehand with the priest or usher.

Will contributions to the church be collected at the ceremony? No.

AFTER THE CEREMONY

Is there usually a reception after the ceremony? There is a reception, usually at the home of the confirmand. Food and soft drinks will be served. Alcoholic beverages may be served. The reception may last between one and two hours.

Would it be considered impolite to neither eat nor drink? No.

Is there a grace or benediction before eating or drinking? No.

Is there a grace or benediction after eating or drinking? No.

Is there a traditional greeting for the family? Just offer your congratulations.

Is there a traditional form of address for clergy who may be at the reception? "Father" if greeting a priest. "Your excellency" if greeting a bishop. "Your eminence" if greeting a cardinal.

Is it okay to leave early? Yes.

Marriage Ceremony

Catholics consider married life, which was created by God, to have a decisive bearing on the continuation of the human race, on the personal development and eternal destiny of individual members of a family, and on the dignity, stability, peace and prosperity of families and society.

Love, the Church teaches, is uniquely expressed and perfected through marriage. Children are the "gift of marriage," although marriage is not instituted solely for procreation. Rather, its essential nature as an unbreakable compact between man and wife and for the welfare of the children that come out of it both demand that the love of the respective spouses be embodied in a manner that grows, thrives and ripens.

The wedding may be a ceremony in itself and not part of a larger service or it may be part of a Mass. (For details on the Mass, see "The Basic Service" section above.) It may last between 30 minutes to more than one hour.

BEFORE THE CEREMONY

Are guests usually invited by a formal invitation? Yes.

If not stated explicitly, should one assume that children are invited? Yes.

If one can't attend, what should one do? RSVP with regrets and send a gift.

APPROPRIATE ATTIRE

Men: Jacket and tie or more relaxed clothing. No head covering required.

Women: Dress or a skirt and blouse or a pants suit. Jewelry and open-toed shoes are acceptable. Clothing should be modest, depending on the fashion and the locale. No head covering required. It is recommended that black not be worn.

GIFTS

Is a gift customarily expected? Yes. Often money is most appropriate, with the exact amount subject to your discretion.

Should gifts be brought to the ceremony? Gifts should be sent to the home or brought to the reception.

THE CEREMONY

Where will the ceremony take place? In the main sanctuary of the church.

When should guests arrive and where should they sit? Arrive on time. An usher will show guests where to sit.

If arriving late, are there times when a guest should *not* enter the ceremony? Ushers may guide latecomers. Do not enter as the wedding party processes into the sanctuary.

Are there times when a guest should *not* leave the service? Do not leave until it ends.

Who are the major officiants, leaders or participants at the ceremony and what do they do?
The priest, who witnesses the vows.

What books are used? The hymnal, the New American Bible (or another authorized translation) or a lectionary that contains selections from the Bible, and a prayer book, which is also called a missal.

To indicate the order of the ceremony: There will be a program.

Will a guest who is not a Catholic be expected to do anything other than sit? Guests are expected to stand with the congregation. It is optional for them to kneel, read prayers aloud or sing with the congregation.

Are there any parts of the ceremony in which a non-Catholic guest should *not* participate? Non-Catholics do not receive Communion.

If not disruptive to the ceremony, is it okay to:
Take pictures? Yes. Verify beforehand with the priest or usher.
Use a flash? Yes. Verify beforehand with the priest or usher.
Use a video camera? Yes. Verify beforehand with the priest or usher.
Use a tape recorder? Yes. Verify beforehand with the priest or usher.

Will contributions to the church be collected at the ceremony? No.

AFTER THE CEREMONY

Is there usually a reception after the ceremony? There is a reception that may last more than two hours. It is usually at a catering hall, where food and beverages will be served and there will be dancing and music.

Would it be considered impolite to neither eat nor drink? No.

Is there a grace or benediction before eating or drinking? Yes, the blessing before the meal.

Is there a grace or benediction after eating or drinking? Usually not.

Is there a traditional greeting for the family? Just offer your congratulations.

Is there a traditional form of address for clergy who may be at the reception? "Father" if greeting a priest. "Your excellency" if greeting a bishop. "Your eminence" if greeting a cardinal.

Is it okay to leave early? Yes.

Funerals and Mourning

Roman Catholicism deeply believes in immortality. Each human does not face utter spiritual dissolution, since God loves him or her. Not only does all love desire immortality, but God's love *is* immortality. On the "last day," when the Messiah has arrived, one's physical body joins the spirit in the beatific vision of heaven or the damnation of hell.

A Catholic funeral may be part of a larger service or a ceremony in itself. If it is part of a service, that will be a Mass. (For details on the mass, see "The Basic Service" section above.)

The first day after a death is usually reserved for the family to make arrangements for the funeral. The second day is often reserved for a wake, which may last for possibly one to two days. It is most commonly held at the funeral home. The style of wake (i.e., food, beverages, mood, prayer) varies widely and usually depends on the ethnicity of the deceased and his or her family. However, common to all wakes is an opportunity for community, friends and relatives to gather, pray and express their sympathies to the family of the deceased, to whom they also pay their respects.

BEFORE THE CEREMONY

How soon after the death does the funeral usually take place? Usually within two to three days. Sometimes as much as one week later.

What should a non-Catholic do upon hearing of the death of a member of that faith? Telephone the bereaved at home or visit them at the funeral home to express condolences.

APPROPRIATE ATTIRE

Men: Jacket and tie. No head covering required.

Women: Dress or a skirt and blouse or a pants suit. Jewelry and open-toed shoes are acceptable. Clothing should be modest, depending on the fashion and the locale. No head covering required.

Black or equally sober colors are recommended.

GIFTS

Is it appropriate to send flowers or make a contribution? Flowers of any kind are appreciated. They may be sent upon hearing the news of the death or shortly thereafter. They may be sent to the home of the deceased before or after the funeral or to the funeral home before the funeral.

Contributions are not customary unless the family indicates they are appropriate.

Is it appropriate to send food? Yes, to the home of the bereaved before or after the funeral.

THE CEREMONY

Where will the ceremony take place? At a church or a funeral home.

When should guests arrive and where should they sit? Arrive on time. Sit wherever you like.

If arriving late, are there times when a guest should *not* enter the ceremony? No.

Will the bereaved family be present at the church or funeral home before the ceremony? Yes.

Is there a traditional greeting for the family? Offer your condolences.

Will there be an open casket? Usually.

Is a guest expected to view the body? Yes.

What is appropriate behavior upon viewing the body? Silent prayer.

Who are the major officiants at the ceremony and what do they do?
The priest, who says the Mass and the prayers at graveside.

What books are used? The hymnal, the New American Bible (or another authorized translation), and a prayer book, which is also called a missal.

To indicate the order of the ceremony: A program will be distributed.

Will a guest who is not a Catholic be expected to do anything other than sit? Guests are expected to stand with the other mourners. It is optional for them to kneel, read prayers aloud and sing with the congregation.

Are there any parts of the ceremony in which a non-Catholic guest should *not* participate? Such guests should not receive Communion or say any prayers contradictory to the beliefs of their own faith.

If not disruptive to the ceremony, is it okay to:
Take pictures? No. Verify beforehand with the priest or usher.
Use a flash? No. Verify beforehand with the priest or usher.
Use a video camera? No. Verify beforehand with the priest or usher.
Use a tape recorder? No. Verify beforehand with the priest or usher.

Will contributions to the church be collected at the ceremony? No.

THE INTERMENT

Should guests attend the interment? Yes.

Whom should one ask for directions? The funeral director.

What happens at the graveside? The priest leads prayers for the deceased.

Do guests who are not Catholics participate at the graveside ceremony? No. They are simply present.

COMFORTING THE BEREAVED

Is it appropriate to visit the home of the bereaved after the funeral? Yes, briefly.

Will there be a religious service at the home of the bereaved? No.

Will food be served? Possibly. Given the broad ethnic mixture of Catholicism, some Catholics may have a gathering at which food (and often, drink) is served.

How soon after the funeral will a mourner usually return to a normal work schedule? Perhaps a week.

How soon after the funeral will a mourner usually return to a normal social schedule? Perhaps a week.

Are there mourning customs to which a friend who is not a Catholic should be sensitive? No.

Are there rituals for observing the anniversary of the death? There is a Mass on the anniversary of the death.

5 · HOME CELEBRATIONS

Not applicable to Roman Catholicism.

25

Seventh-day Adventist

1. HISTORY AND BELIEFS

The Seventh-day Adventist Church stemmed from a worldwide religious revival in the mid-1800s when people of many faiths fervently believed biblical prophecies that they interpreted as meaning that Jesus Christ's Second Coming, or "advent," was imminent.

When Christ did not come in the 1840s, a group of these disappointed Adventists in the United States concluded that they had misinterpreted prophetic events, and that the Second Coming was still in the future. This same group later became known as Seventh-day Adventists, which organized formally as a denomination in 1863.

Adventists anticipate and prepare for the world's end in conjunction with the Second Coming of Jesus Christ. They believe that the end of the world is near and that eternal hell for the wicked is not consistent with the concept of a "loving Father." Instead, they believe in eventual annihilation of the wicked and eternal bliss for the

saved. After a thousand-year reign of the saints with Christ in heaven, the wicked will be raised and, along with Satan, annihilated. Out of the chaos of the old earth will emerge a new earth, which the redeemed will inherit as their everlasting home.

Worldwide, there are about 16 million Seventh-day Adventists. The movement grows by about 3.5 to 4 percent annually and has more than 65,900 congregations in over 203 countries.

In addition to a mission program, the church has the largest worldwide Protestant parochial school system, with over 1.5 million elementary through college students in more than 7,500 schools. It also operates medical schools and hospitals.

U.S. churches: 4,870
U.S. membership: 1 million
(data from the 2010 Yearbook of American and Canadian Churches)

For more information, contact:
The Seventh-day Adventist Church
12501 Old Columbia Pike
Silver Spring, MD 20904-6600
(301) 680-6000
www.adventist.org

Canadian churches: 344
Canadian membership: 59,354
(data from the 2010 Yearbook of American and Canadian Churches*)*

For more information, contact:
Seventh-day Adventist Church
    in Canada
1148 King Street East
Oshawa, ON L1H 1H8
(905) 433-0011

2 · THE BASIC SERVICE

The Adventists' basic religious service is held on Saturday mornings and lasts about 60 minutes. The service is strong on fellowship. About half of it is devoted to readings and teachings from the Old and New Testaments.

APPROPRIATE ATTIRE

Men: Jacket and tie or more relaxed clothing. No head covering required.

Women: Suit, dress, skirt and blouse or conservative pants suits are acceptable. No head covering required. Clothing usually covers the arms and hems are below the knee, but neither is obligatory.

Although Adventists do not ordinarily wear jewelry, guests should feel comfortable wearing it.

There are no rules regarding colors of clothing.

THE SANCTUARY

What are the major sections of the church?
The sanctuary: Where congregants sit.
The speakers' platform: A slightly elevated section for speakers and, at times, the choir.

THE SERVICE

When should guests arrive and where should they sit? It is customary to arrive at the time the service is scheduled. There will usually be someone to help you find a seat; if not, take any open seat.

If arriving late, are there times when a guest should *not* enter the service? If arriving late, do not enter during prayer.

Are there times when a guest should *not* leave the service? Do not leave during prayer.

Who are the major officiants, leaders or participants and what do they do?
The elders, who are elected lay leaders in charge of individual congregations. They are usually elected for one year.
An ordained pastor, although not every congregation has one. Adventists ordain only men.

What are the major ritual objects of the service? There are no specific ritual objects.

What books are used? A hymnal and the Old and New Testaments.

To indicate the order of the ser-

vice: A program will be distributed to congregants and guests.

GUEST BEHAVIOR DURING THE SERVICE

Will a guest who is not a Seventh-day Adventist be expected to do anything other than sit? It is optional for guests to stand, kneel and sing with the congregation. It is also optional for them to join in the washing of feet. During this ritual, men and women will leave the sanctuary and go to rooms reserved, for the sake of modesty, for the separate genders. Guests may remain in the sanctuary, during which time the organist will be playing. The entire ritual may take about 10 minutes. The ritual is based on a passage in the New Testament (John 13:14–15) in which Jesus first washes the feet of his disciples at the Last Supper, then instructs them that they should do the same to one another. Adventists do this almost as a weekly mini-baptism.

Are there any parts of the service in which a guest who is not a Seventh-day Adventist should *not* participate? Guests can participate in all aspects of the service, unless their own faith forbids it.

If not disruptive to the service, is it okay to:

Take pictures? Yes.

Use a flash? Yes.

Use a video camera? Yes.

Use a tape recorder? Yes.

Will contributions to the church be collected at the service? An offering plate will be passed through the congregation. Donations by guests are optional.

How much is it customary to contribute? Contributions from $1 to $5 are customary.

AFTER THE SERVICE

Is there usually a reception after the service? Often, yes, lasting 30 to 60 minutes. A variety of foods may be served. Often, a pot luck luncheon is provided for members and guests, in an activity room. There is usually a benediction or prayer before eating. There will be no alcoholic beverages.

It is not considered impolite to neither eat nor drink, especially if one has dietary restrictions.

Is there a traditional form of address for clergy who may be at the reception? "Elder" or "Pastor."

Is it okay to leave early? Yes.

GENERAL GUIDELINES AND ADVICE

None provided.

SPECIAL VOCABULARY

Key words or phrases that it might be helpful for a visitor to know:

Sabbath School: The study service preceding the worship service.

Prayer Meeting: The midweek service, usually held on Wednesday evenings.

DOGMA AND IDEOLOGY

Seventh-day Adventists believe:

The Scriptures of both the Old and New Testaments are the final authority. The Saturday service focuses on the study of these Scriptures and their exposition. (No specific translation of the Bible is used, since 90 percent of Adventists live outside the United States and use hundreds of different translations of the Bible.)

A basic book to which a guest can refer to learn more about the Seventh-day Adventist Church:
Seventh-day Adventists Believe (Silver Spring, Md.: Ministerial Association, General Conference of Seventh-day Adventists).

3. HOLY DAYS AND FESTIVALS

Seventh-day Adventists' only holy day is the Sabbath, which occurs each Saturday. This is Seventh-day Adventists' central day of worship, on which they avoid labor and secular activities.

The faith recognizes no other holy days because the Sabbath is the only universal holy day mentioned in the Scriptures.

4. LIFE CYCLE EVENTS

Baptism Ceremony

Baptism initiates an adolescent or adult into the church. During the ceremony, which usually lasts less than 30 minutes, the person to be baptized enters a baptismal pool with a pastor or elder and is fully and briefly immersed under the water. The baptism is part of a public service, usually the basic Sabbath worship service.

Baptism is a sign of remission of sin and spiritual rebirth by symbolically participating in Christ's death, burial and Resurrection.

BEFORE THE CEREMONY

Are guests usually invited by a formal invitation? There will be no formal invitation.

If not stated explicitly, should one assume that children are invited? Yes.

If one can't attend, what should one do? One may offer their best wishes to the family.

APPROPRIATE ATTIRE

Men: Jacket and tie or more relaxed clothing. No head covering required.

Women: Dress, skirt and blouse or conservative pants suit are acceptable. No head covering required. Clothing usually covers the arms and hems are below the knee, but neither is obligatory.

Although Adventists do not ordinarily wear jewelry, guests should feel comfortable wearing it.

There are no rules regarding colors of clothing.

GIFTS

Is a gift customarily expected? A gift is neither customary nor expected.

Should gifts be brought to the ceremony? See above.

THE CEREMONY

Where will the ceremony take place? Generally, in the main sanctuary of the church. Sometimes, the baptismal immersion will be at an outdoor site, such as a lake, a stream or even the ocean.

When should guests arrive and where should they sit? It is customary to arrive at the time the service is called. There will usually be someone to help you find a seat; if not, you can take any open seat.

If arriving late, are there times when a guest should *not* enter the ceremony? If arriving late, do not enter during prayer.

Are there times when a guest should *not* leave the ceremony? Do not leave during prayer.

Who are the major officiants, leaders or participants at the ceremony and what do they do?
The elder or pastor, who performs the baptism by immersion.

What books are used? None.

To indicate the order of the ceremony: There may be a program.

Will a guest who is not a Seventh-day Adventist be expected to do anything other than sit? It is optional for guests to stand, kneel and sing with the congregation.

Are there any parts of the ceremony in which a guest who is not a Seventh-day Adventist should *not* **participate?** Guests can participate in all aspects of the service, unless their own faith forbids it.

If not disruptive to the ceremony, is it okay to:
Take pictures? Yes.
Use a flash? Yes.
Use a video camera? Yes.
Use a tape recorder? Yes.

Will contributions to the church be collected at the ceremony? Normally baptism is a part of the regular worship service, during which an offering plate is passed through the congregation. No special offering will be taken in connection with the baptism itself. Donations by guests are optional.

How much is it customary to contribute? Contributions from $1 to $10 are customary.

AFTER THE CEREMONY

Is there usually a reception after the ceremony? No.

Is there a traditional greeting for the family? No.

Is there a traditional form of address for clergy whom a guest may meet? "Elder" or "Pastor."

Initiation Ceremony

Not applicable to Seventh-day Adventists.

Marriage Ceremony

Seventh-day Adventists believe that marriage was divinely established in Eden. To accomplish this most important part of Creation, God performed a miracle and brought forth Eve from the side of Adam, and gave her to Adam as his wife. Jesus later affirmed marriage to be a lifelong union between a man and a woman in loving companionship.

A marriage commitment is to God, as well as to the spouse. Marriage should be entered into only between partners who share a common religious faith. Mutual love, honor, respect and responsibility are the fabric of this relationship.

The marriage ceremony usually lasts between 30 and 60 minutes.

BEFORE THE CEREMONY

Are guests usually invited by a formal invitation? Yes. Occasionally, there will be a general invitation in the local church bulletin.

If not stated explicity, should one assume that children are invited? Yes.

If one can't attend, what should one do? RSVP with your regrets and send a gift to the bride and groom.

APPROPRIATE ATTIRE

Men: Jacket and tie. No head covering required.

Women: Dress or skirt and blouse. No head covering required. Clothing should cover the arms and hems should reach below the knee.

Although Adventists do not ordinarily wear jewelry, guests should feel comfortable wearing it.

There are no rules regarding colors of clothing.

GIFTS

Is a gift customarily expected? Only if the celebrants are close friends or relatives. Money and other gifts are appropriate.

Should gifts be brought to the ceremony? Gifts may be sent to the home before or after the wedding ceremony or brought to the ceremony and placed in the reception area.

THE CEREMONY

Where will the ceremony take place? In a variety of settings, although most commonly in the church sanctuary.

When should guests arrive and where should they sit? Arrive shortly before the ceremony is scheduled to start.

If arriving late, are there times when a guest should *not* enter the ceremony? Latecomers should not enter during the bride's entry.

Are there times when a guest should *not* leave the ceremony? Do not leave during prayer.

Who are the major officiants, leaders or participants at the ceremony and what do they do?
The pastor, who will deliver a few comments.

What books are used? Only the clergyman uses a Bible.

To indicate the order of the ceremony: A program will be distributed.

Will a guest who is not a Seventh-day Adventist be expected to do anything other than sit? It is optional for guests to stand, kneel and sing with the congregation.

Are there any parts of the ceremony in which a guest who is not a Seventh-day Adventist should *not* participate? Guests who belong to other faiths can participate in all aspects of the service, unless restricted from doing so by their own faith.

If not disruptive to the ceremony, is it okay to:
Take photographs? Yes.
Use a flash? Yes.
Use a video camera? Yes.
Use a tape recorder? Yes.

Will contributions to the church be collected at the ceremony? No.

AFTER THE CEREMONY

Is there usually a reception after the ceremony? There is usually a 30- to 60-minute reception. The location varies, but will be announced in advance. Guests greet the participants, visit with other guests and enjoy the food. Usually, there is punch and cake. Sometimes, there is a sit-down meal. There will be no alcoholic beverages.

Would it be considered impolite to neither eat or drink? No, especially if a guest has dietary restrictions.

Is there a grace or benediction before eating or drinking? Wait for a brief prayer of thanks for the food before eating.

Is there a grace or benediction after eating or drinking? No.

Is there a traditional greeting for the family? Just offer your congratulations.

Is there a traditional form of address for clergy who may be at the reception? "Elder" or "Pastor."

Is it okay to leave early? Yes.

Funerals and Mourning

Seventh-day Adventists believe that the deceased sleep until the Resurrection of Jesus. A Seventh-day Adventist funeral usually lasts about 15 to 30 minutes.

BEFORE THE CEREMONY

How soon after the death does the funeral usually take place? Within one week of the death.

What should someone who is not a Seventh-day Adventist do upon hearing of the death of a member of that faith? Telephone or visit to express sorrow. Express such words of comfort as "I sense your grief and share it with you." When speaking with each other, Adventists usually follow this phrase with, "We look for the coming resurrection." One should not consign the deceased to heaven or hell.

APPROPRIATE ATTIRE

Men: Jacket and tie. No head covering required.

Women: Dress or skirt and blouse. No head covering required. Clothing should cover the arms, and hems should be below the knee.

No jewelry should be worn.

Somber colors are recommended.

GIFTS

Is it appropriate to send flowers or make a contribution? It is not appropriate to make a donation, but it is appropriate to send flowers to the funeral or to the deceased's home before or after the funeral. The bereaved can also be helped by offering to transport incoming relatives from airports or bus or train stations or offering to help with errands.

Is it appropriate to send food? It is appropriate to bring food after the funeral to the home of the deceased or to the place of a memorial meal, which could be elsewhere.

THE CEREMONY

Where will the ceremony take place? Either in a church or in a funeral home.

When should guests arrive and where should they sit? It is customary to arrive early. If there is no usher, sit in any seat.

If arriving late, are there times when a guest should *not* enter the ceremony? Do not enter during prayer.

Will the bereaved family be present at the church or funeral home before the ceremony? Often.

Is there a traditional greeting for the family? It is appropriate to offer the family a brief word of encouragement before the funeral.

Will there be an open casket? Usually.

Is a guest expected to view the body? This is optional.

What is appropriate behavior upon viewing the body? Simply stand in silent observation.

Who are the major officiants at the ceremony and what do they do?
A *clergyman,* who leads the service; possibly also an associate clergy or layperson and musician(s).

What books are used? The clergy alone uses the Bible.

To indicate the order of the ceremony: A program will be distributed.

Will a guest who is not a Seventh-day Adventist be expected to do anything other than sit? You are not expected to do anything other than sit respectfully.

Are there any parts of the ceremony in which a guest who is not a Seventh-day Adventist should *not* participate? No.

If not disruptive to the service, is it okay to:
Take pictures? No.
Use a flash? No.
Use a video camera? No.
Use a tape recorder? No.

Will contributions to the church be collected at the ceremony? No.

THE INTERMENT

Should guests attend the interment? This is optional.

Whom should one ask for directions? The funeral director.

What happens at the the grave-side? There will be a brief message of encouragement and prayer from the clergyman.

Do guests who are not Seventh-day Adventists participate at the graveside ceremony? No. They are simply present.

COMFORTING THE BEREAVED

Is it appropriate to visit the home of the bereaved after the funeral? Yes, especially during the first few days after the funeral. More than once is appropriate. One should visit briefly, perhaps ten minutes, to express words of encouragement or to offer to help with any difficulties the bereaved may encounter.

Will there be a religious service at the home of the bereaved? There are no special customs or religious services at the home.

Will food be served? No.

How soon after the funeral will a mourner usually return to a normal work schedule? This is left entirely to the discretion of individual mourners, since the Bible does not mandate specific periods for mourning. Probably within days of the funeral.

How soon after the funeral will a mourner usually return to a normal social schedule? Probably within days of the funeral.

Are there rituals for observing the anniversary of the death? No, since the Bible does not mandate such rituals.

5 · HOME CELEBRATIONS

Not applicable to Seventh-day Adventists.

26

Sikh

1. HISTORY AND BELIEFS

The Sikh faith originated in India in the late 15th century through the life and teachings of Guru Nanak (1469–1539 C.E.), the first Sikh guru. At a time of great religious conflict, he taught that all creation is a part of the One Creator. After Guru Nanak's life, he passed his "light" on successively to nine other gurus who further evolved his teachings. Each guru denounced India's caste system and the oppression of anyone based on class, creed, color or sex.

The 10th and last human guru, Guru Gobind Singh, initiated his followers as the *Khalsa,* which means "the Pure Ones." He instructed the *Khalsa* not to cut their hair (since doing so would tamper with God's image, in which they were created); to dress in white Sikh attire called *bana,* which consists of turbans and dresslike garments called *kurtas* and leggings called *churidars;* to be monogamous; and to live righteously. Before dying in 1708, Guru Gobind Singh "gave" the guruship to the Sikh scriptures known as the *Siri Guru Granth Sahib.* These scriptures were compiled by the fifth guru, Arjan Dev, and contain sacred writings by some Sikh gurus and several Hindu and Muslim saints. Since then, Sikhs have bowed before the *Siri Guru Granth Sahib,* consulted it as their only guru and treated it with reverence.

Today, there are 20 million Sikhs throughout the world.

U.S. temples/*gurdwaras:* 100
U.S. membership: 300,000
(2001 data from the World Sikh Organization)

For more information, contact:
Sikh Gurdwara of North Carolina
3214 Banner Street
Durham, NC 27704
(919) 220-0630

Canadian temples/*gurdwaras:* 100
Canadian membership: 400,000
(2001 data from the World Sikh Organization)

For more information, contact:
Gurdwara
SRI Guru Singh Sabha
4504 Millwoods Road S.
Edmonton, AB T6L 6Y8
(403) 462-7454

2. THE BASIC SERVICE

A Sikh service takes place in a *gurdwara,* which literally means "Gate to the Guru" and is an environment that has been especially readied for uplifting one's consciousness. The service may take place in someone's home, in a rented hall or in a special place built for the purpose. The main focus of any Sikh *gurdwara* is the *Siri Guru Granth Sahib,* a compilation of sacred writings that is covered in cloth and is usually at the front of the room. Sikhs bow to the *Siri Guru Granth Sahib,* which symbolizes the Infinite Word of God, as an act of humility and to acknowledge that an Infinite Power pervades all.

Everyone attending the *gurdwara* sits on the floor as an act of humility, equality and respect. They also sit in a cross-legged position, which is conducive to meditation. If helpful to their comfort, guests do not have to sit with their legs crossed.

The Sikh service consists of *kirtan* (songs of praise to God), an *ardas* (community prayer lead by any one person) and a *hukam* (the "Guru's Command"), which is read from the *Siri Guru Granth Sahib.* The *hukam,* which is a portion of the *Siri Guru Granth Sahib* chosen randomly by the reader, is first read in the original Gurmukhi language and then translated to English (or the main language of the congregation).

Often, guest speakers address the *sangat,* or congregation, on spiritual topics. Many *sangats* hold services every Sunday morning that last more than two hours. Other *sangats* may hold services that last about 30 minutes early every morning and sometimes every evening as well.

APPROPRIATE ATTIRE

Men: A jacket and tie or more casual, modest clothing. Shoes are always removed before entering the *gurdwara,* and the head must always be covered while in the *gurdwara.* Guests may wear any hat, cap or scarf that covers the top of the head.

Women: A modest dress, skirt and blouse, or pants suit. It is best if the legs are covered enough so one can comfortably sit cross-legged. Shoes are always removed before entering the *gurdwara,* and the head must always be covered with a scarf, hat or veil that covers the top of the head while in the *gurdwara.* Modest jewelry is permissible.

There are no rules regarding colors of clothing.

THE SANCTUARY

What are the major sections of the gurdwara? *Gurdwaras* can range from a room or house converted for the purpose of worship to magnificent buildings inlaid with gold and marble. However, many *gurdwaras* have the following sections:

The entry room: Has shelves where shoes can be left before entering the main room. Often, the entry room has bowls or sinks for washing one's hands and feet, since one should purify oneself before being in the presence of the *Siri Guru Granth Sahib*. If there is no entry room, shoes should be left outside the *gurdwara*.

The main room: Congregants sit on the covered floor in this area. In some *gurdwaras*, the men sit on the left and the women sit on the right.

The front or central area: Where the Sikh scriptures, the *Siri Guru Granth Sahib*, presides under a canopy and is elevated above the congregation. To the right or left of the *Siri Guru Granth Sahib* is an area for *kirtanis*, musicians who lead congregants in song.

THE SERVICE

When should guests arrive and where should they sit? Because of the length of the ordinary worship service, it is not required to arrive at the time designated for the start of worship. Guests should sit anywhere in the main area with the men on the left and women on the right, although this may not apply in some *gurdwaras*. Everyone, including guests, must always face the *Siri Guru Granth Sahib*, which is at the front (or central location) of the room.

Before entering the *gurdwara*, remove your shoes and cover your head. It is optional to wash your hands and feet. If desired, the guest may offer money or a gift, such as flowers or fruit, to the *Siri Guru Granth Sahib* and then bow before it. Money may be placed in a box with a slot in it or on an offering plate. Either will be in front of the *Siri Guru Granth Sahib*. Other gifts may be placed in front of the *Siri Guru Granth Sahib*.

Next, guests should sit on the floor facing the front. The feet of all present face away from the *Siri Guru Granth Sahib* as a sign of respect. It is important to refrain from eating, drinking or unnecessary conversation in the *gurdwara*.

If arriving late, are there times when a guest should *not* enter the service? It is best to enter during the *kirtan*, or songs. Do not enter during the *ardas*, or community prayer, when everyone is standing.

Are there times when a guest should *not* leave the service? A guest may leave at any time. However, it is recommended not to leave during the *ardas* (community prayer) or *hukam*, the reading from the *Siri Guru Granth Sahib*. It may be advisable for guests to sit near the door if they plan on leaving the service early.

Who are the major officiants, leaders or participants and what do they do?

The granthi or giani ji, who reads the *hukam* from the *Siri Guru Granth Sahib*.

Attendants, several people who sit behind the *Siri Guru Granth Sahib* and attend to it by frequently waving a long-handled brush made of long horsehair called a *chori sahib* above the *Siri Guru Granth Sahib*, or take out or put away the scriptures. The attendants also serve *prasad*, or sweet pudding, at the end of the service; read the *hukam* translation in English; and assist in the *gurdwara* as needed. Many people from the *sangat*, the congregation, participate in these functions.

Kirtanis, musicians who lead the *sangat* in *kirtan*, songs of praise to God.

The master of ceremonies, the person announcing guest speakers and the order of the service. This role is often fulfilled by the *gurdwara* secretary or *granthi* or *giani ji.*

What are the major ritual objects of the service?

The manji sahib, the "bed" or platform for the *Siri Guru Granth Sahib.* It is covered by ornate cloths called *ramalas.*

The chandoa, the canopy hanging over the *Siri Guru Granth Sahib.*

The adi shakti or khanda, a symbol shaped like a circle surrounded by two swords and cut through by one double-edged sword. It symbolizes the primal, creative energy of the universe. The sword cutting through the circle represents the breaking of the cycle of birth and death.

The kirpan, a special knife used to bless *langar* ("sacred food") and *prasad* (sweet pudding) during the *ardas* (community prayer).

The chori sahib, a long-handled brush made of long horsehair. It is identical to brushes used in ancient India that were waved over royalty to show their state of sovereignty. It is waved over the *Siri Guru Granth Sahib* to symbolize its sovereignty, to purify the energy around it, and to show its status as a living guru.

What books are used? Booklets of sheets containing transliteration and translation of the *kirtan* (songs of praise to God) to be sung may be available, depending on the *gurdwara.* Efforts should be made not to put them on the floor. Since Sikhs respect the written word of God, anything containing it should not be stepped upon or marred in any way.

If these booklets are available, they are often found at the front of the *gurdwara.*

To indicate the order of the service: There may be a written program and/or the master of ceremonies may make periodic announcements.

GUEST BEHAVIOR DURING THE SERVICE

Will a guest who is not a Sikh be expected to do anything other than sit? A guest will be expected to stand and sit at the same time as everyone else. It is entirely optional for the guest to sing or bow to the *Siri Guru Granth Sahib.* Guests are expected to accept *prasad* (sweet pudding), which is considered a blessing from the *Siri Guru Granth Sahib.*

Customarily, *prasad* is placed into one's hands, which are placed together with the palms up. One does not have to be a Sikh to eat the *prasad.*

Are there any parts of the service in which a guest who is not a Sikh should *not* participate? Only Sikhs will be asked to serve *prasad,* read from the *Siri Guru Granth Sahib,* do the *ardas* (prayer) and serve in any way needed. A guest will not be expected to perform any of these functions. Other than this, a guest may participate in every part of the service as desired.

If not disruptive to the service, is it okay to:

Take pictures? Yes, but only if intended solely for personal use.

Use a flash? Yes, but only if intended solely for personal use.

Use a video camera? Yes, but only if intended solely for personal use.

Use a tape recorder? Yes, but only if intended solely for personal use.

Will contributions to the *gurdwara* be collected at the service? Donations collected at each service help fund the *langar* (the food provided after the service), *prasad* (sweet pudding) and the general maintenance and administration of the *gurdwara*. No collection plate is passed through the congregation. Instead, money, flowers or fruit may be offered to the *Siri Guru Granth Sahib*, if one chooses to bow to it, which is optional. Money may be placed in a box with a slot in it or on an offering plate. Either will be in front of the *Siri Guru Granth Sahib*. Other gifts may be placed in front of the *Siri Guru Granth Sahib*.

How much is it customary to contribute? The customary contribution is $1 to $10.

AFTER THE SERVICE

Is there usually a reception after the service? *Langar*, or sacred food, is served after (and sometimes during) each service. It is available to all. *Langar* may be served in the *gurdwara* itself, outside, or in a special hall built for the purpose.

Also, a vegetarian meal is provided and often consists of East Indian cuisine. Since alcohol is prohibited to Sikhs, it will not be served. Guests with dietary restrictions may politely decline food. It is not considered impolite if they decline the offered food for this reason. Smoking is also strictly prohibited within the precincts and no one should have tobacco or cigarettes on his or her person. The reception may last anywhere from half an hour to several hours.

Is there a traditional form of address for clergy who may be at the reception? "Granthi" and then the first name, or "Giani Ji."

Is it okay to leave early? Yes.

GENERAL GUIDELINES AND ADVICE

Many *gurdwaras* do not designate specific people to help guests, but feel free to ask any Sikh to help you or to explain any part of the service you may not understand.

Remember to always face the *Siri Guru Granth Sahib* and to have your head covered throughout the service. Also, shoes are never worn within the *gurdwara*, even when a service is not taking place.

SPECIAL VOCABULARY

Key words or phrases that it might be helpful for a visitor to know:

Siri Guru Granth Sahib ("SEE-ree GOO-roo GRANTH SAH-heeb"): Scriptures compiled by the fifth Sikh guru, Arjan Dev, that contain sacred writings by some Sikh gurus and several Hindu and Muslim saints. Sikhs bow before the *Siri Guru Granth Sahib*, consult it as their only guru, and treat it with reverence.

Prasad ("prah-SAHD"): The sweet pudding served toward the end of the service. It consists of water, honey, wheat flour and clarified butter. *Prasad* is considered to be a blessing from the *Siri Guru Granth Sahib* that everyone can eat.

Ardas ("AHR-das"): Community prayer led by one person in the *gurdwara* service. Blessings for special occasions or events may be requested during the *ardas*.

Sangat ("SAHN-gaht"): The congregation of Sikhs and guests who come together for a worship service.

Langar ("LAHN-gahr"): The vegetarian meal prepared in a prayerful environment and served as an offering after or throughout the worship service to the *sangat*, including guests.

Sat Nam ("SAHT NAHM"): A common phrase and greeting among Sikhs that means "True Name" and acknowledges the God in all.

Wahe Guruji ka khalsa. Wahe Guruji ki fateh ("WAH-heh GOO-ROO-ji kah KAHL-sah. WAH-heh GOO-ROO-ji kee FAH-teh"): A common greeting or phrase that means "The Pure Ones belong to God. Victory be to God!"

DOGMA AND IDEOLOGY

Sikhs believe:

While one God pervades everyone and everything, there are many ways to worship God. Thus, Sikhs respect all religions without trying to "convert" others to Sikhism.

The body is a temple that can serve the spirit. The body should be treated respectfully by not eating meat or eggs, or using alcohol, tobacco or drugs. Yoga and meditation can balance the body, mind and spirit.

Women may fully participate in all *gurdwara* services and in any positions of leadership and ministry.

The *Siri Guru Granth Sahib* is the only guru in a Sikh's life. It is written in Gurmukhi, the language of the 10 Sikh gurus. By reciting these words of the gurus, Sikhs believe they can achieve the same consciousness as

did the gurus. Sikhs will never bow to any man or woman, only to the *Siri Guru Granth Sahib*.

Some basic books to which a guest can refer to learn more about Sikhism:

Kundalini Yoga: The Flow of Eternal Power by Shakti Parwha Kaur Khalsa (New York: Penguin, 1996).

Philosophy and Faith of Sikhism by K. S. Duggal (Honesdale, Pa.: Himalayan Institute Press, 1985).

Sikh Gurus: Their Lives and Teachings by K. S. Duggal (Honesdale, Pa.: Himalayan Institute Press, 1987).

The Sikh Religion: Its Gurus, Sacred Writings and Authors by Max Arthur Macauliffe (Oxford: Oxford University Press, 1909; republished 2008 by Forgotten Books).

3 · HOLY DAYS AND FESTIVALS

Sikhs used to observe a lunar calendar, so the dates for holidays could not be accurately correlated to the solar calendar in use in the West. They now observe a solar calendar, so dates for holidays are fixed.

The birthdays of the 10 Sikh gurus are celebrated throughout the year:

Guru Gobind Singh ("GOH-beend SING"). Celebrated January 5.

Guru Har Rai ("hahr rye"). Celebrated January 31.

Guru Teg Bahadur ("TEHG BAH-hah-door"). Celebrated April 18.

Guru Angad ("Ahn-GAHD"). Celebrated April 18.

Guru Arjan ("AHR-jahn"). Celebrated May 2.

Guru Amar Das ("Ah-MAR DAHS"). Celebrated May 23.

Guru Hargobind ("Hahr-GOH-beend"). Celebrated July 5.

Guru Har Krishnan ("HAHR KRISH-nan"). Celebrated July 23.

Guru Ram Das ("rahm dahs"). Celebrated October 9.

Guru Nanak ("Nah-NAHK"). Celebrated November 23.

There are no traditional greetings for the above holidays.

Other important religious celebrations include:

Bhaisaki ("BHAY-soo-ki"). When the *Khalsa* (the Pure Ones) was formed in 1699. This usually occurs in the middle of April. There is no traditional greeting for this holiday.

Guru Gaddi Day ("GOO-ROO GAHD-dee"). Commemorates the *Siri Guru Granth Sahib* proclamation as the Living Guru. This usually occurs in November. There is no traditional greeting for this holiday.

To obtain a list of the exact days on which these holidays fall, consult with a Sikh center in your area.

Sikhs also observe the sixth of each month as a Holy Day. This day commemorates the attack by the Indian government on June 6, 1984, on the Akal Takhat in Amritsar in northern India. The government had mistakenly assumed that armed rebels were inside the Akal Takhat, a fortress that represents the temporal authority of the Sikhs. The Akal Takhat is adjacent to the Golden Temple, which houses the spiritual authority of the Sikhs. The two shrines are considered the holiest sites for Sikhs throughout the world.

These celebrations take place through the same *gurdwara* service as described earlier. Behavior and expectations for guests at these celebrations are the same as for the typical Sikh service.

4 · LIFE CYCLE EVENTS

Birth Ceremony

Among many Sikhs, it is traditional to name a newborn child by taking a *hukam* from the *Siri Guru Granth Sahib* and picking a name that begins with the first letter of the *hukam*. But this is not done in a religious ceremony. In the Sikh faith, there is no birth ceremony per se.

Initiation Ceremony

The *amrit* ceremony is a baptism that one chooses to undergo when one is ready to commit completely to the Sikh way of life. *Amrit* is given to anyone (usually an adult) who desires this commitment. It is usually administered to a group.

The ceremony focuses on the preparation of the *amrit* (holy water) by five "example Sikhs" called *Panj Piare*, or "Beloved Ones." An "example Sikh" is someone who best lives by the instructions and the example set by Guru Gobind Singh.

The *amrit* is then poured on the top of the head of those who have requested to be baptized, then splashed in their face. At the end of the ceremony, all participants and guests drink whatever water remains.

The ceremony incorporates many elements of a normal *gurdwara*, but adds baptism by water (not by immersion) and instructions for living as a Sikh that are given to the newly baptized by the five *Panj Piare*.

The *amrit* ceremony is given a few times each year between 4:00 and 6:00 A.M. Since the ceremony is primarily for those giving or receiving the baptism, special permission and instruction on conduct should be obtained from the head *granthi* for one to attend the ceremony as a guest.

BEFORE THE CEREMONY

Are guests usually invited by a formal invitation? Outside guests are not usually invited to the ceremony. Permission for them to attend must first be obtained by the person undergoing the *amrit* ceremony from the head *granthi*. Once permission has been granted, guests are invited informally, usually by telephone.

If not stated explicitly, should one assume that children are invited? No.

If one can't attend, what should one do? Politely decline with a note or a telephone call.

APPROPRIATE ATTIRE

Men: A jacket and tie or more casual, modest clothing. Shoes are always removed before entering the *gurdwara*, and the head must always be covered while in the *gurdwara*. Guests may wear any hat, cap, or scarf that covers the top of the head.

Women: A modest dress, skirt and blouse, or pants suit. It is best if the legs are covered enough so one can comfortably sit cross-legged. Shoes are always removed before entering the *gurdwara,* and the head must always be covered with a scarf, hat or veil that covers the top of the head while in the *gurdwara*. Modest jewelry is permissible.

There are no rules regarding colors of clothing.

GIFTS

Is a gift customarily expected? No.

Should gifts be brought to the ceremony? See above.

THE CEREMONY

Where will the ceremony take place? In the main room of the *gurdwara*.

When should guests arrive and where should they sit?
Guests should arrive before the time when the ceremony will begin, since no one is allowed to enter after it starts. Guests should sit where they are instructed to do so by the five *Panj Piare* who administer the ceremony.

Upon entering the *gurdwara*, remove your shoes and cover your head. It is optional to wash your hands and feet. If desired, the guest may offer money or a gift, such as flowers or fruit, to the *Siri Guru Granth Sahib* and then bow before it. Money may be placed in a box with a slot in it or on an offering plate. Either will be in front of the *Siri Guru Granth Sahib*. Other gifts may be placed in front of the *Siri Guru Granth Sahib*.

Next, guests should sit on the floor facing the front. The feet of all present should face away from the *Siri Guru Granth Sahib* as a sign of respect. It is important to refrain from eating, drinking or unnecessary conversation in the *gurdwara*.

If arriving late, are there times when a guest should *not* enter the ceremony? No one is allowed to enter after the ceremony starts.

Are there times when a guest should *not* leave the ceremony? Once entering the *amrit* ceremony, one may not leave until the ceremony has concluded so the commitment and concentration of participants is not disturbed.

Who are the major officiants, leaders or participants at the ceremony and what do they do?

The Panj Piare ("Panj Pee-AR-ay"), five Sikhs who constantly repeat a chant, administer the *amrit* and instruct those being baptized in their duties as Sikhs.

The granthi ("GRAHN-thee") *or giani ji,* who reads the *hukam* from the *Siri Guru Granth Sahib*.

Attendants, who serve *prasad* (sweet pudding) at the end of the ceremony, who read the *hukam* translation in English, and who assist in the *gurdwara*. Many people from the *sangat,* the congregation, participate in these functions.

Kirtanis, musicians who lead the *sangat* in *kirtan*, songs of praise to God.

The master of ceremonies, who announces any guest speakers and the order of the service. This role is often fulfilled by the *gurdwara* secretary or *granthi* or *giani ji.*

What books are used? Booklets of sheets containing transliteration and translation of the *kirtan* (songs of praise to God) to be sung may be available, depending on the *gurdwara*. Efforts should be made not to put them on the floor. Since Sikhs respect the written word of God, anything containing it should not be stepped upon or marred in any way.

If these booklets are available, they are often found at the front of the *gurdwara*.

To indicate the order of the ceremony: There may be a written program and/or the master of ceremonies may make periodic announcements.

Will a guest who is not a Sikh be expected to do anything other than sit? A guest will be expected to stand and sit at the same time as everyone else. It is entirely optional for the guest to sing or bow to the *Siri Guru Granth Sahib*. Guests are expected to accept *prasad* (sweet pudding), which is considered a blessing from the *Siri Guru Granth Sahib*.

Customarily, *prasad* is placed into one's hands, which are placed together with the palms up. One does not have to be a Sikh to eat the *prasad*.

Are there any parts of the ceremony in which a guest who is not a Sikh should *not* participate? Only Sikhs will be asked to serve *prasad*, read from the *Siri Guru Granth Sahib* and serve in any way needed.

If not disruptive to the ceremony, is it okay to:

Take pictures? Only with prior permission of the head *granthi* and if intended solely for personal use.

Use a flash? Only with prior permission of the head *granthi* and if intended solely for personal use.

Use a video camera? Only with prior permission of the head *granthi* and if intended solely for personal use.

Use a tape recorder? Only with prior permission of the head *granthi* and if intended solely for personal use.

Will contributions to the *gurdwara* be collected at the ceremony? Donations collected at each service help fund the *langar* (the food provided after the service), *prasad* and the general maintenance and administration of the *gurdwara*. No collection plate is passed through the congregation. Instead, money or flowers may be offered to the *Siri Guru Granth Sahib* if one chooses to bow to it, which is optional. Money may be placed in a box with a slot in it or on an offering plate. Either will be in front of the *Siri Guru Granth Sahib*. Other gifts may be placed in front of the *Siri Guru Granth Sahib*.

How much is it customary to contribute? The customary contribution is $1 to $10.

AFTER THE CEREMONY

Is there usually a reception after the ceremony?
Langar, or sacred food, may be served after (and sometimes during) the ceremony. It is available to all. *Langar* may be served inside or outside the *gurdwara* or in a special hall built for the purpose.

Also, a vegetarian meal is provided and often consists of East Indian cuisine. Since alcohol is prohibited to Sikhs, it will not be served. The reception may last from 30 minutes to several hours.

Would it be considered impolite to neither eat nor drink? No.

Is there a grace or benediction before eating or drinking? No.

Is there a grace or benediction after eating or drinking? No.

Is there a traditional greeting for the family? The traditional greeting for newly baptized Sikhs is *"Wahe Guruji ka khalsa. Wahe Guru ji ki fateh"* ("WAH-beh GOO-ROO-ji kah KAHL-sah. WAH-heh GOO-ROO-ji kee FAH-teh"), which means "The Pure Ones belong to God. Victory be to God!"

Is there a traditional form of address for clergy who may be at the reception? "Granthi" and then the first name, or "Giani Ji."

Is it okay to leave early? Yes.

Marriage Ceremony

A couple is considered to come together in a Sikh marriage to help each other on the spiritual path. The merging of two identities that takes place in a marriage is an earthly symbol for the more infinite merger between the soul and God.

A wedding can take place as part of the regular *gurdwara* service, but it may be a service in itself. One or more couples may be married at the same time. A minister addresses the *sangat* (the congregation), then explains to the couple the Sikh concept of marriage and commitment. The bride and groom will be called to sit in front of the *Siri Guru Granth Sahib*. The *kirtanis* (musicians) will be seated on one side and the minister on the other side at the front of the *gurdwara*.

A short prayer called an *ardas* is recited to bless the wedding. Only immediate family and the wedding couple stand at this time. A *hukam,* or "Guru's command," for the wedding is then read from the *Siri Guru Granth Sahib*. Next, a special shawl is placed on the shoulder of the groom and in the hands of the bride. The shawl links the couple throughout the wedding ceremony.

The couple is considered to be married when they have circled the *Siri Guru Granth Sahib* four times after reciting four "marriage rounds," which are special verses from the *Siri Guru Granth Sahib,* in Gurmukhi and then in English (or the primary language of the *sangat,* the congregation). The rounds are then sung by the *kirtanis*. These marriage rounds were written by the fourth Sikh guru for his own wedding in the 16th century. They include special instructions for married life. During these rounds, family and close friends (including non-Sikh guests) may be invited to stand around the *Siri Guru Granth Sahib* to show their support for the couple, whom they also encircle. In some *gurdwaras,* as the couple finishes the last round, the congregation may shower the couple with flower petals to show joy and congratulations. At this point, the couple is officially considered to be married and the minister may then make a legal pronouncement of marriage.

The first act of the newly married couple is to feed each other fruit. This illustrates their commitment to nourish and support each other.

If the wedding ceremony is part of a full worship service, the couple and their family and friends now rejoin the *sangat* and the service proceeds as usual.

The wedding itself usually lasts about one hour.

BEFORE THE CEREMONY

Are guests usually invited by a formal invitation? Possibly, but not always. Sikh weddings are open to everyone.

If not stated explicitly, should one assume that children are invited? Yes.

If one can't attend, what should one do? Respond in writing or call, and send a gift if you desire to do so.

APPROPRIATE ATTIRE

Men: A jacket and tie or more casual, modest clothing. Shoes are always removed before entering the *gurdwara,* and the head must always be covered while in the *gurdwara*. Guests may wear any hat, cap, or scarf that covers the top of the head.

Women: A modest dress, skirt and blouse, or pants suit. It is best if the legs are covered enough so one can comfortably sit cross-legged. Shoes are always removed before entering the *gurdwara,* and the head must always be covered with a scarf, hat or veil which covers the top of the head while in the *gurdwara.* Modest jewelry is permissible.

There are no rules regarding colors of clothing.

GIFTS

Is a gift customarily expected? There is no Sikh tradition dictating gift giving for weddings. If one wishes to present a gift, appropriate gifts may include household items (such as sheets, kitchenware or small appliances), a special, inspirational gift or money.

Should gifts be brought to the ceremony? Gifts may either be left in the entry room or brought to a later reception.

THE CEREMONY

Where will the ceremony take place? In the main *gurdwara.*

When should guests arrive and where should they sit? Arrive shortly before the time for which the ceremony has been called, although some *gurdwaras* with primarily Eastern Indian congregants begin weddings much later than what is indicated on an invitation, so it's best to inquire of your host beforehand when the ceremony will actually start.

As with all *gurdwara* services, everyone sits facing the *Siri Guru Granth Sahib,* sometimes with the men on the left and women on the right.

If arriving late, are there times when a guest should *not* enter the ceremony? A guest may enter at any time during the service, except during the *ardas* (community prayer), which is the point during the service when everyone is standing. One should wait at the entrance to the main worship room until these prayers have ended.

Are there times when a guest should *not* leave the ceremony? It is advised not to leave during the *ardas* (prayer), *hukam* (the reading from the *Siri Guru Granth Sahib*) or the "wedding rounds," which are special verses from the *Siri Guru Granth Sahib* recited by the couple in Gurmukhi and then in English (or the primary language of the *sangat,* the congregation).

Guests may wish to sit near the door if they plan on leaving the ceremony early.

Who are the major officiants, leaders or participants at the ceremony and what do they do?
The *granthi or giani ji,* the person reading the *hukam,* or portion, from the *Siri Guru Granth Sahib.* He or she also reads the four wedding rounds.
The minister, the person who officiates at the wedding ceremony.
The bride and groom and their wedding party.
Kirtanis, musicians who lead the *sangat,* or congregation, in *kirtan* (songs of praise to God).

What books are used? Booklets of sheets containing transliteration and translation of the *kirtan* to be sung may be available, depending on the *gurdwara*. These are often found at the front of the *gurdwara* and in front of the *Siri Guru Granth Sahib*. Effort should be made not to place these booklets on the floor. Since Sikhs respect the written word of God, anything containing it should not be stepped upon or marred in any way.

To indicate the order of the ceremony: There may be a written program and/or the master of ceremonies may make periodic announcements.

Will a guest who is not a Sikh be expected to do anything other than sit? A guest is expected to stand and sit at the same time as everyone else, but it is optional to sing or bow to the *Siri Guru Granth Sahib*. Family and close friends wishing to stand behind the *Siri Guru Granth Sahib* to offer support to the couple may do so at the time indicated by the minister.

Are there any parts of the ceremony in which a guest who is not a Sikh should *not* participate? No.

If not disruptive to the ceremony, is it okay to:
Take pictures? Yes, but only if intended solely for personal use.
Use a flash? Yes, but only if intended solely for personal use.
Use a video camera? Yes, but only if intended solely for personal use.
Use a tape recorder? Yes, but only if intended solely for personal use.

Will contributions to the *gurdwara* be collected at the ceremony? Money or flowers may be offered to the *Siri Guru Granth Sahib* if one chooses to bow to it, which is optional.

Money may be placed in a box with a slot in it or on an offering plate. Either will be in front of the *Siri Guru Granth Sahib*. Other gifts may be placed in front of the *Siri Guru Granth Sahib*.

How much is it customary to contribute? The customary contribution is $1 to $10.

AFTER THE CEREMONY

Is there usually a reception after the ceremony? *Langar*, or sacred food, may be served after (and sometimes during) the ceremony. *Langar* may be served inside or outside the *gurdwara* or in a special hall built for the purpose. An additional reception at another location may take place after the *langar*, where a vegetarian meal is provided. This often consists of East Indian cuisine. Since alcoholic beverages are prohibited to Sikhs, they will not be served. It is not considered impolite to decline the offered food for any reason. The reception may last anywhere from half an hour to several hours.

Would it be considered impolite to neither eat nor drink? No.

Is there a grace or benediction before eating or drinking? No.

Is there a grace or benediction after eating or drinking? No.

Is there a traditional greeting for the family? Just offer your congratulations.

Is there a traditional form of address for clergy who may be at the reception? "Granthi" and then the first name, or "Giani Ji."

Is it okay to leave early? Yes.

Funerals and Mourning

Sikhs believe in the cycle of reincarnation and that certain actions and attachments bind the soul to this cycle. The soul itself is not subject to death. Death is only the progression of the soul on its journey from God, through the created universe, and back to God again.

A Sikh tries to be constantly mindful of death so that he or she may be sufficiently prayerful, detached and righteous to break the cycle of birth and death and return to God. Because the soul never dies, there is no mourning at the death of a Sikh. All ceremonies commemorating a death include much prayer to help the soul be released from the bonds of reincarnation and to become one with God again.

After death, Sikhs prepare the body for the funeral with a yogurt bath while reciting prayers. Next the body is dressed in new clothes and the five symbols of a Sikh: *kesh,* or uncut hair; *kirpan,* the Sikh knife that represents compassion and one's task to defend the truth; *kara,* a stainless steel bracelet; *kachera,* special Sikh underwear; and *kanga,* a small comb.

A short ceremony takes place at the funeral home before the cremation. An *ardas,* or community prayer, is recited to begin the service. A minister may be present to offer prayers and say a few words, but this is optional. Two Sikh daily prayers, *Japji* and *Kirtan Sohila,* are recited, and the cremation begins. Although these prayers may be continuously recited throughout the cremation, the basic funeral service ends at this time, and guests may leave. This service usually lasts about 30 to 60 minutes.

Afterward, there may be another service at the *gurdwara,* but this is optional. Traditionally, the word *akal,* which means "undying," is chanted at this service to help release the soul to return to the Infinite. This second ceremony, which is a service in itself, lasts about one hour.

BEFORE THE CEREMONY

How soon after the death does the funeral usually take place? The body of a Sikh is always cremated. This usually occurs within three days after death.

What should a non-Sikh do upon hearing of the death of a member of that faith? It is fine to call the family of the deceased to express your love and concern and offer help or support they may need. In calling or writing, it is best not to focus on loss or sadness, but rather to help the family and friends remember the joy of the soul returning to its true home with God.

APPROPRIATE ATTIRE

Men: A jacket and tie or more casual, modest clothing. Any color is fine. Shoes may be worn inside a funeral home, but not in a *gurdwara* service. The head should be covered with a hat, cap or scarf.

Women: A modest dress, skirt and blouse, or pants suit. It is best if the legs are covered enough to sit comfortably cross-legged. Shoes may be worn inside a funeral home, but not at a *gurdwara* service. The head should be covered with a scarf, hat or veil. Open-toed shoes and modest jewelry are permissible inside the funeral home, but shoes must be removed before entering the *gurdwara*.

There are no rules regarding colors of clothing.

GIFTS

Is it appropriate to send flowers or make a contribution? Flowers, food or contributions to a charity chosen by the family of the deceased may be given, but are not expected.

Is it appropriate to send food? Yes, but do not send food that contains meat, fish, eggs or alcohol.

THE CEREMONY

Where will the ceremony take place? The precremation ceremony will take place at a funeral home. The optional, postcremation ceremony will be at the *gurdwara*.

When should guests arrive and where should they sit? It is best to arrive early enough to be seated before the funeral service begins. At a funeral home, one may sit wherever one wishes, but the family of the deceased will sit in the front. For *gurdwara* services, everyone sits on the floor facing the *Siri Guru Granth Sahib*, sometimes with the men on the left and women on the right.

If arriving late, are there times when a guest should *not* enter the ceremony? One can enter the ceremony in the funeral home and quietly sit anywhere.

Wait at the entrance to the *gurdwara* until the *ardas,* or community prayer, ends and everyone has again been seated.

Will the bereaved family be present at the funeral home before the ceremony? Depending on the customs of a particular Sikh community, the body of the deceased may be displayed at a visitation before the funeral. If this is not the case, the family of the deceased will most likely arrive at the time of the ceremony and not before.

Is there a traditional greeting for the family? Just offer your condolences.

Will there be an open casket? Possibly, depending on the customs of a particular Sikh community.

Is a guest expected to view the body? No.

What is appropriate behavior upon viewing the body? Silently say a short prayer for the soul of the deceased as you pass by the casket.

Who are the major officiants at the ceremony and what do they do?

One person, usually a close family member, officiates at the ceremony at the funeral home and leads the prayers recited there.

Officiating at the service in the *gurdwara* are:

The granthi or giani ji, the person reading the *hukam* from the *Siri Guru Granth Sahib.* The *hukam,* which is a portion of the *Siri Guru Granth Sahib* chosen randomly by the reader, is first read in the original Gurmukhi language and then translated to English (or the main language of the congregation).

Attendants, several people who sit behind the *Siri Guru Granth Sahib* and attend to it by frequently waving a long-handled brush made of long horsehair called a *chori sahib* above the *Siri Guru Granth Sahib* or who take out or put away the scriptures. The attendants also serve *prasad,* or sweet pudding, at the end of the service; read the *hukam* translation in English; and assist in the *gurdwara* in any way. Many people from the *sangat,* the congregation, participate in these functions.

Kirtanis, musicians who lead the *sangat* in *kirtan,* songs of praise to God.

The master of ceremonies, the person announcing guest speakers and the order of the service. This role is often fulfilled by the *gurdwara* secretary or *granthi.*

What books are used? A *Nit Nem,* or daily prayer book of the Sikhs is used to recite the prayers before cremation. Since all prayers are read in Gurmukhi (the original language of the gurus), it is not expected for guests to also recite these. If desired, however, a *Nit Nam* with a transliteration may be available upon request.

To indicate the order of the ceremony: In the funeral home, no one indicates the order of the ceremony that is held there. For the *gurdwara* service, there may be a written program and/or the master of ceremonies may make periodic announcements.

Will a guest who is not a Sikh be expected to do anything other than sit? There are no expectations for guests attending the ceremony in the funeral home. Those guests attending the *gurdwara* ceremony will be expected to stand and sit at the same time as everyone else. It is entirely optional for guests to sing or bow to the *Siri Guru Granth Sahib,* although they are expected to accept *prasad* (sweet pudding), which is considered a blessing from the *Siri Guru Granth Sahib.* Customarily, one receives prasad with both hands together, palms up. One does not have to be a Sikh to eat the *prasad.*

Are there any parts of the ceremony in which a guest who is not a Sikh should *not* participate? Guests may participate in all aspects of the ceremony in the funeral home. In the *gurdwara* ceremony, only Sikhs will be asked to serve *prasad,* read from the *Siri Guru Granth Sahib,* do the *ardas* (prayer) and to serve in any way needed. Other than this, guest may participate in every part of the *gurdwara* ceremony as desired.

If not disruptive to the ceremony, is it okay to:

Take pictures? Only with prior permission of the family of the deceased and if intended solely for personal use.

Use a flash? Only with prior permission of the family of the deceased and if intended solely for personal use.

Use a video camera? Only with prior permission of the family of the deceased and if intended solely for personal use.

Use a tape recorder? Only with prior permission of the family of the deceased and if intended solely for personal use.

Will contributions to the local Sikh temple be collected at the service? No contributions will be collected at a funeral home service. At *gurdwara* services, money or flowers may be offered to the *Siri Guru Granth Sahib* at the time of bowing, but this is optional. Money may be placed in a box with a slot in it or on an offering plate. Either will be in front of the *Siri Guru Granth Sahib*. Other gifts may be placed in front of the *Siri Guru Granth Sahib*.

How much is it customary to contribute? The customary contribution is $1 to $10.

THE CREMATION

Should guests attend the cremation? Usually only close family members remain for the cremation, since it lasts several hours.

Whom should one ask for directions? Friends or the family of the deceased.

What happens at the cremation? An *ardas,* or community prayer, is recited to begin the service. A minister may offer prayers and say a few words, but this is optional. Two Sikh daily prayers, *Japji* and *Kirtan Sohila,* are recited, and the cremation begins.

Do guests who are not Sikhs participate at the cremation ceremony? Not usually, unless they are invited by the family to do so.

COMFORTING THE BEREAVED

Is it appropriate to visit the home of the bereaved after the funeral ceremony? This is optional, though not really expected.

Will there be a religious service at the home of the bereaved? Memorial services are often held at home, especially when the funeral ceremony has taken place in another city. Sometimes, the family of the deceased sponsors an *Akhand Path* (unbroken) or other reading of the *Siri Guru Granth Sahib*. This may take place at their home, at the *gurdwara,* or elsewhere. During the *Akhand Path* service, the entire *Siri Guru Granth Sahib* is read in 48 hours in the Gurmukhi language or in 72 hours in English. People take turns reading the text.

Will food be served? Possibly. Since Sikhs are prohibited from drinking alcoholic beverages, none will be offered.

How soon after the funeral will a mourner usually return to a normal work schedule? Usually one returns to a normal work routine anywhere from a few days to a few weeks after the funeral. This is at the personal discretion of each individual.

How soon after the funeral will a mourner usually return to a normal social schedule? Usually one returns to a normal social routine anywhere from a few days to a few weeks after the funeral. This is at the personal discretion of each individual.

Are there mourning customs to which a friend who is not a Sikh should be sensitive? When visiting, it is best not to focus on loss or sadness, but rather to help the family and friends remember the joy of the soul returning to its true home with God.

Are there rituals for observing the anniversary of the death? No, although some Sikhs may choose to remember a deceased loved one in prayer during a *gurdwara* service on the anniversary of a death. Some Sikhs also choose to hold a special *gurdwara* and *langar* at the anniversary.

5 · HOME CELEBRATIONS

The Home or Business Blessing

When does it occur? Before occupying a new house or apartment or launching a new venture or business.

What is its significance? To bless a new home or enterprise with success and happiness. Many Sikhs may hold a *gurdwara* service called an *Akhand Path,* during which the entire *Siri Guru Granth Sahib* is read in 48 hours in the Gurmukhi language or in 72 hours in English. People take turns reading the text. Other Sikhs may choose to serve *langar,* or sacred food, in the new home or business location.

What is the proper greeting to the celebrants? "Congratulations."

BEFORE THE CEREMONY

Are guests usually invited by a formal invitation? Yes.

If not stated explicitly, should one assume children are invited? Yes.

If one can't attend, what should one do? Politely decline by note or a telephone call. A housewarming gift is appropriate for a new dwelling, but this is entirely optional.

APPROPRIATE ATTIRE

Men: A jacket and tie or more casual, modest clothing. Shoes are always removed before entering the *gurdwara,* and the head must always be covered while in the *gurdwara*. Guests may wear any hat, cap or scarf that covers the top of the head.

Women: A modest dress, skirt and blouse, or pants suit. It is best if the legs are covered enough so one can comfortably sit cross-legged. Shoes are always removed before entering the *gurdwara,* and the head must always be covered with a scarf, hat or veil that covers the top of the head while in the *gurdwara*. Modest jewelry is permissible.

There are no rules regarding colors of clothing.

GIFTS

Is a gift customarily expected? No. This is optional.

If one decides to give a gift, is a certain type of gift appropriate? Anything for a new home or business.

THE CEREMONY

If the hosts choose to have an *Akhand Path,* a 48- to 72-hour reading of the

Siri Guru Granth Sahib, it is preceded by a one-hour *gurdwara* service at which the following officiate:

The granthi or giani ji, the person reading the *hukam* from the *Siri Guru Granth Sahib.*

Attendants, several people who sit behind the *Siri Guru Granth Sahib* and attend to it by frequently waving a long-handled brush made of long horsehair called a *chori sahib* above the *Siri Guru Granth Sahib* or take out or put away the scriptures. The attendants also serve *prasad,* or sweet pudding, at the end of the service; read the *hukam* translation in English; and assist in the *gurdwara* in any way. Many people from the *sangat,* the congregation, participate in these functions.

Kirtanis, musicians who lead those present in *kirtan,* songs of praise to God.

It is customary to arrive for the service at the time for which it has been called.

What are the major ritual objects of the ceremony?

If there is an *Akhand Path,* the following are used:

The manji sahib, the "bed" or platform for the *Siri Guru Granth Sahib.* It is covered by ornate cloths called *ramalas.*

The chandoa, the canopy hanging over the *Siri Guru Granth Sahib.*

The adi shakti or khanda, a symbol shaped like a circle surrounded by two swords and cut through by one double-edged sword. It symbolizes the primal, creative energy of the universe. The sword cutting through the circle represents the breaking of the cycle of birth and death.

The kirpan, a special knife used to bless *langar* ("sacred food") and *prasad* (sweet pudding) during the *ardas* (community prayer).

The chori sahib, a long-handled brush made of long horsehair. It is identical to brushes used in ancient India that were waved over royalty to show their state of sovereignty. It is waved over the *Siri Guru Granth Sahib* to symbolize its sovereignty, to purify the energy around it, and to show its status as a living guru.

What books are used? Booklets of sheets containing transliteration and translation of the *kirtan* (songs of praise to God) to be sung may be available. Efforts should be made not to put them on the floor. Since Sikhs respect the written word of God, anything containing it should not be stepped upon or marred in any way.

Will a guest who is not a Sikh be expected to do anything other than sit? A guest will be expected to stand and sit at the same time as everyone else. It is entirely optional for the guest to sing or bow to the *Siri Guru Granth Sahib.* Guests are expected to accept *prasad* (sweet pudding), which is considered a blessing from the *Siri Guru Granth Sahib.*

Customarily, one receives *prasad* with both hands together, palms up. One does not have to be a Sikh to eat the *prasad.*

Are there any parts of the ceremony in which a guest who is not a Sikh should *not* participate? Only Sikhs will be asked to serve *prasad,* read from the *Siri Guru Granth Sahib,* do the *ardas* (prayer) and to serve in any way needed. Other than this, a guest may participate in every part of the service as desired.

If not disruptive to the ceremony, is it okay to:

Take pictures? Yes, but only if intended solely for personal use.

Use a flash? Yes, but only if intended solely for personal use.

Use a video camera? Yes, but only if intended solely for personal use.

Use a tape recorder? Yes, but only if intended solely for personal use.

EATING AND DRINKING

Is a meal part of the celebration? Possibly.

Will there be alcoholic beverages? No.

Would it be considered impolite to neither eat nor drink? No.

Is there a grace or benediction before eating or drinking? No.

Is there a grace or benediction after eating or drinking? No.

At the meal, will a guest be asked to say or do anything? No.

Will there be:
Dancing? No.
Music? Only *kirtan,* songs of praise to God.

GENERAL GUIDELINES AND ADVICE

None provided.

27

Unitarian Universalist

(also known as Unitarian or Universalist)

1. HISTORY AND BELIEFS

The Unitarian Universalist Association was created in 1961 when the American Unitarian Association and the Universalist Church of America merged. The purpose of the union was "to cherish and spread the universal truths taught by the great prophets and teachers of humanity in every age and tradition, immemorially summarized in the Judeo-Christian heritage as love to God and love to man."

The newly formed Unitarian Universalist Association included both American and Canadian congregations. In the same year, 1961, the Canadian Unitarian Council was organized to provide services to Canadian congregations, which are members of both bodies.

Like its predecessors, the new denomination is committed to living in the tension between humanistic liberalism and Christianity, and prefers following reason, conscience and experience to following creeds. Unitarian Universalist churches make no official pronouncements on God, the Bible, Jesus, immortality or other theological questions that are often answered with finality by more traditional religions. Instead, Unitarian Universalism deems a religious way of life as being too important to be left to rigid creeds and dogmas, and there is frequent discussion among members and clergy about whether the faith has, indeed, grown beyond Judeo-Christianity and become something more universal. Unitarian Universalists reject the attitude that salvation is attainable only through the mediation of Jesus Christ and membership in a Christian church. Thus, many believe that Unitarian Universalism is not a Christian faith today, although its historical and theological roots are undeniably Christian.

Unitarians trace their origins to a movement that began shortly after the death of Jesus Christ. According to present Unitarian teachings, many who personally knew Jesus rejected claims of his divinity. Instead, they focused on his humanity and his teachings, not on his alleged godliness. The movement was eventually named Arianism, after Arius, a priest from Alexandria who preached this belief. After the Council of Nicea adopted in 325 C.E. the concept of

338

the Trinity—God the Father, God the Son, God the Holy Ghost—those who embraced this idea denounced believers in God's unity as heretics.

Nevertheless, by the 16th century, Unitarian ideas had gained a foothold in Switzerland, Britain, Hungary and Italy. In 1683, the first Unitarian church to use that name was established in Transylvania. And by the first decade of the 19th century, 20 Unitarian churches had been established in England.

In the United States, Unitarianism got its impetus from the preaching and writings of William Ellery Channing in the early 19th century. Strongly concerned with liberal social causes, such as abolition and educational reform, the faith also gave birth to the transcendentalism associated with Ralph Waldo Emerson and Henry David Thoreau.

While Unitarianism most often attracted the highly educated and intellectual, especially in New England, Universalism was initially an evangelistic, working-class movement with an uneducated clergy. Their "universalism" rested on a belief that all souls would eventually attain salvation. As with Unitarianism, it dates from the early days of Christianity, most notably the writings of Origen, an early Church father.

In the United States, circuit-rider ministers helped spread the faith so well that by the 1850s there were about 800,000 Universalists. By the 1900s, Universalism was the sixth largest denomination in the United States. After that, membership steadily declined, although its theological development eventually so paralleled that of Unitarianism that the two denominations could merge.

In 19th-century Canada, Unitarian congregations were established in Montreal and Toronto, with the assistance of British Unitarians. Universalism entered Canada from the United States, and was largely centered in the Maritimes and southern Ontario. Many Icelandic Lutherans in Manitoba were attracted to the more liberal Unitarian faith and established a number of congregations there. Unitarianism in Canada remained a very small faith group until the end of World War II, when there was a strong movement away from more traditional faiths, and new congregations and lay-led fellowships were established in many parts of the country.

Each local Unitarian Universalist congregation, which may be called a church, society or fellowship, adopts its own bylaws, elects its own officers and approves its budget. Each local congregation is affiliated with one of the 23 districts of the Unitarian Universalist Association of Congregations.

U.S. churches: 1,046
U.S. membership: 221,476
(data from the 2010 Yearbook of American and Canadian Churches*)*

For more information, contact:

The Unitarian Universalist
   Association of Congregations
25 Beacon Street
Boston, MA 02108
(617) 742-2100
www.uua.org

Canadian churches: 48
Canadian membership: 5,000
(2009 data from the Canadian Unitarian Council)

For more information, contact:
Canadian Unitarian Council
100-344 Dupont Street
Toronto, ON M5R 1V9
(416) 489-4121
www.cuc.ca
info@cuc.ca

2 · THE BASIC SERVICE

Unitarian Universalism teaches that worship invites those present to focus on the transcendental, the intimate and the worthy. It helps us regain a sense of ourselves, and reminds us that we may challenge greed or violence, which pollutes the human condition.

Local culture, inherited traditions, a particular minister or a lay worship team all contribute to the style of Unitarian Universalist worship. Some services are formal, and maintain a sense of decorum and a devotional atmosphere. Other services are marked by applause or a dialogue between congregants and whoever is speaking from the pulpit.

But whatever the style, the community remains the locus of the holy. Unitarian Universalists recognize the power of solitude and personal devotion, but they worship together for the strength gained from the presence and wisdom of others.

Usually, a service begins with an invocation and music. Some services also begin by lighting a candle or a flaming chalice, which is the symbol of the faith. The balance of the service may have Scripture readings, poetry and other readings chosen from the spiritual heritage of many faiths. There may also be a sermon, periods of silence and announcements that share the joys and concerns of individual congregants with the entire community. Services usually end with closing words, benedictions and blessings.

Most congregations hold services on Sunday mornings, although smaller and, especially, relatively new congregations may hold services on Saturday or Sunday evenings. This is done not for theological reasons, but because of the availability of space where services are held. Services may last about 60 to 75 minutes.

APPROPRIATE ATTIRE

Men: A jacket and tie or more casual attire, such as slacks, a sport jacket and an open collar. No head covering is required.

Women: A dress or a skirt and blouse or a pants suit. Hems need not reach below the knees nor need clothing cover the arms. Open-toed shoes and modest jewelry are permissible. No head covering is required.

There are no rules regarding colors of clothing.

THE SANCTUARY

What are the major sections of the church? Unitarian Universalists worship in a variety of settings—from a

Gothic nave to a large living room, from a 19th-century meeting house to a rented school auditorium. The following applies to those services held in a church building:

The podium or dais, which is used by speakers and includes the lectern or pulpit.

The choir loft, where the choir and/or the organist sit and perform.

The pews, where congregants and guests sit.

THE SERVICE

When should guests arrive and where should they sit? Arrive at the time for which the service has been called or shortly before that time. Ushers may be present to advise guests where to sit. If not, sit wherever you wish.

If arriving late, are there times when a guest should *not* enter the service? Do not enter during a meditation or prayer.

Are there times when a guest should *not* leave the service? Do not leave during a meditation or prayer.

Who are the major officiants, leaders or participants and what do they do?

The minister, who officiates at the service.

The director of religious education, who may preside during the children's portion of the service.

The parish chair or president, who may welcome congregants and guests and may colead the service.

The choir and/or music director, who presides over the musical elements of the service.

What are the major ritual objects of the service?

The flaming chalice, which is the symbol of Unitarian Universalism. The chalice symbolizes sharing, generosity, sustenance and love. The flame symbolizes sacrifice, courage and spiritual illumination. The flaming chalice is usually located on the lectern or pulpit.

(A few churches may have a cross. Some have a range of symbols, such as a cross, a Star of David, a Buddhist wheel, a Tao circle and a Sufic winged heart.)

What books are used? Almost all Unitarian Universalist congregations use the hymnals *Singing the Living Tradition* and *Singing the Journey,* while prayers and readings are drawn from a wide variety of sources that can include the Bible, but also Buddhist writings, Native American writings, and poetry.

To indicate the order of the service: A program will be distributed.

GUEST BEHAVIOR DURING THE SERVICE

Will a guest who is not a Unitarian Universalist be expected to do anything other than sit? It is expected for guests to stand with congregants when they rise for songs. It is optional for guests to sing and read prayers aloud with congregants if this does not violate their own religious beliefs. There is no kneeling during a Unitarian Universalist service.

Are there any parts of the service in which a guest who is not a member of the Unitarian Universalist

Church should *not* participate? No.

If not disruptive to the service, is it okay to:
Take pictures? Yes.
Use a flash? No.
Use a video camera? Yes.
Use a tape recorder? Yes.

Will contributions to the church be collected at the service? An offering plate will be passed throughout most congregations during the service. Some congregations prefer to encourage parishioners to contribute to the church community in other ways, such as teaching in the religious education program, working on church committees or hosting church-related meetings at one's home.

How much is it customary to contribute? It is entirely optional for guests to contribute. If they choose to do so, a contribution between $1 and $10 is appropriate.

AFTER THE SERVICE

Is there usually a reception after the service? Yes. This is usually held in the reception area of the church and may consist of coffee, tea, cookies and fruit. There is no grace or benediction before or after eating or drinking. The reception may last about 30 to 60 minutes.

Is there a traditional form of address for clergy who may be at the reception? "Mr.," "Ms.," "Dr.," "Reverend" or simply call the clergyperson by his or her first name.

Is it okay to leave early? Yes.

GENERAL GUIDELINES AND ADVICE

Most Unitarian Universalist services are quite informal and nontraditional.

SPECIAL VOCABULARY

Key words or phrases that it might be helpful for a visitor to know:

UU: Shorthand for "Unitarian Universalist."

YRUU: Shorthand for "Young Religious Unitarian Universalists," a youth group for Unitarian Universalists who are in junior and high school.

P&P: Shorthand for "Principles and Purposes," which are those concepts on which Unitarian Universalism is based.

DOGMA AND IDEOLOGY

Unitarian Universalists believe:

Personal experience, conscience and reason should be the final authorities in religion. Religious authority lies not in a book or a person or an institution, but in ourselves.

One cannot be bound by a statement of belief. Unitarian Universalism does not ask anyone to subscribe to a creed.

Religious wisdom is ever changing, and human understanding of life and death, the world and its mysteries is never final, and revelation is continuous.

All men and women have worth. Differences in opinion and lifestyle should be honored.

One should act as a moral force in the world, and ethical living is the supreme witness of religion. The here and now and the effects that our actions will have on future generations are of great concern. Relations with each other, with other peoples, nations and races should be governed by justice, equity and compassion.

Some basic books and pamphlets to which a guest can refer to learn more about Unitarian Universalism:

A Chosen Faith: An Introduction to Unitarian Universalism by John Buehrens and Forrest Church (Boston, Mass.: Beacon Press, 1998).

The Unitarian Universalist Pocket Guide edited by William Sinkford (Boston, Mass.: Skinner House Books, 2004).

Welcome: A Unitarian Universalist Primer edited by Patricia Frevert (Boston, Mass.: Skinner House Books, 2009).

These may be obtained from The Unitarian Universalist Bookstore, 25 Beacon Street, Boston, MA 02108; (800) 215-9076; www.uuabookstore.org.

3. HOLY DAYS AND FESTIVALS

Easter. Always falls on the Sunday after the first full moon that occurs on or after the Spring equinox of March 21. Commemorates the renewal of life through a service that emphasizes light and rebirth. The traditional greeting is "Happy Easter."

Passover (celebrated in some congregations). Begins with the 15th day of the Hebrew month of Nisan, which is usually in late March or early to mid-April. The holiday celebrates the deliverance of the Jewish people from slavery in Egypt. The celebration may include a Passover *seder,* a festive ritualistic meal, on the Sunday closest to the first day of Passover. The *seders* are usually held at home; some are held in the church. The traditional greeting is "Happy Passover."

Thanksgiving. Celebrated on the fourth Thursday of November. Celebrates harvest and home, usually with a church service that emphasizes thanksgiving and a traditional Thanksgiving dinner at home. The traditional greeting is "Happy Thanksgiving."

Chanukah (celebrated in some congregations). Observed for the eight days beginning with the 25th day of the Hebrew month of Kislev, which is usually in early to mid-December. The celebration may include an evening dinner either at home or in the church reception hall. It is often an intergenerational celebration with youths, parents and elders from the congregation present. The traditional greeting is "Happy Chanukah."

Christmas. Always falls on December 25. Celebrates the promise of all children to be prophets in their own time. Churches usually have at least one Christmas Eve candlelit ceremony as well as ceremonies on Christmas Day. The traditional greeting is "Merry Christmas."

Winter and Summer Solstice (celebrated in some congregations). The winter solstice occurs on either December 21 or 22; the summer solstice occurs on either June 20 or 21. The dates depend on the movement of the earth around the sun. Solstice ceremonies are often informal, and may include dancing and/or chanting. The holidays signify the cosmic cycle and movement from darkness to light and rebirth. The traditional greeting is "Happy solstice."

4. LIFE CYCLE EVENTS

Birth Ceremony

Depending on the specific congregation, this may be called a "christening," a "naming" or a "dedication." "Christening" means "to make Christian" and emphasizes the importance of a faith community to nurture and sustain individuals and families in times of joy and sorrow. "Naming" signifies that each child is a unique individual whose name is a powerful symbol of their individuality. "Dedication" may include these meanings, as well as underscore a covenant with God, the Church and the family, in which parents dedicate themselves to lovingly raise their child in a home that will promote the fullest growth of the child's body, mind and spirit.

The ceremony may contain traditional elements, such as water from a baptismal font. Or the water may come from the sea, thus representing the source of all life. A rose may be presented to the child or the family to represent the beauty and fragility of life.

The ceremony is the same for males and females. It is often performed for an infant, although older children or even adults may desire such a ceremony to publicly experience such a dedication. The 15- to 30-minute long ceremony is usually part of a Sunday worship service.

BEFORE THE CEREMONY

Are guests usually invited by a formal invitation? Sometimes.

If not stated explicitly, should one assume that children are invited? Yes.

If one can't attend, what should one do? RSVP with regrets.

APPROPRIATE ATTIRE

Men: A jacket and tie or more casual attire, such as slacks, a sport jacket and an open collar. No head covering is required.

Women: A dress or a skirt and blouse or a pants suit. Hems need not reach below the knees nor need clothing cover the arms. Open-toed shoes and modest jewelry are permissible. No head covering is required.

There are no rules regarding colors of clothing.

GIFTS

Is a gift customarily expected? No.

Should gifts be brought to the ceremony? See above.

THE CEREMONY

Where will the ceremony take place? In the main sanctuary of the parents' church.

When should guests arrive and where should they sit? Arrive at the time for which the ceremony has been called or shortly before that time. Ushers may be present to advise guests where to sit. If not, sit wherever you wish.

If arriving late, are there times when a guest should *not* enter the ceremony? Do not enter during meditation or prayer or the dedication itself.

Are there times when a guest should *not* leave the ceremony? Do not leave during meditation or prayer or the dedication itself.

Who are the major officiants, leaders or participants at the ceremony and what do they do?
The minister, who officiates at the ceremony.
The director of religious education, who may preside during the child's portion of the ceremony.
The infant and his or her parents and god-parents.

What books are used? The dedication ceremony will probably be printed in the program for the ceremony.

To indicate the order of the ceremony: A program will be distributed.

Will a guest who is not a Unitarian Universalist be expected to do anything other than sit? It is expected for guests to stand with congregants when they rise for songs and to participate in parts of the ceremony that require the congregants to respond to the minister or to the family of the child whose dedication is being observed. It is optional for guests to sing and read prayers aloud with congregants if this does not violate their own religious beliefs. There is no kneeling during a Unitarian Universalist ceremony.

Are there any parts of the ceremony in which a guest who is not a Unitarian Universalist should *not* participate? No.

If not disruptive to the ceremony, is it okay to:
Take pictures? Yes.
Use a flash? No.
Use a video camera? Yes.
Use a tape recorder? Yes.

Will contributions to the church be collected at the ceremony? An offering plate will be passed throughout most congregations during the service. Some congregations prefer to encourage parishioners to contribute to the church community in other ways, such as teaching in the religious education program, working on church committees or hosting church-related meetings at one's home.

How much is it customary to contribute? It is entirely optional for guests to contribute. If they choose to do so, a contribution between $1 and $10 is appropriate.

AFTER THE CEREMONY

Is there usually a reception after the ceremony? Possibly. If so, it may be a small, low-key, casual reception in the reception hall of the church or in the home of the parents whose child was dedicated. There may be light food, possibly alcoholic beverages, and neither singing nor dancing. The reception may last about 30 to 60 minutes.

Would it be considered impolite to neither eat nor drink? No.

Is there a grace or benediction before eating or drinking? Sometimes.

Is there a grace or benediction after eating or drinking? Sometimes.

Is there a traditional greeting for the family? Just offer your congratulations.

Is there a traditional form of address for clergy who may be at the reception? "Mr.," "Ms.," "Dr.," "Reverend" or simply call the clergyperson by his or her first name.

Is it okay to leave early? Yes, whenever one wishes.

Initiation Ceremony

Teens between 14 and 16 years are eligible for what is called a "coming of age" ceremony, which is comparable to confirmation in other faiths and acknowledges the onset of young adulthood. The ceremony varies from congregation to congregation, with each congregation choosing whether to even have one. Usually, the ceremony is the same for males and females and is performed for an entire class of teens, not for individuals.

The ceremony may be a service in itself or part of a regular Sunday worship service. The ceremony lasts slightly more than one hour.

BEFORE THE CEREMONY

Are guests usually invited by a formal invitation? No.

If not stated explicitly, should one assume that children are invited? Yes.

If one can't attend, what should one do? RSVP with regrets.

APPROPRIATE ATTIRE

Men: A jacket and tie or more casual attire, such as slacks, a sport jacket and an open collar. No head covering is required.

Women: A dress or a skirt and blouse or a pants suit. Hems need not reach below the knees nor need clothing cover the arms. Open-toed shoes and modest jewelry are permissible. No head covering is required.

There are no rules regarding colors of clothing.

GIFTS

Is a gift customarily expected? No, although a gift is not inappropriate. If one chooses to give a gift, appropriate items are cash in the range of $25 to $50 or personal or spiritual items, such as books or pins with a flaming chalice motif.

Should gifts be brought to the ceremony? Yes.

THE CEREMONY

Where will the ceremony take place? In the main sanctuary of the church.

When should guests arrive and where should they sit? Arrive at the time for which the ceremony has been called or shortly before that time. Ushers may be present to advise guests where to sit. If not, sit wherever you wish.

If arriving late, are there times when a guest should *not* enter the ceremony? Do not enter during meditation or prayer or the coming of age ceremony itself.

Are there times when a guest should *not* leave the ceremony? Do not leave during meditation or prayer or the coming of age ceremony itself.

Who are the major officiants, leaders or participants at the ceremony and what do they do?
The participating teens.
The minister, who officiates at the ceremony.
The director of religious education, who may preside during part of the ceremony.
A youth group leader.
The youths' teacher or mentor.

What books are used? A hymnal, *Singing the Living Tradition* or *Singing the Journey.*

To indicate the order of the ceremony: A program will be distributed.

Will a guest who is not a Unitarian Universalist be expected to do anything other than sit? It is expected for guests to stand with congregants when they rise for songs. It is optional for guests to sing and read prayers aloud with congregants if this does not violate their own religious beliefs. There is no kneeling during a Unitarian Universalist ceremony.

Are there any parts of the ceremony in which a guest who is not a Unitarian Universalist should *not* participate? No.

If not disruptive to the ceremony, is it okay to:
Take pictures? Yes.
Use a flash? No.
Use a video camera? Yes.
Use a tape recorder? Yes.

Will contributions to the church be collected at the ceremony? An offering plate will be passed throughout most congregations during the service. Some congregations prefer to encourage parishioners to contribute to the church community in other ways, such as teaching in the religious education program, working on church committees or hosting church-related meetings at one's home.

How much is it customary to contribute? If guests choose to contribute, a contribution between $1 and $10 is appropriate.

AFTER THE CEREMONY

Is there usually a reception after the ceremony? No.

Is there a traditional greeting for the family? Just offer your congratulations.

Is there a traditional form of address for clergy whom a guest may meet? "Mr.," "Ms.," "Dr.," "Reverend" or simply call the clergyperson by his or her first name.

Marriage Ceremony

Marriage is the committed joining of two lives as witnessed by the community. Unitarian Universalism does not necessarily consider marriage to be a union that will last for the entirety of one's life. It also supports same-sex marriages, a stance that reflects the faith's longtime call for lesbians and gays to be fully included in the religious community and in society at large.

The wedding ceremony is a ceremony in itself. It may last about 30 to 60 minutes.

BEFORE THE CEREMONY

Are guests usually invited by a formal invitation? Yes.

If not stated explicitly, should one assume that children are invited? No.

If one can't attend, what should one do? Send a written RSVP and a gift.

APPROPRIATE ATTIRE

Men: A jacket and tie. No head covering is required.

Women: A dress. Hems need not reach below the knees nor need clothing cover the arms. Open-toed shoes and modest jewelry are permissible. No head covering is required.

There are no rules regarding colors of clothing.

GIFTS

Is a gift customarily expected? Yes. Small household items such as sheets, small appliances or kitchenware or cash in the amount of $25 to $100 are appropriate.

Should gifts be brought to the ceremony? Gifts may be sent to the home of the newlyweds.

THE CEREMONY

Where will the ceremony take place? In the main sanctuary of the church, in a special area elsewhere in the church or in a home.

When should guests arrive and where should they sit? Arrive shortly before the time for which the ceremony has been called. Ushers will advise guests where to sit. Often, relatives and friends of the bride and of the groom sit on opposite sides of the aisle.

If arriving late, are there times when a guest should *not* enter the ceremony? Do not enter during the processional of the wedding party.

Are there times when a guest should *not* leave the ceremony? Do not leave during the recessional of the wedding party.

Who are the major officiants, leaders or participants at the ceremony and what do they do?

The minister, who officiates at the ceremony and witnesses the vows of the bride and groom.

The bride and groom and members of their wedding party.

Friends of the bride and groom, who may lead those present in a meditation or read aloud a text chosen by the couple.

What books are used? A hymnal, *Singing the Living Tradition* or *Singing the Journey.*

To indicate the order of the ceremony: A program may be distributed.

Will a guest who is not a Unitarian Universalist be expected to do anything other than sit? No.

Are there any parts of the ceremony in which a guest who is not a Unitarian Universalist should *not* participate? Yes. Do not participate in the affirmation or the welcoming of the couple from members of the congregation.

If not disruptive to the ceremony, is it okay to:
Take pictures? No.
Use a flash? No.
Use a video camera? No.
Use a tape recorder? Yes.

Will contributions to the church be collected at the ceremony? No.

AFTER THE CEREMONY

Is there usually a reception after the ceremony? A reception is usually held in the church reception hall, in a catering hall or at a home. Food served may be hors d'oeuvres, a complete meal, coffee, cake and alcoholic beverages. There will probably be music and dancing. The reception may last for two hours.

Would it be considered impolite to neither eat nor drink? Yes.

Is there a grace or benediction before eating or drinking? Yes.

Is there a grace or benediction after eating or drinking? Sometimes.

Is there a traditional greeting for the family? Just offer your congratulations.

Is there a traditional form of address for clergy who may be at the reception? "Mr.," "Ms.," "Dr.," "Reverend" or simply call the clergyperson by his or her first name.

Is it okay to leave early? Yes, but only after the wedding cake has been cut and served.

Funerals and Mourning

There is no specific Unitarian Universalist doctrine about afterlife. Some Unitarian Universalists believe in an afterlife; some doubt that there is one.

The Unitarian Universalist ritual that marks one's death is called a memorial service, not a funeral.

The memorial service is a ceremony in itself and may last about 30 to 60 minutes. Some memorial services may last more than one hour.

BEFORE THE CEREMONY

How soon after the death does the memorial service usually take place? Usually within one week; sometimes up to one month after the death. The length of time between the death and the memorial service is determined solely at the discretion of the family.

What should someone who is not a Unitarian Universalist do upon hearing of the death of a member of that faith? Telephone or visit the bereaved to express your condolences and share your memories of the deceased. Such comments as "I am so very sorry for your loss" are appropriate. Such comments as "Now he/she is with God" or "It was God's will" are not appropriate.

APPROPRIATE ATTIRE

Men: A jacket and tie. No head covering is required.

Women: A dress. Hems need not reach below the knees nor must clothing cover the arms. Open-toed shoes and modest jewelry are permissible. No head covering is required.

Somber colors are recommended for clothing.

GIFTS

Is it appropriate to send flowers or make a contribution? Flowers may be delivered to the home of the bereaved before the memorial service. Also, contributions ranging from $10 to $200 may be made to a fund or charity designated by the family or the deceased.

Is it appropriate to send food? Yes. This may be sent to the home of the bereaved upon hearing of the death or after the memorial service.

THE CEREMONY

Where will the ceremony take place? Usually in a funeral home; sometimes in a church.

When should guests arrive and where should they sit? Arrive shortly before the time for which the memorial service has been called. Sit wherever you wish, except for the first two or three rows, which are usually reserved for the close family of the deceased.

If arriving late, are there times when a guest should *not* enter the ceremony? No.

Will the bereaved family be present at the funeral home or church before the ceremony? Sometimes.

Is there a traditional greeting for the family? Express your condolences. Such comments as "I am so very sorry for your loss" are appropriate.

Will there be an open casket? Rarely.

Is a guest expected to view the body? Guests are not expected or obligated to view the body.

What is appropriate behavior upon viewing the body? If one chooses to view the body, walk slowly and reverently past the casket.

Who are the major officiants at the ceremony and what do they do?
The minister, who delivers a sermon and meditation and commits the body to the grave.
The eulogist, who is chosen by the family of the deceased and delivers a eulogy in honor of the deceased.
The music director and organist, who provide music.

What books are used? A hymnal, *Singing the Living Tradition* or *Singing the Journey.*

To indicate the order of the ceremony: Usually either a program will be provided or a display near the front of the room where the memorial service is held will indicate the order.

Will a guest who is not a Unitarian Universalist be expected to do anything other than sit? It is expected for guests to stand with congregants when they rise for songs or prayer. It is optional for guests to sing and read prayers aloud with congregants if this does not violate their own religious beliefs. There is no kneeling during a Unitarian Universalist memorial service.

Are there any parts of the ceremony in which a guest who is not a Unitarian Universalist should *not* participate? No.

If not disruptive to the ceremony, is it okay to:
Take pictures? No.
Use a flash? No.
Use a video camera? No.
Use a tape recorder? Only with prior approval of the family of the deceased.

Will contributions to the church be collected at the ceremony? No.

THE INTERMENT

Should guests attend the interment? This is entirely optional.

Whom should one ask for directions? The funeral director.

What happens at the graveside? Prayers are recited and the body is committed to the ground.

Do guests who are not Unitarian Universalists participate at the graveside ceremony? No. They are simply present.

COMFORTING THE BEREAVED

Is it appropriate to visit the home of the bereaved after the memorial service? Yes. The length of the visit depends on one's relationship with the bereaved and with the deceased. When visiting, express your sympathy to the bereaved and offer specific help to them. Fond memories of the deceased are especially appreciated.

Will there be a religious service at the home of the bereaved? No.

Will food be served? Yes, possibly including alcoholic beverages.

How soon after the memorial service will a mourner usually return to a normal work schedule? This is left to the discretion of the mourner, but is usually a few days to a few weeks.

How soon after the memorial service will a mourner usually return to a normal social schedule? This is left to the discretion of the mourner, but is usually a few days to a few weeks.

Are there mourning customs to which a friend who is not a Unitarian Universalist should be sensitive? No.

Are there rituals for observing the anniversary of the death? No.

5 · HOME CELEBRATIONS

Not applicable to Unitarian Universalism.

28

United Church of Canada

1 • HISTORY AND BELIEFS

The United Church of Canada was created by an act of Parliament in 1925 as a union of the country's Presbyterian, Methodist and Congregational denominations. In western Canada, in communities unable to afford the luxury of separate churches, a number of informal Union churches had already formed, applying pressure on parent denominations to amalgamate.

Although Presbyterians provided the initial push for the three-denomination Union, in the end they also offered its greatest opposition; approximately one-third of Presbyterian congregations voted not to unite. The Methodist and Congregational denominations entered the Church Union as a whole.

The United Church sees itself as having a mandate to work toward further unions. In 1968, it was joined by the Evangelical United Brethren. A proposed union with the Anglican Church of Canada, however, foundered in the 1970s.

Its worship and policies are, inevitably, a product of its founding traditions. From the Methodists,

the United Church inherited a passion for social justice; from the Presbyterians, a conciliar system for internal governance; from the Congregationalists, a stubborn refusal to be bound by arbitrary doctrine or dogma.

The United Church has been at the forefront of social change in Canada. It was the first mainline denomination in the world to ordain women as ministers. It welcomed draft dodgers during the Vietnam War, lobbied against alcohol and tobacco, urged recognition of the Republic of China, endorsed women's right to reproductive freedoms, including that of abortion, and, most recently, ruled that homosexuality is not, in and of itself, a bar to ordination.

The national court of the United Church is the General Council, which meets every three years. Only the General Council speaks for the United Church. Between councils, elected officials of the church or various committees or divisions may interpret or comment on the council's policies. Surprisingly, there are few doctrinal statements. The *Basis of Union* of 1925 contains "Twenty Articles of

Faith," developed as a statement of the common faith of the three founding denominations. The only statement of faith issued by the United Church itself came in 1940, with a teaching catechism in 1942. In 1968, the General Council authorized a "New Creed" as an authentic expression of the United Church's faith. This creed has since been revised twice, to eliminate exclusively masculine language, and to add concern for the natural environment.

The Congregationalist openness to diverse viewpoints means that ministers are required only to be in "essential agreement" with the "Twenty Articles." As a result, the church's ministry encompasses a wide variety of theological viewpoints.

As a national denomination, the United Church has no branches or subsidiaries in any other country. It does have working partnerships with a number of other churches in other parts of the world. The United Church maintains membership in the world associations to which its predecessors belonged, such as the World Alliance of Reformed Churches.

Canadian churches: 3,405
Canadian membership: 1.4 million
   (data from the 2010 Yearbook of American and Canadian Churches)

For more information, contact:

The United Church of Canada
3250 Bloor Street West, Suite 300
Toronto, ON M8X 2Y4
(416) 231-5931
www.united-church.ca

2 · THE BASIC SERVICE

United Church congregations gather to worship God, to explore God's will and to celebrate the sacraments together. The United Church normally meets for worship Sunday mornings, although some congregations have experimented with midweek services, especially during holiday seasons. The traditional time was 11:00 A.M.; increasingly, services are moving to 10:00 or 10:30 A.M. Most services last about an hour. Children are welcome. Sunday school is commonly held at the same time as the worship service, with the children leaving partway through the service.

APPROPRIATE ATTIRE

Men: Depends on local culture more than on religious standards. The farther west, the more casual the standards; the farther east and/or the bigger the church, the more formal. There are no requirements. Common sense and reasonably good taste are usually sufficient guidelines.

Women: Depends on local culture more than on religious standards. The farther west, the more casual the standards; the farther east and/or the bigger the church, the more formal. There are no requirements. Common sense and reasonably good taste are usually sufficient guidelines.

THE SANCTUARY

What are the major sections of the church?

The chancel: At the front of the church, normally slightly raised. Worship is normally led by ministers, choir and lay members from the chancel.

The nave: Where the people sit. Many churches have fixed pews; some have movable seating.

The narthex or foyer: Usually the area just outside the sanctuary. Normally where people hang coats. In some buildings, also where refreshments are served after the service.

The Christian education area: Rooms where the Sunday school and other groups meet.

THE SERVICE

When should guests arrive, and where should they sit? Arrive at
the time of the service, or earlier. Latecomers may have to sit near the front. If ushers do not guide visitors to a specific seat, visitors may take any vacant seat.

If arriving late, are there times when a guest should *not* enter the service? Yes. Ushers will seat you
when it is appropriate.

Are there times when a guest should *not* leave the service? No.

Who are the major officiants, leaders or participants and what do they do?

The worship leader, who is usually a professional minister, male or female, presides, preaches and celebrates Communion.

Lay members, who may lead prayers, read the Bible or speak.

The choir, choir director and/or organist, who provide leadership in music.

What are the major ritual objects of the service?

The cross, mounted on a wall and/or placed on the Communion table.

The Christ candle (usually one, sometimes several), lit at the beginning of the service.

The Bible, sometimes carried in, commonly opened at the beginning of the service.

The Communion table.

Bread and wine, for Communion services. Practices for distribution vary. In some congregations members come forward to the chancel; others serve members in their seats. Some provide whole bread, and have members break off chunks; others provide precut cubes or balls of bread. Most use small individual cups to serve wine (usually grape juice), for hygienic reasons; those that use a common cup may encourage "intinction," dipping the bread into the wine.

What books are used? Most congre-
gations use *Voices United*, the United Church's hymnbook (Etobicoke, Ont.: The United Church Publishing House, 1996), and *More Voices* (2006), a supplement to *Voices United*. Some congregations also use *Songs for a Gospel People* (Winfield, B.C.: Wood Lake Books, 1987), commonly referred to as "the green book." The most commonly used translation of the Bible is the New Revised Standard Version.

To indicate the order of the service: Most congregations provide a

printed program or bulletin, usually supplemented by announcements from the worship leader.

GUEST BEHAVIOR DURING THE SERVICE

Will a guest who is not a member of the United Church be expected to do anything other than sit? Visitors are invited to participate along with the congregation in all aspects of a worship service. The United Church practices open Communion, meaning that all who profess faith in Jesus Christ are welcome in the Service of the Word (ordinary worship) and at the Service of the Table (Communion).

No one is excluded on the basis of denominational allegiance, age, race, color or for any reason other than personal choice.

Are there any parts of the service in which a guest who is not a member of the United Church should *not* participate? No.

If not disruptive to the service, is it okay to:
Take pictures? Possibly. But ask first.
Use a flash? No, unless you have received permission.
Use a video camera? Possibly. Ask first.
Use a tape recorder? Probably.

Will contributions to the church be collected at the service? Yes. Plates or baskets will be passed, usually after the sermon.

How much is it customary to contribute? Unless you're a child, you should consider $1 a minimum. Most visitors will contribute up to $10.

AFTER THE SERVICE

Is there usually a reception after the service? Many congregations do have some kind of reception after a service, usually in the narthex or an adjoining hall.

Food may or may not be available. There is normally coffee, sometimes tea or juices. You will not find alcoholic beverages. There is no obligation to take anything at a postservice reception. Visitors with dietary restrictions should simply avoid unsuitable foods and beverages.

Unless the reception is a sit-down meal for a special occasion, there will usually be no opening ritual or grace, or any formal closing. People will drift away when they have finished their conversations.

Is there a traditional form of address for clergy whom a guest may meet? Formally, clergy should be addressed as "Mr.," "Mrs." or "Ms.," followed by the last name. It is impolite to refer to them simply as "Reverend." Informally, many prefer to be addressed by their first names.

Is it okay to leave early? Yes.

GENERAL GUIDELINES AND ADVICE

United Church congregations usually stand for hymns and sit for prayers. There are no universal practices. Some have formal refrains or responses to readings; others do not. Some encourage congregations to clap; others discourage it.

The best guideline is simply to do as the people around you are doing. Pay particular attention to any instructions that are given for receiving Communion.

SPECIAL VOCABULARY

None. The United Church is probably the most colloquial denomination in Canada for its language and terminology. It places a greater emphasis than most other denominations on inclusive language, especially when referring to God— but even this varies widely from congregation to congregation, and from minister to minister.

DOGMA AND IDEOLOGY

The United Church is officially Trinitarian. That is, it believes in three primary manifestations of the divine: Father, Son and Holy Spirit. Some congregations and clergy prefer to formulate these as Creator, Sustainer and Nurturer (or some similar wording).

Worship services typically move through a call to worship, confession of sins, assurance of pardon, two or more Bible readings, a sermon and the congregational response in prayers and offerings.

As a general rule, the United Church is liberal in its theology. It emphasizes reason and scholarship along with piety. But individual congregations are highly diverse, ranging from conservative to radical.

Some basic books to which a guest can refer to learn more about The United Church of Canada:

Finding Your Way: A Newcomer's Look at the United Church of Canada by Donna Sinclair (available from the United Church Resource Distribution Center, 1-800-288-7365).

This United Church of Ours by Ralph Milton, 3rd ed. (Kelowna, B.C.: Wood Lake Books, 2008).

3 · HOLY DAYS AND FESTIVALS

Advent. The four weeks preceding Christmas. A time of preparation for the coming of Christ. There are no particular religious observances or any traditional greetings.

Christmas. December 25; includes Christmas Eve, December 24. Usually special services, similar in format to normal worship. Marks the birth of Jesus, the revelation of God in human form (the "Incarnation"). Traditional greeting: "Merry Christmas."

Lent. The seven weeks preceding Easter. Begins on Ash Wednesday. Traditionally a time for repentance and reflection. Abstinence and self-denial as a form of self-discipline are rarely practiced anymore. During the final week before Easter, called Passion Week, there may be special services.

Good Friday. The Friday immediately preceding Easter. Services focus on the suffering of the Crucifixion. The sanctuary is often stripped of its usual symbols. A few congregations celebrate Easter Vigil, Saturday night.

Easter. The Sunday following the first full moon that occurs on or after the spring equinox. Celebrates the Resurrection of Christ. Some congregations will have sunrise services. Traditional greeting: "Happy Easter!"

Christian Family Sunday. Coincides with

the secular Mother's Day in May.

Pentecost. The seventh Sunday after Easter. Celebrates the coming of the Holy Spirit. Often considered the birthday of the Christian church. No traditional greetings.

Thanksgiving. Usually falls on the second Monday of October. Not to be confused with American Thanksgiving, which comes at the end of November. Many congregations celebrate Thanksgiving Sunday with lavishly decorated sanctuaries.

There are no restrictions on any person to participation in any of these services. The same guidelines for behavior apply as for ordinary worship services.

4 · LIFE CYCLE EVENTS

Birth Ceremony

There is no celebration of birth as such, but many infants are baptized within months after birth.

Baptism initiates a person into the universal Christian church. It is a one-time event, recognized as valid in almost all mainline denominations. Persons may be baptized as adults, or as infants (when parents make the vows on the child's behalf). Adults seeking baptism, and parents seeking baptism for a child, normally attend one or more sessions of preparation and study.

Baptism is not an act of magic that protects a child from going to hell. The United Church teaches that God loves all children, baptized or not. Baptism is the affirmation by the person (or by the parents, on his/her behalf) to seek to live a Christian life, in the Christian community.

Some congregations include, as part of the baptismal ceremony, either or both of the following:

Confirmation. Historically the act of a bishop, confirming the actions of a parish priest who had done the actual baptism some time before. Now sometimes combined with baptism to confirm that this person is now a full member of the universal Christian church.

Reaffirmation of faith. A continuation of the baptismal ceremony in which members of the Christian church (that is, anyone who has already been baptized) are invited to renew their baptismal vows. Rarely, the symbolism of water in baptism is repeated by sprinkling the congregation with drops of water (called aspersion).

BEFORE THE CEREMONY

Are guests usually invited by a formal invitation? The family may invite special guests, but the baptism normally takes place during a regular worship service, at which anyone is welcome.

If not stated explicitly, should one assume that children are invited? Yes.

If one can't attend, what should one do? Reply, expressing regrets. Telephone to offer good wishes. Send flowers or a gift to the home.

APPROPRIATE ATTIRE

Men: Depends on local culture more than on religious standards. The farther west, the more casual the standards; the farther east and/or the bigger the church, the more formal. There are no requirements. Common sense and reasonably good taste are usually sufficient guidelines.

If you have been specifically invited to a baptismal celebration, greater formality may be expected.

Women: Depends on local culture more than on religious standards. The farther west, the more casual the standards; the farther east and/or the bigger the church, the more formal. There are no requirements. Common sense and reasonably good taste are usually sufficient guidelines.

If you have been specifically invited to a baptismal celebration, greater formality may be expected.

GIFTS

Is a gift customarily expected? Only if you have been formally invited by the family. For infant baptism, gifts should be comparable to those you would give at a baby shower.

Should gifts be brought to the ceremony? Gifts should be brought to the reception or the home, not to the service.

THE CEREMONY

Where will the ceremony take place? In the United Church of Canada, baptism is seen as initiation into a specific community of faith, a congregation. Therefore, baptism almost always takes place with a congregation present, during a regular worship service, in the home church of the parents (sometimes of the grandparents). It is performed privately only in exceptional circumstances.

The service as a whole will take slightly over one hour; the baptismal portion will probably take about 10 minutes.

When should guests arrive and where should they sit? Invited guests should arrive early, not at the last minute, and will probably gather as a group before the service. Family and friends will be seated in a special block of reserved seats. Others may sit wherever they choose.

If arriving late, are there times when a guest should *not* enter the service? Yes. Ushers will seat you when it is appropriate.

Are there times when a guest should *not* leave the service? The baptismal party (family, friends and invited guests) is expected to be present for the whole service. Some congregations give opportunity for parents and infants (especially crying infants) to leave after the baptism itself, but it is considered discourteous for the whole baptismal party to leave.

Who are the major officiants, leaders or participants at the ceremony and what do they do?
The minister(s), who will baptize the child or adult seeking baptism. A favorite minister from another congregation may be invited to take

part in the ceremony, if the participants wish.

The person being baptized (and his or her parents, if a child), who is the central participant. Baptism is not something done *to* this person, but something this person does as an affirmation of faith in the Triune God.

The United Church does not formally recognize godparents, but if parents wish to have godparents, they may be invited to come forward to stand with the parents during the baptism.

What books are used? Most congregations use *Voices United*, the United Church's hymnbook (Etobicoke, Ont.: The United Church Publishing House, 1996), and *More Voices* (2006), a supplement to *Voices United*. Some congregations also use *Songs for a Gospel People* (Winfield, B.C.: Wood Lake Books, 1987), commonly referred to as "the green book." The most commonly used translation of the Bible is the New Revised Standard Version.

To indicate the order of the ceremony: Most congregations provide a printed program or bulletin, usually supplemented by announcements from the worship leader.

Will a guest who is not a member of the United Church be expected to do anything other than sit? Visitors are invited to participate along with the congregation in all aspects of a baptismal service that do not violate their own personal beliefs.

No one is excluded on the basis of denominational allegiance, age, race, color or for any reason other than personal choice.

Are there any parts of the ceremony in which a guest who is not a member of the United Church should *not* participate? No.

If not disruptive to the service, is it okay to:
Take pictures? Possibly. But ask first.
Use a flash? No, unless you have received permission.
Use a video camera? Possibly. Ask first.
Use a tape recorder? Probably.

Will contributions to the church be collected at the ceremony? Yes. Plates or baskets will be passed, usually after the sermon.

How much is it customary to contribute? Unless you're a child, you should consider $1 a minimum. Most visitors will contribute up to $10.

AFTER THE CEREMONY

Is there usually a reception after the ceremony? If there is a formal reception after a baptismal service, it will probably be held at the parents' or grandparents' home. If it is held at the church, it will probably be informal, open to all.

Would it be considered impolite to neither eat nor drink? At the church, no.

Is there a grace or benediction before eating or drinking? At a private reception, maybe. At the church, after the service, probably not.

Is there a grace or benediction after eating or drinking? No.

Is there a traditional greeting for the family? No.

Is there a traditional form of address for clergy who may be at the reception? Formally, clergy should be addressed as "Mr.," "Mrs." or "Ms.," followed by the last name. It is impolite to refer to them simply as "Reverend." Informally, many prefer to be addressed by their first names.

Is it okay to leave early? Yes.

Initiation Ceremony

Some United Church congregations continue to use confirmation as a ceremony in which young people officially become members of the church. The candidates affirm for themselves the Christian faith and church into which they were baptized, usually as infants.

Other congregations combine confirmation with baptism and have, instead, a Service of Reaffirmation of Baptismal Faith for young people wishing to affirm their baptismal vows as their own.

Either ceremony takes about 10 minutes, as part of a regular worship service, which lasts about an hour.

BEFORE THE CEREMONY

Are guests usually invited by a formal invitation? The family may invite special guests, but the ceremony normally takes place during a regular worship service, at which anyone is welcome.

If not stated explicitly, should one assume that children are invited? Yes.

If one can't attend, what should one do? Reply, expressing regrets.

APPROPRIATE ATTIRE

Men: Depends on local culture more than on religious standards. The farther west, the more casual the standards; the farther east and/or the bigger the church, the more formal. There are no requirements. Common sense and reasonably good taste are usually sufficient guidelines.

If you have been specifically invited by the family, greater formality may be expected.

Women: Depends on local culture more than on religious standards. The farther west, the more casual the standards; the farther east and/or the bigger the church, the more formal. There are no requirements. Common sense and reasonably good taste are usually sufficient guidelines.

If you have been specifically invited by the family, greater formality may be expected.

GIFTS

Is a gift customarily expected? No.

Should gifts be brought to the ceremony? No.

THE CEREMONY

Where will the ceremony take place? At the front of the main sanctuary of the church.

When should guests arrive and where should they sit? Invited guests should arrive early, not at the last minute. Ushers may indicate where to sit. The candidates themselves will probably sit in a block of reserved seats. Otherwise, there are no restrictions on where to sit.

If arriving late, are there times when a guest should *not* enter the ceremony? Yes. Ushers will seat you when it is appropriate.

Are there times when a guest should *not* leave the ceremony? No.

Who are the major officiants, leaders or participants at the ceremony and what do they do?

The minister(s), who will preside at the ceremony.

The candidates, who are the central participants.

Laypersons or mentors, who may participate in laying on of hands.

What books are used? Most congregations use *Voices United,* the United Church's hymnbook (Etobicoke, Ont.: The United Church Publishing House, 1996), and *More Voices* (2006), a supplement to *Voices United.* Some congregations also use *Songs for a Gospel People* (Winfield, B.C.: Wood Lake Books, 1987), commonly referred to as "the green book." The most commonly used translation of the Bible is the New Revised Standard Version.

To indicate the order of the ceremony: Most congregations provide a printed program or bulletin, usually supplemented by announcements from the worship leader.

Will a guest who is not a member of the United Church be expected to do anything other than sit? Visitors are invited to participate along with the congregation in all aspects of the service that do not violate their own personal beliefs.

No one is excluded on the basis of denominational allegiance, age, race, color or for any reason other than personal choice.

Are there any parts of the ceremony in which a guest who is not a member of the United Church should *not* participate? No.

If not disruptive to the service, is it okay to:

Take pictures? Possibly. But ask first.

Use a flash? No, unless you have received permission.

Use a video camera? Possibly. Ask first.

Use a tape recorder? Probably.

Will contributions to the church be collected at the ceremony? Yes. Plates or baskets will be passed, usually after the sermon.

How much is it customary to contribute? Unless you're a child, you should consider $1 a minimum. Most visitors will contribute up to $10.

AFTER THE CEREMONY

Is there usually a reception after the ceremony? Rarely, other than the usual gathering for coffee, tea, etc.

Would it be considered impolite to neither eat nor drink? No.

Is there a grace or benediction before eating or drinking? No.

Is there a grace or benediction after eating or drinking? No.

Is there a traditional greeting for the family? No.

Is there a traditional form of address for clergy who may be at the reception? Formally, clergy should be addressed as "Mr.," "Mrs." or "Ms.," followed by the last name. It is impolite to refer to them simply as "Reverend." Informally, many prefer to be addressed by their first names.

Is it okay to leave early? Yes.

Marriage Ceremony

Marriage is the formal ceremony in which a couple make lifetime vows of commitment to each other, in the presence of God and of their families and friends. The ceremony is rarely combined with a regular worship service. It is both a civil and a religious ceremony, and may last anywhere from 15 minutes to an hour, depending on the number of musical numbers performed, the length of the minister's address to the couple and the time required for signing the official register.

BEFORE THE CEREMONY

Are guests usually invited by a formal invitation? Yes. Anyone may attend the religious ceremony of marriage, without requiring an invitation. But an invitation is required for the reception that follows the wedding ceremony.

If not stated explicitly, should one assume children are invited? No.

If one cannot attend, what should one do? Reply with regrets, and send a gift.

APPROPRIATE ATTIRE

Men: Generally, a suit or jacket and tie.

Women: A dress or pants suit. Clothing and jewelry should be relatively modest.

Dress for both men and women depends more on the local culture than on religious standards. The more elaborate the wedding ceremony, the more formal attire should be. There are no religious rules applicable to attire at wedding ceremonies.

GIFTS

Is a gift ordinarily expected? Yes, if you have received a formal invitation. If you are simply attending a public ceremony, a gift would be appreciated, but is not necessary. Items suitable for helping the couple set up their home—small appliances, bedding, sheets, towels and other household gifts—are appropriate.

Should gifts be brought to the ceremony? No. Gifts should be sent to the home of the newlyweds.

THE CEREMONY

Where will the ceremony take place? Normally, in the sanctuary, the place of worship. However, United Church clergy have shown themselves remarkably adaptable, and may be willing to perform the ceremony outside the church—for example, in a garden or on a beach.

If the ceremony is held in a church, the actual ceremony will take place in front of the congregation, immediately before the chancel.

When should guests arrive and where should they sit? Arrive early. In most weddings, ushers will show guests where to sit. It is still traditional, in many places, to have friends of the groom sit on one side of the sanctuary, and friends of the bride on the other side.

If arriving late, are there times when a guest should *not* enter the ceremony? Ushers will assist latecomers.

Are there times when a guest should *not* leave the ceremony? It is considered poor taste to leave before the ceremony is completed.

Who are the major officiants, leaders or participants at the ceremony and what do they do?
The minister(s), who leads the service.
The couple, who exchange vows.
The wedding party, who provide support and witness the vows.

What books are used? Most likely the congregation's normal hymnbook(s). Often the hymns and other responses are printed out in a special program or bulletin.

To indicate the order of the ceremony: Usually a printed program or bulletin will be provided, supplemented by announcements from the minister.

Will a guest who is not a member of the United Church be expected to do anything other than sit? Guests are invited to participate in all aspects of a marriage ceremony that do not violate their own personal beliefs.

If not disruptive to the service, is it okay to:
Take pictures? Possibly. But ask first.
Use a flash? No, unless you have received permission.
Use a video camera? Possibly. Ask first.
Use a tape recorder? Probably.

Will contributions to the church be collected at the ceremony? No.

AFTER THE CEREMONY

Is there usually a reception after the ceremony? Yes. Sometimes it is held in a hall or room adjacent to the church sanctuary. More commonly, it is catered in an entirely separate location. Food and beverages may be served; there may be dancing or other activities. Alcoholic beverages may be served, if the reception is not on church premises. The reception may last anywhere from an hour to most of a night.

Would it be considered impolite to neither eat nor drink? No. Guests should feel free to apply their own dietary standards.

Is there a grace or benediction before eating or drinking? Sometimes. It depends on the family's preferences.

Is there a grace or benediction after eating or drinking? No.

Is there a traditional greeting for the family? No.

Is there a traditional form of address for clergy who may be at the reception? Formally, clergy should be addressed as "Mr.," "Mrs."

or "Ms.," followed by the last name. It is impolite to refer to them simply as "Reverend." Informally, many prefer to be addressed by their first names.

Is it okay to leave early? Yes, but it's usually expected that you will stay until at least the toasts have been made and the wedding cake served.

Funerals and Mourning

In the United Church of Canada, traditional funerals are often replaced by memorial services, which celebrate the life and faith of the departed person. Funerals, with a casket present, are increasingly rare. If a casket is present, it will more often be closed than open.

More and more, United Church members choose cremation rather than burial.

Beliefs about life after death vary widely across the United Church of Canada. Some believe that after death they will be reunited with their loved ones. Others may believe that this life is all we have, and that death is final.

Officially, the United Church of Canada teaches that the Resurrection of Jesus is symbolic of the Resurrection that is possible for all who believe in him.

BEFORE THE CEREMONY

How soon after the death will the funeral usually take place? Between a few days and a week. There are no religious requirements to have a funeral immediately. A memorial service may be held several weeks after a death, to allow time for mourners to gather from across the country.

What should someone who is not a member of the United Church do upon hearing of the death of a member of that church? Telephone or visit the bereaved to offer sympathy. In some parts of the country, visits are made directly to the family's home. In others, visits are made at specified times to the funeral parlor. Check the obituary notice; if it makes no reference to visiting times at a funeral parlor, then visits may be made at any (reasonable) time in the home.

APPROPRIATE ATTIRE

Funerals call for more formality in dress than almost any other religious occasion in the United Church of Canada.

Men: Mainly suit and tie, dark colors preferred. In more casual cultures, slacks and sweaters may be acceptable.

Women: Dresses, dark colors, plain fabrics. Pants suits may be permissible, again, in darker colors. Arms and heads may be uncovered. Subdued jewelry is permissible.

GIFTS

Is it appropriate to send flowers or to make a contribution? Check the obituary notice to see if the family wants to have donations made to a charity or cause in lieu of flowers.

If they accept flowers, the flowers should usually go to the church or funeral parlor rather than to the family home.

If donations are preferred, send them directly to the chosen charity, marked "In memory of [name]." Some charities send notification of such gifts to the bereaved family; some don't. If you want the bereaved to know that you've made a donation, include a note providing their address so the charity will know where to send a notification.

Is it appropriate to send food? Yes. Send or take it to the home of the bereaved.

THE CEREMONY

Where will the ceremony take place? In a church or in a funeral parlor.

When should guests arrive and where should they sit? Arrive early. Family and friends will be seated in a special block of reserved seats. Ushers will advise where to sit. If there are no ushers, guests may sit wherever they choose.

If arriving late, are there times when a guest should *not* enter the service? Yes. Ushers will seat you when it is appropriate.

Will the bereaved family be present at the church or funeral home before the ceremony? Possibly.

Is there a traditional greeting for the family? No. Express sympathy. If time permits, invite the bereaved to talk about their feelings, and how they're coping with their loss. Share your favorite memories of the deceased person. Funny memories are

just as acceptable as sorrowful ones.

Avoid preaching. Don't offer pat answers about the meaning of life or about God's promises of eternal life. Don't suggest that this is all God's will and will work out for the best in the end.

Will there be an open casket? In the United Church, less and less often.

Is a guest expected to view the body? This is optional, but if it is a memorial service, there will be no body to view.

What is appropriate behavior upon viewing the body? Silence, or silent prayer.

Who are the major officiants at the ceremony and what do they do? *The minister(s),* who will lead the service.

What books are used? Most congregations use *Voices United,* the United Church's hymnbook (Etobicoke, Ont.: The United Church Publishing House, 1996), and *More Voices* (2006), a supplement to *Voices United.* Some congregations also use *Songs for a Gospel People* (Winfield, B.C.: Wood Lake Books, 1987), commonly referred to as "the green book." The most commonly used translation of the Bible is the New Revised Standard Version.

To indicate the order of the ceremony: There will be a printed program or bulletin, and the minister will make announcements or give instructions.

Will a guest who is not a member of the United Church be expected to do anything other than sit? Visitors are invited to participate along with the congregation in all aspects of a funeral or memorial service that do not violate their own personal beliefs.

Are there any parts of the ceremony in which a guest who is not a member of the United Church should *not* participate? No.

If not disruptive to the service, is it okay to:

Take pictures? No, unless you have received prior permission.

Use a flash? No, unless you have received prior permission.

Use a video camera? No, unless you have received prior permission.

Use a tape recorder? Possibly, but ask first.

Will contributions to the church be collected at the ceremony? No.

THE INTERMENT

With the increasing trend to cremation and memorial services, there may not be an interment. If there is, it may take place months later, as a private ceremony for the immediate family.

Should guests attend the interment? This is optional. If it immediately follows a funeral service, probably yes. After a memorial service, no.

Whom should one ask for directions? The funeral director.

What happens at the graveside? If there is a formal interment or burial, of the casket or of ashes, you are simply expected to be present and to participate in the ceremony as you are able. The minister or presider will offer prayers. If responses are expected, they will either be familiar or will be printed in a program or bulletin. The casket or ashes will be lowered into the ground or placed in a vault. Guests may be invited to assist in sprinkling earth or sand; you are not obliged to participate if you do not wish to.

The rites of a fraternal order or of the military may be part of a graveside service.

Do guests who are not members of the United Church participate at the graveside ceremony? Guests are invited to participate along with the congregation in all aspects of an interment or burial that do not violate their own personal beliefs.

COMFORTING THE BEREAVED

Is it appropriate to visit the home of the bereaved after the funeral? Yes. At any mutually convenient time, and as often as you feel appropriate. Too often, families are expected to return to normal right after the ceremony. Grieving takes a lot longer than that. Visiting allows people to talk about their experience, turning painful memories into memories of painful memories.

How long you stay depends on your closeness to the bereaved. An average visit might be 15 to 30 minutes.

Will there be a religious service at the home of the bereaved? No.

Will food be served? Often, refreshments or a light meal will be served at a reception immediately following the memorial, funeral or interment service.

How soon after the funeral will a mourner usually return to a normal work schedule? Depends on the person and the situation. There are no customs requiring a certain period of isolation, or a certain number of days off work. Most mourners will return to work within a week.

How soon after the funeral will a mourner usually return to a normal social schedule? Depends on the person and the situation. Remember that grieving is a process. It can't, and shouldn't, be hurried.

Are there mourning customs to which a friend who is not a member of the United Church should be sensitive? No.

Are there rituals for observing the anniversary of the death? No.

5 · HOME CELEBRATIONS

Not applicable to the United Church of Canada.

29

United Church of Christ

1 • HISTORY AND BELIEFS

Formed in 1957 by the merger of two churches, the United Church of Christ is one of the newer Protestant denominations in the United States.

The merger was between the Congregational Christian Churches, whose roots date back to 16th-century England and to the Puritan and Separatist movements that settled New England, and the Evangelical and Reform Church, which had previously been formed by combining the German Reformed Church and the Evangelical Synod of North America.

According to the constitution of the United Church of Christ, Jesus Christ is the "sole Head" of the Church and each local congregation is its "basic unit." Local churches choose their own pastors and determine policy regarding membership, worship, budget and programs. Congregations cooperate in area groupings called associations and in larger regional bodies called conferences. The General Synod, the Church's central deliberative body, meets biennially to conduct denominational business.

More than half the Church's membership is in the New England and Midwestern states.

U.S. churches: 5,320
U.S. membership: 1.1 million
(data from the 2010 Yearbook of American and Canadian Churches)

For more information, contact:
The United Church of Christ
700 Prospect Avenue
Cleveland, OH 44115
(216) 736-2100
www.ucc.org

2 • THE BASIC SERVICE

The primary components of the Sunday morning service are a "call to worship," which is usually read responsively by the minister and congregants; the reading of Scriptures; a sermon, which may last about 20 minutes and, in some ways, is the centerpiece of the service; prayers, including the Lord's Prayer, some of which are said by the congregation and some by the minister on behalf of the congregation; and a closing benediction, or a "sending forth," said by the minister. The service usually lasts about one hour.

APPROPRIATE ATTIRE

Men: A jacket and tie would never be out of place, although many congregations welcome more casual attire. No head covering is required.

Women: A dress or a skirt and blouse or a pants suit, although many congregations welcome casual attire. Clothing need not cover the arms and hems need not reach below the knees. Open-toed shoes and modest jewelry are permissible. No head covering is required.

There are no rules regarding colors of clothing.

THE SANCTUARY

What are the major sections of the church?

The foyer or narthex: Where worshipers are greeted and receive a church bulletin.

The pews: Where congregants and guests sit.

The chancel: A raised section at the front of the sanctuary for an altar, pulpit and lectern and where ministers and other worship leaders sit.

The choir loft: Where the choir or other musicians sit. Depending on the architecture of the church, this may be to one or both sides of the chancel or in a balcony at the rear of the sanctuary.

THE SERVICE

When should guests arrive and where should they sit? Arrive about five minutes before the scheduled start of the service. In many churches, ushers will advise guests where to sit.

If arriving late, are there times when a guest should *not* enter the service? Do not enter while prayers are being recited, during the reading of Scriptures or during the sermon.

Are there times when a guest should *not* leave the service? Do not leave while prayers are being recited, during the reading of Scriptures or during the sermon.

Who are the major officiants, leaders or participants and what do they do?

The minister(s) or pastor(s), the primary leader of the service. He or she preaches a sermon and presides over the Communion and baptism.

Lector(s) or reader(s), who reads the Scriptures aloud to the congregants.

Ushers, who greet worshipers in most churches and distribute church bulletins and offering plates. In some churches, they also seat worshipers and guests.

Lay leaders, who may greet congregants and guests, make announcements about church activities and lead prayers.

Deacons, who help serve Communion in some churches.

What are the major ritual objects of the service?

A Bible, which is on the altar or pulpit and which worship leaders read during the service.

A cross, which is usually displayed on the altar and reminds worshipers of the suffering, death and Resurrection of Christ.

Candles, which remind worshipers of God's illuminating presence.

Bread and wine or grape juice, which are served to worshipers during Communion. Most United Church of Christ congregations believe that Christ is spiritually present at Communion. Unlike certain other Christian churches, they do not believe that the bread and wine or grape juice are transubstantiated into the actual body and blood of Christ.

The baptismal font, which contains water used during services that include baptisms.

What books are used? The most commonly used of several Protestant Bibles is the New Revised Standard Version (New York: National Council of Churches, 1989). Also used is *The New Century Hymnal* (Cleveland: The Pilgrim Press, 1995).

To indicate the order of the service: A program will be distributed and the minister will make periodic announcements.

GUEST BEHAVIOR DURING THE SERVICE

Will a guest who is not a member of the United Church of Christ be expected to do anything other than sit? Guests are expected to join congregants when they stand during the service. It is entirely optional for them to read prayers aloud and sing with the congregation. In most United Church of Christ congregations, congregants do not kneel. In those churches where kneeling occurs, it is optional for guests to join in. Those guests who do not kneel should remain seated.

Are there any parts of the service in which a guest who is not a member of the United Church of Christ should *not* participate? No, except that local practices regarding the sacrament of Communion vary. In most congregations, Communion is open to all who wish to receive it; in some, it is preferred that only baptized Christians and/or only adults receive it. If you wish to know the practice of a local congregation on this or any other matter, ask the local minister in advance.

If not disruptive to the service, is it okay to:
Take pictures? No.
Use a flash? No.
Use a video camera? No.
Use a tape recorder? No.

Will contributions to the church be collected at the service? Yes. Ushers pass offering plates through the congregation during the service.

How much is it customary to contribute? It is entirely optional for guests to contribute. If they choose to do so, contributions between $1 and $10 are appropriate.

AFTER THE SERVICE

Is there usually a reception after the service? Yes. Some churches serve no food during the reception; some serve such light foods as coffee, tea, juice and pastry; some serve a complete lunch. The reception may last 30 to 60 minutes.

Is there a traditional form of address for clergy who may be at the reception? Some are addressed as "Pastor." Some prefer to be addressed as "Mr." or "Ms." or, if the church bulletin distributed at services so indicates, as "Dr." Many United Church of Christ clergy prefer being addressed by their first name.

Is it okay to leave early? If necessary.

GENERAL GUIDELINES AND ADVICE

Take your cues from those around you. Do not remain standing when congregants have reseated themselves. In many congregations, "amen" is not said or sung at the conclusion of each hymn or prayer.

SPECIAL VOCABULARY

Key words or phrases that it might be helpful for a visitor to know:

"And also with you." The proper response if someone says, "The peace of God be with you."

"That they may all be one." This quote from the Gospel according to John (17:21) appears in the logo of the United Church of Christ. It is part of Jesus' prayer for unity among those who believe in him.

DOGMA AND IDEOLOGY

Members of the United Church of Christ believe:

In the Trinitarian concept of the divinity. This consists of God the Father, God the Son (Jesus) and God the Holy Spirit.

Each person who believes and trusts in Jesus, who is the "head" of the church, has his or her sins forgiven, is endowed with "courage in the struggle for justice and peace," and is granted "eternal life in Your realm which has no end."

A basic book to which a guest can refer to learn more about the United Church of Christ:

A History of the Evangelical and Reform Church by David Dunn and Lowell H. Zuck (New York and Cleveland: The Pilgrim Press, 2010).

3 · HOLY DAYS AND FESTIVALS

Advent. Begins four weeks before Christmas. The purpose is to prepare for Christmas and to focus on Christ. There is no traditional greeting for Advent.

Christmas. Occurs on the evening of December 24 and the day of December 25. Marks the birth of Jesus and the incarnation of God as a human.

Lent. Begins on Ash Wednesday, which occurs six weeks before Easter. The purpose is to prepare for Easter. There is no traditional greeting for Lent. Between Lent and Easter, abstention from entertainment is encouraged, as is increased giving to the poor. Often, there are midweek worship services. Few members of the United Church of Christ engage in a moderate fast (abstaining from certain foods) during Lent.

Easter. Always the Sunday following the first full moon on or after March 21. Celebrates the Resurrection of Jesus Christ. In worship services, the pastor may greet congregants with, "Christ is risen!" Congregants respond with "Christ [or "He"] is risen, indeed!"

Pentecost Sunday. The seventh Sunday after Easter. Celebrates the coming of the Holy Spirit, which is the empowering spirit of God in human life. This is often considered the birth of the Christian church. There is no traditional greeting for this holiday.

4 · LIFE CYCLE EVENTS

Birth Ceremony

The baptism or "dedication" service is the same for males and females. Baptism celebrates the birth of a person into the church, and can occur anytime from birth onward through adulthood. The ceremony is usually integrated into a regular church service and may last about 15 minutes. In the United Church of Christ, baptism is administered only once. Baptism initiates an individual into the Church and is the sign and seal of God's grace upon that person through the power of the Holy Spirit. During the ceremony, the pastor pours or sprinkles water over the candidate's head or dips or immerses him or her in water. Another method of baptism is "immersion," in which the person being baptized is lowered into the water and raised up again.

Baptism is almost always part of a larger Sunday morning service. The baptism itself may last about 15 minutes, while the entire service may last about one hour.

BEFORE THE CEREMONY

Are guests usually invited by a formal invitation? Invitations are usually oral.

If not stated explicitly, should one assume that children are invited? Yes.

If one can't attend, what should one do? RSVP with regrets. While appreciated, gifts are not expected.

APPROPRIATE ATTIRE

Men: A jacket and tie would never be out of place, although many congregations accept more casual attire. No head covering is required.

Women: A dress or a skirt and blouse or a pants suit. Many congregations welcome casual attire. Clothing need not cover the arms and hems need not reach below the knees. Open-toed shoes and modest jewelry are permissible. No head covering is required.

There are no rules regarding colors of clothing.

GIFTS

Is a gift customarily expected? While not inappropriate, gifts are not expected. Should one decide to give a gift, such items as clothing or toys are appropriate for an infant being baptized and books are appropriate for adults being baptized.

Should gifts be brought to the ceremony? No, they should be sent to the home of the person being baptized.

THE CEREMONY

Where will the ceremony take place? Almost always in the church's main sanctuary. Only occasionally does a baptism occur at the parents' home or outdoors.

When should guests arrive and where should they sit? Arrive about ten minutes before the scheduled start of the service. In many churches, ushers will advise guests where to sit.

If arriving late, are there times when a guest should *not* enter the ceremony? Do not enter while prayers are being recited, during the reading of Scriptures or during the sermon.

Are there times when a guest should *not* leave the ceremony? Do not leave while prayers are being recited, during the reading of Scriptures or during the sermon.

Who are the major officiants, leaders or participants at the ceremony and what do they do?

The minister(s) or pastor(s), the primary leader of the service; presides over the baptism.

The person being baptized.

The parents (in the case of a child), who present the child and pledge to raise him or her in Christ's faith.

The sponsor(s) or godparents, who may accompany the child to the baptismal font and pledge to offer special support for him or her.

The congregation, which welcomes the person being baptized into the community of faith.

What books are used? The most commonly used of several Protestant Bibles is the New Revised Standard Version (New York: National Council of Churches, 1989). Also used is *The New Century Hymnal* (Cleveland: The Pilgrim Press, 1995).

To indicate the order of the ceremony: A program will be distributed and the minister will make periodic announcements.

Will a guest who is not a member of the United Church of Christ be expected to do anything other than sit? Upon request of the family of the person being baptized, a guest may be asked to stand at the front of the sanctuary as a sponsor, a family member or a friend. If so, consult the family or the pastor for instructions.

Ordinarily, guests are expected to join congregants when they stand during the service. It is entirely optional for them to read prayers aloud and sing with the congregation. In most United Church of Christ congregations, congregants do not kneel. In those churches where kneeling occurs, it is optional for guests to join in. Those guests who do not kneel should remain seated.

Are there any parts of the ceremony in which a guest who is not a member of the United Church of Christ should *not* participate? No.

If not disruptive to the ceremony, is it okay to:

Take pictures? Practice varies. Ask the pastor in advance.

Use a flash? Practice varies. Ask the pastor in advance.

Use a video camera? Practice varies. Ask the pastor in advance.

Use a tape recorder? Practice varies. Ask the pastor in advance.

Will contributions to the church be collected at the ceremony? Yes. Ushers pass offering plates through the congregation during the service.

How much is it customary to contribute? It is entirely optional for guests to contribute. If they choose to do so, contributions between $1 and $10 are appropriate.

AFTER THE CEREMONY

Is there usually a reception after the ceremony? Sometimes there is a reception. If so, it may be at the home of the person being baptized or in the same building as the baptismal ceremony. There may be a reception line, and light food such as coffee, tea, punch and pastries may be served. Sometimes, a full meal is served. If the reception is not in the church, there may be alcoholic beverages and/or music and dancing.

If at the church, the reception may last 30 to 60 minutes. If at home or elsewhere, it may last two hours or more.

Would it be considered impolite to neither eat nor drink? No.

Is there a grace or benediction before eating or drinking? Grace will be said only if a full meal is served.

Is there a grace or benediction after eating or drinking? No.

Is there a traditional greeting for the family? Just offer your congratulations.

Is there a traditional form of address for clergy who may be at the reception? Some are addressed as "Pastor." Some prefer to be addressed as "Mr." or "Ms." or, if the church bulletin distributed at services so indicates, as "Dr." Many United Church of Christ clergy prefer being addressed by their first name.

Is it okay to leave early? Yes.

Initiation Ceremony

Confirmation is celebrated for teenagers who were baptized as infants. It offers one who was baptized as an infant the opportunity to publicly assent to the baptismal promises and celebrates the affirmation of baptism in the life of the individual. One is usually confirmed with other teens who were in the same confirmation class.

The confirmation is usually part of the regular Sunday worship service. It may last about 15 minutes, although the entire service may last about an hour.

BEFORE THE CEREMONY

Are guests usually invited by a formal invitation? Invitations are usually issued orally.

If not stated explicitly, should one assume that children are invited? Yes.

If one can't attend, what should one do? RSVP with regrets. While appreciated, gifts are not expected.

APPROPRIATE ATTIRE

Men: A jacket and tie would never be out of place, although many congregations accept more casual attire. No head covering is required.

Women: A dress or a skirt and blouse or a pants suit. Many congregations welcome casual attire. Clothing need not cover the arms and hems need not reach below the knees. Open-toed shoes and modest jewelry are permissible. No head covering is required.

There are no rules regarding colors of clothing.

GIFTS

Is a gift customarily expected? While not inappropriate, gifts are not expected. Should one decide to give a gift, appropriate items are a Bible or a book (either fiction or nonfiction).

Should gifts be brought to the ceremony? Either bring or send gifts to the home of the confirmand.

THE CEREMONY

Where will the ceremony take place? In the church's main sanctuary.

When should guests arrive and where should they sit? Arrive about ten minutes before the scheduled start of the service. In many churches, ushers will advise guests where to sit.

If arriving late, are there times when a guest should *not* enter the ceremony? Do not enter while prayers are being recited, during the reading of Scriptures or during the sermon.

Are there times when a guest should *not* leave the ceremony?

Do not leave while prayers are being recited, during the reading of Scriptures or during the sermon.

Who are the major officiants, leaders or participants at the ceremony and what do they do?
The confirmand(s), the person(s) being confirmed.
The minister(s) or pastor(s), the primary leader of the service. He or she preaches a sermon and presides over the Communion and baptism.
Lector(s) or reader(s), who reads the Scriptures aloud to the congregants.
Ushers, who greet worshipers in most churches and distribute church bulletins and offering plates. In some churches, they also seat worshipers and guests.
Lay leaders, who may greet congregants and guests, make announcements about church activities and lead prayers.
Deacons, who help serve Communion in some churches.

What books are used? The most commonly used of several Protestant Bibles is the New Revised Standard Version (New York: National Council of Churches, 1989). Also used is *The New Century Hymnal* (Cleveland, Ohio: The Pilgrim Press, 1995).

To indicate the order of the ceremony: A program will be distributed and the minister will make periodic announcements.

Will a guest who is not a member of the United Church of Christ be expected to do anything other than sit? If the family or the confirmand has specifically asked you to join him or her while standing in front of the congregation, then do so.

Ordinarily, guests are expected to join congregants when they stand during the service. It is entirely optional for them to read prayers aloud and sing with the congregation. In most United Church of Christ congregations, congregants do not kneel. In those churches where kneeling occurs, it is optional for guests to join in. Those guests who do not kneel should remain seated.

Are there any parts of the ceremony in which a guest who is not a member of the United Church of Christ should *not* participate? No.

If not disruptive to the ceremony, is it okay to:

Take pictures? Practice varies. Ask the pastor in advance.

Use a flash? Practice varies. Ask the pastor in advance.

Use a video camera? Practice varies. Ask the pastor in advance.

Use a tape recorder? Practice varies. Ask the pastor in advance.

Will contributions to the church be collected at the ceremony? Yes. Ushers pass offering plates through the congregation during the service.

How much is it customary to contribute? It is entirely optional for guests to contribute. If they choose to do so, contributions between $1 and $10 are appropriate.

AFTER THE CEREMONY

Is there usually a reception after the ceremony? Yes. Some churches serve no food during the reception; some serve such light foods as coffee, tea, juice and pastry; some serve a complete lunch. Grace will be recited only if a meal is served—and then only before the meal, not after it. The reception may last 30 to 60 minutes.

Would it be considered impolite to neither eat nor drink? No.

Is there a grace or benediction before eating or drinking? Grace will be said if a full meal is served.

Is there a grace or benediction after eating or drinking? No.

Is there a traditional greeting for the family? Just offer your congratulations.

Is there a traditional form of address for clergy who may be at the reception? Some are addressed as "Pastor." Some prefer to be addressed as "Mr." or "Ms." or, if the church bulletin distributed at services so indicates, as "Dr." Many United Church of Christ clergy prefer being addressed by their first name.

Is it okay to leave early? Yes.

Marriage Ceremony

The United Church of Christ teaches that the essence of marriage is a covenanted commitment that has its foundation in the faithfulness of God's love. The marriage ceremony is the occasion on which two people unite as husband and wife in the mutual exchange of covenant promises. The presiding official represents the Church and gives the marriage the Church's blessing. The congregation joins in affirming the marriage and in offering support and thanksgiving for the new family.

Usually, the wedding is a ceremony in itself. Only rarely is it part of a regular Sunday worship service. It may last 30 minutes to one hour.

BEFORE THE CEREMONY

Are guests usually invited by a formal invitation? Yes.

If not stated explicitly, should one assume that children are invited? No.

If one can't attend, what should one do? RSVP with regrets and send a gift.

APPROPRIATE ATTIRE

Men: A jacket and tie. No head covering is required.

Women: A dress or a skirt and blouse. Clothing need not cover the arms and hems need not reach below the knees. Open-toed shoes and modest jewelry are permissible. No head covering is required.

There are no rules regarding colors of clothing.

GIFTS

Is a gift customarily expected? Yes. Cash or bonds or household items (such as sheets, kitchenware or small appliances) are appropriate.

Should gifts be brought to the ceremony? Bring gifts to the reception that follows the wedding ceremony.

THE CEREMONY

Where will the ceremony take place? In the church's main sanctuary or a special room in the church, or in a home, a catering hall or outdoors.

When should guests arrive and where should they sit? Arrive shortly before the time for which the wedding has been scheduled. Usually, ushers will advise guests where to sit.

If arriving late, are there times when a guest should *not* enter the ceremony? Do not enter during the processional or recessional of the wedding party or during the recitation of wedding vows. Follow the ushers' guidance for entering the ceremony.

Are there times when a guest should *not* leave the ceremony? Do not leave during the processional or recessional of the wedding party or during the recitation of wedding vows. Follow the ushers' guidance for leaving the ceremony.

Who are the major officiants, leaders or participants at the ceremony and what do they do?

The minister(s) or pastor(s), who presides over the ceremony.

The bride and groom.

Other members of the wedding party.

Lector(s) or reader(s), who, at some weddings, may read the Scriptures aloud to those present.

Deacons, who help serve Communion, which is not served at all weddings.

Ushers, who greet and seat guests at most weddings.

What books are used? The most commonly used of several Protestant Bibles is the New Revised Standard Version (New York: National Council of Churches, 1989). Also used is *The New Century Hymnal* (Cleveland: The Pilgrim Press, 1995).

To indicate the order of the ceremony: The minister will make periodic announcements.

Will a guest who is not a member of the United Church of Christ be expected to do anything other than sit? Guests are expected to join congregants when they stand during the service. It is entirely optional for them to read prayers aloud and sing with the congregation. In most United Church of Christ congregations, congregants do not kneel. In those churches where kneeling occurs, it is optional for guests to join in. Those guests who do not kneel should remain seated.

Are there any parts of the ceremony in which a guest who is not a member of the United Church of Christ should *not* participate? No.

If not disruptive to the ceremony, is it okay to:
Take pictures? Practice varies. Ask the pastor in advance.
Use a flash? Practice varies. Ask the pastor in advance.
Use a video camera? Practice varies. Ask the pastor in advance.
Use a tape recorder? Practice varies. Ask the pastor in advance.

Will contributions to the church be collected at the ceremony? Only if the wedding is part of a regular Sunday worship service. If so, ushers will pass offering plates through the congregation during the service.

How much is it customary to contribute? If guests choose to do so, contributions between $1 and $10 are appropriate.

AFTER THE CEREMONY

Is there usually a reception after the ceremony? Yes. It is usually in a catering hall, at a home or in a church reception hall. There is usually a reception line and a full meal is served. If the reception is not in the church, there may be alcoholic beverages and/or music and dancing. The reception may last two hours or more.

Would it be considered impolite to neither eat nor drink? No.

Is there a grace or benediction before eating or drinking? Grace will be said if a full meal is served.

Is there a grace or benediction after eating or drinking? No.

Is there a traditional greeting for the family? Just offer your congratulations.

Is there a traditional form of address for clergy who may be at the reception? Some are addressed as "Pastor." Some prefer to be addressed as "Mr." or "Ms." or, if the church bulletin distributed at services so indicates, as "Dr." Many United Church of Christ clergy prefer being addressed by their first name.

Is it okay to leave early? Yes.

Funerals and Mourning

A United Church of Christ funeral service, states the Church's *Book of Worship*, "recognizes both the pain and sorrow of the separation that accompanies death and the hope and joy of the promises of God to those who die and are raised in Jesus Christ. The service celebrates the life of the deceased, gives thanks for that person's life, and commends that life to God…. Its purpose is to affirm once more the powerful, steadfast love of God from which people cannot be separated, even by death."

The funeral service is almost always a service in itself. Ordinarily, it lasts about 15 to 30 minutes, although it may sometimes last up to 60 minutes.

BEFORE THE CEREMONY

How soon after the death does the funeral usually take place? Within one week.

What should someone who is not a member of the United Church of Christ do upon hearing of the death of a member of that faith? Telephone or visit the bereaved family or send a card to them to express your condolences.

APPROPRIATE ATTIRE

Men: A jacket and tie. No head covering is required.

Women: A dress or a skirt and blouse. Clothing need not cover the arms and hems need not reach below the knees. Open-toed shoes and modest jewelry are permissible. No head covering is required.

Dark, somber colors of clothing are advised. Bright, flashy tones are strongly discouraged.

GIFTS

Is it appropriate to send flowers or make a contribution? Flowers may be sent to the home of the bereaved upon hearing of the death or after the funeral, or they may be sent to the church or funeral home where the funeral service will be held. Contributions to a church or organization designated by the family may be made after the funeral.

Is it appropriate to send food? Yes. This may be sent to the home of the bereaved.

THE CEREMONY

Where will the ceremony take place? In either a church or a funeral home.

When should guests arrive and where should they sit? Arrive 15 minutes before the time for which the service has been scheduled. Sit wherever you wish, unless a specially marked section has been reserved for immediate family.

If arriving late, are there times when a guest should *not* enter the ceremony? Do not enter during prayers, the sermon or the eulogy. Follow ushers' guidance about entering the service.

Will the bereaved family be present at the church or funeral home before the ceremony? Not usually, though sometimes family members do greet guests beforehand.

Is there a traditional greeting for the family? No. Just offer your condolences.

Will there be an open casket? Rarely. This depends on local customs and the preference of the family. "Viewing" time is sometimes scheduled in the days or hours before the funeral. "Viewing" may also be offered during or at the end of the funeral service itself.

Is a guest expected to view the body? This is entirely optional. If there is a "viewing" at the funeral and you do not wish to participate, excuse yourself from the line that forms to pass the casket. If you happen to be in the line that passes the casket and you do not wish to view the body, simply avert your eyes.

What is appropriate behavior upon viewing the body? View it silently and somberly. Do not touch it or place any flowers or memorabilia in the casket.

Who are the major officiants at the ceremony and what do they do?
A minister or pastor, who officiates and delivers the sermon.
A family member or a close friend, who may also deliver a eulogy.

What books are used? The minister will use a Bible. Of several Protestant Bibles, the most commonly used in the United Church of Christ is the New Revised Standard Version (New York:

National Council of Churches, 1989). Also used is *The New Century Hymnal* (Cleveland: The Pilgrim Press, 1995).

To indicate the order of the ceremony: Usually a program will be distributed; sometimes the minister will make periodic announcements.

Will a guest who is not a member of the United Church of Christ be expected to do anything other than sit? Guests are expected to join congregants when they stand during the service. It is entirely optional for them to read prayers aloud and sing with the congregation. In most United Church of Christ congregations, congregants do not kneel. In those churches where kneeling occurs, it is optional for guests to join in. Those guests who do not kneel should remain seated.

Are there any parts of the service in which a guest who is not a member of the United Church of Christ should *not* participate? No.

If not disruptive to the ceremony, is it okay to:
Take pictures? No.
Use a flash? No.
Use a video camera? No.
Use a tape recorder? No.

Will contributions to the church be collected at the ceremony? No.

THE INTERMENT

Should guests attend the interment? Yes, unless the minister announces at the funeral service that the interment is only for the family.

Whom should one ask for directions? The minister or funeral director.

What happens at the graveside? Scriptures are read and the casket is placed in the ground.

Do guests who are not members of the United Church of Christ participate at the graveside ceremony? No, they are simply present—although rarely, guests may be invited to say a few words about the deceased.

COMFORTING THE BEREAVED

Is it appropriate to visit the home of the bereaved after the funeral? Often, there is a reception at the home of the bereaved after the funeral. If not, visiting a few days after the funeral is appropriate.

Will there be a religious service at the home of the bereaved? No.

Will food be served? Yes, possibly a dinner if there is a reception immediately after the interment.

How soon after the funeral will a mourner usually return to a normal work schedule? The Church has no religious prescriptions specifying the number of days that one should formally be in mourning. Local, ethnic and cultural customs are more relevant than any particular religious tradition of the Church.

How soon after the funeral will a mourner usually return to a normal social schedule? The Church has no religious prescriptions specifying the number of days that one should formally be in mourning. Local, ethnic and cultural customs are more relevant than any particular religious tradition of the Church.

Are there mourning customs to which a friend who is not a member of the United Church of Christ should be sensitive? No. Local, ethnic and cultural customs are more relevant than any particular religious tradition of the Church.

Are there rituals for observing the anniversary of the death? No. Local, ethnic and cultural customs are more relevant than any particular religious tradition of the Church.

5 . HOME CELEBRATIONS

Not applicable to the United Church of Christ.

Glossary of Common Religious Terms and Names

'Abdu'l-Bahá ("Ab-DOOL-bah-HAH"): [Arabic] The son of Bahá'u'lláh, the founder of the Bahá'í Faith. His name means "Servant of Baha."

Advaita: The Vedanta notion of nonduality, or the essential oneness of God, individual soul, and universe. Also the name of a school of Vedanta teaching.

Aliyah ("ah-lee-YAH"): [Hebrew] Literally translated as "going up," it is the honor of being called to participate in the reading of the Torah in a synagogue/temple.

Allah'u'Abhá ("Ah-lah-oo-ab-HAH"): [Arabic] A Bahá'í phrase that means "God is most glorious."

Apostles' Creed: The most widely used creed, or declaratory affirmation, in the Christian church in the West. Based on a creed used in Rome in the third century and given its present form in France in the sixth or seventh century. States that one believes in God, "the Father Almighty"; in Jesus Christ, the "Son of the Lord," who was conceived in a virgin birth and eventually rose to heaven after his crucifixion, where he will judge the dead; and in "the Holy Ghost; … the Forgiveness of sins; the Resurrection of the body; and the Life everlasting."

Ardas ("AHR-das"): [Gurmukhi] Community prayer led by one person in a Sikh *gurdwara* service. Blessings for special occasions or events may be requested during the *ardas*.

Atman ("AHT-mahn"): [Sanskrit] In Hinduism, the individual soul.

Ayyám-i-há ("Ah-yah-mee-HAH"): [Arabic] "Days of Ha," which Bahá'ís celebrate from February 26 through March 1. The holiday is devoted to hospitality, charity and gift-giving and to spiritually preparing oneself for the annual fast that lasts for all 19 days of the last month in the Bahá'í calendar.

The Báb ("Bob"): [Arabic] Literally means "Gate" or "Door" and is used in the Bahá'í Faith to refer to Mírzá'Ali-Muhammed, a direct descendent of the Prophet Muhammad, who announced in mid–19th-century Persia that he was the forerunner of the Universal Messenger of God.

Bahá'í ("Ba-HIGH"): [Arabic] A follower of Bahá'u'lláh.

Bahá'u'lláh ("Bah-HAH-oo-LAH"): [Arabic] The founder of the Bahá'í Faith, whose name means "Glory of God."

Baptism: In Christianity, a ritual washing for initiation; a sign of remission of sin and of spiritual rebirth by symbolically participating in Christ's death, burial and Resurrection. Depending on the specific Christian denomination, baptism may occur at birth, during the preteen or teen years or as an adult.

Baptistery: The place for administering baptism. Some churches have baptisteries adjoining or near their entrance. This position indicates that through baptism, one is initiated, or "enters," the church.

Benedict XVI, Pope: Elected in 2005, known for his conservative approach to doctrine.

Bhagavad Gita ("BAHG-ah-vahd GEE-tah"): [Sanskrit] The epic Hindu poem in which Krishna, god in human form, expounds the nature of reality.

Bible: As used by Judaism, applies to the Hebrew Scriptures and ascribes primary authority to the Torah (the first five books of the Bible); secondary authority to the Books of the Prophets; and tertiary authority to the Kethubim, whose 13 books include Psalms, Proverbs and Daniel. As used by Christianity, *Bible* refers to the Hebrew and Christian Scriptures known as the Old and New Testaments.

Bimah ("BEE-mah"): [Hebrew] The part of the sanctuary in a Jewish synagogue or temple from which the service is led and where the rabbi and cantor stand and sit. It is usually raised above the level where congregants sit and is at the front or in the middle of the sanctuary.

Blessingway Ceremony: A ceremonial chant that recounts the Navajo creation story and is usually recited over two nights. It is performed to maintain a positive or healthy environment and to prevent imbalance or disharmony.

Book of Mormon: Joseph Smith's translation of God's revelations. First published in 1830.

Brahman ("BRAH-mahn"): [Sanskrit] In Hinduism, the One, All-Encompassing soul.

Breviary: A Roman Catholic book that contains the prayers, psalms and readings of the Liturgy of the Hours (daily prayers).

Brit ("breet"): [Hebrew] The Jewish birth ceremony. The term literally means "covenant." For boys, the *brit milah* ("breet mee-LAH"), or the "covenant of circumcision," occurs on the eighth day of a male child's life. The *brit bat* or *brit hayyim* ("breet baht" or "breet hy-YEEM"), the "covenant of a daughter" or the "covenant of life," is a naming ceremony for a girl.

Censer: An incense burner holder. Smoke from the incense represents prayers being carried to heaven. Used in Greek Orthodox and other liturgical churches.

Chalice: In Christianity, a cup, sometimes covered with gold and often with a tall stem. Held by a priest or other clergy and contains the holy wine, which, depending on the Christian denomination, either symbolizes the blood of Christ or is believed to have become transubstantiated into the actual blood of Christ.

Christian Greek Scriptures: The term Jehovah's Witnesses use for the Scriptures written in the time of the early Christian church; see "New Testament."

Chumash ("KOOH-mahsh"): [Hebrew] The first five books of the Torah, also known as the Five Books of Moses. These are the biblical books of Genesis, Exodus, Leviticus, Numbers and Deuteronomy. It also contains the traditional sections from Prophets that are associated with each Torah section and are read after the Torah reading.

Communion: A rite through which Christians believe they receive either the symbolic or the real body and blood of Christ.

Confirmation: A church rite in which one who was previously baptized expresses his or her faith in Jesus Christ.

Congregation Elders: Deliver talks on the Bible and lead Bible discussions with congregants at meetings of Jehovah's Witnesses.

Creed: A statement of belief. Christian churches generally use one of the early Christian creeds, either the Apostles' Creed or the Nicene Creed.

Dalai Lama, H.H.: The spiritual and de facto political leader of the Tibetan people. Tenzin Gyatso (1935–) is the current Dalai Lama. "H.H." is the abbreviation for "His Holiness."

Dedication: The term in Pentecostal churches for a ceremony for infants or young children during which the child's parents publicly commit themselves to raise the child in the teachings of Jesus.

Dhammapada Dharma: Literally righteousness, duty. Also refers to the accumulated teachings of Buddhism.

Dynamis ("THEE-nah-mees"): [Greek] Used in the Orthodox churches; means "with greater power."

Eddy, Mary Baker: (1821–1910) Founder of the Church of Christ, Scientist.

Epistles: Generally refers to the letters of St. Paul or another New Testament writer.

Error: The Christian Science term for "evil."

Eucharist: The most widely accepted name for Communion, the central act of Christian worship, in which Christians believe they receive either the symbolic or the real body and blood of Christ.

Feast: The centerpiece of the Bahá'í community is the Nineteen Day Feast, which is held every 19 days and is the local community's regular worship gathering—and more. The feast day is held on the first day of each of the 19 months in the Bahá'í calendar and helps sustain the unity of the local Bahá'í community. A Bahá'í feast always contains spiritual devotion, administrative consultation and fellowship. "Feast" does not imply that a large meal will be served, but that a "spiritual feast"—worship, companionship and unity—will be available.

Feast days: Days set aside in liturgical churches to commemorate significant events in the life of Jesus Christ, the saints or the Christian people.

Festival of Ridván ("RIZ-von"): [Arabic] A 12-day Bahá'í holiday celebrated from April 21 through May 2; it commemorates the 12 days in 1863 when Bahá'u'lláh, the prophet-founder of the Bahá'í Faith, publicly proclaimed in a garden in Baghdad his mission as God's messenger for this age.

First Reader: The man or woman who conducts a Christian Science service. Reads mainly from *Science and Health* on Sunday and equally from the King James Bible and *Science and Health* on Wednesday. The Second Reader, who is elected by members to read from the Bible at the Sunday service, shares the platform with the First Reader and presides in the absence of the First Reader.

Foot Washing: Commemorates Christ's washing of His disciples' feet at the Last Supper. In some Pentecostal churches, men and women are in separate rooms and each gender washes the feet of other members of the same gender. Depending on their church's tradition, they may wash the feet of just one individual or of all those present. Individual churches in each faith determine the form and the frequency with which they will practice foot washing.

Gospel: The New Testament Books of Matthew, Mark, Luke and John, which record the life and ministry of Jesus. *Gospel* literally means "good news." For Christians, the "good news" is that the Son of God became a man in the person of Jesus and suffered for the sins of humanity so people will not have to undergo that suffering.

Haftarah ("hahf-TOH-rah"): [Hebrew] In Judaism, the Torah reading during a service in a synagogue or temple.

Haggadah ("hah-GAH-dah"): [Hebrew] The Jewish text, usually in Hebrew and English, that tells the Passover story and its meaning for each generation. Read at the Passover *seder*.

Hajj ("hahj"): [Arabic] A pilgrimage to Mecca that a Muslim must make at least once in his or her lifetime if physically and financially able.

Hatha-yoga: One of the schools of yoga—the one that focuses on physical health and well-being.

Healing: In Christian Science, a realization of God's goodness and the perfection of humanity; regeneration of thought reflected on the body.

Holy Communion: Also called the Lord's Supper. A rite through which Christians believe they receive either the symbolic or the real body and blood of Christ as assurance that God has forgiven their sins.

Holy Spirit: In Christianity, the empowering spirit of God; the third person of the Triune God.

Huppah ("hoo-PAH"): [Hebrew] The canopy under which a Jewish wedding ceremony takes place. Symbolizes the canopy of the heavens under which all life transpires.

Icons: Two-dimensional artistic images of saints. Found primarily in Orthodox churches.

Imam ("EE-mahm"): [Arabic] In Islam, the person who leads prayers and delivers a sermon.

Jehovah: According to Jehovah's Witnesses, the one true name for God.

John XXIII, Pope: (1881–1963) Known for his role in the Second Vatican Council.

John Paul II, Pope: (1920–2005) Known for his international, interfaith efforts.

Jumma ("JUH-mah"): [Arabic] In Islam, noon prayer on Friday. This congregational prayer is recited at a central mosque designated for that purpose.

Kaddish ("KAH-dish"): [Hebrew] The Jewish prayer for the dead.

Karma-yoga: One of the schools of yoga—the one that focuses on doing one's duty, which is unselfish action to help others.

Kiddush Cup ("kee-DOOSH"): [Hebrew] Used to drink ritual wine at certain Jewish ritual events, such as the *shabbat* meal or by the bridal couple during a wedding ceremony.

Kingdom Halls: The name of Jehovah's Witnesses' meeting halls.

Kosher ("KOH-sher"): [Hebrew] Food deemed fit for consumption according to Jewish dietary laws, which prohibit such foods as pork or shellfish and the mixing of dairy and meat products at the same meal or within several hours after eating either one of these dishes.

Langar ("LAHN-gahr"): [Gurmukhi] The vegetarian meal prepared in a prayerful environment and served as an offering after or throughout a Sikh worship service to the *sangat,* or community of worshipers.

Lectio divina: The ancient Christian practice of spiritual reading, once only the practice of monks, now commonly practiced by laypeople.

Mantra: A sacred word of syllable. In Hinduism, the most sacred sound, often used as a mantra, is OM. (OM is also a symbol of God, or Brahman.)

Meeting: The Quaker term for worship service.

Menorah ("min-OHR-ah"): [Hebrew] A seven-branched candelabra, which has become a central motif in the consciousness of the Jewish people. Often placed on the *bima,* or pulpit, in a synagogue or temple.

Mohel ("MOH-hail"): [Hebrew] A specially trained male who performs a ritual Jewish circumcision. The *mohel* may also be a rabbi or physician.

Muazzin ("MOO-ah-zin"): [Arabic] In Islam, the person who calls Muslims to prayer.

Naw-Rúz ("Naw-ROOZ"): [Arabic] The Bahá'í New Year's Day, which occurs on March 21. The day is astronomically fixed so the new year commences on the first day of spring.

New Testament: Scriptures written in the time of the early Christian church. Comprises four Gospels, the Acts of the Apostles, 21 epistles, and the Apocalyptic revelations of John.

Nhat Hanh, Thich: (1926–) With H.H. Dalai Lama, the most popular Buddhist religious leader in the West in the second half of the 20th century.

Nicene Creed: A declaratory affirmation in the Christian church that states the full deity of Jesus Christ.

Nirvana ("neer-VAH-nah"): [Sanskrit] In Buddhism, the extinction of worldly illusions and passions.

Offertory: The portion of a Christian service set apart for the collection from congregants.

Old Testament: The Christian name for the collection of writings sacred to Christians and Jews. Its 39 books, beginning with Genesis and ending with Malachi, include history, law and poems.

Ordinance: The term used by the Assemblies of God Church for water baptism and Communion because they were practices ordained or established by Jesus.

Paten: Holds the consecrated bread or wafer of the Eucharist during a Christian service. Depending on the denomination, the wafer either symbolizes the body of Christ or is believed to have been transubstantiated into the actual body of Christ.

Pope: The Bishop of Rome and the leader of the worldwide Roman Catholic Church.

Potlatch Ceremony: A diverse, complex series of ceremonies practiced by the Native Peoples of the northwest coast of North America. Their central function is to maintain balance and harmony among one's community. It generally consists of a community feast during which the host, typically a family, presents gifts to guests and also reenacts the family's oral history from mythic times to the present.

Prasad ("prah-SAHD"): [Gurmukhi] The sweet pudding served toward the end of a Sikh service that consists of water, honey, wheat flour, and clarified butter. Prasad is considered to be a blessing from the *Siri Guru Granth Sahib* that everyone can eat.

Prasad ("PRAH-sahd"): [Sanskrit] In Hinduism, sacramental food served to those present at certain rituals and ceremonies.

Prokimenon ("Proh-KEE-min-non"): [Greek] Used in the Orthodox churches; means "offertory."

Proskomen ("PROS-koh-men"): [Greek] Used in the Orthodox churches; means "Let us attend."

Puja ("POO-jah"): [Sanskrit] In Hinduism, a ritual worship held before a specific deity.

Qiblah ("KIHB-lah"): [Arabic] In Islam, the direction to which the imam, or prayer leader, faces while praying.

Qur'an ("koo-RAHN"): [Arabic] Islam's holy book, also known as *The Recitation*. Consists of 114 chapters or suras and a total of 6,000 verses. Divinely revealed to the Prophet Muhammad during the 22 years from 610 to 632 C.E.

Raka'ah ("RAH-kah"): [Arabic] In Islam, a way to "greet" and honor the mosque upon entering it. A full *raka'ah* consists of recitations during which one first stands, then makes one bow, followed by two prostrating motions (separated by a short sitting). Each prayer time requires a specific number of *raka'ah*.

Ramakrishna, Sri: (1836–1886) A great Hindu saint of Bengal, inspiration for the founding of the Ramakrishna Order, and source of the modern renaissance of Vedanta.

The Rapture: The "catching away" of believers by the Lord upon the return of Jesus Christ.

Regeneration: Also known as "born again." Occurs when a person has fully accepted Jesus Christ as savior.

Requiem: All or part of a Christian funeral service. In the Episcopal Church, if a funeral service is part of a larger service, it is called a requiem.

Sacrament Meeting: Mormons' term for their basic service.

Sacred Circle: A symbolic representation of many Native Peoples' conception of the world and life. It captures ecological cycles of life and death and represents one's journey along the path of life.

Sacred Sites: Sites that Native Peoples recognize as being imbued with a specific or special aspect of the sacred.

Salvation: Also known as *saved* and *born again*. Different terms for accepting Christ as one's savior and his teachings as guiding principles.

Samsara ("SAHM-sah-rah"): [Sanskrit] In Buddhism and Hinduism, recurrent birth-and-death from which one is finally liberated.

Sanctification: Pentecostal doctrine in which holiness is considered to be a progressive work of God's grace beginning with regeneration.

Sangat ("SAHN-gaht"): [Gurmukhi] The congregation of Sikhs and guests who come together for a Sikh worship service.

Sat Nam ("SAHT NAHM"): [Gurmukhi] A common phrase and greeting among Sikhs that means "True Name" and acknowledges the God in all.

Seder ("SAY-dihr"): [Hebrew] The festive dinner during the Jewish holiday of Passover during which the story of the Jewish people's liberation from slavery in Egypt is told. Rituals precede and follow the meal.

Shabbat ("shah-BAHT"): [Hebrew] The Jewish word for "Sabbath." Commemorates the day on which God rested after creating the world during the previous six days. *Shabbat* begins at sundown on Friday and ends at sundown on Saturday.

Shahadah ("SHAH-hah-dah"): [Arabic] The Islamic Declaration of Faith. One becomes a Muslim by saying and believing the *shahadah:* "There is no god but God and Muhammad is the messenger of God."

Shiva ("SHIH-vah"): [Hebrew] The seven days immediately after the burial of a family member during which Jews sit in mourning.

Shoghi Effendi ("SHOW-gey Eh-FEN-dee"): The grandson of 'Abdu'l-Bahá, who was the founder of the Bahá'í Faith. Shoghi Effendi was also called "the Guardian."

Shraddha ("SHRAD-dah"): [Sanskrit] A Hindu ceremony, held 10 to 30 days after death, intended to liberate the soul of the deceased for its ascent to heaven.

Siri Guru Granth Sahib: [Gurmukhi] Scriptures compiled by the fifth Sikh guru, Arjan Dev, which contain sacred writings by several Sikh gurus and Hindu and Moslem saints. Since then, Sikhs have bowed before the *Siri Guru Granth Sahib,* consulted it as their only guru, and treated it with reverence.

Speaking in Tongues: Speaking in a language unknown to those speaking it, a phenomenon associated with the coming of the Holy Spirit (the empowering quality of God) and common to Pentecostal faiths.

Sri: Literally, blessed, holy. A prefix commonly attached to the names of male religious leaders in India.

Stomp Dances: A common style of dance with Native tribes that are originally from the southeastern United States. The primary rhythm is provided by singing, the use of gourds rattled by men, and turtle shells that are filled with pebbles and tied to women's legs.

Sun Dance Ceremony: The most important annual religious ceremony for about thirty Plains tribes. Its meaning varies somewhat from tribe to tribe, but it is basically a test of courage and a demonstration of personal sacrifice. During the three-day ceremony, men undergo "piercing," or being suspended from a sacred pole by skewers of wood inserted into their chests.

Sweat Lodge Ceremony: A ceremony common to many Native religions. Its functions vary from tribe to tribe, but it is generally intended to provide purification and healing and to restore balance in one's life.

Theotokos ("Thee-oh-TOH-kohs"): [Greek] Used in the Orthodox churches; means "Mother of God."

Torah ("TOH-rah"): [Hebrew] Most commonly used to refer to the scroll of the Five Books of Moses, but its broader meaning includes the full body of rabbinic contributions to Judaism.

Upanishads: Hindu scriptures.

Wadu ("WAH-doo"): [Arabic] In Islam, ablutions of the hands, face and feet performed before prayer.

Williams, Rowan: (1950–) The current Archbishop of Canterbury, the symbolic head of the Church of England and the Anglican Communion (although with little real power to instruct dioceses other than his own).

Wisdom Keepers: Also known as Elders. Living repositories of Native Americans' traditional wisdom, ceremonial practices and customs. The title does not necessarily imply old age, for the title is earned through extensive training and practice.

Yahrzeit ("YAHR-tzite"): [Yiddish] In Judaism, the yearly anniversary of the death of a member of the immediate family. Upon the *yahrzeit,* a wife, husband and/or children attend services at synagogue and light a *yahrzeit* candle at home.

Yoga ("YOH-gah"): [Sanskrit] Specific disciplines in Hinduism to achieve enlightenment that address the intellect, emotions and labor and service to others.

The Meanings of Popular Religious Symbols of Major Traditions

 Arabic calligraphic writing of the name of God, "Allah."

 Bahá'í "ringstone" (a symbol often worn on a finger ring). The two stars represent The Báb and the Bahá'u'lláh, the founder and most important prophet of the Bahá'í Faith.

 Bahá'í star, always nine-pointed. Nine is a sacred number in the Bahá'í Faith; as the highest single number it is considered perfect.

 Buddhist *enso,* always hand-drawn with one brush stroke. Symbolizes timelessness and enlightenment.

 Buddha's foot, symbolizing his teachings and divine human, or buddha, nature.

 Celtic Christian symbol of the Trinity, or God in three persons (God the Father, Jesus Christ, and Holy Spirit).

 Celtic cross, which combines the traditional Christian cross with a circle symbolizing eternity.

Chakras, energy centers throughout the body. Common in many Eastern religious and healing traditions, most of all in Hinduism.

Chi-ro, early Christian symbol for Christ. *Chi* and *ro* are the first two letters in Christ's name in Greek. Roman Emperor Constantine said that he saw this symbol before him in 312 C.E. in battle and credited it with his victory. Afterward, Constantine converted to Christianity and brought it to the Empire.

Christian fish symbol, representing Jesus as the "fisher of men," according to the Christian gospels. Like many religious symbols, this one has pagan origins.

Crescent and star, the most visible symbol for Islam, but without doctrinal or sacred meaning for Muslims. The five points of the star are often said to symbolize the five pillars, or essential elements, of Islam, and the moon may symbolize time, or the importance of the seasons of the calendar, in Muslim life.

Cross and flame, a combined symbol of the United Methodist Church in America. The cross symbolizes Jesus Christ, and the flame represents the Holy Spirit who gives all spiritual gifts.

Dancing Shiva, one of the principal deities of Hinduism, together with Brahma and Vishnu, forms the trinity of Hinduism. Symbolizes the Divine balancing between creation and destruction.

Dharma wheel, each spoke represents one aspect of Buddhist commitment (known as "The Eightfold Path"): Right faith, right intention, right speech, right action, right livelihood, right endeavor, right mindfulness, and right meditation.

Dove, symbolic of the presence of the Holy Spirit, the third person of the Trinity, in Christianity.

Kirpan, a ceremonial dagger for fighting oppression. A symbol, not a weapon, sometimes worn more as jewelry is worn, other times as a traditional sword or dagger in a sheath at the waist.

Menorah, an ancient symbol of Judaism. The Hanukkah menorah (nine lights) is an adaptation of the Temple menorah (seven lights). The Temple menorah's seven branches symbolize the Tree of Life in the Garden of Eden and the seven days of creation.

Star of David, symbol of the Jewish faith. Possibly originated with King David, hence the other name for it: Magen David (shield of David, i.e., God). Always represented as two interlocking triangles (with overlapping lines), not simply as a six-pointed star, which is a hexagram.

The Three Jewels of Buddhism, the Buddha, the Dharma (teachings), and the Sangha (the community of practitioners).

The Tree of Life, the primary symbol of Kabbalah in Jewish mysticism. Each circle represents one of ten *sefirot,* or aspects of God's personality.

Om, in Hinduism and other Eastern traditions, the most sacred sound in the universe, the first sound, and a symbol for unity with the Divine.

Calendar of
Religious Holidays and Festivals

The Gregorian calendar, in use throughout the world, was first introduced in 1582 by Pope Gregory XIII as a corrected form of the old Julian calendar.

The Hindu calendar is lunisolar and governs Hindu religious life and almost all Indian festivals.

The Jewish calendar is the official calendar of the Jewish religious community and is used to mark the dates of annual religious events and holidays.

The Muslim calendar is the official calendar in many Muslim countries, and is used throughout the Islamic world to mark religious events and festivals.

The following chart describes the basic structure of these calendars. Each list begins with the first month of the year.

GREGORIAN

The solar year of the Gregorian calendar consists of 365 days, except in a leap year—occuring every four years, in an even-numbered year—which has 366 days. (Centenary years are leap years only if they are evenly divisible by 400.)

Month	Number of Days
January	31
February	28
in leap year	29
March	31
April	30
May	31
June	30
July	31
August	31

September 30
October 31
November 30
December 31

HINDU

In the Hindu calendar, the solar year is divided into 12 lunar months in accordance with the successive entrances of the sun into the signs of the zodiac; the months vary in length from 29 to 32 days. An intercalary month is inserted after every month in which two new moons occur (once in three years), and this intercalary month has the name of the month that precedes it. The months correspond approximately to the Gregorian months shown in parentheses in this chart.

Months

Chai (March–April)
Baisakh (April–May)
Jeth (May–June)
Asarh (June–July)
Sawan (July–August)
Bhadon (August–September)
Asin (September–October)
Kartik (October–November)
Aghan (November–December)
Pus (December–January)
Magh (January–February)
Phagun (February–March)

JEWISH

The Jewish calendar is based on both the solar and the lunar cycles. The lunar year, averaging 354 days, is adjusted to the solar year by periodic leap years, occuring approximately once every three years, which contain an intercalary month and ensure that the major religious holidays fall in the proper season. The months correspond approximately to the Gregorian months shown in parentheses in this chart.

Month	Number of Days
Tishrei (September–October)	30
Chesvan (October–November)	29
in some years	30

Kislev (November–December) 29
  in some years 30
Tevet (December–January) 29
Shevat (January–February) 30
Adar (February–March) 29
  in some years 30
Adar II 29
  (intercalary month
  in leap year only)
Nisan (March–April) 30
Iyar (April–May) 29
Sivan (May–June) 30
Tammuz (June–July) 29
Av (July–August) 30
Elul (August–September).............29

MUSLIM

The Muslim calendar is based on the lunar year. Each year consists of 354 days or 355 days (in leap years). The number of days per month is adjusted throughout the year, in accordance with each lunar cycle. The beginning of the Muslim year retrogresses through the solar year; it completes a full cycle every $32^{1}/_{2}$ years.

Month	Number of Days
Muharram	29 or 30
Safar	29 or 30
Rabi I	29 or 30
Rabi II	29 or 30
Jumada I	29 or 30
Jumada II	29 or 30
Rajab	29 or 30
Sha'ban	29 or 30
Ramadan	29 or 30
Shawwal	29 or 30
Dhu al-Qa'dah	29 or 30
Dhu al-Hijjah	29 or 30

The following list presents the dates, on the Gregorian calendar, of major religious holidays and festivals of Buddhists, Christians, Hindus, Jews, Muslims, Bahá'ís and Sikhs.

Since, in the Muslim calendar, the actual beginning of the new month is determined by the appearance of the new moon, the Gregorian dates given here may vary slightly.

All Jewish holidays and festivals begin at sundown the evening before the date shown and conclude at nightfall on the last day.

In Orthodox churches that use the old Julian calendar, observances are held 13 days later than the dates that are listed below.

B: Buddhist

Ba: Bahá'í Faith

H: Hindu

J: Jewish

M: Muslim

O: Orthodox churches (Christian)

S: Sikh

W: Western churches (Christian)

Religious Holiday/Festival	2011	2012	2013
New Year's Day (B, O, W)	Jan. 1	Jan. 1	Jan. 1
Birth of Guru Gobind Singh (S)	Jan. 5	Jan. 5	Jan. 5
Christmas (O—Armenian)	Jan. 6	Jan. 6	Jan. 6
Epiphany (O, W—Roman Catholic, Episcopalian/ Anglican, Lutheran)	Jan. 6	Jan. 6	Jan. 6
World Religion Day (Ba)	Jan. 16	Jan. 15	Jan. 20
Birth of Guru Har Rai (S)	Jan. 31	Jan. 31	Jan. 31
Nirvana Day (B)	Feb. 15	Feb. 15	Feb. 15
Mawlid al-Nabi (M)	Feb. 15	Feb. 4	Jan. 24
Ayyám-i-Há/Days of Ha (Ba)	Feb. 26	Feb. 26	Feb. 26
Shiva Ratri (H)	Mar. 3	Feb. 20	Mar. 10
Ash Wednesday (W)	Mar. 9	Feb. 22	Feb. 13
Lent begins (O)	Mar. 13	Feb. 26	Feb. 17
Purim (J)	Mar. 20	Mar. 8	Feb. 24
Naw-Rúz (Ba)	Mar. 21	Mar. 21	Mar. 21
Annunciation (Christian)	Mar. 25	Mar. 25	Mar. 25
Hanamatsuri/Buddha Day (B)	Apr. 8	Apr. 8	Apr. 8

Religious Holiday/Festival	2011	2012	2013
Rama Navami (H)	Apr. 12	Apr. 1	Apr. 20
Palm Sunday (O)	Apr. 17	Apr. 8	Apr. 28
Palm Sunday (W)	Apr. 17	Apr. 1	Mar. 24
Birth of Guru Angad (S)	Apr. 18	Apr. 18	Apr. 18
Birth of Guru Teg Bahadur (S)	Apr. 18	Apr. 18	Apr. 18
First Day of Passover (J)	Apr. 19	Apr. 7	Mar. 26
First Day of Festival of Ridván (Ba)	Apr. 21	Apr. 21	Apr. 21
Holy Thursday (O)	Apr. 21	Apr. 12	May 2
Holy Thursday (W)	Apr. 21	Apr. 5	Mar. 28
Holy (Good) Friday (O)	Apr. 22	Apr. 13	May 3
Good Friday (W)	Apr. 22	Apr. 6	Mar. 29
Easter (Pascha) (O)	Apr. 24	Apr. 15	May 5
Easter (W)	Apr. 24	Apr. 8	Mar. 21
Birth of Guru Arjan (S)	May 2	May 2	May 2
Birth of Guru Amar Das (S)	May 23	May 23	May 23
Declaration of The Báb (Ba)	May 23	May 23	May 23
Ascension Day (W)	June 2	May 17	May 9
Ascension Day (O)	June 2	May 24	June 13
First Day of Shavuot (J)	June 8	May 27	May 15
Pentecost (W)	June 12	May 27	May 19
Race Unity Day (Ba)	June 12	June 10	June 9
Pentecost (O)	June 12	June 3	June 23
Summer Solstice	June 21	June 20	June 21
Birth of Guru Hargobind (S)	July 5	July 5	July 5
Martyrdom of The Báb (Ba)	July 9	July 9	July 9
Birth of Guru Har Krishnan (S)	July 23	July 23	July 23
First Day of the Month of Ramadan (M)	Aug. 1	July 20	July 9
Krishna Janmashtami (H)	Aug. 22	Aug. 10	Aug. 28
Id al-Fitr (M)	Aug. 30	Aug. 19	Aug. 8
Buddhist Churches of America Founding Day (B)	Sept. 1	Sept. 1	Sept. 1
Holy Cross Day (O, W—Roman Catholic, Episcopalian/Anglican, Lutheran)	Sept. 14	Sept. 14	Sept. 14

Religious Holiday/Festival	2011	2012	2013
First Day of Rosh Hashanah (J)	Sept. 29	Sept. 17	Sept. 5
Yom Kippur (J)	Oct. 8	Sept. 26	Sept. 14
Birth of Guru Ram Das (S)	Oct. 9	Oct. 9	Oct. 9
Thanksgiving (Canada)	Oct. 10	Oct. 8	Oct. 14
First Day of Sukkot (J)	Oct. 13	Oct. 1	Sept. 19
Birth of The Báb (Ba)	Oct. 20	Oct. 20	Oct. 20
Shemini Atzeret (J)	Oct. 20	Oct. 8	Sept. 26
Simchat Torah (J)	Oct. 21	Oct. 9	Sept. 27
Reformation Sunday (W—Lutheran)	Oct. 30	Oct. 28	Oct. 27
Reformation Day (W—Lutheran)	Oct. 31	Oct. 31	Oct. 31
Duhsehra/Durga Puja (H)	Nov. 6	Oct. 24	Oct. 14
Id al-Adha (M)	Nov. 6	Oct. 26	Oct. 15
Birth of Bahá'u'lláh (Ba)	Nov. 12	Nov. 12	Nov. 12
Birth of Guru Nanak (S)	Nov. 23	Nov. 23	Nov. 23
Thanksgiving (United States)	Nov. 23	Nov. 22	Nov. 27
The Day of the Covenant (Ba)	Nov. 26	Nov. 26	Nov. 26
First Day of the Month of Muharram (M)	Nov. 26	Nov. 15	Nov. 4
First Sunday of Advent (O, W)	Nov. 27	Dec. 2	Dec. 1
Bodhi Day (B)	Dec. 8	Dec. 8	Dec. 8
First Day of Chanukah (J)	Dec. 21	Dec. 9	Nov. 28
Winter Solstice	Dec. 22	Dec. 21	Dec. 21
Christmas Eve (W)	Dec. 24	Dec. 24	Dec. 24
Christmas (O, except Armenian; W)	Dec. 25	Dec. 25	Dec. 25

Summary of Proper Forms for Addressing Leaders of Various Faiths

When you are introduced to the spiritual leader, member of the clergy or officiator of the religious ceremony that you are attending, what do you say after "I am so pleased to meet you—"? Most leaders of congregations or other religious groups are very understanding and sympathetic about visitors' confusion over what form of address to use, but checking this list will give you a head start.

African American Methodist churches: "Pastor" or "Reverend" followed by last name

Assemblies of God: "Pastor" or "Reverend" followed by last name

Bahá'í Faith: There are no clergy

Baptist: "Pastor" or "Reverend" followed by last name

Buddhist: "Reverend," "Lama" or "Roshi"

Christian Church (Disciples of Christ): "Pastor" or "Reverend" followed by last name

Christian Science (Church of Christ, Scientist): There are no clergy

Churches of Christ: "Mr.," "Mrs." or "Ms." followed by last name

Episcopalian and Anglican: "Mr.," "Mrs.," "Ms." or "Miss" followed by last name is sufficient; "Reverend" in more formal situations

Hindu: "Swamiji" if a monk, "Panditji" if a priest

Islam: "Imam" or the imam's name

Jehovah's Witnesses: "Brother" or "Mr." followed by last name

Jewish: "Rabbi" or "Cantor" followed by last name

Lutheran: "Pastor" followed by last name

Mennonite/Amish: "Pastor" followed by last name

Methodist: "Pastor" or "Reverend" followed by last name

Mormon (Church of Jesus Christ of Latter-day Saints): "Bishop" followed by last name; for the bishop's counselors, "Brother" followed by last name

Native American/First Nations: "Mr.," "Mrs." or "Ms." followed by last name

Orthodox churches: "Father" followed by last name

Pentecostal Church of God: "Pastor," "Minister" or "Brother" followed by last name

Presbyterian: "Reverend" followed by last name; in Canada, "Mr.," "Mrs." or "Ms." followed by last name

Quaker (Religious Society of Friends): There are no clergy

Reformed Church in America/Canada: "Pastor" or "Reverend" followed by last name

Roman Catholic: "Father" followed by last name; for a monsignor, "Monsignor" followed by last name; for a bishop or archbishop, "Your Excellency"; for a cardinal, "Your Eminence"

Seventh-day Adventist: "Elder" or "Pastor" followed by last name

Sikh: "Granthi" followed by first name or "Giani Ji"

Unitarian Universalist: "Mr.," "Ms.," "Dr." or "Reverend" followed by last name, or informally by first name

United Church of Canada: "Mr.," "Mrs." or "Ms." followed by last name, or informally by first name

United Church of Christ: "Pastor," "Mr.," "Mrs.," "Ms." or "Dr.," followed by last name, or informally by first name

AVAILABLE FROM BETTER BOOKSTORES.
TRY YOUR BOOKSTORE FIRST.

Bible Stories / Folktales

Abraham's Bind & Other Bible Tales of Trickery, Folly, Mercy and Love *by Michael J. Caduto*
New retellings of episodes in the lives of familiar biblical characters explore relevant life lessons.   6 x 9, 224 pp, HC, 978-1-59473-186-0 **$19.99**

Daughters of the Desert: Stories of Remarkable Women from Christian, Jewish and Muslim Traditions *by Claire Rudolf Murphy,*
Meghan Nuttall Sayres, Mary Cronk Farrell, Sarah Conover and Betsy Wharton
Breathes new life into the old tales of our female ancestors in faith. Uses traditional scriptural passages as starting points, then with vivid detail fills in historical context and place. Chapters reveal the voices of Sarah, Hagar, Huldah, Esther, Salome, Mary Magdalene, Lydia, Khadija, Fatima and many more. Historical fiction ideal for readers of all ages.
5½ x 8½, 192 pp, Quality PB, 978-1-59473-106-8 **$14.99**   Inc. reader's discussion guide
HC, 978-1-893361-72-0 **$19.95**

The Triumph of Eve & Other Subversive Bible Tales
by Matt Biers-Ariel
These engaging retellings of familiar Bible stories are witty, often hilarious and always profound. They invite you to grapple with questions and issues that are often hidden in the original texts.
5½ x 8½, 192 pp, Quality PB, 978-1-59473-176-1 **$14.99**

Also available: **The Triumph of Eve Teacher's Guide**
8½ x 11, 44 pp, PB, 978-1-59473-152-5 **$8.99**

Wisdom in the Telling
Finding Inspiration and Grace in Traditional Folktales and Myths Retold
by Lorraine Hartin-Gelardi
6 x 9, 192 pp, HC, 978-1-59473-185-3 **$19.99**

Religious Etiquette / Reference

How to Be a Perfect Stranger, 5th Edition: The Essential Religious Etiquette Handbook *Edited by Stuart M. Matlins and Arthur J. Magida*
The indispensable guidebook to help the well-meaning guest when visiting other people's religious ceremonies.
6 x 9, 432 pp, Quality PB, 978-1-59473-294-2 **$19.99**

The Perfect Stranger's Guide to Funerals and Grieving Practices: A Guide to Etiquette in Other People's Religious Ceremonies *Edited by Stuart M. Matlins*
6 x 9, 240 pp, Quality PB, 978-1-893361-20-1 **$16.95**

The Perfect Stranger's Guide to Wedding Ceremonies: A Guide to Etiquette in Other People's Religious Ceremonies *Edited by Stuart M. Matlins*
6 x 9, 208 pp, Quality PB, 978-1-893361-19-5 **$16.95**

Or phone, fax, mail or e-mail to: SKYLIGHT PATHS Publishing
Sunset Farm Offices, Route 4 • P.O. Box 237 • Woodstock, Vermont 05091
Tel: (802) 457-4000 • Fax: (802) 457-4004 • www.skylightpaths.com
Credit card orders: (800) 962-4544 (8:30AM–5:30PM ET Monday–Friday)
Generous discounts on quantity orders. SATISFACTION GUARANTEED. Prices subject to change.

Children's Spirituality

ENDORSED BY CATHOLIC, PROTESTANT, JEWISH, AND BUDDHIST RELIGIOUS LEADERS

Remembering My Grandparent: A Kid's Own Grief Workbook in the Christian Tradition *by Nechama Liss-Levinson, PhD, and Rev. Molly Phinney Baskette, MDiv* 8 x 10, 48 pp, 2-color text, HC, 978-1-59473-212-6 **$16.99** *For ages 7 & up*

Does God Ever Sleep? *by Joan Sauro, CSJ*
A charming nighttime reminder that God is always present in our lives.
10 x 8½, 32 pp, Full-color photos, Quality PB, 978-1-59473-110-5 **$8.99** *For ages 3–6*

Does God Forgive Me? *by August Gold; Full-color photos by Diane Hardy Waller*
Gently shows how God forgives all that we do if we are truly sorry.
10 x 8½, 32 pp, Full-color photos, Quality PB, 978-1-59473-142-6 **$8.99** *For ages 3–6*

God Said Amen *by Sandy Eisenberg Sasso; Full-color illus. by Avi Katz*
A warm and inspiring tale that shows us that we need only reach out to each other to find the answers to our prayers.
9 x 12, 32 pp, Full-color illus., HC, 978-1-58023-080-3 **$16.95*** *For ages 4 & up*

How Does God Listen? *by Kay Lindahl; Full-color photos by Cynthia Maloney*
How do we know when God is listening to us? Children will find the answers to these questions as they engage their senses while the story unfolds, learning how God listens in the wind, waves, clouds, hot chocolate, perfume, our tears and our laughter.
10 x 8½, 32 pp, Full-color photos, Quality PB, 978-1-59473-084-9 **$8.99** *For ages 3–6*

In God's Hands *by Lawrence Kushner and Gary Schmidt; Full-color illus. by Matthew J. Baek*
9 x 12, 32 pp, Full-color illus., HC, 978-1-58023-224-1 **$16.99*** *For ages 5 & up*

In God's Name *by Sandy Eisenberg Sasso; Full-color illus. by Phoebe Stone*
Like an ancient myth in its poetic text and vibrant illustrations, this award-winning modern fable about the search for God's name celebrates the diversity and, at the same time, the unity of all the people of the world.
9 x 12, 32 pp, Full-color illus., HC, 978-1-879045-26-2 **$16.99*** *For ages 4 & up*

Also available in Spanish: El nombre de Dios
9 x 12, 32 pp, Full-color illus., HC, 978-1-893361-63-8 **$16.95**

In Our Image: God's First Creatures
by Nancy Sohn Swartz; Full-color illus. by Melanie Hall
A playful new twist on the Genesis story—from the perspective of the animals. Celebrates the interconnectedness of nature and the harmony of all living things.
9 x 12, 32 pp, Full-color illus., HC, 978-1-879045-99-6 **$16.95*** *For ages 4 & up*

Noah's Wife: The Story of Naamah
by Sandy Eisenberg Sasso; Full-color illus. by Bethanne Andersen
Opens young readers' religious imaginations to new ideas about the well-known story of the Flood. When God tells Noah to bring the animals of the world onto the ark, God also calls on Naamah, Noah's wife, to save each plant on Earth.
9 x 12, 32 pp, Full-color illus., HC, 978-1-58023-134-3 **$16.95*** *For ages 4 & up*

Also available: Naamah: Noah's Wife (A Board Book)
by Sandy Eisenberg Sasso; Full-color illus. by Bethanne Andersen
5 x 5, 24 pp, Full-color illus., Board Book, 978-1-893361-56-0 **$7.95** *For ages 0–4*

Where Does God Live? *by August Gold and Matthew J. Perlman*
Helps children and their parents find God in the world around us with simple, practical examples children can relate to.
10 x 8½, 32 pp, Full-color photos, Quality PB, 978-1-893361-39-3 **$8.99** *For ages 3–6*

* A book from Jewish Lights, SkyLight Paths' sister imprint

Children's Spirituality—Board Books

Adam & Eve's New Day
by Sandy Eisenberg Sasso; Full-color illus. by Joani Keller Rothenberg
A lesson in hope for every child who has worried about what comes next.
Abridged from *Adam & Eve's First Sunset.*
5 x 5, 24 pp, Full-color illus., Board Book, 978-1-59473-205-8 **$7.99** *For ages 0–4*

How Did the Animals Help God?
by Nancy Sohn Swartz; Full-color illus. by Melanie Hall
God asks all of nature to offer gifts to humankind—with a promise that they will
care for creation in return. Abridged from *In Our Image.*
5 x 5, 24 pp, Full-color illus., Board Book, 978-1-59473-044-3 **$7.99** *For ages 0–4*

How Does God Make Things Happen?
by Lawrence and Karen Kushner; Full-color illus. by Dawn W. Majewski
A charming invitation for young children to explore how God makes things happen
in our world. Abridged from *Because Nothing Looks Like God.*
5 x 5, 24 pp, Full-color illus., Board Book, 978-1-893361-24-9 **$7.95** *For ages 0–4*

What Does God Look Like?
by Lawrence and Karen Kushner; Full-color illus. by Dawn W. Majewski
A simple way for young children to explore the ways that we "see" God.
Abridged from *Because Nothing Looks Like God.*
5 x 5, 24 pp, Full-color illus., Board Book, 978-1-893361-23-2 **$7.99** *For ages 0–4*

What Is God's Name?
by Sandy Eisenberg Sasso; Full-color illus. by Phoebe Stone
Everyone and everything in the world has a name. What is God's name?
Abridged from the award-winning *In God's Name.*
5 x 5, 24 pp, Full-color illus., Board Book, 978-1-893361-10-2 **$7.99** *For ages 0–4*

Where Is God? *by Lawrence and Karen Kushner; Full-color illus. by*
Dawn W. Majewski A gentle way for young children to explore how God is
with us every day, in every way. Abridged from *Because Nothing Looks Like
God.*
5 x 5, 24 pp, Full-color illus., Board Book, 978-1-893361-17-1 **$7.99** *For ages 0–4*

What You Will See Inside ...

Fun-to-read books with vibrant full-color photos show children ages
6 and up the who, what, when, where, why and how of traditional
houses of worship, liturgical celebrations and rituals of different
world faiths, empowering them to respect and understand their own
religious traditions—and those of their friends and neighbors.

What You Will See Inside a Catholic Church
by Rev. Michael Keane; Foreword by Robert J. Kealey, EdD
Full-color photos by Aaron Pepis
8½ x 10¼, 32 pp, Full-color photos, HC, 978-1-893361-54-6 **$17.95**

Also available in Spanish: **Lo que se puede ver dentro de una iglesia católica**
8½ x 10¼, 32 pp, Full-color photos, HC, 978-1-893361-66-9 **$16.95**

What You Will See Inside a Hindu Temple
by Mahendra Jani, PhD, and Vandana Jani, PhD; Full-color photos by Neirah Bhargava and Vijay Dave
8½ x 10¼, 32 pp, Full-color photos, HC, 978-1-59473-116-7 **$17.99**

What You Will See Inside a Mosque
by Aisha Karen Khan; Full-color photos by Aaron Pepis
8½ x 10¼, 32 pp, Full-color photos, Quality PB, 978-1-59473-257-7 **$8.99**

What You Will See Inside a Synagogue
by Rabbi Lawrence A. Hoffman, PhD, and Dr. Ron Wolfson; Full-color photos by Bill Aron
8½ x 10¼, 32 pp, Full-color photos, Quality PB, 978-1-59473-256-0 **$8.99**

Judaism / Christianity / Islam / Interfaith

Getting to the Heart of Interfaith
The Eye-Opening, Hope-Filled Friendship of a Pastor, a Rabbi and a Sheikh
by Pastor Don Mackenzie, Rabbi Ted Falcon and Sheikh Jamal Rahman
Offers many insights and encouragements for individuals and groups who want to tap into the promise of interfaith dialogue. 6 x 9, 192 pp, Quality PB, 978-1-59473-263-8 **$16.99**

Hearing the Call across Traditions: Readings on Faith and Service
Edited by Adam Davis; Foreword by Eboo Patel Explores the connections between faith, service and social justice through the prose, verse and sacred texts of the world's great faith traditions. 6 x 9, 352 pp, HC, 978-1-59473-264-5 **$29.99**

How to Do Good & Avoid Evil: A Global Ethic from the Sources of
Judaism *by Hans Küng and Rabbi Walter Homolka; Translated by Rev. Dr. John Bowden*
Explores how Judaism's ethical principles can help all religions work together toward a more peaceful humankind. 6 x 9, 224 pp, HC, 978-1-59473-255-3 **$19.99**

Blessed Relief: What Christians Can Learn from Buddhists about Suffering
by Gordon Peerman 6 x 9, 208 pp, Quality PB, 978-1-59473-252-2 **$16.99**

The Changing Christian World: A Brief Introduction for Jews
by Rabbi Leonard A. Schoolman 5½ x 8½, 176 pp, Quality PB, 978-1-58023-344-6 **$16.99***

Christians & Jews in Dialogue: Learning in the Presence of the Other *by Mary C. Boys and Sara S. Lee; Foreword by Dorothy C. Bass* 6 x 9, 240 pp, Quality PB, 978-1-59473-254-6 **$18.99**; HC, 978-1-59473-144-0 **$21.99**

Disaster Spiritual Care: Practical Clergy Responses to Community, Regional and National Tragedy *Edited by Rabbi Stephen B. Roberts, BCJC, and Rev. Willard W.C. Ashley, Sr., DMin, DH* 6 x 9, 384 pp, HC, 978-1-59473-240-9 **$40.00**

InterActive Faith: The Essential Interreligious Community-Building Handbook
Edited by Rev. Bud Heckman with Rori Picker Neiss; Foreword by Rev. Dirk Ficca
6 x 9, 304 pp, Quality PB, 978-1-59473-273-7 **$16.99**; HC, 978-1-59473-237-9 **$29.99**

The Jewish Approach to God: A Brief Introduction for Christians
by Rabbi Neil Gillman, PhD 5½ x 8½, 192 pp, Quality PB, 978-1-58023-190-9 **$16.95***

The Jewish Approach to Repairing the World (*Tikkun Olam*): A Brief Introduction for Christians *by Rabbi Elliot N. Dorff, PhD, with Rev. Cory Willson*
5½ x 8½, 256 pp, Quality PB, 978-1-58023-349-1 **$16.99***

The Jewish Connection to Israel, the Promised Land: A Brief Introduction for Christians *by Rabbi Eugene Korn, PhD* 5½ x 8½, 192 pp, Quality PB, 978-1-58023-318-7 **$14.99***

Jewish Holidays: A Brief Introduction for Christians *by Rabbi Kerry M. Olitzky and Rabbi Daniel Judson* 5½ x 8½, 176 pp, Quality PB, 978-1-58023-302-6 **$16.99***

Jewish Ritual: A Brief Introduction for Christians
by Rabbi Kerry M. Olitzky and Rabbi Daniel Judson 5½ x 8½, 144 pp, Quality PB, 978-1-58023-210-4 **$14.99***

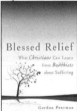

Jewish Spirituality: A Brief Introduction for Christians *by Rabbi Lawrence Kushner*
5½ x 8½, 112 pp, Quality PB, 978-1-58023-150-3 **$12.95***

A Jewish Understanding of the New Testament *by Rabbi Samuel Sandmel;*
New preface by Rabbi David Sandmel 5½ x 8½, 368 pp, Quality PB, 978-1-59473-048-1 **$19.99***

Modern Jews Engage the New Testament: Enhancing Jewish Well-Being in a Christian Environment *by Rabbi Michael J. Cook, PhD* 6 x 9, 416 pp, HC 978-1-58023-313-2 **$29.99***

Talking about God: Exploring the Meaning of Religious Life with Kierkegaard, Buber, Tillich and Heschel *by Daniel F. Polish, PhD* 6 x 9, 160 pp, Quality PB, 978-1-59473-272-0 **$16.99**

We Jews and Jesus: Exploring Theological Differences for Mutual Understanding
by Rabbi Samuel Sandmel; New preface by Rabbi David Sandmel
6 x 9, 192 pp, Quality PB, 978-1-59473-208-9 **$16.99**

Who Are the *Real* Chosen People? The Meaning of Chosenness in Judaism, Christianity and Islam *by Reuven Firestone, PhD*
6 x 9, 176 pp, Quality PB, 978-1-59473-290-4 **$16.99**

* A book from Jewish Lights, SkyLight Paths' sister imprint

Spirituality & Crafts

Beading—The Creative Spirit: Finding Your Sacred Center through the Art of Beadwork *by Rev. Wendy Ellsworth*
Invites you on a spiritual pilgrimage into the kaleidoscope world of glass and color. 7 x 9, 240 pp, 8-page color insert, 40+ b/w photos and 40 diagrams, Quality PB, 978-1-59473-267-6 **$18.99**

Contemplative Crochet: A Hands-On Guide for Interlocking Faith and Craft *by Cindy Crandall-Frazier; Foreword by Linda Skolnik*
Illuminates the spiritual lessons you can learn through crocheting.
7 x 9, 208 pp, b/w photos, Quality PB, 978-1-59473-238-6 **$16.99**

The Knitting Way: A Guide to Spiritual Self-Discovery
by Linda Skolnik and Janice MacDaniels Examines how you can explore and strengthen your spiritual life through knitting.
7 x 9, 240 pp, b/w photos, Quality PB, 978-1-59473-079-5 **$16.99**

The Painting Path: Embodying Spiritual Discovery through Yoga, Brush and Color *by Linda Novick; Foreword by Richard Segalman*
Explores the divine connection you can experience through art.
7 x 9, 208 pp, 8-page color insert, plus b/w photos,
Quality PB, 978-1-59473-226-3 **$18.99**

The Quilting Path: A Guide to Spiritual Discovery through Fabric, Thread and Kabbalah *by Louise Silk*
Explores how to cultivate personal growth through quilt making.
7 x 9, 192 pp, b/w photos and illus., Quality PB, 978-1-59473-206-5 **$16.99**

The Scrapbooking Journey: A Hands-On Guide to Spiritual Discovery
by Cory Richardson-Lauve; Foreword by Stacy Julian Reveals how this craft can become a practice used to deepen and shape your life.
7 x 9, 176 pp, 8-page color insert, plus b/w photos, Quality PB, 978-1-59473-216-4 **$18.99**

The Soulwork of Clay: A Hands-On Approach to Spirituality
by Marjory Zoet Bankson; Photos by Peter Bankson
Takes you through the seven-step process of making clay into a pot, drawing parallels at each stage to the process of spiritual growth.
7 x 9, 192 pp, b/w photos, Quality PB, 978-1-59473-249-2 **$16.99**

Kabbalah / Enneagram
(Books from Jewish Lights Publishing, SkyLight Paths' sister imprint)

Cast in God's Image: Discover Your Personality Type Using the Enneagram and Kabbalah
by Rabbi Howard A. Addison 7 x 9, 176 pp, Quality PB, 978-1-58023-124-4 **$16.95**

Ehyeh: A Kabbalah for Tomorrow *by Dr. Arthur Green*
6 x 9, 224 pp, Quality PB, 978-1-58023-213-5 **$16.99**

The Enneagram and Kabbalah, 2nd Edition: Reading Your Soul
by Rabbi Howard A. Addison 6 x 9, 192 pp, Quality PB, 978-1-58023-229-6 **$16.99**

The Gift of Kabbalah: Discovering the Secrets of Heaven, Renewing Your Life on Earth
by Tamar Frankiel, PhD 6 x 9, 256 pp, Quality PB, 978-1-58023-141-1 **$16.95**

God in Your Body: Kabbalah, Mindfulness and Embodied Spiritual Practice
by Jay Michaelson 6 x 9, 272 pp, Quality PB, 978-1-58023-304-0 **$18.99**

Kabbalah: A Brief Introduction for Christians
by Tamar Frankiel, PhD 5½ x 8½, 208 pp, Quality PB, 978-1-58023-303-3 **$16.99**

Zohar: Annotated & Explained *Translation & Annotation by Daniel C. Matt;*
Foreword by Andrew Harvey 5½ x 8½, 176 pp, Quality PB, 978-1-893361-51-5 **$15.99**

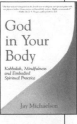

Prayer / Meditation

Sacred Attention: A Spiritual Practice for Finding God in the Moment
by Margaret D. McGee
Framed on the Christian liturgical year, this inspiring guide explores ways to develop a practice of attention as a means of talking—and listening—to God.
6 x 9, 144 pp, Quality PB, 978-1-59473-291-1 **$16.99**

Women Pray: Voices through the Ages, from Many Faiths, Cultures and Traditions
Edited and with Introductions by Monica Furlong
5 x 7¼, 256 pp, Quality PB, 978-1-59473-071-9 **$15.99**

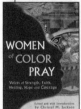

Women of Color Pray: Voices of Strength, Faith, Healing, Hope and Courage
Edited and with Introductions by Christal M. Jackson
Through these prayers, poetry, lyrics, meditations and affirmations, you will share in the strong and undeniable connection women of color share with God.
5 x 7¼, 208 pp, Quality PB, 978-1-59473-077-1 **$15.99**

Secrets of Prayer: A Multifaith Guide to Creating Personal Prayer in Your Life   *by Nancy Corcoran, CSJ*
This compelling, multifaith guidebook offers you companionship and encouragement on the journey to a healthy prayer life.   6 x 9, 160 pp, Quality PB, 978-1-59473-215-7 **$16.99**

Prayers to an Evolutionary God
by William Cleary; Afterword by Diarmuid O'Murchu
Inspired by the spiritual and scientific teachings of Diarmuid O'Murchu and Teilhard de Chardin, reveals that religion and science can be combined to create an expanding view of the universe—an evolutionary faith.
6 x 9, 208 pp, HC, 978-1-59473-006-1 **$21.99**

The Art of Public Prayer, 2nd Edition: Not for Clergy Only
by Lawrence A. Hoffman, PhD 6 x 9, 288 pp, Quality PB, 978-1-893361-06-5 **$19.99**

A Heart of Stillness: A Complete Guide to Learning the Art of Meditation
by David A. Cooper 5½ x 8½, 272 pp, Quality PB, 978-1-893361-03-4 **$18.99**

Meditation without Gurus: A Guide to the Heart of Practice
by Clark Strand 5½ x 8½, 192 pp, Quality PB, 978-1-893361-93-5 **$16.95**

Praying with Our Hands: 21 Practices of Embodied Prayer from the World's Spiritual Traditions *by Jon M. Sweeney; Photos by Jennifer J. Wilson; Foreword by Mother Tessa Bielecki; Afterword by Taitetsu Unno, PhD*
8 x 8, 96 pp, 22 duotone photos, Quality PB, 978-1-893361-16-4 **$16.95**

Three Gates to Meditation Practice: A Personal Journey into Sufism, Buddhism, and Judaism *by David A. Cooper* 5½ x 8½, 240 pp, Quality PB, 978-1-893361-22-5 **$16.95**

Prayer / M. Basil Pennington, OCSO

Finding Grace at the Center, 3rd Edition: The Beginning of Centering Prayer   *with Thomas Keating, OCSO, and Thomas E. Clarke, SJ; Foreword by Rev. Cynthia Bourgeault, PhD* A practical guide to a simple and beautiful form of meditative prayer. 5 x 7¼, 128 pp, Quality PB, 978-1-59473-182-2 **$12.99**

The Monks of Mount Athos: A Western Monk's Extraordinary Spiritual Journey on Eastern Holy Ground   *Foreword by Archimandrite Dionysios*
Explores the landscape, monastic communities and food of Athos.
6 x 9, 352 pp, Quality PB, 978-1-893361-78-2 **$18.95**

Psalms: A Spiritual Commentary   *Illus. by Phillip Ratner*
Reflections on some of the most beloved passages from the Bible's most widely read book.   6 x 9, 176 pp, 24 full-page b/w illus., Quality PB, 978-1-59473-234-8 **$16.99**

The Song of Songs: A Spiritual Commentary   *Illus. by Phillip Ratner*
Explore the Bible's most challenging mystical text.
6 x 9, 160 pp, 14 full-page b/w illus., Quality PB, 978-1-59473-235-5 **$16.99**
HC, 978-1-59473-004-7 **$19.99**

Women's Interest

New Feminist Christianity: Many Voices, Many Views
Edited by Mary E. Hunt and Diann L. Neu

Insights from ministers and theologians, activists and leaders, artists and liturgists who are shaping the future. Taken together, their voices offer a starting point for building new models of religious life and worship.
6 x 9, 384 pp, HC, 978-1-59473-285-0 **$24.99**

New Jewish Feminism: Probing the Past, Forging the Future
Edited by Rabbi Elyse Goldstein; Foreword by Anita Diamant

Looks at the growth and accomplishments of Jewish feminism and what they mean for Jewish women today and tomorrow. Features the voices of women from every area of Jewish life, addressing the important issues that concern Jewish women.
6 x 9, 480 pp, HC, 978-1-58023-359-0 **$24.99***

Dance—The Sacred Art: The Joy of Movement as a Spiritual Practice
by Cynthia Winton-Henry 5½ x 8½, 224 pp, Quality PB, 978-1-59473-268-3 **$16.99**

Daughters of the Desert: Stories of Remarkable Women from Christian, Jewish and Muslim Traditions
by Claire Rudolf Murphy, Meghan Nuttall Sayres, Mary Cronk Farrell, Sarah Conover and Betsy Wharton
5½ x 8½, 192 pp, Illus., Quality PB, 978-1-59473-106-8 **$14.99** Inc. reader's discussion guide
HC, 978-1-893361-72-0 **$19.95**

The Divine Feminine in Biblical Wisdom Literature
Selections Annotated & Explained
Translation & Annotation by Rabbi Rami Shapiro; Foreword by Rev. Cynthia Bourgeault, PhD
5½ x 8½, 240 pp, Quality PB, 978-1-59473-109-9 **$16.99**

Divining the Body: Reclaim the Holiness of Your Physical Self
by Jan Phillips 8 x 8, 256 pp, Quality PB, 978-1-59473-080-1 **$16.99**

Honoring Motherhood: Prayers, Ceremonies & Blessings
Edited and with Introductions by Lynn L. Caruso 5 x 7¼, 272 pp, HC, 978-1-59473-239-3 **$19.99**

ReVisions: Seeing Torah through a Feminist Lens
by Rabbi Elyse Goldstein 5½ x 8½, 224 pp, Quality PB, 978-1-58023-117-6 **$16.95***

The Triumph of Eve & Other Subversive Bible Tales
by Matt Biers-Ariel 5½ x 8½, 192 pp, Quality PB, 978-1-59473-176-1 **$14.99**

Also available: **The Triumph of Eve Teacher's Guide**
8½ x 11, 44 pp, PB, 978-1-59473-152-5 **$8.99**

White Fire: A Portrait of Women Spiritual Leaders in America
by Malka Drucker; Photos by Gay Block 7 x 10, 320 pp, b/w photos, HC, 978-1-893361-64-5 **$24.95**

Woman Spirit Awakening in Nature
Growing Into the Fullness of Who You Are
by Nancy Barrett Chickerneo, PhD; Foreword by Eileen Fisher
8 x 8, 224 pp, b/w illus., Quality PB, 978-1-59473-250-8 **$16.99**

Women of Color Pray: Voices of Strength, Faith, Healing, Hope and Courage
Edited and with Introductions by Christal M. Jackson
5 x 7¼, 208 pp, Quality PB, 978-1-59473-077-1 **$15.99**

Women Pray: Voices through the Ages, from Many Faiths, Cultures and Traditions
Edited and with Introductions by Monica Furlong
5 x 7¼, 256 pp, Quality PB, 978-1-59473-071-9 **$15.99**

The Women's Haftarah Commentary: New Insights from Women Rabbis on the 54 Weekly Haftarah Portions, the 5 Megillot & Special Shabbatot *Edited by Rabbi Elyse Goldstein*
6 x 9, 560 pp, Quality PB, 978-1-58023-371-2 **$19.99***

The Women's Torah Commentary: New Insights from Women Rabbis on the 54 Weekly Torah Portions *Edited by Rabbi Elyse Goldstein*
6 x 9, 496 pp, Quality PB, 978-1-58023-370-5 **$19.99**; HC, 978-1-58023-076-6 **$34.95***

* A book from Jewish Lights, SkyLight Paths' sister imprint

Spirituality

Creative Aging: Rethinking Retirement and Non-Retirement in a Changing World *by Marjory Zoet Bankson*
Offers creative ways to nourish our calling and discover meaning and purpose in our older years.   6 x 9, 160 pp, Quality PB, 978-1-59473-281-2 **$16.99**

Laugh Your Way to Grace: Reclaiming the Spiritual Power of Humor
by Rev. Susan Sparks A powerful, humorous case for laughter as a spiritual, healing path.   6 x 9, 176 pp, Quality PB, 978-1-59473-280-5 **$16.99**

Living into Hope: A Call to Spiritual Action for Such a Time as This
by Rev. Dr. Joan Brown Campbell; Foreword by Karen Armstrong
A visionary minister speaks out on the pressing issues that face us today, offering inspiration and challenge.   6 x 9, 144 pp (est), HC, 978-1-59473-283-6 **$21.99**

Claiming Earth as Common Ground: The Ecological Crisis through the Lens of Faith *by Andrea Cohen-Kiener; Foreword by Rev. Sally Bingham*
Inspires us to work across denominational lines in order to fulfill our sacred imperative to care for God's creation. 6 x 9, 192 pp, Quality PB, 978-1-59473-261-4 **$16.99**

Bread, Body, Spirit: Finding the Sacred in Food
Edited and with Introductions by Alice Peck 6 x 9, 224 pp, Quality PB, 978-1-59473-242-3 **$19.99**

Creating a Spiritual Retirement: A Guide to the Unseen Possibilities in Our Lives
by Molly Srode 6 x 9, 208 pp, b/w photos, Quality PB, 978-1-59473-050-4 **$14.99**

Finding Hope: Cultivating God's Gift of a Hopeful Spirit
by Marcia Ford; Foreword by Andrea Jaeger 8 x 8, 176 pp, Quality PB, 978-1-59473-211-9 **$16.99**

Hearing the Call across Traditions: Readings on Faith and Service
Edited by Adam Davis; Foreword by Eboo Patel 6 x 9, 352 pp, HC, 978-1-59473-264-5 **$29.99**

Honoring Motherhood: Prayers, Ceremonies & Blessings
Edited and with Introductions by Lynn L. Caruso 5 x 7¼, 272 pp, HC, 978-1-59473-239-3 **$19.99**

Journeys of Simplicity: Traveling Light with Thomas Merton, Bashō, Edward Abbey, Annie Dillard & Others *by Philip Harnden*
5 x 7¼, 144 pp, Quality PB, 978-1-59473-181-5 **$12.99**; 128 pp, HC, 978-1-893361-76-8 **$16.95**

Keeping Spiritual Balance as We Grow Older: More than 65 Creative Ways to Use Purpose, Prayer, and the Power of Spirit to Build a Meaningful Retirement
by Molly and Bernie Srode 8 x 8, 224 pp, Quality PB, 978-1-59473-042-9 **$16.99**

The Losses of Our Lives: The Sacred Gifts of Renewal in Everyday Loss
by Dr. Nancy Copeland-Payton 6 x 9, 192 pp, HC, 978-1-59473-271-3 **$19.99**

Money and the Way of Wisdom: Insights from the Book of Proverbs
by Timothy J. Sandoval, PhD 6 x 9, 192 pp, Quality PB, 978-1-59473-245-4 **$16.99**

Next to Godliness: Finding the Sacred in Housekeeping
Edited by Alice Peck 6 x 9, 224 pp, Quality PB, 978-1-59473-214-0 **$19.99**

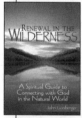

Renewal in the Wilderness: A Spiritual Guide to Connecting with God in the Natural World *by John Lionberger*
6 x 9, 176 pp, b/w photos, Quality PB, 978-1-59473-219-5 **$16.99**

Sacred Attention: A Spiritual Practice for Finding God in the Moment
by Margaret D. McGee 6 x 9, 144 pp, Quality PB, 978-1-59473-291-1 **$16.99**

Soul Fire: Accessing Your Creativity
by Thomas Ryan, CSP 6 x 9, 160 pp, Quality PB, 978-1-59473-243-0 **$16.99**

A Spirituality for Brokenness: Discovering Your Deepest Self in Difficult Times
by Terry Taylor 6 x 9, 176 pp, Quality PB, 978-1-59473-229-4 **$16.99**

Spiritually Incorrect: Finding God in All the *Wrong* Places *by Dan Wakefield; Illus. by Marian DelVecchio* 5½ x 8½, 192 pp, b/w illus., Quality PB, 978-1-59473-137-2 **$15.99**

A Walk with Four Spiritual Guides: Krishna, Buddha, Jesus, and Ramakrishna
by Andrew Harvey 5½ x 8½, 192 pp, b/w photos & illus., Quality PB, 978-1-59473-138-9 **$15.99**

The Workplace and Spirituality: New Perspectives on Research and Practice
Edited by Dr. Joan Marques, Dr. Satinder Dhiman and Dr. Richard King
6 x 9, 256 pp, HC, 978-1-59473-260-7 **$29.99**

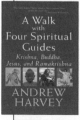

Spiritual Practice

Laugh Your Way to Grace: Reclaiming the Spiritual Power of Humor
by Rev. Susan Sparks A powerful, humorous case for laughter as a spiritual, healing path. 6 x 9, 176 pp, Quality PB, 978-1-59473-280-5 **$16.99**

Haiku—The Sacred Art: A Spiritual Practice in Three Lines
by Margaret D. McGee Introduces haiku as a simple and effective way of tapping into the sacred moments that permeate everyday living.
5½ x 8½, 192 pp, Quality PB, 978-1-59473-269-0 **$16.99**

Dance—The Sacred Art: The Joy of Movement as a Spiritual Practice
by Cynthia Winton-Henry Invites all of us, regardless of experience, into the possibility of dance/movement as a spiritual practice.
5½ x 8½, 224 pp, Quality PB, 978-1-59473-268-3 **$16.99**

Spiritual Adventures in the Snow: Skiing & Snowboarding as Renewal for Your Soul *by Dr. Marcia McFee and Rev. Karen Foster; Foreword by Paul Arthur*
Explores snow sports as tangible experiences of the spiritual essence of our bodies and the earth. 5½ x 8½, 208 pp, Quality PB, 978-1-59473-270-6 **$16.99**

Divining the Body: Reclaim the Holiness of Your Physical Self *by Jan Phillips*
8 x 8, 256 pp, Quality PB, 978-1-59473-080-1 **$16.99**

Everyday Herbs in Spiritual Life: A Guide to Many Practices
by Michael J. Caduto; Foreword by Rosemary Gladstar
7 x 9, 208 pp, 20+ b/w illus., Quality PB, 978-1-59473-174-7 **$16.99**

The Gospel of Thomas: A Guidebook for Spiritual Practice
by Ron Miller; Translations by Stevan Davies 6 x 9, 160 pp, Quality PB, 978-1-59473-047-4 **$14.99**

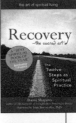

Hospitality—The Sacred Art: Discovering the Hidden Spiritual Power of Invitation and Welcome *by Rev. Nanette Sawyer; Foreword by Rev. Dirk Ficca*
5½ x 8½, 208 pp, Quality PB, 978-1-59473-228-7 **$16.99**

Labyrinths from the Outside In: Walking to Spiritual Insight—A Beginner's Guide
by Donna Schaper and Carole Ann Camp
6 x 9, 208 pp, b/w illus. and photos, Quality PB, 978-1-893361-18-8 **$16.95**

Practicing the Sacred Art of Listening: A Guide to Enrich Your Relationships and Kindle Your Spiritual Life *by Kay Lindahl* 8 x 8, 176 pp, Quality PB, 978-1-893361-85-0 **$16.95**

Recovery—The Sacred Art: The Twelve Steps as Spiritual Practice *by Rami Shapiro; Foreword by Joan Borysenko, PhD* 5½ x 8½, 240 pp, Quality PB, 978-1-59473-259-1 **$16.99**

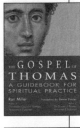

Running—The Sacred Art: Preparing to Practice *by Dr. Warren A. Kay; Foreword by Kristin Armstrong* 5½ x 8½, 160 pp, Quality PB, 978-1-59473-227-0 **$16.99**

The Sacred Art of Bowing: Preparing to Practice
by Andi Young 5½ x 8½, 128 pp, b/w illus., Quality PB, 978-1-893361-82-9 **$14.95**

The Sacred Art of Chant: Preparing to Practice
by Ana Hernández 5½ x 8½, 192 pp, Quality PB, 978-1-59473-036-8 **$15.99**

The Sacred Art of Fasting: Preparing to Practice
by Thomas Ryan, CSP 5½ x 8½, 192 pp, Quality PB, 978-1-59473-078-8 **$15.99**

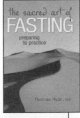

The Sacred Art of Forgiveness: Forgiving Ourselves and Others through God's Grace
by Marcia Ford 8 x 8, 176 pp, Quality PB, 978-1-59473-175-4 **$16.99**

The Sacred Art of Listening: Forty Reflections for Cultivating a Spiritual Practice
by Kay Lindahl; Illus. by Amy Schnapper 8 x 8, 160 pp, b/w illus., Quality PB, 978-1-893361-44-7 **$16.99**

The Sacred Art of Lovingkindness: Preparing to Practice
by Rabbi Rami Shapiro; Foreword by Marcia Ford 5½ x 8½, 176 pp, Quality PB, 978-1-59473-151-8 **$16.99**

Sacred Attention: A Spiritual Practice for Finding God in the Moment
by Margaret D. McGee 6 x 9, 144 pp, Quality PB, 978-1-59473-291-1 **$16.99**

Sacred Speech: A Practical Guide for Keeping Spirit in Your Speech
by Rev. Donna Schaper 6 x 9, 176 pp, Quality PB, 978-1-59473-068-9 **$15.99**
HC, 978-1-893361-74-4 **$21.95**

Soul Fire: Accessing Your Creativity
by Thomas Ryan, CSP 6 x 9, 160 pp, Quality PB, 978-1-59473-243-0 **$16.99**

Thanking & Blessing—The Sacred Art: Spiritual Vitality through Gratefulness
by Jay Marshall, PhD; Foreword by Philip Gulley 5½ x 8½, 176 pp, Quality PB, 978-1-59473-231-7 **$16.99**

AVAILABLE FROM BETTER BOOKSTORES.
TRY YOUR BOOKSTORE FIRST.

About SKYLIGHT PATHS Publishing

SkyLight Paths Publishing is creating a place where people of different spiritual traditions come together for challenge and inspiration, a place where we can help each other understand the mystery that lies at the heart of our existence.

Through spirituality, our religious beliefs are increasingly becoming a part of our lives—rather than *apart* from our lives. While many of us may be more interested than ever in spiritual growth, we may be less firmly planted in traditional religion. Yet, we do want to deepen our relationship to the sacred, to learn from our own as well as from other faith traditions, and to practice in new ways.

SkyLight Paths sees both believers and seekers as a community that increasingly transcends traditional boundaries of religion and denomination—people wanting to learn from each other, *walking together, finding the way.*

For your information and convenience, at the back of this book we have provided a list of other SkyLight Paths books you might find interesting and useful. They cover the following subjects:

Buddhism / Zen	Global Spiritual	Monasticism
Catholicism	Perspectives	Mysticism
Children's Books	Gnosticism	Poetry
Christianity	Hinduism /	Prayer
Comparative	Vedanta	Religious Etiquette
Religion	Inspiration	Retirement
Current Events	Islam / Sufism	Spiritual Biography
Earth-Based	Judaism	Spiritual Direction
Spirituality	Kabbalah	Spirituality
Enneagram	Meditation	Women's Interest
	Midrash Fiction	Worship

Or phone, fax, mail or e-mail to: SKYLIGHT PATHS Publishing
Sunset Farm Offices, Route 4 • P.O. Box 237 • Woodstock, Vermont 05091
Tel: (802) 457-4000 • Fax: (802) 457-4004 • www.skylightpaths.com
Credit card orders: (800) 962-4544 (8:30AM–5:30PM ET Monday–Friday)
Generous discounts on quantity orders. SATISFACTION GUARANTEED. Prices subject to change.

For more information about each book,
visit our website at www.skylightpaths.com